D1598599

THE SECOND COMING

THE SECOND COMING

POPULAR MILLENARIANISM
1780–1850

J. F. C. HARRISON

Professor of History, University of Sussex

ROUTLEDGE & KEGAN PAUL

LONDON AND HENLEY

First published in 1979
by Routledge & Kegan Paul Ltd
39 Store Street, London WC1E 7DD and
Broadway House, Newtown Road,
Henley-on-Thames, Oxon RG9 1EN
Set in 11 on 13 pt Bembo by
Computacomp (UK) Ltd, Fort William, Scotland
and printed in Great Britain by
Unwin Brothers Ltd
The Gresham Press
Old Woking, Surrey
A member of the Staples Printing Group
Plates printed by
Headley Brothers Ltd, Ashford, Kent

British Library Cataloguing in Publication Data

Harrison, John Fletcher Clews

The Second Coming
1. Millenialism — England — History
2. Millenialism — United States — History
I. Title
236'.3'0942   BR758

ISBN 0 7100 0191 6

CONTENTS

ILLUSTRATIONS

(between pages 118 and 119)

PREFACE

In the writing of this book I have incurred many obligations. To my own University of Sussex I am indebted for leave of absence in which to write and research. Much of the preliminary work was done while on a research fellowship at the Charles Warren Center for Studies in American History, Harvard University, in 1972–3. A social science research fellowship from the Nuffield Foundation in the autumn of 1975 enabled me to get ahead with the writing. Further substantial progress was made at Canberra during the (northern hemisphere) summer of 1977, thanks to a visiting research fellowship in the History Department, Research School of Social Sciences, Australian National University. And the book was completed at Madison, Wisconsin, USA, while I was Herbert F. Johnson Research Professor at the Institute for Research in the Humanities, University of Wisconsin, for the academic year 1977–8. To these institutions I am grateful for financial support and the provision of ideal working conditions.

Many friends, colleagues and acquaintances have helped me with information, comments and expert opinions, and I would like to thank them all: Patricia Allderidge, Richard Bushman, A. W. Exell, Robert Fogarty, Clarke Garrett, H. J. Haden, Ann Hone, Dafydd Ifan, Beynon John, Peter Lineham, David Lovejoy, Ernest Martin, Ted Milligan, Howard Murphy, Marcia Pointon, Marsha Keith Schuchard, Malcolm Thomas, Edward Thompson, Malcolm Thorp, and Michael Wadsworth. Barry Smith read all except the final chapter of the manuscript, and I have benefited greatly from his advice.

J.F.C.H.

ACKNOWLEDGMENTS

The author wishes to thank the following for their help in providing photographs and granting permission for the use of material in the plates shown: The National Gallery of Art, Washington, DC; the Rosenwald Collection (3); the Trustees of the British Museum, London (7, 8); the Tate Gallery, London (4, 5, 6); Houghton Library, Harvard University (9).

INTRODUCTION

This book is an experiment in the writing of popular history — a contribution to the history of the people who have no history. It stems in part from a sympathy with the view expressed by an old Yorkshireman in 1886:

> Surely, Sir, if it is the people who form the nation ..., what they do, suffer, enjoy, think and feel ... is real history, far more than the story of a few who have borne titles and made laws, the benefit of which has been mostly for themselves.[1]

History from below is in fact no more 'real' than history from above; but it is still largely true that 'the people' in this sense are a dimension missing from many interpretations of the past. Even when some attention is paid to 'what they do, suffer, enjoy', it is rare to find any analysis of what they 'think and feel'.

The reasons for this neglect are not far to seek. It is not easy for the historian to hear the voices of the people, for they have left relatively few records, and their views and opinions are drowned or crowded out by the louder and more insistent voices of the educated classes. In the records of the past the labouring man or small shopkeeper only seldom speaks for himself, and when he does it is to mention briefly the externals of his life, not what he 'thinks and feels'. He appears upon the stage of history indirectly, via the speeches of others. We see him only through the eyes of outsiders who, even when sympathetic, were far removed from his mental world. The problem of understanding the mind of the 'lower orders' is not new. Henry Moseley, an inspector of schools, observed in 1845:

> The fact is that the inner life of the classes below us in society is never penetrated by us. We are profoundly ignorant of the springs of public

opinion, the elements of thought and the principles of action among them – those things which we recognise at once as constituting our own social life.[2]

Such insight was rare among the educated classes, who normally showed little interest in, or appreciation of labouring men – especially those who did not conform to expected patterns of thought and behaviour: why bother to take seriously the views of people who were 'ignorant' and 'credulous'; and who in any case were effectively excluded from the decision-making processes of politics and economic life? So the historian has a double obstacle to surmount: first, the inarticulateness of ordinary men and women, and then the ignoring or distortion of their views by articulate observers. To these must be added a third hazard. Even when we have documentary evidence we cannot be sure that we are interpreting it correctly; there is a danger for the historian in assuming that the written word was actually what people believed. We know, for instance, that many thousands of labouring people sang hymns which enshrined the basic doctrines of Methodism. But we are not warranted in assuming that when humble Methodists sang of grace, salvation, and the blood of the lamb, these words had the same meaning for them as for John Wesley, or the same significance that theologians, psychologists and historians have attributed to them later. To some extent this is a problem which besets all history; but it seems to be particularly acute in popular history.

We all have what may be loosely termed a philosophy of life: a bundle of attitudes, beliefs and values with which we navigate our way through the pleasures and perils of everyday living. At any given moment the responses we make, the decisions we take, the things we do or do not do, are determined according to our notions about ourselves and the physical and social world. For much of the time this process is instinctive and automatic, and not subject to conscious reasoning. But on other occasions – as when people differ from us – we become aware that there are some things we believe and others which we do not. Beliefs are not held singly, but in clusters, organized in a structure and having behavioural consequences.

A belief system may be defined as having represented within it, in some organised psychological but not necessarily logical form, each and every one of a person's countless beliefs about physical and social reality. By definition, we do not allow beliefs to exist outside the belief system for the same reason that the astronomer does not allow stars to remain outside the universe.[3]

Not all beliefs are of equal importance to us. Some are central, and reach down deep into our being. They concern basic truths about our own existence and the nature of the world in which we find ourselves. They are largely taken for granted, and to question them would cause a serious disruption in our lives. Other beliefs are not so central, and do not have the same taken-for-granted character. They are beliefs derived from the authority of family, class or religious group, and we recognize differences of opinion about them. Beyond these are beliefs which are no more than matters of taste, and which are inconsequential in their relation to our central or primary beliefs. Many questions arise as to the nature of such a belief system: whence comes the stimulus to formulate it?; what elements are available for its construction?; what are its functions?. We have only to ask these questions to realize the formidable nature of any attempt to probe into the mental world of people in the past, especially people who have left few records of what they 'think and feel.' Nor is there good reason to suppose that people who led apparently simple lives necessarily held simple beliefs. The ways of thinking of labouring men and women are as complicated and difficult to unravel as for the more educated classes. But we are less familiar with the problems involved.

As a way round the barriers to understanding the popular mind, I propose to examine one particular set of concepts and the people who held them in the late eighteenth and first half of the nineteenth centuries. The material is mainly British, with some American sources added for comparison. The choice of millenarianism was not fortuitous, but arose out of previous work in which I observed that many Owenites and other social reformers in the nineteenth century used millenarian ideas and vocabulary. An investigation of this phenomenon seemed likely to be fruitful; and in the event has led into unsuspected places. It seemed possible that the study of millenarianism might yield information not just about religious beliefs but also about the structure of popular thought. If this were so, then millenarianism might be used as a means of penetrating the mental world of some ordinary men and women who were otherwise inarticulate. My concern with millenarianism therefore has been not theological but methodological. Millenarianism is used as a conceptual tool with which to explore some aspects of popular thought and culture in the age of Romanticism.

In particular I have been attracted by the possibility that such a study might elucidate some of the more obscure aspects of social change. It has often been noted that millenarianism appealed to the socially deprived, and that it was viewed with suspicion or enmity by the authorities. The doctrine of the millennium and the second advent implied an overturning of the world as at present constituted. Might we not have here at least the elements of an ideology of social change? The late eighteenth and early nineteenth centuries were a period of acute social and economic change, a time when it might be expected there would be need for some reshaping of men's perception of themselves and their world. Today we are so deeply inured to the idea of change, so accustomed to the assumption that our lives will be different from our fathers', that we have to make a conscious effort to remember that this was not always so. In pre-industrial society concern with social change was unusual; and when change was sought it had to be presented as a restoration of former conditions, not as something new (which was not, *per se*, regarded as desirable). Ideology explained and justified stability and equilibrium in society. An ideology of social change was scarcely necessary since the rate of change was relatively slow. But from the late eighteenth century this stability was upset, and traditional attitudes and beliefs were felt to be increasingly inadequate. There was need for a new ideology to take account of the changes, but where could ordinary people find a system of beliefs which would give meaning to their new and bewildering experiences? Millenarianism was one attempt at an answer. It was not directed to restoring the past, to going back. Instead it openly looked forward to a future which would be completely new. It provided a vision, a philosophy of radical social change.

Starting with this hypothesis (for it is really little more) I have tried to explore the world of popular millenarianism. The material is so fascinating in itself – so rich in unusual characters and extreme doctrines – that the story which emerges has its own intrinsic interest and validity. Nevertheless, the exploration will have failed in its purpose if it does not suggest ways in which the history of millenarianism raises wider issues of historical analysis: the social forms in which beliefs occur; the way in which beliefs relate to social action; attitudes to, and expectations of social change. The temptations of facetiousness and of knowing better than, or seeing through the millenarians are great; and we have always to be on our guard lest we adopt superior and anachronistic attitudes. I hope also I have avoided the dangers of a shallow functionalism, while not abdicating the social historian's duty to look at the effects of an action or belief with the advantage of hindsight.

The core of the book (part II) is a study of Richard Brothers, Joanna Southcott and their successors and followers. But in order to account for many aspects of millenarianism between 1790 and 1840 I found it necessary to look for roots in an earlier period, and ultimately to examine what happened to the millenarian tradition in the eighteenth century.

The results of this investigation are set out in part I. Part III attempts an overall assessment of millenarianism as an aspect of popular culture. By drawing on American Shakers, Mormons and Millerites a comparative dimension is introduced; and a final chapter pulls together earlier themes, suggests several levels of explanation, and returns to the central proposition that the culture of millenarianism provided a way of looking at one's self and the world which has to be taken seriously. But first we need an introduction to the whole idea of the millennium and millenarianism.

PART I

THE MILLENARIAN TRADITION

THE HOPE OF THE MILLENNIUM

Historical understanding of millenarianism does not come easily these days. In the first place, it is couched largely in the language of theology, and employs technical terms with which we are no longer familiar. Our vocabulary is provided by the sociologist and psychologist rather than the theologian. We have to make a conscious effort at translation even to grasp what the millenarians are saying. More formidable, however, is a second obstacle. In our present secular age many people find it difficult to take seriously a belief in the millennium, and by projecting this disbelief into their view of the past they preclude themselves from a sympathetic understanding of earlier millenarians. It is puzzling when we find intelligent people expressing beliefs which we can see only as errors and delusions; but this is often a measure of our anachronistic blindness. We simply fail to see the force or logic of something which does not rest on our own intellectual assumptions, and so we are incredulous.[1] Even if the beliefs were in fact mistaken or delusional, it is still important to try to understand them, for history is full of examples of erroneous or evil ideas which were all too effective. In the case of millennialism its longevity and capacity for adaptation should be a caution against dismissing it as an intellectual oddity. A great many people in all walks of life in the eighteenth and nineteenth centuries took the idea of the millennium seriously, and accordingly worked out a variety of intellectual positions and established millennial institutions. In general this book will be an exploration of belief in the millennium rather than an examination of millennial theories themselves. Nevertheless, the two are obviously intertwined, and some definition of the millennium is necessary.

At the start it is perhaps useful to remember the strength and persistence of millennialism in the Christian church at all times from its beginning. Millennialism is to be regarded not as an aberration but rather as an extreme form of one aspect of orthodox faith. Jesus' teachings about the kingdom, the last days and the coming of the messiah in glory and majesty were taken literally by his disciples, and after His death the Apostolic church continued to believe in a second coming which would not long be delayed. When the great promises of the second advent were not literally fulfilled they were subjected to interpretation, so that the apocalyptic tradition was not discarded but adjusted to the new situation. From the early church there was handed down a body of inspired prophecy, the core of which was contained in the books of Daniel and Revelation, the Apocrypha and the 'synoptic Apocalypse' of Jesus himself.[2] Throughout the history of the Christian church the interpretation of this prophetic literature was the basis of innumerable theories and speculations. In particular, the symbolic prophecies of Daniel 7 and 8 and Revelation 14 fascinated generations of Christians, who exercised untold ingenuity in their exposition of the meaning of the 'beasts' and 'horns' and the 'mother of the harlots'. The object of this interpretation was to throw light on the nature of the millennium and its relation to Jesus' second coming, a doctrine to which all professed Christians were, in some form or other, committed.

There was general agreement in millennial theology that the world was to be transformed by the second coming of Christ and the establishment of the kingdom of God on earth. This state would last for 1,000 years, after which would come the last judgment. During the period of the millennium the saints (i.e., the Christian martyrs and all faithful Christians who have suffered) would reign with Christ. There were differences of view, however, between those Christians who believed that Christ's second coming would precede the millennium (premillennialists) and those who thought that the second advent would follow the millennium (postmillennialists). From these differences stemmed others. The premillennialists were predisposed towards the establishment of the millennium by divine, cataclysmic action, whereas the postmillennialists were prone to think that the kingdom of God would come gradually as the result of Christian, human instrumentalities. For either of these views there was ample scriptural support, so that the choice between a revolutionary or reformist interpretation had to be made on other than theological grounds. Among premillennialists there was a further division between those who believed that the second advent had already occurred and the millennium had begun, and those who still looked for these events in the future. Again, among both pre- and postmillennialists anticipation of the millennium could provoke either pessimism or optimism, depending on whether the imminent end of the world was dreaded or welcomed.

4

From these differences in interpretation and emphasis a variety of types of millennial concern was possible, ranging from sophisticated study of the biblical books of prophecy to divine revelations concerning the immediate arrival of Christ on earth. Throughout the eighteenth and first half of the nineteenth centuries the first of these forms never lacked able exponents. Contemporary events like the Lisbon earthquake of 1755 were interpreted as evidence of the fulfilment of biblical prophecies. Above all, the French Revolution excited a spate of interpretations on both sides of the Atlantic designed to show that the world was entering upon the last days. Millennialism was widely espoused by leading scholars and divines. In America the names of Timothy Dwight (President of Yale), John H. Livingston (President of Rutgers) and Joseph Priestley come to mind: in Britain, George Stanley Faber, Edward King, and Edward Irving.[3] A spate of pamphlets and sermons by Church of England clergy and orthodox American ministers poured forth from the 1790s; and there was constant reference back to the prophetical studies of Sir Isaac Newton, Joseph Mede, and William Whiston. The usual method of interpretation was some variant of the year–day theory, by which days mentioned in the prophecies were counted as years, weeks as seven-year periods, and months as thirty years. There was general agreement in the late eighteenth century that the 1,260 days mentioned in Revelation 12:6 were to be interpreted as 1,260 years, and that this period was now ended. An alternative theory, which became increasingly popular after 1800, emphasized the importance of the 2,300-year period of Daniel 8:14 and the 'cleansing of the sanctuary' which would fall due some time in the 1840s. The fulfilment of the time prophecies meant that mankind was living in the last days, that the 'midnight cry' might soon be heard, and that the coming of the messiah might be expected shortly. Such beliefs had an influence far beyond the members of explicitly adventist sects. They were part and parcel of everyday evangelical religion.

Our concern, however, is not with these, the intellectually sophisticated millennialists; but with the popular, largely self-educated, adventist millenarians.[4] They are the people condemned by the opulent classes as fanatics and imposters, and by historians as cranks and the lunatic fringe. The distinction between what may be called respectable, orthodox, scholarly millennialism on the one hand, and popular (or folk) millenarianism on the other is useful for analytical purposes,[5] but the division is not hard and fast. Those who believed in the millennium had the option of combining so many variables that a millennialist or a millenarian could be placed at any point along a continuum of belief.

Millennialism and millenarianism were ways of looking at the world, rather than specific doctrines.[6] This was at the root of the difference between the millennialism of seventeenth- and eighteenth-century divines and scholars (many of them fellows of Cambridge colleges), and the popular millenarian tradition stemming from the radical sects of the English Revolution. It is the tone and temper of the popular millenarians, the way in which they used the texts and symbols from Daniel and Revelation, which is distinctive. They were the enthusiasts, the fanatics, the come-outers. Their beliefs were derived from a literal, eclectic interpretation of the prophetic scriptures, and a divine revelation vouchsafed to them directly. A simplicity, often crudity, seemed to mark their mentality, for their reliance on the supernatural enabled them to dispense with many of the limitations imposed by logic and reason. Moderation and gradualness did not commend themselves as virtues, but rather were signs of lack of faith. The basic principles of good and evil in the world were crystal clear, and life was to be lived by the light of this absolute standard, with no compromises.

The relationship between these popular millenarians and the more respectable millennialists illuminates several aspects of belief in the millennium in the late eighteenth and early nineteenth centuries. Both types accepted the same canonical writings, and disagreement was over interpretation, not the sources themselves. Millennialists and millenarians had a common set of symbols, texts and assumptions – many of which they also shared with the Protestant evangelical community at large. On matters of biblical prophecy, for instance, there were divisions over the timing and the sense in which prophecies would be fulfilled. But underlying these differences were more fundamental questions of the social functions of prophecy at a particular time and for a particular group of people. The millennium provided a common language and set of images and concepts in which people could express both individual and collective needs (and in which at times the two might even be merged[7]); but it remained a mode of expression, a means of communication, rather than an end with an agreed meaning and programme. The deepest differences between the millennialists and the millenarians were not about the interpretation of the millennium, but about the purposes for which such interpretation was made.

In comparison with the millennialists, the millenarians seem somewhat old-fashioned. From a postmillennial position it is easy to assume that the kingdoms of this world will eventually become those of Christ, that through the endeavours of Christians the world will get better and better, until finally it is worthy to receive Christ at his second coming. In the eighteenth century millennialists increasingly came to equate this doctrine with the idea of progress. The millennium was secularized into a utopia or perfect state of society, to be attained through a gradual and steady march of improvement. Providence was integrated into the concept of natural law.[8] In sharp contrast with this optimistic, reassuring, Augustan view, the premillennialist (or millenarian) expected no such comforting progression. Convinced that the world was evil, he looked for sudden divine intervention to destroy the existing order and establish the millennium. Such a view was out of step with the usual Enlightenment thinking on political events and historical causation. It has the air of an old-fashioned, popular ideology, unaffected by contemporary intellectual and theological trends – more suited to the seventeenth than to the eighteenth century, until the revolutionary upheavals of the 1790s suddenly made it seem attractive again. One is reminded of the famous theory of Dixon Ryan Fox that the ideas of the educated and upper classes of one generation are cast off and picked up by the next generation of lower classes: 'the cast-off garments of the intellectuals of one age are found, albeit soiled and ragged, on the backs of the ignorant many in the next.'[9] The millennial ideas of the learned New England divines of the 1790s, argued Fox, appeared a generation or so later among the Mormons and Millerites. On reflection, however, the model of ideas dropping down from one social layer to another (Fox's 'stratigraphical chart' of intellect) scarcely fits the case. Fox made no distinction between millennialists and millenarians, since he was concerned solely with the ideas of the millennium and not with how and why those ideas were held. Moreover, his supposition of a time-lag in the transmission of ideas between classes does not square with the chronology of millennialists and millenarians, who flourished contemporaneously in the period 1780 to 1850. We cannot argue that millenarians derived their doctrines from the millennialists of a previous generation, for millenarian ideas flourished in the sixteenth century and in the Middle Ages. The context in which doctrines are held is of course a vital factor in their historical evaluation. To be a millenarian in the mid nineteenth century meant something different from holding similar millenarian views two centuries earlier. The doctrines of the millennium could remain more or less the same: the hope of the millennium changed greatly.

The traditional meaning of millenarianism was derived from Revelation 20, the events therein being taken in a strictly literal sense. Satan was to be bound fast and the saints would reign with Christ on earth for 1,000 years; after which Satan would be released and finally defeated. But millenarianism also has a wider meaning, extending beyond its theological or doctrinal origins. It is a type of salvationism. The search for salvation, variously defined, is a main preoccupation of most religious movements, and millenarianism can be identified by its distinctive characteristics in this respect. At least five such qualities appear to be present in most millenarian movements.[10] First, the salvation sought is conceived as being for the faithful as a group – the saints, the true believers – and not as each individual seeking by himself to save his own soul. Next, this salvation is to be enjoyed in a kingdom on this earth, and it is to come soon and suddenly. It will be total in its effects: the present evil world will not be improved, but utterly destroyed, and replaced by a perfect society. Lastly, the change will come about by divine agency, not by human efforts. Men seek salvation for many reasons, and look for it in many forms. One man's concern will be to find salvation from illness, anxiety or grief: another's will be to save the world. Men will seek to be healed, to be recognized as important, to protect themselves from adversity, to change the social order. What they have in common is the hope that through the millennium these things will be realized.

For most of this book we shall be occupied, as historians usually are, with very specific examples of millenarian belief and activity. Only by naming names (often quite obscure ones) and relating them closely to a particular context can we hope to attain historical understanding. But millenarianism can be (and is being) studied from many different angles by anthropologists, psychiatrists, sociologists, political scientists, and theologians; and the historian is not in such a strong position that he can afford to ignore the benefits of interdisciplinary study. Thus in considering millenarianism as a type of salvationism we may gain from the sociologists some useful hints on typology which would stand us in good stead when examining specific millenarian sects later. By the use of theoretical models we may be able to sort out some of the divergent and confusing positions of those who are loosely grouped together as millenarians.

For this purpose Bryan R. Wilson's approach in his *Magic and the Millennium* is perhaps the most useful.[11] Wilson classifies the seekers after salvation by their responses to the world, and identifies seven types of response. The conversionist believes that only by changing men can the world be changed, and he looks for salvation through an experience of conversion which will profoundly alter a man's heart. He is saved now, even though the objective world is not yet changed. In contrast, the revolutionist is convinced that only the destruction of the world (and usually he means the present social order) will suffice to save men. This will be brought about by divine, cataclysmic intervention, and believers know that they can really do little more than prepare themselves and others for this imminent overturning. A third response is to withdraw from the world, since it is so hopelessly evil. The introversionist may do this as an individual or as a member of a community, and in the latter case the source of salvation is the community itself. Less radical in rejecting the world and all its works is the belief that salvation is possible in the world if men will adopt the right means to deal with their problems. This is the manipulationist's response. It is not at all other-worldly, and consists basically of applying religious techniques which allow men to see the world differently and explain evil away. A similar, but narrower type of response is the thaumaturgical. Relief from present ills is sought by means of magic. Such salvation is personal and local, and does not as a rule call for any elaborate doctrine. Another response, the reformist, is close to the position of secular social reformers, and in fact differs only in positing divine guidance. The intention is to amend the world gradually in the light of supernaturally given insights. Lastly, there is the utopian response in which men seek to construct a perfect society, free from evil. The utopian does not wait for a divine cataclysm, he is not satisfied with anything less than a complete replacement of present society, and he is too active to simply withdraw from the world. Wilson summarizes these 'prescriptions for changing the relation of men to "the world" ' in a threefold way. To the objectivists it seems that God will overturn the world (revolutionists) or that he calls us to abandon it (introversionists), amend it (reformists) or reconstruct it (utopians). The subjectivists believe that God will change us (conversionists). And the relationists claim that God calls us to change our perception of the world (manipulationists), or that God will grant special dispensations and work specific miracles (thaumaturgists).

These seven responses are not descriptions of salvationist sects, but are ideal-type constructs. They present a range of possible positions which salvationists might adopt, not only in Western cultures but also in the Third World. Applying these models to British and American millenarians, c. 1780–1850, we do not have to suppose that any particular sect exactly fitted any of the seven types, nor that any particular millenarian sought salvation in exactly the manner laid down. Religious believers, even within the same sect, are often inconsistent or contradictory, and almost any combination of variables from the seven types is imaginable. Among the followers of Joanna Southcott and her successors we shall have little difficulty in recognizing several of these different responses to the world at some stage or in a particular individual. We are, however, involved in classifying groups of millenarians only to the extent necessary for understanding their historic role, and it is not our purpose to study millenarianism through sociological models. Nevertheless, the sociologists' emphasis on the need for classification and generalization is a valuable corrective to historical studies, and a reminder that after we have examined millenarianism in specific and local contexts we need to go further in the search for historical explanation and meaning.

The hope of the millennium has also another dimension. In addition to its theological origin and subsequent widening into salvationism, it has a secular aspect. Some types of postmillennialism, as Wilson noted, can easily shade off into social reform movements which are not thought of as religious. Certain utopian movements are of this nature, and it has been suggested that utopianism is a kind of 'secular millennial equivalent'.[12] Millenarian movements which have shed virtually all association with traditional religious belief – and which indeed may proclaim themselves anti-Christian – may be labelled secular.[13] It is also possible for reformers and others to use the rhetoric of millenarianism as a means of communication, to refer to the images and concepts of the millennium without implying assent to a particular religious belief. But this analytical device of dividing religious from secular millenarianism runs a grave risk of tempting us to fall into the historians' sin of anachronism. Many of the millenarians who will appear later seem to have made little if any distinction between what we now commonly call the religious and the secular. They condemned the world as evil, as being in the grip of Satan, not as being neutral or outside the power of supernatural forces. The division was between Christ and anti-Christ, rather than between areas of life in which God did or did not operate. Evangelical Christians of fairly orthodox persuasion were prone to separate the sacred from the profane, the faithful believer from the infidel. But the more extreme and non-respectable millenarians went out of their way to deny any such distinctions. In a world turned upside down who could say what was religious and what was not? With this caveat, however, it is possible to accept the notion of a secularization of the millennium, and to regard it as potentially useful for tackling some of the problems of millenarianism which will be encountered.[14] Millenarian modes of thinking were applied to a variety of social issues, and affected people beyond the millenarians' ranks. The hope of the millennium caught their imagination in different ways and for different reasons. But for all of them there was the compelling vision of 'a new heaven and a new earth', and the great promise: 'Behold, I make all things new.'

CHAPTER TWO

PROPHETS AND PROPHESYINGS

The hope of the millennium and a yearning for salvation do not by themselves result in a millenarian movement. Other causative factors are present in most situations where such movements arise. A prophet or messiah is usually necessary to give the movement coherence. He is the bearer of the millenarian ideas, his presence gives them a sense of immediacy, and he becomes the centre round which the movement revolves. Certain socio-economic factors and a situation in which unusual distress, anxiety, and feelings of relative deprivation can develop are also associated with the appearance of prophets and millenarian movements – and may indeed be necessary conditions for that emergence. They will be considered later. At this preliminary stage of our inquiry we are concerned to observe and record the presence of prophets, prophetesses and prophesyings and to relate them to millenarianism. First we shall consider very briefly the role of the prophet from a sociological perspective. Then in more detail we shall examine some aspects of the seventeenth- and eighteenth-century manifestations of prophetism and prophecy.

To the greatest of the sociologists who has written on this theme, Max Weber, a prophet is 'a purely individual bearer of charisma, who by virtue of his mission proclaims a religious doctrine or divine commandment.'[1] By charisma is meant not a personal quality or attribute, but rather a relationship. It is the recognition and acceptance of a leader by his followers, and is a sociological, not a psychological, concept.[2] Not all would-be prophets find acceptance; many are regarded as lunatics or imposters and are therefore denied charisma. But when the special claims of a prophet are acknowledged by a group of followers his leadership becomes charismatic. (For this reason, if for no other, it is as important to study the followers as the prophets in millenarian movements). The prophet bases his claims on divine revelation. He receives a personal call, and is 'commanded' to do and say what he does. In this respect he is different from a priest or minister, whose authority derives from a sacred tradition or religious institution. Usually the prophet is a layman, is unpaid, and stands outside the normal religious structure. Proof of his gift of the spirit is required from the prophet, and he provides this by divination, healing, counselling and raising the dead. Through such 'signs' he first attracts and then holds his followers. Around him there gathers a small band of personal devotees, some of whom may also possess charismatic qualifications. A wider circle of believers supports the prophet with time and money, and actively seeks to proselytize and organize congregations.

The prophet's message may take many forms. But his revelation involves for both himself and his followers 'a unified view of the world derived from a consciously integrated and meaningful attitude toward life'.[3] It is an attempt to systematize all the manifestations of life in the light of the need for salvation, and is essentially practical, even at the expense of logical consistency. In a priestly system the canon of sacred scriptures is closed, and the era of genuine prophecy lies only in the past. This view is strongly rejected by the prophet and his followers. His message cannot be bound by the past, but involves a new interpretation of old scriptures and, if necessary, the addition of new ones. Prophecy is not primarily an intellectual exercise, and the prophet is seldom a highly educated person. Inevitably he finds himself in opposition to the priesthood and the canon of religious orthodoxy; and like Jesus he can but repeat, 'It is written ..., but I say unto you.' Through his role and his message the prophet is committed to break with the established order; to this extent he stands apart in society, he is abnormal, alienated, and is a potential agent of change. His enemies say that he is insane or seditious. After his death his followers are faced with a crucial choice. They have accepted him charismatically, and have believed in his supernatural powers (even though he may often have denied such powers) and the likelihood of his resurrection. For his followers he may therefore live on as the incarnation in some way of the divine. Alternatively the followers may preserve only such aspects of the prophet's teaching as they need; or transfer their allegiance to a new prophet.

Such in outline is our sociological model. We do not have to suppose that any particular prophet was possessed of all these characteristics or that prophesying necessarily involved all such features. The model provides an 'ideal type', to which specific instances may approximate in a greater or lesser degree. It is a generalized statement, an imposed pattern of order, derived from observation of individual cases. Its use is as a corrective to the historian's necessary concern for the specific and particular. There is a very real danger, especially when dealing with such colourful and eccentric characters as the millenarians, of being overwhelmed by the fascinating details of each particular case, to the exclusion of the broader implications of the material. The wood is perceived only dimly because of the sharp focus on each of the splendid trees. Yet we need to know many things about the wood (meaning in this case society as a whole) before we can account for the trees (i.e. individuals and their behaviour). Why, for instance, have some societies apparently been more congenial than others to prophets and millenarian movements? A society which highly regards prophets or which is tolerant of millenarian movements will be blessed with examples of them, for cultural values serve to regulate their incidence. The millenarians of the 1790s did not appear out of nowhere; they were conscious of belonging to a society which had a long experience of prophets and prophesying.

In the seventeenth century this experience was wide-spread, and it has been acknowledged and documented by historians.[4] The assumption (often implicit rather than explicit) has been, however, that millenarianism, prophetism, and other sectarian beliefs did not for the most part survive the end of the century; and that such remnants as did remain faded rapidly in the eighteenth-century reign of reason, toleration and latitudinarianism. This view is at best only partly true. Certainly the strength of the sects had been greatly reduced since the days of the Commonwealth, but sectarian views – even quite extreme ones – persisted into the eighteenth century. As Ronald Knox reminded us,

> we ought not to judge the religious temper of the eighteenth century
> by the religious temper of its political idols or of its literary
> interpreters. There were deeper currents below the surface; the age of
> enlightenment was also an age of fanaticisms.[5]

When we probe below the surface into popular beliefs in the eighteenth century we find much that is familiar from the previous age. A popular (should one fashionably say underground?) tradition of sectarian belief and practice runs continuously from the seventeenth century (and probably earlier) to the 1790s and beyond. This tradition was outside respectable Dissent, though sometimes embarrassingly close to it. The Quakers in the later eighteenth century were a much more staid body than they had been in the time of George Fox; but it would be interesting to know how many Friends had to be disowned for professing views which would have been tolerated or even accepted 100 years earlier.[6] Robert Hindmarsh, the Swedenborgian, recalled meeting a man from Shoreditch in the 1780s whose doctrines were those of the Ranters: he said 'that there was no God in the universe but man', and 'that he himself was a God.'[7] There is no way of estimating accurately the size and strength of this tradition. But it is not difficult to show the continuance of certain seventeenth-century sectarian beliefs in various forms and institutions, and these provided the ground in which might be nurtured prophets and (even more importantly) their followers. The millenarian inheritance from the seventeenth century was twofold: primarily it was a matter of ideas and beliefs, an intellectual milieu favourable to eschatological interpretation of events: secondarily it was institutional, in that some sects (Quakers, Muggletonians, Ranters) remained as visible links with the enthusiasts and fanatics of the past.

It goes almost without saying that this tradition was heavily anti-clerical. The very idea of an established church with a paid, university-educated priesthood, was anathema. God spoke directly to believers, to women no less than to men, and 'mechanick preachers' were to be preferred to hireling ministers. The Bible was an indisputable authority to which all men could appeal (though a right understanding of the scriptures was usually held to be dependent on the guidance of the Spirit within each believer). Not only was the Bible believed to be divinely inspired, and accepted in an intensely literal sense: it was also treated non-historically and used as a handbook to the events of the contemporary world. Alternatively, the Bible was allegorized, and its stories interpreted as internal states of the human mind. In the English Revolution this mixture of bibliolatry, theological heterodoxy, anti-priestcraft, and religion of the heart had helped to produce a rich harvest of prophets and millenarianism; and its continuance, even in a much weakened form, into the eighteenth century gives meaning to some otherwise unexpected outbursts of millenarianism in the Age of Reason. Among the millenarians of 1790 to 1850 can be recognized doctrines and beliefs which were prominent among the sectaries of the seventeenth century: England the chosen nation (the new Israel of God), the everlasting gospel, deification (the divine humanity), and the allegorization or spiritual interpretation of scripture. Two aspects of the tradition in particular – antinomianism and mysticism – will repay closer scrutiny.

In his *Journal* for 23 March 1746 John Wesley recorded a conversation with an antinomian at Birmingham:

'Do you believe you have nothing to do with the law of God?'

'I have not; I am not under the law: I live by faith.'

'Have you, as living by faith, a right to do everything in the world?'

'I have; all is mine, since Christ is mine.'

'May you, then, take anything you will anywhere? Suppose out of a shop, without the consent or knowledge of the owner?'

'I may, if I want it; for it is mine. Only I will not give offence.'

'Have you also a right to all the women in the world?'

'Yes, if they consent.'

'And is not that a sin?'

'Yes, to him that thinks it is a sin; but not to those whose hearts are free.'[8]

Antinomianism, or freedom from the restraints of the moral law, was in one sense no more than an extreme extension of the great Protestant doctrine of justification by faith. But its practical results, from the Anabaptists' establishment of a communistic New Jerusalem in Münster onwards, were such as to scare all but extreme radicals. Wesley was no radical, and he fiercely condemned the antinomians as 'the first born children of Satan'.[9] He feared that 'speculative' antinomianism (meaning rejection of the restraints of scriptural law and of the necessity of good works) would lead to practical antinomianism which would subvert the existing social and political order.[10] He was particularly embarrassed and angry by antinomianism among some of his own followers and preachers – William Cudworth, James Relly, Roger Ball – and he feared the effects on the faithful. At Wednesbury he met the antinomian preacher, Stephen Timmins, and wondered

> whether pride had not made him mad. An uncommon wildness and fierceness in his air, his words and the whole manner of his behaviour, almost induced me to think God had for a season given him up into the hands of Satan.[11]

Wesley's critics were not the least surprised by such evidence. They had maintained all along that Methodism was but the latest form of enthusiasm and fanaticism, a breeding ground for antinomianism and other sectarian heresies. And to an extent they were right. In so far as Methodism was a popular movement in the eighteenth century, reaching down into the labouring poor, it drew upon some of the same sort of people as had the sects earlier. It may also have served to revive some of the controversies and shibboleths of the Commonwealth. However much Wesley was opposed to enthusiasm, it was in fact strengthened by the Methodist revival. Edmund Gibson, Bishop of London from 1720 to 1748, defined enthusiasm as 'a strong persuasion on the mind of persons that they are guided in an extraordinary manner by immediate impressions and impulses of the Spirit of God'; and he noted that the Methodists were true enthusiasts

> when they tell us of extraordinary communications they have with God, and more than ordinary assurances of a special Presence with them; when they talk the language of those who have a special and immediate commission from God; when they profess to think and act under the immediate guidance of a divine inspiration; ... when they claim the spirit of prophecy; when they speak of themselves in the language and under the character of the Apostles of Christ, and even of Christ himself.[12]

A cruder opponent of Methodism was George Lavington, Bishop of Exeter from 1747 to 1762. He attacked the Methodists for their field-preaching, prophesying, visions and ecstasies, which amounted to a 'wild and pernicious Enthusiasm'. Their emphasis on faith rather than works, their arrogance in claiming 'absolute freedom from corruption', was antinomian and could lead only to vice and immorality.[13] It does not matter that Wesley repudiated enthusiasm as strongly as his critics, nor that Lavington's charges are valid, if at all, for George Whitefield rather than Wesley. The point is that enthusiasm and antinomianism, far from having died out after the Restoration, were recognized to be still alive and even flourishing, especially among some of the 'people called Methodists'. Lavington, on the strength of chiliastic statements by Wesley in his early days, detected millenarian tendencies among Methodists. And Lavington's latter-day disciple, Richard Polwhele, later described the followers of Joanna Southcott as a 'sect of Methodism'.[14]

Antinomian was used as a bogey word, usually implying sexual promiscuity. If a man believed that he had attained perfection and was no longer capable of sin ('Whosoever is born of God doth not commit sin; for his seed remaineth in him: and he cannot sin because he is born of God', I John 3:9), he was free to do all manner of things which were normally forbidden. Free love, for instance, was a sign or symbol of spiritual emancipation. Similarly the antinomian did not feel constrained to abide by social conventions or political laws. He claimed an area of freedom which was frightening to all in authority. The diagnosis of antinomianism was that it stemmed from enthusiasm (another term of opprobrium), which, said John Locke, was but the conceit 'of a warmed or overweening brain'. Since immediate revelation is much easier than hard thinking, he argued, 'it is no wonder that some have been very apt to pretend to revelation, and to persuade themselves that they are under the peculiar guidance of heaven', especially in those matters which they cannot account for by the ordinary methods of knowledge. And he continued:

> Their minds being thus prepared, whatever groundless opinion comes to settle itself strongly upon their fancies, is an illumination from the spirit of God, and presently of divine authority: and whatsoever odd action they find in themselves a strong inclination to do ... is a commission from above, and they cannot err in executing it. This I take to be properly enthusiasm.[15]

Locke was writing in 1700, but the same warnings were being repeated 100 years later.

Enthusiasm and antinomianism were not specific doctrines so much as broad clusters of opinions, attitudes and beliefs. Some of these beliefs had their echoes in the late eighteenth and early nineteenth centuries. Antinomians believed that God was essentially in every man, and perhaps in every created thing. Some, like the seventeenth century Ranters, said that God existed only in man, and that they themselves were God (to which George Fox, the Quaker, gave short shrift: 'They said they were God, but I asked them whether it would rain tomorrow and they could not tell. I told them God could tell!'[16]). The consequences of this were either materialism and a vague pantheism, or else mysticism and the idea of God as indwelling. Both of these positions are traceable among the followers of Zion Ward in the 1830s. And about 1820 William Blake wrote: 'God is Man and exists in us and we in him.'[17]

It was Blake, too, who entitled his last great poem, 'The Everlasting Gospel'. The phrase is from the Book of Revelation 14:6, where an angel is seen to 'fly in the midst of heaven, having the everlasting gospel to preach unto them that dwell on the earth, and to every nation.' This gospel was not the same as the New Testament, but a new revelation of religious truth which would appear in the last days. It was a sign that the millennium was near, and also a means of bringing it about.[18] The form which the everlasting gospel would take was open to interpretation. For Blake and others in the antinomian tradition it meant an inward revelation: God would be in man, and there would be no need for the existing institutions of religion. To Southcottians the everlasting gospel was Joanna's dispensation: it was 'the final revelation of [God's] will, previous to the destruction of Satan and the establishment of Christ's

Kingdom'. England was to be 'the place from whence the everlasting gospel will be sent to every part of the habitable globe.'[19]

In the antinomian tradition nakedness had a special significance. Clothes were associated with the fall of man, for Adam and Eve in their original state of innocence had been naked and unashamed. To go naked, therefore, was to put off the old, or fallen Adam, and to assert the new, or regenerate man. Nakedness was also a symbol of equality, and of the 'naked truths' of the gospel. Thus some of the early Quakers ran naked through the streets, 'going naked for a sign', as they said. The well-known story of Blake and his wife sitting naked in their garden at Lambeth may have been more than a rare instance of sun-bathing; for Blake invited Thomas Butts, who had discovered them, to 'Come in! it's only Adam and Eve you know.'[20] William Huntington (the 'Sinner Saved'), when wrestling with the Devil before his conversion, stripped himself stark naked to read and pray.[21] Joanna Southcott in 1804 'was ordered to undress and go to bed, and never to arise to put on her clothes more, before she heard the voice of the Lord call her aloud.' When after four days she had heard no voice, she got out of bed and washed, thinking 'perhaps the Lord would call her when she was naked, as he called Adam.'[22] Nakedness, the everlasting gospel, divine humanity – these scattered instances do not demonstrate anything like the widespread antinomianism of the seventeenth century. But they do suggest that, perhaps just below the surface of current thought, were beliefs and attitudes familiar enough in the earlier period.

The second strand in this popular tradition was mysticism. This is a difficult word to use, and it is employed here to mean an inward, spiritual religion based on the experience of direct, immediate awareness of God.[23] The mystic seeks oneness with the Divine Reality, direct communion with the Absolute. 'We speak the wisdom of God in a mystery, even the hidden wisdom ... revealed unto us by his Spirit', wrote St Paul, and his words in I Corinthians 2:7–15 were taken as an invitation and assurance by those who sought a type of religion which, they felt, could not be found through the traditional institutions of churches. This religion was essentially personal and emphasized experience rather than theology. It could produce people whose lives were quiet, introverted, and intensely devout. It also produced those whose visions, voices and ecstacies caused a great stir. As with St Paul and the early church, the 'gift' of prophesying was highly esteemed by the mystically inclined, and they looked to prophets, not priests, for leadership. The New Testament provided the model of the prophet who, through visions, was able to reveal the commands of the Spirit – together with the corresponding 'gift of discernment' among the people who were thereby enabled to accept the prophet's message. There is a strong likelihood, however, that the manifestations of hysteria which often accompanied mysticism have served to obscure or distort the real nature of the phenomenon. While critics could easily inveigh against the outward signs, the inward experience of God which the mystic claimed, was valid only for the individual concerned and quite beyond the critics' reach. Most of the men and women who sought the path of inward religion were not prophets, and only some were cases of hysteria. What of those who quietly tried to 'take Christ within you', who believed 'the Kingdom of heaven is within you', and who came to the conclusion that heaven and hell were not places but inward states of the soul? Their voices had been heard from time to time in the seventeenth century, and continued thereafter, though somewhat muted. Among Quakers and among the descendants of the sectaries the practice of inward religion was maintained. But the greatest inspiration to mystics in the eighteenth century, the name most frequently mentioned as exemplar, was Jacob Boehme.

The writings of Boehme (or Behmen) were translated into English by John Sparrow and John Ellistone in the 1640s and 1650s, and various editions and selections were available in the early eighteenth century. A four-volume reissue of the works (sometimes called William Law's edition) appeared from 1764 to 1781, and it was probably from this that William Blake and his contemporaries derived their knowledge of Boehme. Almost everything about Boehme was well calculated to appeal to the sort of man or woman best described as a seeker. His humble and unlettered origins, his persecution by the clergy, the tremendous claims of his new revelation, and the utter obscurity of great passages in his writings – all found a sympathetic response in men looking for guidance towards an inward religion, and at the same time set a precedent for would-be mystical leaders. Boehme (1575–1624) was a shoemaker from Görlitz in Silesia, the recipient of mystical experiences and the author of writings which were the result of divine illumination. Typically, he said of his first book, *Aurora* (1612) that it was dictated to him by the Spirit, and that he (Boehme) did but hold the pen. To the extent that the essential experience of all mystics is the same, Boehme was taken as the representative mystic for Protestants interested in exploring this way of approach to God. His works were a powerful protest against institutional, formal religion, and against the claims of the intellect over experience. 'The entire bible lies in me if I have Christ's Spirit in me', he wrote. 'What do I need of more books?'[24] Boehme described himself as a seeker, to whom suddenly 'the gate was opened.' In an experience of illumination, he recorded,

> I saw and knew more [in one quarter of an hour] than if I had been
> many years together at an university. .... For I saw and knew the
> Being of all Beings, the Byss (the ground or original foundation), and
> Abyss (that which is without ground, or bottomless and fathomless);
> also the birth [or eternal generation] of the holy Trinity; the descent,
> and original of this world, and of all creatures, through the divine
> wisdom.[25]

Boehme believed that he was able to penetrate the deepest mysteries of God, man and the universe.

Two of his central ideas in particular impressed his English readers and were repeated in various guises: first, that all things have an outward and an inward form, and the former is a reflection or parable of the latter; and second, that God is made manifest within men. 'The whole outward visible world with all its being', wrote Boehme, 'is a signature, or figure of the inward spiritual world.'[26] Boehme believed, like Paracelsus, that all objects in nature (as for example plants, minerals, and the stars) might be comprehended by this inward way of approach. 'The inward power and property' may be known 'by the outward signs; for nature has given marks and notes to everything, whereby it may be known; and this is the Language of Nature, which signifies for what everything is good and profitable.'[27] When applied to man this idea produces the concept of microcosm: 'man is a little world out of the great world (*microcosmus ex macrocosmus*) and hath the property of the whole great world in him.'[28] Everything lies within man; 'for he is a complete image of God, or of the Being of all Beings.'[29] Something of the same idea of microcosm was expressed by Blake in his 'Auguries of Innocence':

> To see a World in a Grain of Sand
> And a Heaven in a Wild Flower,
> Hold Infinity in the palm of your hand
> And Eternity in an hour.[30]

Christ, too, was for Boehme both outward and inward. In the outward and visible world He had a temporal manifestation; but He also has an eternal, invisible presence. 'He [Christ] is become that which I am, and has made me that which he is', declared Boehme.[31] Christ dwells within man; God is everywhere; and heaven or hell are states of the soul. Every man creates his own real world. Like Adam, the first man, he may 'fall' by cutting himself off from God through the pursuit of self; or he may follow the light, which is to be Christ.

Beyond a certain point the words of mystics become obscure to most people. It is difficult to explain a musical experience to one who has never tried to listen to music. Only those who have tried are likely to understand. Boehme is no exception to this rule, and for the modern reader the difficulty of understanding him is increased by his use of the vocabulary and symbolism of alchemy, astrology, and humoral physiology. Yet it is possible that in the eighteenth century these references to the stars and magic and the philosopher's stone were endearing rather than repelling qualities to his more humble readers. The seeker after inward religion did not expect an easy journey; he was not to be put off by the more arid parts of Boehme's work, and was already sufficiently advanced along the mystic way to be able to gather valuable gems from the master: 'he that seeketh, findeth.' Moreover, Boehme's astrological and alchemical language harmonized well with popular traditions of magic and the supernatural, with herbalism and popular medicine. Among the intellectually sophisticated such notions were increasingly scorned after the seventeenth century, though elements of folk belief retained a firm hold in the minds of men as highly educated as Wesley and Dr Johnson. And popular religion contained until much later many beliefs which are supposed by some historians to have 'died out' in the age of Enlightenment.

How extensive was the influence of Boehme among the 'lower orders'? It would be unwarranted to attribute every manifestation of mysticism or neo-Platonism in eighteenth-century popular thought to Behmenist ideas. But there are straws in the wind to suggest that Boehme's influence, either directly or indirectly, was quite wide-spread among a certain type of seeker. The similarity between some of Boehme's ideas and the doctrines of Swedenborg will become apparent later when we examine the relation between Swedenborgianism and the millenarians of the 1790s. The same sort of people who earlier were interested in Boehme, in the later eighteenth century were likely to be attracted by Swedenborg. In a valuable survey made in 1775, Ralph Mather, an early Swedenborgian missionary from Bolton, testified to the existence of seekers in various parts of the country who had been influenced in their search for an inward religion by Boehme and William Law.[32] At Carrickfergus, Ireland, was

Edward Pendril, shoemaker, a married man who under great
persecution lives in continence and abstinence from animal food ...

He is tender minded. He was with the Quakers but now fully believes in restitution, and the universality of God's power and love.

In Hercules Lane, Belfast, lived William Forde: 'a poor man, he is not so solid as E.P. but teachable and lives on roots and water.' In Warrington it was 'not impossible to find some simple minds. James Worrall and Richard China, both well-meaning Methodists, and my loving friends, can soon direct thee.' At Leigh were to be found William Crompton, farmer, and others — 'poor people [who] love J. Behme and Wm. Law.' Bolton had a number of seekers, and 'several more coming on: these I think are in general but low in the world, but 'tis a school of female philosophers.' In Chester the inquirer should seek out Elizabeth Letsham: 'she has a most tender mind. She was with the Methodists, and though [she has] a pretty handsome annuity, sits alone and keeps silence.' In the same town 'a poor woman has had a large experience.' And 'J. Leadbetter, a painter, and many (5 or 6) others have been visited. These are also held in derision as mystics, but though some do not come forward as one would wish, yet they are not gone from simplicity.' At Manchester Mather mentions Sarah Lee of St Anne's Square, 'one highly elevated in the world but of a large experience'; Sam Mann of Radcliffe Street, who 'has been about 18 years in the way'; and Thomas [sic] Clowes, 'a rector of one of the churches, a pious solid young man'. But 'some others in this place who would feign the name of mystics I fear are deceiving themselves.'

Mather's list of 'those in whose minds the light of God has arisen or is graciously arising' cuts across denominational loyalties. In these and other cases he mentions are Quakers, Methodists, Anglicans — men and women, often 'simple and low in the world', who were seeking an inward way to God independently of the established religious channels. Sometimes they abstained from flesh food and practised sexual continence; always they tried to avoid too great a preoccupation with earthly things. They longed for a 'visitation' from the Spirit, and watched eagerly for signs and wonders. How many they were it is impossible to say. Twenty years earlier Stephen Penny, a Bristol correspondent of William Law, had referred to acquaintances in Dartmouth who were familiar with the works of Boehme:

> what is remarkable ... they are of the simple and illiterate sort. Others of school-learning despise us, and ridicule them. It was of the first sort the followers of the Saviour of the world consisted, when clothed with humanity.[33]

Their significance for this study is that they were people who, in certain circumstances, might be drawn to prophets and prophetesses, and to the support of millenarian causes.

In a letter of 1779 Mather refers to his reading of tracts by Jane Lead – another way in which Behmenist ideas continued to be circulated in the eighteenth century. Mrs Jane Lead (1623–1704), the author of several works which were greatly admired by the mystically inclined, was head of the small Philadelphian Society which flourished in London at the end of the seventeenth century.[34] She had been influenced by Boehme (probably in the first instance through the writings of Dr John Pordage, a Behmenist) and her own 'prophetic visions' were in a similar mould. The Philadelphians (named after the sixth of the seven churches in Asia mentioned in Revelation 1:4 and 3:7) were chiliastic mystics who believed in the imminence of the millennium, though not in a violent, cataclysmic sense. Jane Lead's *A Fountain of Gardens* (1696–1701) is one of the few works mentioned occasionally by later millenarians who were attracted to Brothers and Joanna Southcott.[35] The book is a spiritual diary beginning in 1670, written as a series of letters. In form it is similar to the writings of Joanna: visions and dreams relating to homely, every-day occurrences are followed by interpretations of their spiritual significance. But the interpretations are more mystical than those of Joanna Southcott or Richard Brothers, who in comparison appear somewhat coarse and crude.

Another voice from the late seventeenth century was that of the prophet, Lodowicke Muggleton (1609–98). With his cousin, John Reeve (1608–58), who was a tailor like himself, Muggleton proclaimed they were the two witnesses of Revelation 11:3 ('And I will give power unto my two witnesses, and they shall prophesy a thousand two hundred and threescore days'). They were the Lord's last messengers before the second coming, mandated to declare a new system of faith and empowered to pronounce eternal life or death on individuals. Muggleton was first attracted and then repelled by Boehme, and a good deal of his (Muggleton's) efforts were directed against the Behmenists and Quakers. Like Joachim of Fiore in the twelfth century, Muggleton and Reeve had a trinitarian conception of the whole of history, which they interpreted in three ages (or 'commissions') of the Father, the Son and the Spirit. The third age, to which they were the witnesses appointed by divine communications, began in 1652. They also elaborated the doctrine of the 'two seeds' in man, the divine and the diabolic. According to this philosophy every man is a mixture of the seed of God (faith) and the seed of the devil (reason), and according to the proportion of the one to the other so will a man be in a state of eternal life or damnation. The main items of Muggletonianism are summed up in the 'six principles': 1 God and the man Jesus Christ are synonymous expressions; 2 the devil and human reason are synonymous; 3 the soul dies and rises again with the body; 4 heaven is a place above the stars; 5 at present hell is nowhere, but this earth, darkened after the last judgment, will be hell; 6 angels are the only beings of pure reason.

The early history of the Muggletonians is a chapter in the history of Commonwealth sectarianism and does not belong here. But Muggletonians survived until very much later, indeed until recent times; and their subsequent history is relevant to our theme.[36] In the 1750s and 1760s – and again in the 1820s – Muggletonian works were reprinted,[37] in much the same way that Boehme's works were reprinted by William Law. It is unlikely that the Muggletonians were ever very numerous. Their abandonment of prayer and any form of public worship meant that they had no need of chapels, ministers or weekly meetings. Muggletonian gatherings ('holidays') were simply occasions on which the faithful met to commemorate events in the prophets' lives, notably the giving of the 'commission' to John Reeve on 3–5 February 1652, and Muggleton's release from prison on 19 July 1677. With such a weak institutional structure, and with little, if any, attempt at proselytizing, their numbers were hardly likely to grow. Nevertheless, there was sufficient life in the Muggletonian body in the 1770s to promote schism. James Birch, a Welsh watch-motion maker living in London, defected with a group of followers (known as the Birchites or Anti-church); and when he went on in 1778 to claim divine prophetic powers, he was in turn repudiated by Martha Collier and others, who formed a third group, the Collierites. Muggletonians were to be found in London, Kent, Wales, and in small numbers elsewhere. In the neighbourhood of Ilam and Blore, on the Derbyshire–Staffordshire border, they were still to be found in 1863 – descendants of converts made by Thomas Tomkinson (1631–1710?), a local yeoman who was perhaps the ablest of all the followers of Muggleton.

The Muggletonian faith was preserved obscurely in the families of believers, who handed down the printed works and circulated among themselves the manuscripts of the two prophets – rather as the old Southcottians cherished the teachings of Joanna in the late nineteenth century. In this way a minority sectarian tradition could continue long after its more public and formal existence had disappeared. The significance of Muggletonianism in the eighteenth century is that it witnessed to the existence of beliefs and attitudes which, in certain circumstances, could be given a new twist and direction.[38] If it familiarized millenarian-type thinking and strengthened acceptance of the idea of latter-day prophets, it may have contributed to that milieu of popular religious culture into which we are probing.[39] To that extent it helps towards an understanding of those undercurrents of fanaticism and sectarian belief which erupted from time to time in the Age of Reason.

Other forms of enthusiasm attracted greater public attention. The French prophets (Camisards), who arrived in London in 1706, 'made a great noise', and immediately collected an English following.[40] After the revocation of the Edict of Nantes (which had secured toleration for French Protestants) in 1685, persecution of the Huguenots led to a bitter struggle, especially in the Cévennes, where armed rebellion continued from 1702 to 1705. In a situation of misery, oppression and seemingly hopeless struggle against powerful tyrants – the classic conditions for the emergence of chiliasm – appeared a strong millenarian movement, complete with prophets, prophesyings and messianic promises. Pierre Jurieu, a Huguenot leader living in Rotterdam and with close English connections, forecast that the millennium would begin in 1690. In the Cévennes there was an outpouring of manifestations of the Spirit – visions, miracles, antinomianism, and ecstatic states. After the collapse of the Camisard revolt, some of the Cévenole prophets came to England, where they continued in their same role, but soon widened the area of their denunciations to include all who refused to accept the authority of their revelations. The Huguenot church in London repudiated them: and in 1707 three of their leaders were sentenced to the pillory. By this time they had made converts (the English prophets), and the notoriety of their activities made their name a by-word for extravagant enthusiasm.

Meetings of the French and English prophets were characterized by 'enthusiastic agitations'. States of religious exaltation were followed by prophetic utterances, speaking with tongues, and violent actions of the body – convulsions, tremblings, jumping, laughing, and bizarre physical acts. Samuel Keimer, a young printer, was attracted to the prophets and describes a typical incident:

> Another time I have seen my sister [Mary Keimer], who is a lusty young woman, fling another prophetess upon the floor, and under agitations, tread upon her breast, belly, legs, etc., walking several times backwards and forwards over her, and stamping upon her with violence. This was adjudged to be a sign of the fall of the whore of Babylon.[41]

On another occasion he recorded how, 'at the house of Francis Moult I have seen a prophet tear a prophetess by the hair of the head, leading her up and down in a very frightful manner, both being under violent agitations.' At other meetings the prophets impersonated God, the devil, the arch-angel Gabriel, and the church, and fought and struggled with each other on the floor. Keimer later emigrated to Philadelphia, where he set up as a printer (and was incidentally the employer for a time of the young Benjamin Franklin); but for several years he and his sister and friends were deeply implicated with the prophets. 'For my part', he recalls, 'I had such a thorough belief of the divinity of the spirit presiding, that had John Potter ['a great prophet'], under operation, commanded me to kill my father, mother, or even the late Queen on the throne, I sincerely believe I should immediately have attempted it.' At this time he (like many others, he says) 'could not relish any preaching but what came immediately from the spirit', and so eschewed all who 'preached for hire': even the Quakers were unacceptable, 'considering [their] tautology and meanness of expression'. He also lived in daily hope of the millennium:

> All this while, which was about three years after I was out of my time, I, with the rest of the believers, continued in great expectations of approaching changes, according to what the spirit had so often said ... should happen.

The prophets did not confine themselves to uttering vague generalities about the coming of the millennium. In December 1707 Dr Thomas Emes, a believer, died, and several prophecies were made that he would be resurrected five months later. The crowds who went to Bunhill Fields cemetery in May 1708 to witness the event were disappointed; but for the faithful there was, as always in such cases, an acceptable explanation of the failure. The miracle had been cancelled, said John Lacy, because of the danger that the crowd would cause a disturbance and molest the risen prophet. Lacy, a wealthy justice of the peace, was a leading prophet and the author of several pamphlets. He was guided by the Spirit to make prophetic utterances, and also claimed the gift of speaking with tongues. Among the prophets he caused some dissension by following the command of the Spirit to leave his wife and co-habit with Elizabeth Gray, a young prophetess. It was prophesied that the child of this adultery would be a son who would work miracles; but Elizabeth bore a daughter − and likewise with the second child. Keimer, after later reflection and parting from the prophets, testified: 'For my own part, I now sincerely believe that John Lacy did not leave his wife from any lustful desire, but solely in obedience to the Spirit's commands.' The outside world was not so charitable in its assessment of such antinomianism; and the rumours of 'indecencies' and 'lewd posturings' in the prophets' meetings confirmed the worst suspicions.[42]

Dissension within the movement also centred on another wealthy convert, Sir Richard Bulkeley, an Irish baronet. His body was short and crooked, and it was prophesied that he would be miraculously made straight, and cured of other ailments by the Spirit acting through Lacy. According to Keimer, Bulkeley fell under the influence of Abraham Whitrow, a prophet who 'preaches up the doctrine of levelling, or that the rich must part with all their estates, and become poor, if ever they designed to enter the Kingdom of Heaven.' Lacy vainly opposed this doctrine of social equality; Bulkeley, convinced of the divine nature of Whitrow's messages, accompanied him on journeys through England and Ireland, providing lavish financial support.[43]

The prophets and their followers were never a large sect – to be numbered perhaps by hundreds rather than thousands – and their significance lies elsewhere than in their numbers. They were in some ways a bridge between the millenarians of the seventeenth and the eighteenth centuries. The Philadelphians (at first glance rather different in tone and temperament) in 1707 'came out of their retirement, and combined with the Camisards to announce once again in public that the Last Days had already begun.'[44] Richard Roach, rector of St Augustine's, Hackney, and a follower of Jane Lead, regarded the prophets as God's instruments but also as a divine sport or jest. He made fun of Lacy's 'wedding' with Elizabeth Gray, but accepted that it was a droll example of the Spirit's leading. For Roach the prophets, with their denunciations and agitations, were yet one more sign of the approaching millennium, which he continued to proclaim until his death in 1730.[45]

The prophets made missionary tours into the provinces. Bristol, Coventry, Worcester, Oxford, Cambridge, Scotland, Ireland and Wales were visited. 'Nor were they without success in their several progresses, deluding many sincere people into a belief of the strange revolutions approaching', said Keimer; and he observed that their preaching and prophesying produced the same results as in London. Not much is heard of the prophets as a body after about 1713, but individual prophets continued their testimony for several decades. Lacy, who settled in Lancashire, was still producing tracts on prophecy in the 1720s.[46] A younger generation may also have carried on the tradition, for Wesley records visiting Mary Plewit, 'one of the French Prophets', aged about twenty-four or twenty-five, in 1739. Her body was convulsed by contortions for about ten minutes. Then

she spoke much (all as in the person of God, and mostly in Scripture

27

words) of the fulfilling of the prophecies, the coming of Christ now at hand, and the spreading of the gospel over all the earth ... Two or three of our company were much affected, and believed she spoke by the Spirit of God. But this was in no wise clear to me.

Wesley considered that 'the motion might be either hysterical or artificial. And the same words any person of a good understanding and well versed in the Scriptures might have spoken.'[47] His suspicion hardened into opposition when he saw similar manifestations produced by some Methodist preaching.

The continuance of the French prophets' tradition is also evidenced in the early history of the Shakers. In their own account of their origins, the Shakers accepted Cévenole prophesying as the source from which the Shaker movement sprang. Although the testimony of the prophets in England declined after the peak years, 1706–13, a handful of believers remained, who 'stood as living witnesses of God, and, like faithful watchmen of the night, waited the approaching dawn.' This saving remnant came from Lancashire.

> About the year 1747, a small number who were endowed with the spirit of these witnesses, were led by the influence of the Divine Spirit to unite themselves into a small society, in the neighborhood of Manchester, under the ministry of James and Jane Wardley. These were both sincerely devoted to the cause of God, and were blest with great manifestations of divine light. ... They boldly testified, that the second appearing of Christ was at hand; and that the Church was rising in her full and transcendant glory, which would effect the final downfall of Antichrist. They affirmed that the work of the great day of God was then commencing, and would increase until every promise of God should be fulfilled.[48]

The Wardleys were Quaker tailors from Bolton, who in 1747 joined John Townley, a well-to-do builder, and his wife, Ann, in Manchester, who had likewise come under the influence of the prophets. A small group of millenarians, mostly ex-Quakers, met regularly at the Townleys' house, under the spiritual leadership of the Wardleys. Their devotions included trances, agitations of the body, shouting, and apocalyptic-style preaching. They soon became known to their scandalized neighbours as Shaking Quakers or Shakers. In 1758 they were joined by Ann Lee, a young woman who had been one of George Whitefield's 'hearers'. For some years she was not a very active member of the society; but in 1770 she was imprisoned for profaning the Sabbath, and while in gaol received a great revelation. She soon realized that she was a new, female messiah, and asserted her leadership in the sect as Mother Ann. In 1774, following another revelation, she emigrated with eight of her followers to America.[49]

By the end of the eighteenth century the French prophets and their followers were extinct, but not forgotten. In the spate of re-publication of old prophecies in the 1790s their names were recalled and their works revived.[50] Many of their experiences and doctrines were similar to those of the later millenarians. The doom-laden prophecies of the French prophets were echoed by Brothers' denunciations of London as Babylon. Keimer describes a ceremony by Nicholas Faccio (one of the Camisards who was pilloried in 1707) which is reminiscent of Joanna Southcott's sealing of believers, and also of Brothers' and John Wroe's assigning their followers to the tribes of Israel.[51] Widow Hughes, an illiterate prophetess from St Martin's-le-Grand, claimed, like Joanna Southcott later, to be the 'Woman clothed with the Sun' of Revelation 12. In their concern for ecstatic states, visions, millenarian expectations, and the role accorded to prophetesses as well as prophets, the earlier movement had much in common with the later. Moreover, if Keimer's sample of the membership of the French and English prophets in London is reliable, the social composition was not unlike the followers of Brothers and Joanna.[52] There was the same mixture of artisans (watchmaker, staymaker, printer) and tradesmen (tallow-chandler, book-seller), interspersed with merchants, professional men, and a handful of wealthy disciples. About a third of the names belong to women. As with the later millenarians, the prophets had quite often belonged formerly to other sects, in this case usually the Quakers or Philadelphians. There is no reason to suppose that the millenarians of 1790–1850 deliberately imitated the French prophets, even though they may have been aware of them. Any similarities can be accounted for by their common relation to a popular tradition of millenarianism and enthusiastic religion. The significance of the French prophets was that they helped to keep alive that tradition in the first decades of the eighteenth century.

It is not easy to set institutional bounds to this tradition. As in the seventeenth century,[53] prophets and prophetesses appeared from many parts of the sectarian milieu and in many different parts of the country. To attempt a catalogue of them here would be tedious and unnecessary; but by way of illustration we may turn again to Wesley's *Journal*.[54] In a letter of 7 June 1739 he describes his visit to Mrs Cooper, 'the supposed prophetess' in Bristol, and comments:

> Her agitations were nothing near so violent as those of Mary Plewit are. She prayed awhile (as under the hand of God) and then spoke to

me above half an hour. What spirit she spoke of I know not. The words were good. ... I felt no power while she spoke. Appearances are against her, but I judge nothing before the time.

In 1744 Wesley visited Thomas Newans, a Shropshire prophet; and again in April 1746 he recorded:

I rode with Mr Piers to see one who called himself a prophet. We were with him about an hour; but I could not at all think that he was sent of God: 1 Because he appeared to be full of himself, vain, heady and opinionated. 2 Because he spoke with extreme bitterness, both of the King, and of all the bishops and all the clergy. 3 Because he aimed at talking Latin, but could not; plainly showing he understood not his own calling.

These prophets and prophetesses were not Methodists, but at times Wesley had to encounter similar claims among his own followers. John Brown, of Tanfield Leigh, after his conversion, declared to the people of Newcastle that God had revealed to him that he should be a king and would tread all his enemies beneath his feet. George Bell, an ex-life-guardsman, and Methodist lay preacher, claimed extraordinary revelations, and attempted divine healing. He was accepted as a true prophet by a small group of the more visionary Methodists under the leadership of Thomas Maxfield; and Bell went on to proclaim that the world would end on 28 February 1763.[55] Wesley repudiated – though somewhat reluctantly – these aberrations of spirituality, and declared that he was not willing to bear the reproach of enthusiasm. Yet the doctrines which Methodism emphasized – Christian perfection, assurance, and sanctification – encouraged in some believers the very tendencies which Wesley deplored. Methodism was essentially a religion of experience. Its appeal was not to specific doctrines as such, but rather to 'a profound emotional and mystical experience achieved by methods not requiring learning or analysis ... an experience more accessible to the humble and unsophisticated than to their better situated or better educated fellows.'[56] Thus did Methodism become the bearer, and much the most influential disseminator, of the qualities of popular enthusiastic religion in the eighteenth century. The autobiographies of most working-class millenarians and seekers in the period record contact at some stage with a local Methodist society. If one was searching for an inward, spiritual religion the natural place to inquire in the first instance seemed to be among the people called Methodists.

The incidence of prophetism generally appears to have increased in the 1780s, and still more so in the 1790s. Samuel Best (1738–1825) was typical of a certain type of prophet, and was visited by the same kind of people who were attracted to Richard Brothers. Best, who called himself Poor-Helps, had been a Spitalfields weaver, but some time before 1787 became an inmate of Shoreditch workhouse. He lived on a meagre diet of bread and cheese, and gin tinctured with rhubarb, but recouped his strength by nightly converse with celestial powers. Visitors were impressed by the decorations in straw which adorned his apartment and by his combination of biblical knowledge with palmistry, but usually concluded that he was partly out of his mind. He was convinced that it was his mission to lead the children of Israel and to rebuild Jerusalem.[57]

It is a well-established characteristic of enthusiastic religion that the Spirit operates impartially as between the sexes. Women, whether in the role of prophetess or wealthy patroness or adoring disciple appear prominently in millenarian movements. The later eighteenth century produced its full share of prophetesses. From Joanna Southcott's own West Country came a contemporary known as the Cornish Trumpeter who claimed that she was one of the seven trumpeters of Revelation 8 who were to proclaim the second coming.[58] The same chapter of Revelation was used by another prophetess, Mrs Sarah Flaxmer, to interpret the events of 1795 as the fulfilment of the apocalyptic prophecies. She had known since 1779 that God had chosen her to 'reveal Satan', and more recently she had been guided by dreams and visitations.[59] When she told the minister under whom she sat about 'the Lord's gracious dealings with me' he only laughed and called her an enthusiast. But her convictions were unshaken, and she declared that the war with France was 'the great War in the Revelations, by which this Government was to be overturned.' She recognized Brothers as 'the Lord's prophet', but argued that he had temporarily fallen into the power of Satan, and that she was destined to 'reveal Satan' and thereby free Brothers, as foretold in Revelation 12 and in her dream of 1779. For this reason she refused to see John Wright, an apostle of Brothers, and denounced the Avignon Society, which Wright had visited, as 'the synagogue of Satan'.[60] Her doctrines embodied a sturdy feminism. It was by a woman (namely, herself) that Satan was to be overcome in these last days; and she found confirmation of feminine pre-eminence in the Apocryphal book I Esdras 4, where Zorobabel lists the powers of women over men. Her mission was a complement or perhaps a challenge to Brothers. This was also the case with Mrs S. Eyre of Cecil Street, London, who, in 1794–5, believed that she was commanded to announce the pouring out of the vials in the last days and to warn against France (the beast of Revelation) and Brothers. There is no evidence that these prophetesses attracted much of a following, and they may be taken as symptomatic of a general interest in millennialism rather than of commitment to specific millenarian movements.

It was otherwise with two prophetesses in Wales and Scotland. About 1780 there appeared in Merioneth a woman named Mary Evans (Mari Evan) who was known as *Mari y fantell wen* (Mary of the white cloak).[61] She had come from Anglesey, having left her husband, and declared that she was now the bride of Christ. A group of followers (some sixty to seventy has been suggested) soon gathered in the country between Ffestiniog and Harlech, and acknowledged her as a prophetess. Members of the sect wore white mantles on Sundays, and met in houses and 'on hill tops'; but reliable evidence about beliefs, practices and membership is lacking. She died in 1789 aged fifty-four and was buried at Llanfihangel y traethau, where her grave may still be seen. According to local legend (usual in such cases) her followers delayed the burial in hopes of her speedy resurrection. Little as is known about Mary, her impact on the local community was sufficient to be remembered in the area for several generations,[62] and her following attests the strength of the will to believe in a prophetess and her message.

Far stronger is the documentation of her Scottish contemporary, Mrs (Luckie) Buchan (*c.* 1738–91).[63] Born Elspeth Simpson, her parents kept a small way-side inn at Fatmacken on the road between Banff and Portsoy. Her mother died when she was two and her father married again; and Elspeth (or Elspath) was brought up in the family of a relation, by whom she was taught reading and sewing. During a visit to Greenock she met Robert Buchan, a working potter from Ayr, whom she married. 'Many children' were said to have been born to the couple, who lived first in Ayr and then in Banff, but only three were alive when Elspeth separated from her husband in 1781 and went to live in Glasgow. The causes of the separation are not entirely clear: both Elspeth's 'licentious conduct' and Robert's need to search for employment are mentioned. A more likely explanation is Elspeth's religious state. There is no need to take too seriously her later recollection of how, at the age of between five and seven, she was troubled by the scriptures and by the problem of how death came into the world. But by the 1770s she had become a seeker. 'In the year 1774 the power of God wrought wonderfully upon all my senses.'[64] For several weeks she could not eat, and nearly starved to death. She was a regular attender at 'fellowship meetings' – societies of persons who met weekly for religious purposes, rather like the Methodists – and her unorthodox interpretations of scripture alienated the clergy and attracted a few kindred souls. She went from kirk to kirk but found no spiritual rest. Then one Sunday in December 1782 she heard the Reverend Hugh White preach at a sacrament service in Glasgow, and was immediately captivated: 'my soul filled with love for him.' She corresponded with him for four months and accepted his invitation to stay with him at his home in Irvine in Ayrshire.

White was minister of the Relief congregation at Irvine, a secessionist body which had left the Church of Scotland in 1761. He apparently had some reputation as a scholar and theologian, though in his preaching he was described as 'a coarse hewer'. After meeting Mrs Buchan he affirmed that she was a saint and a mystic who would bring light to disperse the darkness of Antichrist that had long lain over the land. More explicitly he shortly recognized her as the 'Woman clothed with the Sun' (Revelation 12); and she reciprocated by declaring that he was the man-child whom she had (figuratively) brought forth, and who was to rule all nations with a rod of iron. The congregation at first welcomed her, but these claims were too much for the majority, who asked White to dismiss Mrs Buchan and repudiate her doctrines. This he refused to do, and accordingly he was suspended from the ministry by the presbytery. The doors of his church were closed against White in the summer of 1783, but some of his old congregation followed him into the wilderness and declared their allegiance to the new prophetess.

The Buchanites (as the new sect was called) did not have an easy passage. At first they met in White's house or in the home of one of the members in Irvine. But local opposition to the supposed 'immoral' relationship between White and Mrs Buchan, as well as to her prophetical claims was strong. Merchants, tradesmen and labourers who were known Buchanites suffered loss of trade and unemployment. Mrs Buchan herself was set upon by a crowd and driven out of town, returning the next morning 'bare-headed, bare-footed, with scarcely a rag to cover her nakedness, and all her person covered with blood'.[65] Fearing more riotous behaviour, the magistrates banished her from the town, and in May 1784 the sect left, firmly believing that Irvine would shortly be destroyed by a Sodom-like judgment.[66] The Buchanites made their way to New Cample, a farm in Nithsdale, Dumfriesshire, where they lived in an empty barn until they could build a rough community house, dubbed derisively 'Buchan Ha''. Here again they were attacked at night by a crowd who smashed the doors, windows and furniture, and drove the members out into the December snow. However, they survived this and other harassments until March 1787, when they were compelled to leave because of the county magistrates' requirement of security against poor-law entitlement. This time they moved to Auchengibbert, a wild moorland farm in the parish of Urr, Kirkcudbrightshire. After four years their pecuniary state was flourishing, but in 1791 Mrs Buchan died and the community broke up. White and about thirty of the members emigrated to America in June 1792; but a remnant of fourteen others remained in Scotland, living first at Larghill in the same parish, and (from 1808) at Crocketford. There, Andrew Innes, the last of the Buchanites, died in 1846.

The central belief of the sect was the divinity of Friend Mother, as they called their leader. She claimed that she was the third person of the Godhead (the Holy Ghost) and that Christ, as the second person of the Godhead, was her elder brother. She was also the mysterious woman of Revelation 12, in whom the light of God was restored to the earth. At the second coming of Christ she was to meet Him in the clouds with her followers, and to take them direct to heaven without tasting death. She could also impart the Holy Spirit to others by breathing on them, and such persons were held to be in a state of grace from which they could not fall. No attempt was made to work miracles. The apostles, she argued, had not required a sign for them to answer Jesus' call. They simply had faith. On her death-bed she assured her followers that she would be resurrected after six days if their faith were sufficiently pure; otherwise they would have to wait for ten or even fifty years before she returned to take them to heaven. To facilitate her ascension the lid of her coffin was not nailed down for several days; but when nothing happened she was buried secretly.

The faith of the Buchanites had been severely tried earlier by their experiences at New Cample. White and Mrs Buchan were convinced – and persuaded their followers – that the second coming could be expected at any moment. When this took place the whole body of believers would be raised by supernatural power to heaven, where they would dwell with the angels and all redeemed saints. This was the eagerly awaited and ardently prayed-for consummation of the little society:

Oh! hasten translation, and come resurrection!
Oh! hasten the coming of Christ in the air!

After several false hopes and alarms that the 'Midnight Cry' was to be heard, Mrs Buchan declared a forty-day fast as a preparation for the great event. The community cut itself off from the outside world: the door was bolted and the windows nailed down and screened. A total abstinence from food was enjoined, and only the needs of extreme thirst were to be met. During the fast the time was spent in singing hymns and reading aloud. At the end of the forty days the members, weak and emaciated, staggered out of Buchan Ha' and assembled before sunrise on the top of a nearby hill to await the coming of the Lord in glory and ascension with him to heaven. But, like the American Millerites later, they were disappointed. Mrs Buchan explained that their faith was too weak. To the faithful disciple, Andrew Innes, it seemed that the failure was not without precedent:

> she [Mrs Buchan] was under the necessity of doing with us, as Jesus did with his disciples, Peter, James and John, when they would not be satisfied without a sight of his Father. He ascended with them to the top of the mount, and allowed them to be sensible of their unfitness to receive what they so much desired. The same was it with us[67]

The Buchanites, unlike most millenarians in Britain, lived in a community. Originally there were forty-six members, but after the establishment of Buchan Ha' the numbers increased to over sixty. Following the example of the early Apostles (Acts 2:44–5; 4:32–5) they 'had all things common.' Their money was put into a common stock and placed at the disposal of the treasurer; unused clothing was pooled and issued to members as required; and the washing, mending, knitting and cooking were undertaken by the women communally. A rough equality prevailed. All sat at the same table and ate the same food, with the exception of Friend Mother who either served those at table herself or was employed in directing others to do so. No titles were used; members were known by their Christian names; and married women reverted to using their maiden names. At first little thought was given to the economic basis of the community, which lived off the funds provided by the wealthier disciples. Members were happy to work gratuitously for neighbouring farmers, thereby demonstrating their renunciation of worldly considerations. The arrangements were in any case regarded as temporary, since the second coming was imminent. But later, when the funds were exhausted and when it had become clear that the necessities of life would have to be provided for some years at least, a new regime was introduced. Members hired themselves out to local farmers for work in the fields; and after the removal to Auchengibbert the community set about farming on their own account. Duncan Robertson, a wheelwright and leader of the community, made spinning-wheels, and the women found regular employment in spinning yarn for factories. Later still, after the remnant of the community settled at Larghill, the Buchanite women became famous for their use of the two-handed spinning-wheel and the fineness of their yarn. They also acquired local fame for their skill in medicine and herbal cures. Moreover, they refused all rewards or even thanks for any benefits they were able to bestow upon their neighbours, quoting Mrs Buchan to the effect that thanks were due only to God. Despite their oddities, such as always wearing home-spun clothes of a light green colour, and working on Sundays, local opposition to the Buchanites died down, and they were tolerated if not approved.

Opposition in the early days at New Cample concentrated on the suspicion of practical antinomianism. 'All things common' was thought to include women as well as material goods, and the community was accused of gross sexual immorality. Mrs Buchan's teachings on marriage did nothing to allay such fears. She held that

> the same law that finished the carnal service at the altar, and bestial sacrifices, put an end to carnal marriages. ... Where the Holy Spirit of God occupies all the person, and reigns throughout the flesh, it matters not much whether they marry or not.[68]

Members of the community gave up their married status and declared that they were no longer subject to 'the bondage of what they [i.e. the world outside] call matrimony.' Hugh White brought his wife and two small children to Buchan Ha', but the family did not live separately, and White and Mrs Buchan slept in the same bed. Katherine Gardner, formerly a housemaid in the family of one of the richer members, Peter Hunter, became pregnant by Andrew Innes, whom she later married, and their daughter was brought up in the community. It was intended that children should be taken from their mothers and reared communally, but in practice the exclusiveness of mother-love proved difficult to overcome.

The social composition of the Buchanites was mixed. Peter Hunter, who had belonged to White's old congregation, was writer and town clerk of Irvine, as well as having business interests in shipping and the coal trade. John Gibson, a wealthy builder, was in a similar position. They and their wives and families were influential members of the community. But also among the leading disciples were two working men from Muthill, Duncan Robertson, a wheelwright, and Andrew Innes, a carpenter. Innes (1757–1846) became acquainted with Mrs Buchan in 1783, and then formed an attachment to her person and her mission which lasted until his death. After the departure of White for America, Innes took possession of the bones of Mrs Buchan and guarded them in the small reorganized community. He told an inquiring antiquary in 1843 that he expected the return of Friend Mother that same year.[69] The original band of disciples at New Cample was joined by others. George Hill, a well-educated young man, who had been clerk to the Closeburn Lime Works, became a Buchanite, despite strong dissuasion from his brothers. And in the north of England recruits were attracted from among the Methodists, notably James Brown, a merchant tailor from Sunderland, and Thomas Bradley, a farmer from Stranton, near Hartlepool. Rather less welcome was Charles Edward Conyers, who claimed to be a marine officer on half pay, but who turned out to be a moneyless rake. In general the Buchanites were typical of most millenarian movements of the period – a mixture of labouring men and women, domestic servants, and some wealthier tradesmen and professibnals.

Clearly the most important person among the Buchanites, after Mrs Buchan herself, was Hugh White. A native of Stirlingshire, he had been a 'professor of logic in an American college' before being called as minister to the Relief congregation in Irvine. At Buchan Ha' he supervised all arrangements for the running of the community, but apparently spent most of his time preaching to the members and writing hymns and theological works. He was very disappointed by the failure of the attempted ascension to heaven, which necessitated a reorientation of his expectations and plans. The refusal of Mrs Buchan to rise from the dead in 1791 completed this transformation. He proposed to the community that they should abandon all expectations of her return, and accept the fact that her mission was now done. In her place he would assume the leadership, playing the role of Joshua to finish the work of the dead Moses. A majority of the members accepted this proposal; but about a third of them, led by Andrew Innes, Duncan Robertson and George Kidd (a ploughman) dissented strongly. White and some thirty of his followers then emigrated to America, where apparently the community broke up and the members went their separate ways. White made his way to Virginia and established an academy, first in Richmond and then, in 1808, in Charlottesville, where he remained until 1815. He died in 1827 at Milton, near Monticello. Some time before 1812 he became a Swedenborgian, and in that year was ordained a minister in the New Jerusalem Church. He does not appear to have exercised a very active ministry; but he documented his spiritual and theological development in two pamphlets, *Philotheos* and *Cosmogenia*.[70]

Several aspects of the Buchanite movement are worth noting, in relation both to earlier millenarians and to those who came after. Most obvious is the similarity between Mrs Buchan and other prophetesses, especially Mother Ann Lee, Mary Evans, and Joanna Southcott. Hugh White's position is also closely paralleled by leading disciples among the

Shakers and Southcottians. The tendency to antinomianism and unorthodox views on sex, marriage and the family is characteristic of millenarian sects generally, and will recur in later chapters. Recruitment of the Buchanites from the Relief congregation and the Methodists is again according to type, for millenarians came principally from existing churches and sects rather than from those completely outside institutional religion. The response of the outside world to the Buchanites was predictable, and the charges of witchcraft and Satanism to account for Mrs Buchan's 'hold' over her followers were repeated against most prophetesses who claimed supernatural powers. In two respects, however, the Buchanites were unusual in comparison with the Southcottians and followers of Brothers to be examined later. First, they were largely local and confined to a small area in the west of Scotland. Second, they emphasized their withdrawal from the world much more strongly by their communitarianism. All in all the story of Friend Mother is a strong confirmation of the power of a local prophetess to appeal successfully to those who sought salvation through the guidance of prophesyings.

The wider social significance of the kind of prophetism described in this chapter is complex. It is easy to say that prophets' actions are functional phenomena related to the needs of a particular historical situation, and that as the context changes so does the behaviour. But this does not take us very far. The prophets concerned differed widely in their teachings and in their actions. One might be commanded, after his awakening or rebirth, to preach (George Fox); another to be quiet and still (Lodowicke Muggleton, for some time); others to withdraw into a community (Mrs Buchan), to set down her visions in writing (Jane Lead), to organize a sect (the French and English prophets). All of them had charisma, all were in some way abnormal or deviant in the eyes of orthodox contemporaries, all provided something for which there was a felt need. In particular they were bearers of a millenarian ideology. They related to, and were witnesses of, certain strands of popular belief – strands which, despite attempts to discredit them, persisted until late in the nineteenth century and beyond. In relation to these millenarians, Richard Brothers, Joanna Southcott and their followers appear not simply as strange products of the French revolutionary ferment or the social dislocation of early industrialism, but as part of a recognized and recognizable tradition.

CHAPTER THREE

SIGNS AND WONDERS

So far we have tried to relate millenarianism to various currents of enthusiastic or inner-light religion. But this is not the whole story. There is also a close connection between millenarian-style belief and certain elements of popular culture. The folklore which was first discovered and exposed to public view in the sixteenth and seventeenth centuries had a remarkable resilience and tenacity – as attested by the huge amount of material collected in the last hundred years by enthusiastic folklorists. Some of the constituents of this folklore, such as omens and auguries, dreams and divinations, magic, witchcraft and demons, will repay examination. Similarly the popular literature of chapbooks and almanacs lies close to the world of millenarian manifestations. The enemies of millenarianism linked it with popular culture, and condemned them both in the same terms: vulgar, crude, ignorant and superstitious. For it was often observed that the followers of millenarian prophets and prophetesses were drawn from people who were already prone to belief in signs and wonders and who had a deep respect for the supernatural. Folk culture provided a matrix in which millenarian yearnings could be nourished.

Popular belief in the supernatural found expression in many forms. At its most general it was a simple, unintellectual type of neo-Platonism: all forms of life are animated by a spirit, and there is an essential oneness of all God's creatures. Further, there is no clear distinction between matter and spirit: the earth is not an inanimate mass but is deemed to be alive, and the universe is peopled by a hierarchy of spirits. The cosmos is an organic unity, in which every part is related to the rest.[1] These things can be but dimly perceived, for the veil of the world obscures them. But occasionally the veil may be lifted, and men may glimpse something of the mysteries and occult qualities of nature, the virtues of plants, metals and minerals. Given these assumptions, other beliefs follow, and assume

39

a plausibility which is otherwise difficult to appreciate today. Two such beliefs which we shall encounter later among the millenarians were in correspondences and signatures.

The doctrine of correspondences held that every part of the physical world corresponds to some aspect of the spiritual. This relationship is not only general but also particular; so that everything in nature has a spiritual meaning. There is an outward and inward significance to all things. Spiritual reality is mirrored in the homely, everyday events of life if we can but see it. Words — including the words of scripture — have an internal or spiritual meaning as well as their outward sense. Visions and dreams are to be interpreted spiritually by those competent to do so. The mystical implications of this doctrine were apparent in Boehme; and further refinements will be met with in Swedenborg. For millenarian prophets the doctrine of correspondences provided a means of interpreting their own and their followers' experiences. It was a familiar and acceptable part of folk tradition.

Similarly the doctrine of signatures, with its very practical applications, was a constant reminder of the reality of supernatural power. The resemblance in the shape of the root, leaf or fruit of any plant to a particular part of the human body was taken to indicate its possessing some beneficial or hurtful power over the corresponding part. For example a decoction of maidenhair fern was good for washing the head and making the hair grow. Balm and wood-sorrel, representing the heart in figure, were cardiacal. The walnut, which bore the signature of the whole head, was good for the brain and mental disease. 'Thus did Divine Providence, by natural hieroglyphics, read lectures to the rude wit of vulgar man.'[2]

In a world so thoroughly subject to invisible spiritual influences, the claims of conjurors, magicians and astrologers were entirely credible. After all, to conjure meant originally to compel the spirits of men and angels. Magic is the ancient occult science which once led its devotees, the magi, to follow a star which took them to the cradle at Bethlehem: 'we have seen his star in the east and are come to worship him.' Astrology is referred to many times in the scriptures, and in a universe so completely one and interdependent it was reasonable to assume that the stars might influence earthly bodies. Beliefs of this kind were not, however, part of acknowledged religion. But neither were they scientific or secular. Usually they are called superstitions, but perhaps it is more useful to classify them as popular (or people's) religion.[3] Many such beliefs have existed for centuries, despite official disapproval and sometimes condemnation by the churches. Theologians separated 'religious' from 'superstitious' belief, though philosophically the distinction is by no means clear-cut, and all ceremonial religion contains some elements of magic. It is unlikely that popular religion would have survived so long unless it had a fairly powerful functional role. Untidy, confused and incomplete as this collection of beliefs was, it nevertheless provided a fabric which held together folk memories, the meaning of daily joys and suffering, the hopes and expectations for the future. Little of this was specifically millenarian. Yet it fixed the bounds of popular comprehension in such a way that millenarianism could be acceptable in certain circumstances. For many labouring people in the eighteenth century the sense of the impossible had not yet been redrawn (as it had for some of the educated classes) to exclude belief in magic, divination and occult forces. Despite Newton, for many of his humbler fellow-countrymen, 'Nature and Nature's laws lay hid in night.' There is a danger in exaggerating the extent to which the Newtonian revolution in intellectual outlook involved changes in statements of religious belief. We do not know how many people, like William Blake, rejected 'Single vision and Newton's sleep'.[4] In the long run, and more immediately for intellectuals, the simple conception of the cosmos which had come from Aristotle and Aquinas had to be abandoned. But at the popular level heaven and the angels remained just above the sky, thunder was the voice of God, and Satan could be encountered in darkness and storm. Without such beliefs the millenarian movements of 1780–1850 could not have taken the form which they did.

There is abundant evidence of the persistence of folk belief and popular religion in the nineteenth century, and that not only in rural areas. 'Those who are not in daily intercourse with the peasantry', it was reported from Lincolnshire in 1856, 'can hardly be made to believe or comprehend the hold that charms, witchcraft, wise men and other relics of heathendom have upon the people.'[5] The autobiographies of working men almost invariably refer to such beliefs in their childhood.[6] Thomas Cooper, whose home was in Gainsborough during the second decade of the nineteenth century, described how he acquired herbal lore from a friend whose father was a fisherman and herb-gatherer; and how a little later he was attracted to an old man, George White (known as the 'Wise Man of Retford') who was an astrologer and devotee of the 'higher knowledge'. William Lovett, living at the same time in Cornwall, attested his firm belief in ghosts and recalled an old woman, Aunt Tammy, 'who was reputed to be a white witch, one who, from the ill she was believed able to inflict, was regarded by some with superstitious dread.' During the same period at Bramley, near Leeds, Joseph Barker noted many instances of magic and the use of charms.

> My parents were both believers in witchcraft and fairies, as well as in
> some other superstitions. They believed that some persons, especially
> certain women, had the power of causing diseases in men and cattle,
> and of harassing and injuring people in various other ways, by an evil
> wish, or by diabolical influence.

Interestingly, they had no difficulty in reconciling these beliefs with a
strong attachment to Methodism: 'though they were foolish enough to
cling to the superstitions of their childhood, their religious belief was, in
general, the great ruling principle of their lives.' The richest collection of
folklore in these autobiographies, however, is Samuel Bamford's *Passages
in the Life of a Radical*, in which he recalled his memories of Middleton,
Lancashire. His friend and fellow radical, George Plant of Blackley,

> was a firm believer in ghosts, witches, and hobgoblins; in the virtues
> of herbs under certain planetary influences; and in the occult
> mysteries of Culpepper and Sibly. He was entirely self-taught; had
> been a great reader, knew something of arithmetic, was a botanist,
> and a dreary minded wanderer in lonely dells, on moors and heaths;
> searching after herbs of surpassing virtue, of mysterious growth and
> concealment, and of wonderful and unaccountable power.

Another of Bamford's acquaintances was Limping Billy, a noted seer
residing at Radcliffe Bridge. These accounts could be matched by other
local reminiscences from all parts of Britain. The list is endless – for we
are chronicling something which had once existed everywhere and
which still existed perhaps more widely than any other set of beliefs.

A general acceptance of folk beliefs and customs, however, does not of
itself provide more than a cultural climate which may be predisposed in
favour of millenarianism. Is it possible to establish closer links between
millenarian belief and specific aspects of folk culture? In the case of some
millenarians and with certain of the constituents of popular culture such
a relationship can be established; though at other times millenarians
found that their beliefs compelled them to reject 'ignorant superstition'.
Signs and wonders were especially tempting to millenarians. Any
instance in which the laws of nature appeared to have been set aside, any
abnormal or inexplicable happening, any unusual behaviour in man or
beast aroused wide-spread interest and speculation. It created wonder in
itself, and prompted thoughts as to what it might portend as a 'sign of the
times'. Wesley had an insatiable curiosity about such things, and would
always turn out of his way to see, for instance, a man born without

arms, or a 'monster' at Bristol fair.[7] Two famous cases of wonders (which proved in fact to be impostures) attracted more than local attention.

The first was Mary Toft (or Tofts), the rabbit woman of Godalming in Surrey.[8] She was the wife of a poor journeyman clothworker and she claimed that in April 1726, when she was five weeks pregnant, she was startled by a rabbit while working in the fields. In September she had what seemed to be a miscarriage, and then gave birth to sixteen rabbits at intervals of several days. The local apothecary, who had practised midwifery for thirty years, believed the case to be genuine, as also did Nathanael St André and Cyriacus Ahlers, surgeons to George I. A controversy broke out between believers and doubters, but the matter appeared to be settled when Mary was brought to London, allegedly confessed her imposture, and was committed to the bridewell in Tothill Fields. However, William Whiston (Newton's successor at Cambridge) revived the issue in 1752 with a declaration that she had fulfilled a prophecy in Esdras. The case was remarkable for the number of people, including members of the medical profession, who were prepared to consider seriously the possibility of such a happening. In the controversy surrounding the last days and pregnancy of Joanna Southcott in 1814 the Mary Toft case was recalled, and it is possible that Joanna and her followers were familiar with its details.[9]

In the second case, that of Ann Moore of Tutbury, Joanna and the Southcottians were directly involved. Ann was the deserted wife of a farm labourer, and with a large family to support she had to subsist on a minimum amount of food.[10] From November 1806 she gave up eating altogether, and in 1807 took permanently to her bed. She claimed that she could live without food and apparently fasted for several years. In 1808 her claims were verified by a committee of doctors and local inhabitants, and for the next four years she was visited by people from all parts of the country who left offerings for her. But in 1813 a stricter investigation was made and after nine days she was reduced to a state of extreme prostration. She then gave up her claims and confessed to receiving nourishment secretly. As with Mary Toft, the main interest of the case is not the successful imposture but the number of people who were ready to believe that she existed miraculously and that this was a sign. One of Joanna's chief followers, the Reverend Thomas Philip Foley, went to see Ann Moore in August 1809. He reported that she was sitting up in bed, resting upon pillows, and looked well in the face, but that the lower parts of her frame were dried up and totally dead. She told him she had lived two years and five months without food, and that from

October 1808 she had never even wetted her mouth. He believed what she said, and concluded, 'she is a living miracle.' Joanna accepted Foley's report, and her Spirit told her that the fasting woman was a sign of the three years famine which was to come and also evidence that nothing is impossible for God.[11] But in 1813 the Spirit revised this interpretation and told Joanna that Ann Moore was an imposter.[12]

Even more wide-spread than signs and wonders was belief in the significance of dreams. From time immemorial it had been taken for granted that dreams were related to the world of the supernatural, and as long as the latter was accepted there was little reason to doubt the traditional view of dreams. It was believed that dreams must serve some special purpose, and that as a rule they predicted the future. The great diversity in the content of dreams and of their impact on the dreamer necessitated an elaborate system of classification and yet baffled attempts at formulating a coherent explanation of their nature. Most popular interest in dreams was directed towards their interpretation, for which two methods were employed.[13] The first method was to see the dream as a whole and as symbolic of something else. Many dreams in the Bible were treated in this manner; for example Joseph interpreted Pharaoh's dream of the seven fat and seven lean kine as symbolic of the seven years of famine in Egypt which would consume all the surplus produced in the seven years of plenty. John Bunyan, when writing *The Pilgrim's Progress* 'in the similitude of a dream', was using this technique of interpretation. The second method was quite different. Instead of interpreting the dream in its entirety, individual items were interpreted separately. The dream was treated as a kind of secret code, to be translated by means of an established key. To decipher this code one had to consult a 'dream book' or 'book of fate'. 'Hawkers and small shops sell a vast quantity of penny dream-books in Lancashire', it was reported as late as 1867.[14] Typical of this type of popular literature was *Mother Shipton's Legacy* (York, 1797), subtitled *A favourite Fortune-book, in which is given a pleasing interpretation of dreams, and a collection of prophetic verses, moral and entertaining.* In the chapter on dreams the reader is warned that interpretation is not always obvious, and may in fact be contrary to the content of the dream. Thus, to dream of joy denotes grief; of fine clothes, poverty; of sweetmeats, a whipping; of gold, death; of drinking water, good entertainment. And the moral is inescapable:

Though plain and palpable each subject seems,
Yet do not put your trust too much in dreams;
Events may happen, which in dreams you see,

44

And yet as often quite contrary be:
This learned hint observe, for Shipton's sake –
Dreams are but interludes which fancies make.

Nevertheless, once the old Lancashire adage had been grasped ('Dreams always go by contraries'), dreams were to be taken as omens. In folk culture, dispute was not about the validity but the interpretation of dreams.

Millenarians were able to draw heavily upon this body of dream lore. Given acceptance of the belief that dreams contained a hidden meaning, millenarian prophets had strong sanction for their policies when they described their dreams, visions or communications. Sometimes they were very close to the traditional wisdom. For example, it was believed that morning dreams were more to be relied on than those of any other time; and those of the morning twilight were the most highly valued of all. Significantly, Joanna Southcott received most of her communications at daybreak.[15] The followers of millenarian prophets and prophetesses frequently recounted their dreams, and in such cases it is probably useful to see such dreams as the fulfilment of wishes. Proverbially (and also for Freud) dreams are often interpreted as wish-fulfilment, as we might remember when we find that reality surpasses our expectations and we exclaim delightedly, 'I should never have imagined that in my wildest dreams.' Belief in the millennium was in some respects one of such wildest dreams; and it is perhaps not too fanciful to see in it an alternative form of this ancient wisdom.

Dreams, like signs and wonders, could always be interpreted on a do-it-yourself basis, with the aid of a chapbook, an almanac or a bit of rule-of-thumb advice from friends. But in difficult and serious cases, such as those concerned with love, death and disease, help of a more expert kind was required; and then the services of magicians, witches, astrologers and herbalists were in demand. 'A cunning man, or a cunning woman, as they are termed, is to be found near every town, and though the laws are occasionally put in force against them, still it is a gainful trade', reported Robert Southey in 1807.[16] From all over the country in the nineteenth century detailed examples confirmed Southey's report.[17] White witches, or wise men, used their magic powers benevolently; whereas black witches were malicious, and devoted their art to evil ends. But in both cases they operated to control supernatural forces. Generally speaking, wise men and cunning women provided a service in areas of life where people felt insecure, anxious, and at a loss to know what to do for the best. They were adjusters, protectors, providers of relief in time of

45

misfortune. The wise man had remedies for diseases of man and beast; he could detect thieves and recover stolen goods. The wise woman could counteract spells laid by unknown enemies, could advise in affairs of the heart, and was skilled in midwifery and women's ailments. At the best, witches were useful depositories of folk knowledge who were trusted at times when no outsider's advice or help would be considered; at the worst they were miserable, poor old people, on whom all the hatred and frustration of the neighbourhood could be vented. Robert Burton, though he looked on all conjurors and magicians as agents of the devil, saw clearly how they were regarded by many people.

> Sorcerers are too common; cunning men, wizards, and white-witches, as they call them, are in every village, which if they be sought unto will help almost all infirmities of body and mind. ... 'Tis a common practice of Some men to go first to a witch and then to a physician; if one cannot the other shall. 'It matters not', saith Paracelsus, 'whether it be God or the devil, angels or unclean spirits cure him, so that he be eased.' If a man fall into a ditch ... what matter is it whether a friend or an enemy help him out?[18]

This was written in 1621; but it was a practical sentiment that could still be echoed 300 years later.

Such, however, was but a minimal claim on behalf of witchcraft: if it works, what harm can there be in it? John Wesley put the case on a higher plane: 'I cannot give up to all the Deists in Great Britain the existence of witchcraft till I give up the credit of all history, sacred and profane.'[19] The evidence in its favour, he argued, was too strong to allow of doubt. To those who asked him, 'Did you ever see an apparition yourself?' he replied: 'No; nor did I ever see a murder; yet I believe there is such a thing.' He regretted that most learned men 'have given up all accounts of witches and apparitions as mere old wives' fables.' But his belief in the reality of the world of spirits precluded any abandonment of witchcraft; and he added ominously, 'the giving up witchcraft is, in effect, giving up the Bible.'

Educated millenarians were in a similar position to Wesley: committed to a thorough-going acceptance of outward manifestations of supernatural power, yet uncomfortable about the abracadabra of witchcraft. At the popular level there was less hesitation in recognizing a similarity between witchcraft and millenarianism. Joanna Southcott was at first regarded as a local wise woman; and later she was distressed to find that her seals were being sought after as magic charms. One element in popular magic particularly confused the issue, and that was divination. Many of the wise man's clients came to him for predictions which could guide them in their business and personal affairs; and nothing enhanced the reputation of a wise man more than prophecies that were fulfilled. Fortune-telling and crystal gazing were unlikely to produce more than a local trade; but pronouncements about dearth and plenty, wars, plagues and the significance of comets could raise the status of a cunning man until he was looked upon as a prophet. It seems likely that some of the 'prophets' reported from time to time in local newspapers in the first half of the nineteenth century were of this order.

The more sophisticated wise men were often also astrologers, known colloquially as 'planet rulers'.[20] By the end of the seventeenth century astrology was seldom taken seriously by educated men, but it retained its hold among labouring people. It had an obvious practical utility, and intellectually the all-embracing nature of its claims made it attractive to men who had little opportunity for study. Even today we still use its vocabulary to describe temperaments (jovial, mercurial, saturnine), states of mind (lunacy), or diseases (influenza). Astrology is basically the study of the influence of the relative positions of the moon, sun and stars on human affairs. It is assumed that each of the celestial bodies has a special influence or quality, which varies according to its position in the heavens. By ascertaining the movements of the stars and drawing a map of their positions at a given time (casting a horoscope) the astrologer can study the situation and draw certain conclusions. In the nineteenth century astrology had four main branches.[21] First were nativities, or figures of the heavens at the moment of birth, from which could be calculated the character and fate of individuals. Second was mundane astrology, which was the art of foreseeing the 'circumstances of nations', meaning wars, pestilences, and natural disasters of all kinds. Third, by means of atmospherical astrology the quality of the weather at any required time or place could be known. Fourth was horary astrology which enabled the astrologer to foresee the result of any circumstance or undertaking from the position of the heavens at the time of the query. The great names in English astrology – William Lilly, Nicholas Culpeper, John Gadbury – belong to the seventeenth century, and their works were reprinted and used as text-books in the eighteenth and nineteenth centuries.[22] However, for our purposes it will be more useful to look briefly at a later example.

Ebenezer Sibly's *A Complete Illustration of the Celestial Science of Astrology* was published in London in 1784–8, and its four parts totalled 1,128 pages. The details of Sibly's astrology follow his seventeenth-century masters. He described the qualities of the signs of the zodiac, the properties of the twelve houses of heaven, the characters and aspects of the planets, and the utility of horary astrology in resolving a great range of personal questions. But for our study it is his attempt to justify astrology to his contemporaries of the 1780s which is of most interest. How – and why – could an apparently discredited system of belief be seriously put forward at this time? At the beginning Sibly is on the defensive: 'sensible as I am of the rooted prejudices of the times against the venerable science of Astrology, and sensible also of the reproach and obloquy that will be levelled against me', nevertheless he will seek to rehabilitate the science by arguments 'founded on the principles of religion and morality', showing that 'God is a God of order, and created nothing in vain.'[23] This is his starting point: the familiar eighteenth-century notion of God, the divine watchmaker.

> It would be derogatory to the attributes of the Deity, not to believe that the minutest events of this world were foreseen and provided for in that most perfect frame or model of nature, which ... may be compared to the construction of a watch, consisting of many small wheels, regulated by one master-wheel, or first mover.

This great watch was wound up at the creation and has been unwinding ever since. Every man is a little wheel within the great world, and yet is also a little world within himself, containing 'many thousands of wheels'. It follows from this

> that every occurrence of our lives, and all the various productions of nature, however strange or incomprehensible they may appear, are brought to pass by a regular and established means, decreed by the wisdom of God, at the beginning of the world.

The key to understanding these events is astrology, which 'comprehends every operation that proceeds out of the master-wheel or frame of nature, and furnishes us with a knowledge of the occult virtues of all earthly substances, and of the nature and end of every particle of God's creation.'

These were very large claims indeed. Yet their very comprehensiveness was in part the reason why astrology was attractive. There was literally nothing it could not explain. At the same time on its practical side it was not too difficult for any intelligent person to master. Sibly assured his readers that the mathematics required was quite minimal: 'every person who can make use of a *Ready Reckoner* or *Trader's Sure Guide* may with equal ease understand all the tables calculated for this work.' Despite some problems of astral determinism (which he attempted to deal with), Sibly saw no need for conflict between astrology and Christian doctrine. He regarded theology as 'the sister science of astrology'; and found plenty of scriptural confirmation of the influence of the stars in human affairs. When the great watch was finally unwound, the signs of the last days were that the sun and moon would be darkened and 'the stars shall fall from heaven' (Matthew 24:29).

Astrology was also a necessary component of folk-medicine. Particular parts of the body were thought to be under the rule of the different signs of the zodiac, and treatment of diseases was therefore directly linked to the stars.[24] A favourable time for taking medicine, blood-letting or any other treatment could be found by consulting the almanac. The collection, preparation and administration of herbs was governed by similar considerations, for the occult properties of plants were under the influence of the heavens. The folklorists discovered in 1867 that:

> More copies of Culpepper's *Herbal* and Sibly's *Astrology* are sold in Lancashire than all other works on the same subjects put together, and this principally on account of the planetary influence with which each disease and its antidote are connected.[25]

In his later work, *A Key to Physic, and the Occult Sciences*, Sibly collected more material on popular medicine, which he mixed with astrology, physiology, animal magnetism, curious stories and sex.[26]

Astrology and witchcraft did not directly support millenarian beliefs; but neither did they conflict with them. There is evidence that some millenarians were, or had been attracted to astrology, and that others were prone to listen to wise men who ventured into prophesying. Brothers in his later years was committed to very unorthodox views about the stars.[27] Joanna Southcott had to warn her followers not to 'seek after stargazers or astrologers'.[28] In Yorkshire it seemed natural to outside observers to link John Wroe and his followers with wise men and astrologers.[29] Functionally there may have been some support for this view. If the rationale of witchcraft and belief in the occult was to explain and cope with many of the problems and disasters of daily life, the same might be said of belief in millenarianism. The wise man's predictions and charms were replaced by Joanna's communications and seals. From this perspective millenarianism becomes a substitute for, or alternative to witchcraft.

On second thoughts, however, this argument will not do. It may be useful in explaining individual cases but it is inadequate for understanding millenarianism as a whole. Witchcraft and sorcery seek to provide remedies for particular problems on an individual basis. The object is to satisfy a demand for personal service. Since evil is seen as spasmodic and random, rather than as the consequence of deficiencies in a society which has departed from God's ways, the requirement is for repeated performances, *ad hoc* and *ad hominem*, rather than a prophecy of complete transformation involving everyone.[30] Millenarianism is directed to the destruction of existing society and its replacement by something new; thaumaturgy is concerned not to change the world but to manipulate it for man's advantage. The millenarian prophet appeals to all who will listen, and he attracts followers and disciples. The wise man speaks to individuals, rather than to the community as a whole: he does not have followers, only clients. Men are not as a rule mobilized for social action by astrologers or wise men; but millenarian movements can be disruptive and are viewed with suspicion by governments. Ultimately there is a profound gap between the person who turns to magical agencies in order to get something for himself, and he who obeys an inner command of the Spirit to give himself in a mystic way to God. It was a peculiarity of millenarianism that it attracted people from both camps.

Folk culture was largely part of an oral tradition; but not entirely so. There was a popular literature of almanacs, chapbooks and street ballads, which reflected the values and interests of labouring people and which flourished in the eighteenth and nineteenth centuries. The almanac was perhaps the most popular book in England for over three and a half centuries, and together with the Bible was the work most likely to be found in a cottage home.[31] Moore's *Almanack*, it was noted in 1810 by an observer in Reading, 'may be found not only in every house in the town but also in every one in the neighbourhood and partakes nearly of the same degree of belief in its prognostications as the Bible itself.'[32] An almanac consisted of three parts: the calendar, which showed the days and weeks for each month and indicated the church festivals; the almanac proper, giving general astronomical information for the year and an ephemeris or tables showing the daily position of the stars; and the prognostication or forecast of events for the coming year. These were bound together, and there was also information about the tides, and lists of kings and queens. An anatomical diagram of a man's body (showing which parts were under the dominion of the different signs of the zodiac), a ready reckoner, snippets of miscellaneous information, and weather forecasts completed the volume. Sometimes blank sheets were interleaved or bound in at the end, the whole serving as a working guide and notebook. Another form was the sheet almanac, intended to be pinned on the wall like a modern calendar. The practical significance of the almanac is today obscured, for we forget the overwhelming importance of the weather for past generations. The lives of farmers – and of labourers, artisans and tradesmen who were close to them – were geared to the rhythm of the seasons. Most personal diaries and letters of the eighteenth and nineteenth centuries (and not only of people living on the land) contain constant observations about the weather. The almanac catered to the needs of a great part of the nation, and in its peculiar form served to keep alive the ancient traditions of folk astrology.

It has been estimated that in the seventeenth century there were over 2,000 separate almanacs published and more than 200 authors were involved.[33] By the mid eighteenth century the trade seems to have settled into the hands of such steady favourites as Partridge's *Merlinus Liberatus*, Moore's *Vox Stellarum*, Rider's *British Merlin*, Saunders' *English Apollo*, Season's *Speculum Anni Redivivum*, Poor Robin's *Almanack*, and others under the names of Tycho Wing, White, Pearse, Gadbury, Andrews and Coley. Eighty years later at least five of these were still going strong, with a sale of half a million copies – and in addition there was a huge sale of unstamped (and therefore illegal) almanacs.[34] A newcomer in the field was *Raphael's Prophetic Messenger*, begun by Robert Cross Smith in 1826. This was a very complete almanac of up to 120 pages, with a large coloured hieroglyphic full of mystical signs and apocalyptic figures. It was an attempt to provide something less crude and bucolic than the old almanacs, rather as Zadkiel's *Astrology* was intended for Victorian readers who wanted something more up-to-date than reprints of the seventeenth-century astrologers. The continuing popularity of almanacs in the nineteenth century is evidenced by the fierceness of the attacks on them and by the number of imitators. Almanacs were exhibitions of 'palpable imposture, impudent mendacity, vulgar ignorance, and low obscenity', thundered the *Athenaeum* in 1828. They

> have continued wholly unchanged; precisely of the same character
> that they held in the days when witches were burnt and horoscopes
> were drawn; utterly uninfluenced by any of the modes of thinking
> which have marked the emancipation of the present generation from
> ignorance and credulity.[35]

Yet so indigenous were they that the Society for the Diffusion of Useful Knowledge issued their counter-propaganda in the same form, *The British Almanac*. Others who wished to take their cause to the people – political radicals, Anti-Corn Law Leaguers, phrenologists – also adopted the form of the almanac.[36] Only later in the century was the old popularity of the almanac eclipsed by newer publications.

In view of the wide circulation of almanacs it may seem unsurprising that millenarians bought and read them. But there is evidence of deeper interest. In the first place, the subject matter of the almanac (prophecies, wonders, occult references) was bound to intrigue men who were pondering over the Book of Revelation and listening to the claims of latter day prophets.[37] Despite Joanna's condemnation of astrology, her followers had no compunction in studying their almanacs.[38] Second, there were some millenarians who, while not necessarily accepting the full claims of astrology, were nevertheless happy to accept confirmation of their beliefs from astrological sources. Such a one was William Tozer, a Southcottian preacher.[39] He was sufficiently impressed by Moore's *Almanack* to issue a pamphlet of his own, *Scriptural and Hieroglyphic Observations*, in 1812.[40] In this chapbook-like production he mixed illustrations from the almanacs with scriptural prophecies concerning millennial signs, the restoration of the Jews, and the French Revolution.

Chapbooks (or penny histories, as they were sometimes called) had a wider variety of content than almanacs. They were sold by chapmen (pedlars) at a price of 1d to 6d, and were small, paper-covered booklets, embellished with a crude, and sometimes highly coloured woodcut illustration. The type was of all styles and sizes, the paper was thick and rough, and each production had a vigour and individuality of its own. The contents were seldom original, and as befitted folk art the authorship was anonymous. Romances, often of great antiquity, were always popular: *Guy of Warwick, The History of Valentine and Orson, Bevis of Southampton*; so also were lives and executions of criminals, song and jest books (often bawdy), and legendary histories.[41] Other chapbooks dealt with dreams, fortune-telling, demonology, witchcraft, and the world of spirits. Little manuals on household and farm economy, sex and practical medicine, herbals, and advice for the young of both sexes were legion. Love in all its ramifications (seduction, elopement, separation), marriage and the family figured prominently. Sermons, prophecies, signs and wonders were printed and reprinted. Acquaintance with this literature began in childhood,[42] and indeed such parts of it as have survived have done so as nursery tales. But until the mid nineteenth century chapbooks and chapbook-style literature was the common reading of adults of all ages.[43] In cities, especially London, street literature included all forms of the chapbook, as well as ballads, broadsheets and handbills.[44] At this point urban and rural folklore were very close together.

Millenarians related to chapbook culture in various ways. Joanna

Southcott, as we shall see later, was thoroughly familiar with traditional romances and ballads, and used them for her own purposes. At the time of her final illness and death several accounts of her life were issued as chapbooks, and subsequently her name was used by the ballad-mongers.[45] Two categories of chapbook were well calculated to interest millenarians, namely those dealing with the supernatural and with prophecies. George Sinclair's *Satan's Invisible World Discovered* (1685) was not originally a chapbook; but this collection of apparitions, ghosts and inexplicable happenings was exactly the mixture to appeal to popular taste, and the little book was therefore reissued in 1769 and 1808, and in various local editions. John Tregortha's *News from the Invisible World; or Interesting Anecdotes of the Dead* (1813) was a similar production which circulated in Yorkshire and the Midlands.[46] Cases of demonic possession appear in various places in Wesley's *Journal*, and the devil figures prominently in other accounts of religious conversion and healing. A typical chapbook example is *The Expulsion of Seven Devils, who had taken diabolical possession of G. Lukins, a taylor of Yatton in Somersetshire, and for eighteen years tormented him* ... Lukins was first afflicted when performing in a Christmas mummery play, and it was assumed that he was being punished for such buffoonery. He declared that he was the devil, and roared, barked, howled and blasphemed. But in June 1788, through the efforts of seven clergymen assembled at Temple Church, Bristol, the devil was successfully cast out, 'in the name of Jesus Christ, Father, Son and Holy Ghost', and Lukins was restored to health.[47] Dreams and visions were another staple of the chapbook printer. A common title was *Dreams and Moles with their Interpretation and Signification ... to which is prefixed A Collection of choice and valuable Receipts concerning love and Marriage*, which contained, among other things, recipes for determining whether a young woman was a virgin or a young man a chaste bachelor. For the religiously inclined reader there were many accounts of people who had been in a trance, sometimes for several days, during which time they had seen visions of heaven.[48]

Chapbooks of prophecies were of two kinds. First, there was a steady trade in the ancient prophecies of Mother Shipton, Merlin and Nostradamus, together with relative newcomers from the seventeenth century like Robert Nixon, 'the Cheshire prophet'. These prognostications were of a sufficiently general nature to excite wonder, and speculation about their applicability, in any decade. The second kind were predictions of the events of the 1790s, either by contemporary prophets or culled from millenarian writers of the past. Such were *The remarkable prophecies and predictions for the Year 1795, of the great and*

wonderful Prophet, Don Johannes Gautier, that now lives in this neighbourhood.
... Also the true account of a wonderful star which appears in the sky every
evening (London [1794?]); and *Strange and wonderful prophecies for 1801;*
fortelling all the alarming events of battles by land and sea; plagues,
earthquakes, etc., in various parts of the world. ... To which is added an account
of the dreadful fire at Manchester, with the remarkable appearance of the word,
God, during that shocking conflagration (London [n.d.]). Sometimes the
prophecies were more specifically millennial, as in the following example
which forecast the last days and the end of the world: *The Christian's*
Diary: or an Almanack for one Day. Predicting that there will be great wars and
commotions in several parts of the world ... (Glasgow, 1790). More common
were the collections of prophecies from the past which seemed to predict
the events of the French Revolution and the wars in Europe, such as *The*
Prophetical Mirror, being a collection of prophecies chiefly predictive of the
present tumultuous times, and particularly relative to the Revolution in France
... to which are added the whole of Nixon's Prophecies ... (London [n.d.]). The
writings selected were twelve millennial extracts from Christopher Love,
Peter Jurieu, Robert Fleming, John Lacy, and others.[49] Here the
traditional chapbook style of prophecy begins to overlap with popular
millenarianism, and the whole development is to some extent in the
(intellectual) shadow of the general, fashionable interest in millennialism
sparked off by the American and French Revolutions. The chapbook
provided a medium, familiar and acceptable, by which millenarian ideas
could reach the people.

Belief in millenarianism was thus facilitated, and its forms determined
by folk culture. Like Methodism, it was close to the idiom of the people.
Wesley's *Primitive Physic* was a wonderful collection of old-wive's
remedies (Cure for lunacy: 'rub the head several times a day with
vinegar in which ground-ivy leaves have been infused').[50] 'Mother
Southcote' was referred to in popular parlance rather like Mother
Shipton. Ghosts and witches, signs and wonders, astrology and dream
books might be pooh-poohed by the educated classes, but that only
served to demonstrate the gulf between polite and popular culture – and
also between polite and popular religion, for there was a range of popular
spiritual experiences, embracing visions and supernatural manifestations,
quite outside the orthodox churches. Millenarian prophets, no less than
the early Methodist preachers, when they took their message to the
people, found a basis for understanding and sympathy in some elements
of folk culture and popular religion.

PART II

WORLD'S DOOM

NEPHEW OF THE ALMIGHTY

In 1795 there appeared in London two small volumes entitled *The World's Doom*.[1] They comprised reprints of twenty pamphlets relating to prophecy, and in particular to the claims of a prophet named Richard Brothers who in 1794–5 was attracting considerable attention. The justification for this collection, argued the anonymous editor, is the great contemporary interest in prophecy arising from the French Revolution and the subsequent events in Europe. Men's minds have turned towards the ancient prophecies. The fulfilment of old predictions and even the commencement of the millennium itself have been widely canvassed. Above all, 'men have lately arisen among us pretending to divine communications and to the gift of prophecy.' The established church has held aloof from these attempts to relate prophecy to the modern world, but some Dissenters (notably Dr Price and Dr Priestley) expect the completion of Old Testament and millennial prophecies in the near future. However, the modern prophets have arisen independently of either church or dissent, and enjoin their followers simply to 'search the scriptures'.

Their claims may sound odd to our ears, he adds, but they cannot be dismissed out of hand. For instance, it is irrelevant to argue that these prophets are madmen. 'That the men may be mad forms no solid objection to their prophetic character; for the very term prophetic, is derived from a Greek word signifying madness.' Again, it is indisputable that 'strange prodigies, the never-failing precursors of dire and calamitous events' have been seen by many persons:

> Armies, both horse and foot, have been seen passing over the moon; numerous companies of soldiers have been seen to pass through turnpikes by night, and were never afterwards heard of; and spectres, clad in terrible array, have come into the world, to denounce [*sic*] bloody vengeance upon the wicked and the oppressor.

All the signs suggest that the age of prophecy is at hand, or, as the editor (reverting to the language of a previous age) puts it, 'that there is a sour and atrabilious humour fermenting in the minds of men, the operation of which no human power can check'. The exact nature of that humour, and how and why it was related to prophecy, is illumined by the career of Richard Brothers.

Biographical details of Brothers are scarce.[2] Unlike his successor, Joanna Southcott, whose homely experiences and early reminiscences are woven into her spiritual 'communications', Brothers' writings contain few references to the first thirty years of his life. His obvious gentlemanly qualities and the known fact that he had been a naval lieutenant apparently satisfied any curiosity of his friends to probe into his past; and his enemies had little need of his early history to show that he was mad. His prophetic mission, from February 1792 to May 1795, was very brief; and once the doors of the madhouse had closed upon him he ceased to be of interest to any but a tiny handful of disciples. Nevertheless the outline of his career can be pieced together, though with some tantalizing gaps.

Brothers was born in Placentia, Newfoundland, in 1757, on 25 December (a highly significant omen, he thought later, of his divine mission). His father was a gunner in the local garrison, and sent the boy back to England to join the navy. Richard Brothers entered Woolwich, and in 1771 went to sea as a midshipman. He served as master's mate at the indecisive battle with the French off Ushant in July 1778, and in the following year was transferred to the *St Albans*, a sixty-four gun ship, which in 1781 was commissioned for the West Indies. He fought under Rodney at the battle of the Saints, off Dominica, in April 1782, and was promoted to lieutenant. Following the peace of Versailles (1783), the *St Albans* was put out of commission, and Brothers was retired on half-pay at £54 per annum. Little is known about his life during the next six years, which were in some way crucial for his metamorphosis from naval officer to prophet. He may have joined the mercantile marine, and he appears to have travelled in France, Italy and Spain. In 1786 he married Elizabeth Hassall at Wrenbury, near Nantwich, but immediately after the wedding he rejoined his ship. On his return home some years later he found that his wife was living with another man and that she was the mother of several children. She was not mentioned by him subsequently, but after his death in 1824 she claimed such property as he had left. Brothers went to live in London after discovering his wife's infidelity. It is probable that about this time he became interested in millennial and prophetical religion, but the exact stages of his development are not clear. He may have worshipped at Long Acre chapel or at a Baptist chapel in the Adelphi. He evidently studied his Bible carefully, and pondered the meaning of what he read. He also became acquainted with mystical and prophetical writings, perhaps including Mrs Jane Lead's *A Fountain of Gardens* (1696–1701) and John Lacy's *Prophetical Warnings* (1707). Then 'in the year of 1790 the Spirit of God began first (although I always had a presentiment of being sometime or other very great) to enlighten my understanding, and teach me to distinguish right from wrong.'[3] By this Brothers meant that he had become convinced that the profession of arms was inconsistent with Christian teaching; and he adopted the further Quakerly doctrine that oath-taking was barred by Christ's injunction, 'Swear not at all.' The consequence was that he could not draw his half-pay from the Admiralty, as payment was conditional on taking an oath that he had not received any other employment under the Crown during the previous six months. With his only source of income cut off, Brothers soon fell into debt. The landlady of his lodgings in Dartmouth Street, Mrs Green, complained to the local governors of the poor that she was owed £33 for rent, though the arrears of pay due to Brothers amounted to upwards of £130. After examining him (during which time he kept his hat on), the governors admitted Brothers to the workhouse, where he was allowed to have 'a small room to himself, which he furnished with his sea cot, portmanteau, earthenware, etc.'[4] The workhouse board arranged to draw his pension for him, and he remained in the workhouse for six months, though his liabilities were soon settled. In February 1792 he decided to leave, and took lodgings in Compton Street, Soho. Here he was soon in trouble again, as he still refused to take the oath, and his landlady sued for arrears of rent. This time he was committed to Newgate and was confined in a small room with fourteen others. The food was insufficient; there were no beds, blankets, coals or candles; light and air came only from a small barred window. After eight weeks of this Brothers agreed to sign letters of attorney authorizing his pay to be drawn on his behalf, and in November 1792 he was released.

He was now chastened and dispirited, and he decided to leave England for ever and abandon his interest in prophesying. At eight o'clock one morning he set out to walk to Bristol. He carried a rod that he had cut (in emulation of Moses), but after about sixteen miles he threw it away in anger. When he had gone about twenty-five miles, he tells us,

> on a sudden, God by his power stopped the action of every joint and limb, and turned me feelingly round with more ease than a strong

man would a young child; commanding me, at the same instant, to return and wait his proper time.[5]

On his journey back he found his rod where he had abandoned it. He arrived in London about 10.30 p.m., having walked over fifty miles from Hyde Park corner. But he now knew that from his prophetic call, symbolized by the rod, there was no escape. He took fresh lodgings at 57 Paddington Street, and busied himself with interpreting the dreams and visions which came to him with increasing force. He became aware that he was no ordinary prophet, but was the Prince of the Hebrews and nephew of the Almighty – for his surname of Brothers denoted that he was descended from King David through James, one of the *brothers* of Jesus. In 1794 he published *A Revealed Knowledge of the Prophecies and Times. Book the First*, followed shortly by *Book the Second*. Hitherto Brothers had not attracted much attention – though his attempts to heal the blind in 1792 must have brought some local notoriety. But *A Revealed Knowledge* sold quickly, was rapidly reprinted, and established the identity and claims of the Great Prophet of Paddington Street (as *The Times* dubbed him). From the summer of 1794 to spring 1795 Brothers was visited daily by many people; his writings circulated all over the kingdom and were published in America and France. Pamphlets defending and attacking him proliferated, and followers began to declare themselves.

The political mood of 1794–5 was such that the government viewed Brothers' activity with apprehension, and in March 1795 he was taken into custody and examined before a committee of the Privy Council. He was 'taken up', explained the *Gentleman's Magazine*, because his publications 'have for several months alarmed and agitated the minds of the people (crowds of whom have resorted to him daily).'[6] The outcome was that he was declared insane, and in May he was removed to Fisher House, Islington, the private asylum of Dr Samuel Foart Simmons. He remained there for the next eleven years, despite attempts from time to time to secure his release. His prophetic writings continued to appear, but his followers were reduced to a handful. In 1806 they succeeded in getting the release of Brothers, who lived with Busby, a well-to-do friend, until 1815, and thereafter with John Finlayson. Brothers died in 1824 and was interred in St John's Wood cemetery – where Joanna Southcott had also been buried some ten years previously.

Such in outline was the career of Richard Brothers. On the surface it seems to be little more than a case of a rather gentlemanly, mild-mannered eccentric whose 'religious delusions' proved to be evidence of insanity – just another example of those perennial madmen who scribble crazy little books which they pay to have published. But if we turn from Brothers himself to the manner in which his claims and prophecies were received some interesting questions arise. Why were people who were not themselves insane prepared to take seriously the words of a madman? What sort of people were they who believed in Brothers, and what effect did their belief have on their lives? How many believers were there? Was Brothers' case an isolated phenomenon or was he but the latest in a continuing tradition of inspired or mad prophets? Is it possible to establish exactly his social role? To answer these and similar questions we have to look first at his claims and teachings, and then at the social context in which they were received.

The gist of Brothers's teachings was contained in the two parts of *A Revealed Knowledge*, but this has to be supplemented by later works. Moreover, Brothers enjoined his followers to publish their beliefs, which in turn provoked further pamphlets from opponents. The ensuing polemics, while but a pale reflection of the sectarian exchanges of the seventeenth century, nevertheless produced some lively titles[7] and a small corpus of popular millenarian literature. *A Revealed Knowledge*[8] consists of extracts from the Bible interspersed with passages of comment by Brothers. It is the usual millennial mixture from the scriptures: the great passages from Isaiah about the coming of the messiah; the prophecies of Daniel; Jesus' promises in the gospels; the apocalyptic passages in John's gospel; and the Book of Revelation. None of this was very original: it would have been perfectly familiar to regular church- or chapel-goers. Nor was the interpretation out of line with the accepted Protestant teachings of the day: the great whore of Revelation 17, is Rome; the scarlet-coloured beast is the pope; the ten horns are the cardinals, and so on. Brothers' teaching was based on a knowledge of scripture; but it was not dependent upon any deep study of the Bible. Like most millennialists he made his own calculation as to when the millennium was due, and fixed the date as 19 November 1795, 'at or about sun-rise, in the latitude of Jerusalem'.[9] The last days were now at hand: Revelation 6 (the opening of the seven seals) was 'now fulfilling', and Daniel 12 (the time of the end) had arrived. In these momentous times a special task was assigned to Brothers: he was to lead the return of the Jews to the Holy Land and undertake the rebuilding of Jerusalem. This was to take place in 1798. The Jews he was to lead, however, were not principally the 'visible Hebrews' who professed the Jewish faith, but the 'invisible Hebrews' who were descendants of the ten lost tribes of Israel, many of whom were living in England. Thus Brothers himself was of the house of David, and he identified his followers as belonging to the various tribes. Later he drew up detailed arrangements for the great migration and elaborated plans for the new city of Jerusalem.

More compelling than his theories of the Hebrew origin of the British people are those parts of *A Revealed Knowledge* in which Brothers recounts his visions and divine communications. The millenarian mind appears vividly in the autobiographical fragments.

> The very loud and unusual kind of thunder that was heard in the beginning of January 1791, was the voice of the angel mentioned in the eighteenth chapter of the Revelation, proclaiming the judgement of God and the fall of Babylon the Great.[10]

This thunder, explains Brothers, was a sign of God's anger with the people of London (identified as Babylon). Indeed, so angry was He, that he decided to destroy London, and he ordered Brothers to travel eighteen miles from the city to avoid the holocaust.

> Had London been destroyed ... the place where it stands would have formed a great bay or inlet of the Channel: all the land between Windsor and the Downs would have been sunk, including a distance of eighteen miles each side ... to the depth of seventy fathoms ... that no traces of the city might be ever found, or even so much as looked for.

As a sign of his special favour towards Brothers, God agreed to spare those whom the prophet desired – and he accordingly mentioned several names, including Pitt, Fox, Wilberforce, the royal family and obscure persons who had been kind to him. Brothers was then 'carried up to heaven in a vision', and shown the Holy Spirit in the shape of a Dove. He also saw Satan, 'walking leisurely into London: his face had a smile, but under it his looks were sly, crafty and deceitful. On the right side of his forehead were seven dark spots; he was dressed in white and scarlet robes'. After another vision of a large river running through London, 'coloured with human blood', Brothers was so upset that he asked God to spare London. But 'the Lord God was so highly displeased' that he refused to listen to Brothers' prayers for three days. In a vision ten days later, however, God spoke to him from the middle of a large white cloud: 'All, All. I pardon London and all the people in it, for your sake: there is no other man on earth that could stand before me to ask for so great a thing.'

Two years later Brothers was again interpreting the thunder. This time (3 August 1793) it was the voice of the angel mentioned in Revelation 19:17. On 7 August the thunder was the fulfilment of

Revelation 7:2 ('And I saw another angel ascending from the east, having the seal of the living God; and he cried with a loud voice'). The flashes of lightning 'proceeded from the glory of the angel.' The last thunder, due on 11 August, would have been the 'fourth angel pouring out his vial on the sun' (Revelation 16:8) with the resulting desolation of the world; but God spared London again because of 'his great mercy and regard for me, that I may be esteemed.'

Brothers had other visions. 'It is from visions and revelation, and through the Holy Ghost, that I write this book', he explained. He searched the scriptures for 'some of the prophecies which mean myself': he was the 'man coming up from the midst of the sea' of II Esdras 13:25; the 'prophet' of Deuteronomy 18:15; the man promised by God in Haggai 2:23; the 'great prince' of Daniel 12:1. God's prophecies, he declared, are concealed from men until the proper time; but now they are revealed through me. 'I am the prophet that will be revealed to the Jews.' Brothers claimed divine authority to alter, where necessary, the wording or the commonly accepted interpretation of the scriptures. 'There is no other man under the whole heaven', declared the Lord God, 'that I discover the errors of the Bible to, and reveal a knowledge of how to correct them.' Brothers' sense of intimacy with God comes through at many points. At first, he says, he wrote in the language of scripture, using 'thee' and 'thou'; but God told him: 'write in the same manner as I speak to you; write as other men do ... according to the custom of the country you live in.' Powers of prediction were also vouchsafed to him; and among his prophecies which, he claimed, had been fulfilled were the death of Louis XVI and the abolition of the monarchy in France, the acknowledgment of the French Republic by Prussia and Holland, and the French defeat in the West Indies.[11] His method of receiving the revealed knowledge is indicated by one of his landladies, Mrs S. Green:

> Mr Brothers had several visions while in our house; ... in 1791 ... he lay three days and three nights on his face, and never ate nor drank in this interval. I have often gone into his room when he had been on his knees at prayers, and I have returned out entirely unobserved by him.[12]

The nature of the impact made by Brothers and his teachings can be gauged by the reaction of his followers and critics. This impact was not for the most part verbal or personal. True, he held court for a time at his lodgings in Paddington Street where he was visited by, among others, 'members of parliament and ladies of quality'.[13] But he did not preach or hold any kind of public meeting. He made no attempt to organize a separate sect or church, nor did he travel about the country to gain support. His personality was pleasant but in no sense compelling. Brothers' influence came from his writings in the first instance, and from his reputation which was spread by his followers. Many believers were convinced solely by reading of Brothers' claims, without ever having seen him. To find the secret (if any) of his appeal we have to look also at the reverse side of the coin. Of equal importance with what Brothers wrote is what the believers wanted to read and thought they were reading. The ground, to use an appropriate biblical metaphor, is no less important than the seed that is sown in it. Fortunately we have some testimony which throws light on the minds and life situations of believers.

Foremost among these was Nathaniel Brassey Halhed. In fact, had it not been for Halhed's support, thought a kindly critic, Joseph Moser, Brothers would have remained in the oblivion he rightly merited. Once Halhed took up Brothers' cause he brought to it all the weight and prestige of a distinguished oriental scholar and member of parliament. He came of an old Oxfordshire family, was educated at Harrow and Christ Church, and was a friend of Richard Brinsley Sheridan. During his service with the East India Company he established himself as an authority on Indian philology. Returning to England, he was elected to parliament as member for Lymington. In January 1795 he announced his testimony 'to the authenticity of the prophecies and mission of Richard Brothers as Prince and Prophet of the Hebrews', and went on to acknowledge publicly his 'deep sense of obligation for the light and life communicated to my soul through his inspired writings.'[14] Before an amazed and completely unresponsive House of Commons he twice raised the matter of Brothers' arrest and confinement; and defended him in a flurry of short pamphlets throughout 1795. Halhed was rewarded by the prophet with the promise that three months hence he should have the choice of being either Governor General of India or President of the Board of Control in England. He was also assured that he belonged to the tribe of Judah and house of David.

At this period of his life Halhed appears to have had two main concerns – or, perhaps more accurately, obsessions: the war with France and the interpretation of prophecy.[15] He felt that the great task required of his generation was 'to read the modern history of Europe in the prophetic records of the Old and New Testaments'. On reading *A Revealed Knowledge* he was convinced that he had found the clue for which he was looking. He followed Brothers' advice to 'search the scriptures' and satisfied himself of the validity of his interpretations and claims. This was a scholarly, purely intellectual exercise. Halhed does not mention having any dreams or visions, and he is at pains to present his case logically and unemotionally. He found in Brothers confirmation of his view that the war was a disaster and that peace should be made with revolutionary France. He also found Brothers' interpretation of the prophecies in Daniel, Esdras and Revelation entirely acceptable — particularly the identification of the four beasts of Daniel 7 with the collapse of the four kingdoms of Russia, France, Prussia and England. Halhed checked Brothers' calculation of the date of the millennium and satisfied himself of its correctness. For the rest, he had little difficulty in explaining to his own satisfaction the genuineness of Brothers' revelation. The very crudity of Brothers' writing ('replete with grammatical faults; destitute alike of harmony and arrangement, and elegance of diction') was 'precisely suited to the comprehension of the most ordinary capacity', and showed that God intended it to reach the multitudes. That Brothers was rejected by the authorities was only to be expected — 'by how many crowned heads and powerful countries was Columbus rejected when he offered practically to demonstrate the existence of the western continent?' And how could Brothers be a false prophet when already his prophecies were being fulfilled?

The case of Halhed demonstrates the ease with which a belief in scriptural prophecy and a desire for 'vital', practical Christianity could, in certain circumstances, lead to millenarianism. Halhed's success in his researches into ancient Hindu writings ('not widely dissimilar in style and manner from the prophetical treatises in our own Bible') may have encouraged him to believe that he was uniquely qualified to explicate the biblical prophecies. With almost gnostic delight he confirms from his erudition the truths stated so crudely and simply by Brothers from direct revelation. All prophecies, argues Halhed, are enigmas, in which the meaning is deliberately obscure or ambiguous. Only when we are supplied with the proper clue by the inventor himself can we unravel them. God does not allow us to do this until the proper time, which is why all previous attempts at deciphering the millennial prophecies have come to grief. Thus, the Babylon of Revelation 18 is not Rome, as previous expositors have supposed, but (as Brothers says) London; and the clue to this new and correct interpretation is the phrase 'slaves and souls of men' (verse 13) which is a reference to the 'notorious and abominable traffic in slaves' which is organized from London. Similarly, who can doubt that England is 'in scripture spiritually called Egypt', so that the prophet of Deuteronomy 18:18 is Brothers, who 'will lead the Hebrews again out of captivity this very year?' Halhed was so sure of the logic of his argument that he could not conceive how any fair-minded Christian who acknowledged the force of biblical prophecies could doubt that Brothers was a true prophet, and not a madman or an imposter. He was astonished that his motions on Brothers in the House, on 31 March and 21 April 1795, were not even seconded. But, on further reflection, he realized that this refusal to recognize the messiah was one of the central themes of scripture.

These arguments of Halhed were to be rehearsed many times over by followers of Brothers and by other millenarians. In each case there were individual variations, but they were all part of a common pattern. The most extreme example of devotion to Brothers' cause was John Finlayson, a well-to-do Scots lawyer from Edinburgh. Like Halhed, he became a believer after reading Brothers' works (in 1797) and then experienced a divine call to give up his 'extensive and lucrative practice at law' in order to go to London to serve the prophet.[16] This he did for the rest of his life. He looked after the publication of Brothers' works during the latter's confinement, worked tirelessly for his release in 1806, and from 1815 took him into his own house in Upper Baker Street, Marylebone, where Brothers died in 1824. He was persuaded by Brothers to change the spelling of his name to Finleyson on the grounds that it signified the 'fine leys' of land granted to his ancestors. Brothers, on his death-bed, ordered Finlayson to write a refutation of an unorthodox work on astronomy by Bartholomew Prescot of Liverpool who had been a believer. Finlayson obeyed this request and, until his death in 1854, spent his time defending Brothers' views and fighting the government for the arrears of Brothers' maintenance costs. Although Finlayson for some years conducted a flourishing business as a house-agent, his fortune melted away, and in old age he was reduced to living on a parish allowance. His wife, Elizabeth Anne, whom he married in 1808, was the daughter of Colonel Basil Bruce, who was also a disciple of Brothers.

In the testimonies of most of Brothers' followers several areas of concern occur fairly regularly: opposition to the war – with or without general liberal sympathy for the French republicans; an interest in prophecy and desire to use it to interpret contemporary events; experience of (or dabbling in) mystical, inner-light doctrines through visions, voices, dreams and direct communications; and a generalized puritan condemnation of society and its godless values and behaviour. These interests identified the people who came forward to acknowledge Brothers in 1794–5. Some were intellectuals or professional men, like Halhed and Finlayson. Captain Hanchett, a wealthy ex-naval follower, was specially mentioned in *A Revealed Knowledge* for his 'acts of friendship'. He financed the printing of Brothers' early works and tried unsuccessfully to get the Swedenborgian printer, Robert Hindmarsh, to print *A Revealed Knowledge*. George Riebau, the publisher who actually did undertake the job, was probably a believer ('Bookseller to the Prince of the Hebrews') and was friendly with many leading intellectuals. William Roundell Wetherell was a surgeon from Highgate. Henry Francis Offley, 'late of Oxford', contributed a pamphlet.[17] Several Anglican clergy were attracted: the Reverend Thomas Philip Foley, rector of Oldswinford, Worcestershire, who later became a leading Southcottian; the Reverend Stanhope Bruce, vicar of Inglesham, and father of Colonel Basil Bruce mentioned above; and the Reverend Thomas Webster, lecturer in two City churches, who had a vision while taking a funeral in Bermondsey in 1794.[18] In the north, Brothers gained disciples among business men: George Turner, a merchant of Leeds, who published *A Testimony to the Prophetical Mission of Richard Brothers* in 1795; Peter Morison, a Liverpool cotton-printer; and George Coggan, a merchant of Hull. Turner's testimony is little more than a rambling collection of biblical sentences and thus-saith-the-Lord pronouncements (he was later confined in an asylum in York). But Coggan is a more coherent case-study in the making of a millenarian.

'Four years ago', he says, 'I was under strong impressions ... that there was something of importance awaited us.'[19] In March 1791 he had a 'peculiar manifestation' of future events, but his religious friends refused to take him seriously and dubbed him an enthusiast. The events of the French Revolution convinced him that the hand of God was directly responsible for the downfall of the pope and the overthrow of Louis XVI. Since God is righteous, and is using France to execute his divine will, it is wrong (and also futile) he urged, to try to destroy the French republic by war. He sent letters to Pitt, Grenville and the Queen explaining this. But the only result was that 'they issued a warrant and sent the runners after me.' He then came upon Brothers' books, and after reading them through four times became a believer. Here was the prophet who could, through revelation, interpret the mysterious passages of scripture which had been hidden for so long. Moreover, he too admonished the government to abandon the war. Coggan saw nothing ridiculous in Brothers' intercession with God to spare London, for 'was not this the case with Moses?' The scriptures inform us of the manner in which God speaks to men: it is 'by visions, dreams and inward communications'. The Church of England was for Coggan 'a dead body'; and the Quakers and Methodists had fallen away from their early adherence to the things of the spirit (as outlined in I Corinthians 12). The only recourse was to 'attend much to closet prayer'; for then God 'communicates more largely and intimately his secret operations.' From what he tells us, it seems that Coggan had arrived independently at a religious position very similar to Brothers'. Coggan's reading of *A Revealed Knowledge* confirmed and strengthened that position, and he had no difficulty in accepting Brothers as the prophet who would herald the second coming.

Much the same sort of complaints about the lapsed state of professing Christians and the immorality of society are echoed by other followers of Brothers. Each made his own selection. Coggan condemned the swearing and 'all manner of uncleanness' among sailors ('can such be a defence to a country?') Henry Offley dwelt largely upon the enormity of the slave trade. And Thomas Taylor listed the vices of each group of inhabitants in turn – from the idleness and luxury of the nobility to the cheating, short-changing and monopolizing of merchants and tradesmen, and the bull-baiting, dancing and cock-fighting of the populace.[20] Having condemned all the whoremongers, adulterers and false priests who neglect their flocks, he vows 'not to take up any carnal weapon whatever with any design to injure or destroy any of my fellow creatures'; and to abstain from imported luxuries, such as rum and sugar, which are the product of slavery. A further sample of the testimonies of those who came forward to attest their belief in Brothers in 1795 strengthens the impression that his appeal was to sectarians and 'seekers' of various kinds.[21] Such people wanted to find a prophet who made the type of claims that Brothers did. Having found him, they were already well equipped to answer from scripture all the usual objections. His mission, they argued, was no more improbable than many of the basic teachings of Christianity, such as the virgin birth. If a humble carpenter's son had been King of the Jews, why could not Brothers be accepted as Prince of the Hebrews? Previous interpreters could not explain the prophecies because they were not intended to be known until the time was ripe; and even Daniel was denied this understanding ('Go thy way Daniel: for the words are closed up and sealed till the time of the end.'). But now the time of the end was at hand. With the toppling of European thrones and empires, and the binding of Antichrist the millennial prophecies were being fulfilled. In this setting Brothers was entirely credible.

Some (though what proportion we do not know) of Brothers' followers were working people. In *A Revealed Knowledge* he mentions Isabella Wake, a poor woman who brought him a threepenny loaf every morning when he was in Newgate goal, and who would be rewarded when he entered into his kingdom: 'in my palace you shall always have an apartment, and at my table you shall always have a seat.' There is also mention of John Luke, 'a poor Quaker'. Mrs Green, his landlady, became a believer after Brothers had left her house, being convinced by dreams and visions. John Mason, a brushmaker, was one of the few who remained a believer even after Brothers' death. But the most interesting of his workingmen disciples were two artisans, John Wright and William Bryan. They have left two autobiographical fragments which show clearly the quietist element in the making of popular millenarianism.[22] In simple language they set down their spiritual progress and concerns, interwoven with their family problems and working experiences.

Wright was a carpenter of Leeds, and a seeker after religious truth. His journal is sprinkled liberally with 'the Holy Spirit told me', and 'I was directed by the Holy Spirit', which led Southey to remark (somewhat unkindly) that 'Wright mistook strong inclination for inspiration.' After listening to the two travelling Swedenborgian preachers, Mather and Salmon, mentioned earlier, he determined to go to London to find the New Jerusalem Church. By dint of hard saving and working overtime during the summer he collected enough money for the journey, and in July 1788 he left his wife and four children. He obtained work with a master in Tottenham Court Road, and his family joined him in London. The Swedenborgians disappointed him – 'I saw nothing but old forms of worship, established by men's will and not according to the will of God.' However, at the New Jerusalem Church he met a converted Jew, who after listening to Wright's talk about the imminent restoration of the Jews, gave him the address of William Bryan, who, he said, had similar views. Wright immediately recognized Bryan as a man after his own heart: 'we had a very satisfactory meeting together, for our experience operated with each other, as face answers face in a glass.'

Bryan was a copper-plate printer. He was born in Shrewsbury and came to London when he was twenty-one. 'As I grew up', he says, 'I was religious.' His parents brought him up in the established church, but he did not find there the spiritual life for which he sought. In London he tried the different sects of Dissenters, and at length became a Quaker. But Bryan followed the doctrine of the inner light so exclusively that it led him to give up going to meetings for worship on the ground that they savoured too much of 'church craft'. In December 1789, after about four years with the Quakers, he was disowned by the Westminster Monthly Meeting. But by then he had been 'led by the Spirit' in a new direction. In the autumn of 1788 he told Wright about a 'society at Avignon, who were favoured with divine communications'; and after turning it over in their minds for some time they both concluded that the spirit required them to go to Avignon in France.

This was no small undertaking. They both felt guilty at leaving their families without any money to support themselves. Bryan's wife was in an extremely weak state after giving birth to a child who had died, and she was being nursed by Wright's wife – who had four children of her own. Neither of the men had any money for the journey, nor did they know the route or a word of French. But the power of the Holy Spirit came upon Wright so strongly while he was at work that he was prevented from doing any more; while Bryan 'lay on the floor in a great agony' and tried vainly to argue with God. They therefore concluded that they had to go; and after a friend had providentially given Bryan five guineas, they caught the coach to Dover and crossed to Calais in January 1789. The account of their journey across France on foot and by boat reads like a veritable Pilgrim's Progress, with each hazard overcome by faith and God's help. Dreams, unexpected generosity from unknown persons, and warnings and chastenings from the Holy Spirit occurred daily, until at last they arrived at Avignon, where they were welcomed by the brethren.

The *illuminés* of Avignon were part of that shadowy European world of freemasonry, occultism, mesmerism and spiritualism that flourished in the 1780s. The sect had originated in Berlin, under the leadership of Pernety, a French Benedictine monk who was subsequently librarian to Frederick II, Morveau (brother of the chemist, Guitton de Morveau), and Tadeusz Grabianka, a Polish count,[23] Guided by visions, they established themselves in 1786 at Avignon as a freemasons' lodge, and attracted followers from all over Europe. Their doctrines were a blend of Swedenborgianism and Roman Catholicism, salted with occultism.[24] To the cold intellectualism of the Swedish visionary was added the veneration of the Virgin Mary and recital of the Athanasian creed; while individual members studied Renaissance alchemy, the theurgy of Alexandria, hermetic authors, the philosopher's stone, the divine science of numbers, and the mystical interpretation of dreams. How much of this curious mixture Wright and Bryan absorbed, and what they made of the European savants who came to the society is not clear. They were of course pledged 'to keep the society secret until the appointed time' – which confirmed Southey's suspicions that it was part of an international secret conspiracy ('political Jesuits') and that Wright and Bryan were its unsuspecting tools. During their six months' stay they spent their time reading and making extracts from the journals of the society, which Wright afterwards published. From this oracle they were informed that the world was now in the last days and that the prophecies were being fulfilled preparatory to the Lord's second coming: the Mohammedan empire would fall; Grabianka would become king of Poland; and 'enlightened Jews will embrace the catholic faith.' Wright discloses few details of the daily life of the society, except that mass was said each evening at seven o'clock and that very often the furniture in the room was shaken by the presence of angels. He does relate one incident, however, which particularly impressed him. The members were ordered by the 'Holy Word' to go to a mountain, 'on a religious duty', and despite their precautions to ensure secrecy they were observed by a man who, when questioned, said he was a traveller from Italy. The brethren gave him some money and left. But one of them, 'having some thoughts that he was something more than man, enquired at the word of the Lord; and the answer was, that it was the archangel Raphael.'

Wright and Bryan returned from Avignon greatly strengthened in 'the knowledge of spirits and the spiritual world'. They were also convinced millenarians. Wright had no difficulty in resuming his job as a carpenter, and continued to be guided (much to his wife's upset) by the unpredictable vagaries of the Holy Spirit. In July 1794 he learned of Brothers from his foreman's son, who had been reading *A Revealed Knowledge*; and on visiting the prophet Wright immediately acknowledged him as he 'whom Moses and the prophets, and John in the Revelations, spoke of as the true representative of Jesus Christ.' Moreover, Wright recognized Brothers as the person foretold by the Puritan minister, Christopher Love, who had been executed in 1651, and of whom the brethren at Avignon had spoken.

Bryan did not have such an easy passage. He could not get regular work as a copper-plate printer because everyone thought he was insane and not to be trusted. For two years he existed by doing odd jobs, and then moved to Bristol. He borrowed money from a friend to open a shop as a druggist and 'vendor of the patent medicines'. In his work as an apothecary he was led by the Holy Spirit to practise sympathetic healing. By this he meant that by the power of love he was able to experience in his own body the symptoms of the disease in his patients, and prescribe medicines accordingly. He was known as a mesmerist and herbal doctor, and later (after removing to Hertfordshire) acquired local fame as 'the Galen of Hoddesden'. When he first heard of Brothers he was sceptical of his claims, and regretted that Wright had accepted them. However, in December 1794 he felt that he could not rest until he had investigated the matter for himself. He went to London and visited Brothers, but the only result was that he felt tempted to stab him to see if he was mortal. But these 'powers of darkness' which were loosed upon him gradually passed away; and after calming himself down at Wright's house he recognized Brothers' claims to be true.

Presented thus starkly, the exotic if not bizarre ramblings (both physical and mental) of Wright and Bryan seem interpretable only as the aberrations of two cranky sectarians on the borders of insanity. But if we probe a little deeper into some of the allusions in their story we begin to discover the threads of wider social and intellectual patterns. The ramifications of the Avignon society are obscure. Brothers knew about it, independently of Wright and Bryan.[25] The latter also mentions a Major Tieman, a Russian, whom he had met in England two years earlier, and who, he says, acted as interpreter at Avignon.[26] Where and how these contacts were made is at present a fascinating puzzle; but it was probably through Jacob Duché, who was certainly known to several of those who later became followers of Brothers. Duché was an Anglican clergyman from Philadelphia. He supported the American Revolution and was made chaplain to the Continental Congress; but after the Declaration of Independence he lost his enthusiasm, became a loyalist, and in 1777 came to England, where he was soon made secretary and chaplain of an orphan asylum at St George's Fields, Lambeth. He was attracted to the writings of Jacob Boehme and Swedenborg. 'Universal benevolence' Duché considered to be 'the sublime of religion; the true taste for which can only be derived from the fountain of infinite love, by inward and spiritual communications.'[27] He warmly welcomed students of Swedenborg to his Lambeth circle, which was also visited by Grabianka in 1786. Wright knew Duché[28] – as also did another Brothers' disciple, William Sharp, the engraver (to whom we shall return shortly).[29] At this point we make contact with the world of a much more famous visionary, William Blake, with whom Sharp was friendly. Blake, too, was living in Lambeth from 1790, and had been attracted to Swedenborg. It will be helpful therefore at this stage to look briefly at the New Jerusalem Church which has already been mentioned in the lives of several of Brothers' followers.

Emanuel Swedenborg, a Swedish scientist and mystic, died in London in 1772. His voluminous writings were translated from the Latin and published during the 1780s; and in 1787 his followers, led by five ex-Wesleyan preachers, organized the New Jerusalem Church in London. There was also support for Swedenborg's teaching elsewhere, notably in Lancashire. Two Anglican clergymen, Thomas Hartley, rector of Winwick, Northamptonshire, and John Clowes, rector of St

John's, Manchester, were among the earliest disseminators of his views. Certain elements in Swedenborg's life and 'theosophic' doctrines were well calculated to appeal, at least prima facie, to artisan seekers like Wright and Sharp. In the first place, Swedenborg made very large claims. He attested that 'the Lord manifested himself before me his servant ... and let me into the spiritual world, permitting me to see the heavens and the hells, and also to converse with angels and spirits, and this now continually for many years.'[30] In *The True Christian Religion*, under the heading, 'Memorable Relations', he described many conversations with angels. He declared that God had begun to form a New Church which was the New Jerusalem descending out of heaven (Revelation 21: 1–2). The last judgment occurred in 1757 and the second advent (in a spiritual sense) was already fulfilling. Swedenborg wrote with the authority of a learned man, and in a logical and unemotional manner. His doctrines were presented as eminently reasonable, but they carried the sanction of revealed truth. He offered no less than a key to understanding the universe and man's place in it, by means which, though not original, were couched in novel terms.

At the heart of Swedenborg's teaching was his doctrine of correspondences. 'The whole natural world', he wrote, 'corresponds to the spiritual world, not only the natural world in general, but also in particular. Whatever, therefore, in the natural world exists from the spiritual, is said to be its correspondent.'[31] Even the separate parts of the human body correspond with the angelic societies of heaven; 'man's spiritual world is visible in his natural world.' Every object in the universe, argues Swedenborg, has an interior meaning, is representative of some truth, and corresponds to some inner spiritual order. The Bible is written by 'correspondences': it has an internal, spiritual sense, as well as an outward, literal meaning. 'The Word', he writes, 'has a spiritual sense, which is within the natural sense, just as the soul is within the body.'[32] This revelation of the spiritual sense of the Bible, of which Swedenborg was the human instrument, was in fact the second coming; for the 'clouds of heaven' (in which the Lord is to come) signify the Word in its literal sense, and the 'power and great glory' its spiritual meaning. The second advent is not a destruction of the material world, but the opening of divine truths which have not previously been revealed. This, says Swedenborg, is the descent of the Holy City, New Jerusalem, from God out of heaven, foretold in the book of Revelation.

Other aspects of Swedenborg's teaching – his doctrines of degrees, uses, and divine influx – rounded out a complete theology for the New Church. Here was provided 'the key to open the causes of things'[33] and an explanation of the purpose for which everything exists – always with the insistence that the eye itself does not see, that meaning is not to be found in the outward form of things but in the inward and spiritual. The intricacies of Swedenborgian theology were mastered by mystically inclined seekers like Blake; but the actual New Jerusalem Church, with its sacraments and corporate worship, did not satisfy him (or Wright and Sharp) for very long.[34] Swedenborgianism presented in a new form the ancient argument by analogy, and offered an allegorical interpretation of scripture. The doctrine of correspondence would be not unfamiliar to readers of Boehme, nor indeed to anyone who had pondered on the idea that the visible world is a mirror of the invisible. For some millenarians Swedenborg was the prophet who had announced the millennium, in a spiritual sense. But for others, more literally minded, he represented only a stage in their spiritual odyssey, and as they moved on to some new position they looked back on him as one of the false prophets who would arise in the last days. In some cases the progression was even broader, and the millenarian impulse became entangled with political radicalism. Such was the position of certain followers of Brothers, and notably of William Sharp.[35]

'Fully believing this to be the Man whom GOD has appointed, I engrave his likeness', wrote Sharp on the handsome engraving of 'Richard Brothers, Prince of the Hebrews', which he published in April 1795. By that date Sharp was a well-established London engraver, with an international reputation, the friend of John Flaxman, Henry Fuseli, Philip de Loutherbourg, Blake and others in the world of artists and illustrators. He had been a Swedenborgian, and possibly also a mesmerist. In 1794 he was examined before the privy council for his involvement in the radical republican movement. He next declared his belief in Brothers, and later became a leading supporter of Joanna Southcott. Such a career indicates some of the multifarious ways in which a penchant for millennial belief could find practical expression. The problem is, however, to establish the exact relationship between these different expressions and test the meaning of, say, political as opposed to religious millenarianism.

Sharp, the son of a London gunmaker, was born in 1749 and apprenticed to an engraver.[36] He married a French woman who died early, and there were no children. Sharp had his own business and engaged in 'the superior branches of his art'. By the time of the American Revolution he was a radical reformer and a member of the Society for Constitutional Information when it was formed in 1780.[37] How and when he became a Swedenborgian is not clear. The first public meeting of Swedenborg's followers was in London in December 1783, and Sharp's friend, Flaxman, became attached to them at that time. They did not at first form a separate sect, but worshipped in Duché's chapel at the orphan asylum in St George's Fields. In May 1787 some Swedenborgians in London organized the New Church as a separate body and opened a chapel in Great East Cheap in January 1788. A general conference was held in April 1789. Sharp had joined them by 1787. But from the spring of 1789 the French Revolution completely changed the thinking of men like Sharp. The Society for Constitutional Information, which had fallen into the doldrums, was revived early in 1791, and from March 1792 until the trials of 1794 Sharp was actively involved in it. During this period he was in close touch with Horne Tooke, Brand Hollis, Thomas Holcroft, and other republicans; and was familiar with the views of Godwin, Paine, Barlow and the English Jacobins. When, therefore, the government decided in May 1794 to move against the reformers in London it was not surprising that 'Citizen Sharp' was called before the Privy Council for examination.[38] He confessed friendship with John Thelwall, the Reverend Jeremiah Joyce and Horne Tooke, but denied any support for the 'bold men' (meaning Gerrald, Sinclair and Margarot). He tried to play down his involvement with the SCI, particularly his membership of a committee to meet with the London Corresponding Society; and said that he was 'very unsettled in his ideas'. In general he left the impression of being something less than candid.[39] His friends thought that he was lucky not to be indicted along with Hardy, Horne Tooke and the others.

The government repression beginning in 1793 meant that implication in political radicalism was no light matter. Prosecutions for selling Paine's works brought imprisonment and fines. William Winterbotham, a dissenting minister from Plymouth, was tried at Exeter in July 1793 for seditious sermons and given four years' imprisonment, plus a fine of £200. In August 1793 Thomas Muir, a Scottish lawyer and republican, was sentenced to fourteen years' transportation for sedition, and the following month the Reverend Thomas Palmer, a Unitarian minister received seven years for the same offence. Arising out of the activities of the British Convention held in Edinburgh in November 1793 three leading reformers – Joseph Gerrald, Maurice Margarot, and William Skirving – were also each sentenced to fourteen years' transportation. In the spring of 1794 Thomas Walker, a Manchester radical, was brought to trial for high treason and acquitted. And in May Thomas Hardy and other London reformers were arrested. After a thorough investigation the government selected seven members of the LCS and six of the SCI for trial. In October 1794, after five months' imprisonment, and within a week of the execution of the Scots radical, Robert Watt, for treason, Hardy was tried for high treason, and acquitted – as also were the other prisoners. The treason trials were an effective form of intimidation, for apart from the trial itself the accused had to undergo the ordeal of interrogation and, in some cases, imprisonment before the trial. Sharp was well aware of all this, and was much concerned lest his business and apprentices should suffer.

Sharp's friend, William Tooke Harwood, was in a similar position.[40] He was from Norwich (a noted centre of radical reformism) and was a captain (later colonel) of dragoons. His uncle, William Tooke of Purley, was a radically inclined business man, whose protégé was John Horne Tooke, an eccentric reformer and conversationalist from the days of Wilkes onwards. Harwood was a member of the SCI and gave evidence on behalf of Horne Tooke when his friend was brought to trial. He was friendly with Godwin and married Holcroft's eldest daughter in 1796. Like Sharp he was attracted to millenarianism and was shortly to appear as a follower of Joanna Southcott. Another whose millenarian convictions took him to the edge of radical republicanism, if not beyond, was the Reverend Joseph Lomas Towers (not to be confused with his father, Dr Joseph Towers, an old dissenting radical of the Price–Priestley variety, who was pulled in for questioning before the Privy Council in June 1794). Apparently the Pitt government sought to suppress Towers' *Illustrations of Prophecy* (1796), which welcomed the French Revolution as the fulfilment of biblical eschatology.[41] Towers was not a follower of Brothers, and his work, which examines previous writers on the subject, belongs to the scholarly tradition of millennialism. But his radical conclusions and his sentiments on 'the overthrow of tyranny' and 'the restoration of a people to their rights' were well calculated to alarm a government which was suspicious of a link between millenarian and radical activity.

Such suspicions were fairly wide-spread, and appeared to have some foundation in reality. *The Times* noted that the French Revolution had been preceded by sects, mesmerists, somnambulists, prophets and prophetesses who had prepared the public mind for changes;[42] and the story of Wright and Bryan's contact with the Avignon society could only have strengthened suspicions of a secret international conspiracy.[43] Halhed, in his speech in the Commons in April 1795, felt it necessary to deny that Brothers had any connection with the popular democratic societies ('formed on principles resembling those of the Jacobin clubs in France'), or had ever been a field-preacher.[44] But the impression persisted (for those who wished to believe it) that Brothers and his followers were dupes of the French revolutionaries, whose aim was the overthrow of all (not only papal) religion and the establishment of atheism, deism, and materialism.[45] Too many rumours and reports associating Brothers with radicalism appeared for the government to feel altogether comfortable in ignoring him. For instance, in May 1795 the Mayor of Hastings wrote to the Home Office about a suspicious stranger who had come to the town about three weeks ago. His name was Leigh and he was 'employed generally' (when not distributing seditious handbills) 'in reading Paine's *Rights of Man*, Brothers' *Prophecies* and other books of that description'.[46] Whether or not such reports were correct, they testify to an expectancy in certain quarters that support for millenarianism was likely to come from the same sort of people who were attracted to radical republicanism and reform movements.

Despite Halhed's denials, Brothers' writings contained opinions and prophecies which had strong political implications. 'The Lord God commands me to say to you, George the Third, King of England that immediately on my being revealed ... to the Hebrews as their Prince ... your crown must be delivered to me, that all your power and authority may instantly cease.'[47] The Lord God also commanded him to declare that the radical reformers on trial for high treason were innocent; that the war with France should be ended since the French people had 'the judgement of God in their favour'; and that in any case Britain and her allies would be defeated, in fulfilment of the prophecies in Daniel and Revelation. A glance at the Home Office papers for 1794–5 indicates the mood in government circles at this time:[48] fear of a French invasion and the urgent need for plans to thwart it; apprehension at the spread of anti-war feeling among all ranks of society; anger against the 'treasonable' practices and views of the radical reformers and the suspected disloyalty of Dissenters. Shortages of corn and high bread prices were causing concern; and there were local riots of miners in Cornwall, colliers in Leicester and 'mobs' in Newcastle and Bristol. At the opening of parliament in October 1795 the King's coach was attacked, amid cries of 'Bread, Peace, No Pitt'. The Habeas Corpus Act had been temporarily suspended in May 1794, and the Seditious Meetings and Treasonable Practices Acts followed the peace demonstrations of 1795. In a climate of repression and, at times, hysteria, it was not difficult for the administration to believe that millenarian writings and prophecies might be sufficient to spark off the explosive mixture of social discontent and radical sentiment. In March 1795 Brothers was arrested and brought before the Privy Council. He was examined on suspicion of treason.[49]

But his interrogators found insufficient evidence to substantiate the charge and decided therefore to proceed on medical rather than political grounds. Evidence of madness was produced and Brothers was committed to a lunatic asylum.

There were also more intellectually substantial arguments for associating millenarianism with radicalism than personal friendships and common membership of the reform societies. To the millenarian who identified the Church of Rome with Antichrist, the French attack on Catholicism could only be welcomed. It was evidence that the last days were nigh, and the French revolutionaries were the agents of Providence in fulfilling the prophecies.[50] For radical reformers the events in France similarly confirmed the democratic and republican principles they had held since the time of the American Revolution. There was room here for some overlap with the millenarian position, despite the religious infidelity (usually Deism) of popular radicalism. It was this which alarmed William Hamilton Reid, an ex-radical, into denouncing the 'Mystics, Muggletonians, Millennaries' as auxiliaries of infidelity. He instanced popular speakers in Spitalfields, where 'the French system of politics insensibly attached itself to the auxiliary ideas of prophecies fulfilling on the Continent'; and gave details of a circle of 'infidel mystics' at Hoxton, known as the Ancient Deists, which he alleged was composed of 'alchemists, astrologers, calculators, mystics, magnetizers, prophets and projectors of every class'.[51] Reid wrote of a 'Millennium of Infidelity', and was disgusted with the inconsistency of 'infidels' who attended Christian worship. Yet he well knew that dissenting Christians (including millenarians) who believed in 'the sufficiency of the spirit's teaching' were, in some respects, not far removed from the position of Thomas Paine. In the first part of The Age of Reason which appeared in 1795, Paine declared, 'My own mind is my own church'; and admitted that revelation from God might have a personal (but not general) validity. It is possible therefore, following Reid, to see in the popular radicalism of the mid-1790s a sort of synthesis of Christian and infidel millenarianism. In the case of individuals such as Sharp, however, it is not easy to distinguish the various elements or types of millenarianism at any one time. It is tempting to look for a progression from a radical-political millenarianism to a religious, non-political millenarianism, or vice versa. But on close examination this breaks down. Sharp had been a radical since the days of the American Revolution and was a Swedenborgian in the 1780s. His involvement with the radical reformers of the 1790s and with Brothers appears to be a continuation of his earlier interests, and he was later to transfer his allegiance to Joanna Southcott.

Political radicalism and religious millenarianism were not alternatives so much as different aspects of the same phenomenon. From the personal angle millenarianism has to be seen, not as a progression, but as a generalized belief about the world and the changes going on in it, which could be expressed in varying modes at different times, but which remained a constant for the individual concerned.

The same steadiness of purpose is observable in the reactions of Brothers' followers to his confinement in an asylum. While his incarceration put an end to the personal publicity which had alarmed the government, it did nothing to invalidate the beliefs of millenarians. Rather, it confirmed their faith in Brothers' prophecies and in his role as a true prophet who would be persecuted by his own people, like Jesus and the prophets of the Old Testament. For the next six years (until the appearance of Joanna Southcott in 1801) Brothers remained the central figure in their millenarian world. The prophet continued to write, and his works were printed through the efforts of the faithful Finlayson. In these later pamphlets Brothers developed further some of the doctrines put forward in *A Revealed Knowledge*, notably the restoration of the Jews, British Israelism, and a social programme.

His plans for the return of the Jews to the Holy Land were extremely explicit. The Kings of England, Denmark, Sweden and Prussia, the Emperor of Turkey, and other countries from Abyssinia to Japan, were required to help with the operation. For if God spares the world, argued Brothers, great quantities of stores and building materials will be needed, and each state will have to provide its quota: 300 shiploads of timber, 20,000 tents, 100 large wagons, 800 wheelbarrows, 2,000 bolts of canvas, 500 hand spikes, 600 stone saws – and so on in great detail.[52] The rebuilding of Jerusalem ('with the garden of Eden in the centre') was described exactly, in accordance with the vision of the city in Ezekiel 40–8. *A Description of Jerusalem* contains a vast amount of information on the streets, squares and buildings in the restored city: even the thickness of the walls and the size of the windows is prescribed.[53] Palestine, which used to be very fertile, is now largely desert, notes Brothers, and much hard work will be necessary to make it prosper again. And he adds that to many people it will no doubt be 'astonishing that I should be so perfect on a sudden in architectural delineation, never having studied it ... I confess I am astonished myself. But God is my instructor.'[54] Improbable as the details of Brothers' scheme must have seemed, the basic idea of the return of the Jews in the last days was part of accepted millennial belief. It was inherently no more impossible than the binding of Antichrist, which appeared to have already taken place. If the last days had indeed arrived it was but logical to expect the full implementation of the eschatological programme as laid down in scripture. It is perhaps in this light that we should view Henry Crabb Robinson's story that John Flaxman told him in 1799 that Sharp invited him (Flaxman) to join Brothers' mission to the Holy Land and promised that he should have the building of the Temple in Jerusalem.[55]

The literal-mindedness of Brothers' interpretation of Jerusalem, however, should not be allowed to obscure the importance of the theme for millenarians. John's great vision of 'the holy city, new Jerusalem, coming down from God out of heaven' was not a matter of bricks and mortar, but the dwelling of God with man ('behold, the tabernacle of God is with men'). Jerusalem was a symbol which evoked an imaginative response in the minds of believers. It could be personalized and used to signify a state of blessedness or pure and innocent belief, as in Blake's *Jerusalem* or in Joanna Southcott's 'communications'.[56] The 'building of Jerusalem', whether literally or metaphorically, figured prominently in millenarian writing, and was part of a wider mythology. Brothers, as a minor prophet who claimed to be the Prince of the Hebrews, has to be set in the context of this mythology. And his theory of British Israelism relates directly to the school of speculative mythologists.

The 'invisible' Hebrews, whom he was to lead back to the Holy Land, were accounted for by Brothers in two ways.[57] First, were the descendants of those Israelites who had been carried into captivity at various times by the Assyrians,[58] together with some who had travelled freely into foreign lands. Second, some Jews had been converted to Christianity by Jesus and the apostles. They had been persecuted, taken to Rome, sold into slavery, and dispersed throughout Europe. In remote times many of these exiles had found their way to Britain. Hence a large part of the present British population was of Hebrew extraction, and Brothers had no difficulty in assigning his friends and supporters to one or other of the ten lost tribes of Israel. He himself (and also Miss Cott) were, of course of the kingly house of David. Fanciful as this theory may sound, it was no less credible than other contemporary speculations. Consider, for example, the following quotation from Blake's *Jerusalem*:

To the Jews
Jerusalem the Emanation of the Giant Albion! Can it be? Is it a Truth that the Learned have explored? Was Britain the Primitive Seat of the Patriarchal Religion? If it is true, my title-page is also True, that Jerusalem was and is the Emanation of the Giant Shore.

Your Ancestors derived their origin from Abraham, Heber, Shem and
Noah, who were Druids ...[59]

And in the beautiful and well-known poem from *Milton* Blake imagines
England as the place where man was created and first walked with God
in Paradise:

And did those feet in ancient time
Walk upon England's mountains green?
And was the Holy Lamb of God
On England's pleasant pastures seen?

And did the Countenance Divine
Shine forth upon our clouded hills?
And was Jerusalem builded here
Among these dark Satanic Mills?[60]

The pedigree of these ideas is to be traced in the writings of the
speculative mythologists, whose antiquarian discoveries provided a
slender basis for a highly romantic view of the early history of Britain.[61]
It was claimed that England was the seat of antediluvian religion, and
even that the Garden of Eden was situated in the British Isles. The
patriarchal religion of Abraham was preserved among the Druid
priesthood. 'Adam was a Druid, and Noah', wrote Blake. The ground
for these claims lay in a euhemerist view of mythology, which regarded
myth not as an explanation of some mysterious phenomenon of nature
but as history presented in a special (sometimes distorted and obscure)
way. Biblical chronology imposed a foreshortened time-scale on human
history, given the generally accepted calculation of Archbishop Ussher
that the world was created in 4004 BC. Acceptance of the story of the
deluge meant that the whole world, civilized and uncivilized, had to be
repopulated from Noah and his family. To these restrictions was added
new knowledge derived from the study of philosophy and comparative
religion. The speculative mythologists provided explanations of early
history and cultural diversity which at the same time harmonized with
the scriptural accounts. Not all problems of chronology could be
satisfactorily dealt with in these terms. But by the late eighteenth century
there was general confidence that by further study it would be possible to
elucidate completely the secrets of pre-history. That reliable 'evidences'
were in much shorter supply than the profusion of speculative theories in
no way checked the spread of these ideas. Poets and antiquarians seized
upon them, each adding his own pet theory about the roots of Greek
verbs, the bardic class of patriarchal Druids or Phoenician place names.

Characteristic of the extravagance to which this speculation could run was the rumour of a Welsh speaking tribe of Indians, descendants of the followers of a Welsh prince, Madoc, who had sailed to America and settled along the Missouri river.[62] Robert Southey based two romances, 'Madoc in Wales' and 'Madoc in Aztlan' on the idea; and although he had to admit in 1815 that it had no basis in fact, the notion had by then gained sufficient credence to support a scheme for sending out missionaries to the Welsh Indians.

In the context of this intellectual milieu Brothers' theories of British Israelism do not appear unusually far-fetched; and there is evidence that both he and some of his followers were interested in antiquarian and mythological researches. His *Description of Jerusalem* is based on some reading of ancient history together with accounts by Wood and Bruce of travels in the Near East, including the theory that the ruins of Balbec and Palmyra were the palaces of Solomon.[63] Towards the end of his life he published *A Correct Account of the Invasion and Conquest ... by the Saxons* in which he linked Britons with their forgotten Israelite ancestors.[64] Halhed's reputation as a Sanskrit scholar has already been mentioned. But it is perhaps also worth noting that he was a pupil of Sir William Jones, whose work in comparative philology provided an important element in theories of population migration and cultural diffusion. Halhed's own work was on similar lines, and was thus sympathetic, if not contributory to, some aspects of speculative mythology. Every man could make his own selection from this material and use it in his own special way — as did Blake:

> The antiquities of every Nation under Heaven is no less sacred than that of the Jews. They are the same thing, as Jacob Bryant and all antiquaries have proved. ... All had originally one language, and one religion: this was the religion of Jesus, the Everlasting Gospel.[65]

In the case of William Owen Pughe we can document even more directly the connection between millenarian beliefs and mythological theories. Pughe, a Welsh antiquary and lexicographer, explored bardic culture, using the theories of the mythologists to weave a fantastic pattern of Druidic history and Arthurian lore. After his childhood in Merionethshire, during which he acquired an early interest in Welsh poetry, he lived in London, but details of this period of his life (from 1776) are scanty.[66] He may have associated with the political radicals of the 1790s; but whether or not he was an 'active' millenarian at that time is difficult to determine.[67] Certainly by 1804 he was a believer in Joanna Southcott, and many of her early disciples had been followers of

Brothers.[68] Likewise it seems probable that Pughe was acquainted with Blake, who may have been indebted to him for some of his writings about Druids and patriarchal religion.[69] Since we do not have any autobiographical help, it is not possible to trace precise arguments or experiences by which Pughe related his millenarian beliefs to his mythology. The general problem is how to elucidate the sensibility of the age to millenarian claims, to explain the modes of perceiving the millennium. If, as has been suggested, there was a new sensibility to millenarianism in the 1790s and early 1800s, it may perhaps be related to the same intellectual currents and social impulses as account for the popularity of speculative mythology. But whereas for us at present this is only a general, undifferentiated sensibility, for Pughe, Sharp, Blake and their contemporaries it was a specific mode of perception. In the investigation of their different ways of using the concept of the millennium we return to the age of early romanticism and away from later, anachronistic assumptions about millenarianism. The object of investigation, however, is not to try to match the apparent craziness of the millenarians with the bizarreness of the mythologists in order to show the relative normality of the former, nor to suggest that odd ideas were more common then than now. Rather we search for meaning by taking seriously what the millenarians and mythologists said and did, as a clue in the larger exploration of popular belief.

The third element in Brothers' later writings – the formulation of a social programme – emerges from his plans for the restored Hebrew kingdom. At his death in 1824 he left a manuscript, later published by Finlayson, containing a constitution of ninety-three articles and a variety of arrangements for the conduct of daily life.[70] Hidden in the interstices of this document are such provisions as come nearest to being Brothers' ideas on social problems. They do not amount to a coherent social philosophy or platform, but rather represent personal grievances: no arrest for debt, safeguards for lunacy, and facilities for divorce and remarriage. There are to be no tithes, circumcision is forbidden, and houses are not to remain empty for more than three years. The same type of approach to social policy – demand for the abolition of certain social evils, apparently chosen from personal experience or predilection – appears in Brothers' followers. Thus Thomas Taylor, in addition to his general puritan condemnation of the vices mentioned earlier, also attacked militarists, doctors, lawyers and wet-nurses.[71] The general tone of this literature is critical of the rich and powerful, and sympathetic to the needs and claims of the poor. Always, just below the surface, is the independence and radicalism of the dissenting spirit; and also the conviction that social ills can be cured if men would individually follow God's inward revelation. Ultimately, social evil is inseparable from present society, which is Babylon the Great, the Mother of Harlots; and in these last days she will be destroyed. Already war has been let loose, and will end only with England's defeat. Death on a pale horse (Revelation 6:8) rides out, with authority 'to kill with sword, and with famine, and with death, and by the wild beasts of the earth.'

Brothers' interpretation, that this passage 'relates to the present war',[72] is strikingly similar to Blake's painting, 'Death on a Pale Horse', which makes very much the same comment. And indeed the comparison between Blake and Brothers, which has been suggested earlier, may at this point be taken a little further.[73] Blake was not a follower of Brothers, but he presumably heard about him from friends like Sharp and John Gabriel Stedman. A few years later Blake certainly knew about Joanna Southcott,[74] and there is a story that Sharp tried to convert him to her views.[75] More fundamental than the question of possible personal contacts is Blake's concern with the concept of the millennium and his visionary approach. He spoke of 'my visions', and the theme of the millennium appears constantly in his major works, especially Night IX of *The Four Zoas*. 'He is not so much a disciple of Jacob Böhmen and Swedenborg as a fellow visionary', wrote Henry Crabb Robinson: 'He lives as they did in a world of his own. Enjoying constant intercourse with the world of spirits, he receives visits from Shakespeare, Milton, Dante, Voltaire, and has given me repeatedly their very words in their conversations. His paintings are copies of what he sees in his visions.'[76] Both Blake and Brothers interpreted the Bible as a series of 'types and shadows' (to use Joanna Southcott's phrase), archetypes for the people and events of the modern world. *A Revealed Knowledge* echoes many of the sentiments found in Blake's poetry: the horrors of war, oppression and despotism; defence of the French republic; condemnation of commerce and slavery; anti-clericalism; and apocalyptic warnings. There is a common stock of ideas, images and vocabulary. In this respect Blake and Brothers were part of a wider millenarian tradition stretching back to the sectaries of the seventeenth century, and embodying (via popular mystics, antinomians, prophets and prophetesses) an alternative to the dominant rational assumptions and teachings of the Enlightenment. This millenarian tradition surfaced in the 1790s. But within it were various and conflicting positions; and ultimately the views of Blake and Brothers were very different. The intense literal-mindedness of Brothers was quite foreign to Blake's conception. Whereas for Brothers Jerusalem was an actual city to which he was to lead the 'invisible' Hebrews, for Blake it was a symbol, an imaginative statement about the conditions of human liberty, to be realized in the millennium:

In my Exchanges every Land
Shall walk, and mine in every Land,
Mutual shall build Jerusalem,
Both heart in heart and hand in hand.[77]

The main point of comparing Blake and Brothers is not to try to enlist Blake into the ranks of Brothers' (or Joanna's) disciples, but to establish the nature of millenarianism in the late eighteenth and early nineteenth centuries. The case of Blake serves to remind us of the existence of millenarian belief outside the 'normal' institutions of millenarianism – or, to put the problem in another way, it suggests the weakness of millenarian institutions and the need to assess exactly what their role was.

Through the eyes of Brothers and his followers we have a view of the 1790s which is not often presented. The stance of a millenarian was distinct from the stance of those more usually used as mouthpieces for the period, such as the romantic poet or the political radical; for the millenarian used a different language and had a different set of priorities. In this chapter the tendency has been to emphasize the distinctiveness of the millenarian position. And yet, as we have seen, there were surprising overlaps and common interests. The millenarian was by no means so cranky, isolated and 'unrepresentative' (whatever that means for the historian) as a first reading of millenarian pamphlets might suggest. In relation to his social and political context his views soon become explicable, and perhaps even acquire a simple functional validity.

CHAPTER FIVE

THE WOMAN CLOTHED WITH THE SUN

(i) THE PROPHETESS

The confinement of Brothers and the government repression of radical dissent, whether political or religious, discouraged most of the followers of the Nephew of the Almighty. They did not abandon their millennial beliefs, but they were uncertain where to look for salvation. Convinced that the time of the end was near, they looked anxiously for the sign of a prophet or messiah. Perhaps Brothers was only a herald, a latter-day John the Baptist, and not the Saviour himself, after all. Then, early in 1801, the answer came. A ninepenny pamphlet, called *The Strange Effects of Faith* by Joanna Southcott was published in Exeter. It was followed, during the year, by five further parts; but already by the time of the third part (May 1801) it had become known to some of the followers of Brothers. The three clergymen, Foley, Bruce and Webster, wrote to the author, as also did Sharp, Turner and Morison. 'By reading only her first three Books', Sharp testified, 'I was convinced ... that the visitation to her [was] not of human wisdom.'[1]

Joanna Southcott was a farmer's daughter from Devon. Born in 1750 at Tarford (or Taleford) near Ottery St Mary, she was brought up in the village of Gittisham. She worked on the farm with her sisters and then went into domestic service in various households in Exeter and the neighbouring area. Through her employment in the homes of several upholsterers she became proficient as an upholsteress. Her upbringing was religious, and her father made his children read a chapter of the Bible daily and repeat to him what they had learnt. But it was the death of her mother, when Joanna was twenty-two, that was the first stage in the deepening of her religious development. Hannah Southcott had been a God-fearing woman, and her dying blessing strongly impressed Joanna, who prayed that she might be given 'some assurance'. Thereafter, she said later, 'I began to rejoice in the God of my salvation, and began to have a lively and strong faith in the Lord.'[2] Joanna had been brought up in the established church, and always remained faithful to its tenets. But sometime around 1780 she made contact with the Methodists, and became involved with the notorious ex-Wesleyan preacher, Hugh Saunderson. He had been expelled from the Society by Wesley in 1777 but continued to cause schism among the Methodists, first in Edinburgh and then (from 1782) in Exeter. Joanna attended his class meetings, and described his conduct:

> He used to terrify all the people when he was in prayer; and was often telling what wondrous miracles he had wrought by prayer; and that he had, at a meeting, made the whole society lie stiff upon the floor, till he had got the evil spirits out of them; and I remember myself, once at a class meeting, a religious, good man shrieked out in such a manner as though he had sent an evil spirit into him; but I cannot say he ever had any power over me; only I used to think the room was full of spirits, when he was in prayer.[3]

Joanna, indeed, soon had good cause to believe that this miracle-worker was anything but a man of God: on the contrary she was informed, in answer to her prayer, that he was an instrument of Satan. For Saunderson lodged in the house of Joanna's employer, an upholsterer named Wills, and seduced Wills' wife – 'a lewd woman, whose heart was roving after every man she could make her prey' declared Joanna. Wills was reputed 'a truly religious man', though he had greatly shocked Joanna some time previously by telling her that he loved her. After discovering Saunderson's misconduct Joanna decided to inform Wills, but he refused to believe her and asserted his wife's virtue. Joanna thereupon left, and took a place with a minister at Musbury. But Wills blackened her character to her new employer, and she was then dismissed. Joanna sued Wills for defamation and won her case.

At the trial Wills called Joanna an enthusiast, and it would seem that, despite her experiences with Saunderson and Wills, she remained drawn to the Methodists. She explained her position thus:

> My religion is that of the established church of England; but being of St. Paul's mind, to try all, prove all things, and to hold fast that which is good ... I attended constantly my church, forenoons and afternoons, and received the sacrament; at the same time I also attended Mr. Wesley's preachers at eight o'clock in the mornings and at six in the evenings; these hours not interfering with the service of

the established church; but did not then join their society, though I
was much invited to do so.[4]

At Christmas 1792, however, she was ordered 'by divine command' (as
she said afterwards) to join the society, and so became a member of the
small group of Wesley's followers in Exeter. She continued to work as a
domestic servant for several different employers, but particularly for the
Taylors who were also upholsterers and who later became friends and
believers. Joanna was now forty-two, unmarried, and compelled to
work hard to support herself and also, from time to time to support her
father. But suddenly the pattern of her life was interrupted: 'in 1792 I
was strangely visited, by day and night, concerning what was coming
upon the whole earth. I was then ordered to set it down in writing.'[5] She
obeyed; and from this date began her career as a prophetess.

The decision to write had momentous consequences. Without it
Joanna could hardly have escaped the oblivion which overtook scores of
humble prophetesses and wise women in the villages and towns of
Britain. But the existence of a body of writings, which would later be
published, ensured that her message could be considered more widely and
seriously than was possible by means of local and oral tradition. Joanna
had had little opportunity for practising literary skills. Her reading had
been mainly in the Bible, and her handwriting was virtually illegible.
Nevertheless in the twenty-two years between 1792 and her death in
1814 she produced sixty-five pamphlets, containing some 4,500 pages,
and perhaps twice as much again in unpublished manuscripts.[6] About a
quarter of the printed works are concerned with her own history and
comments on contemporary events, the remainder being
communications from the Spirit and interpretations of scripture.
Scattered throughout her works are passages of autobiography which
together constitute a rare historical record. Here we have, in her own
words, the story of a labouring woman in the later part of the eighteenth
century. In simple language and with artless honesty she portrays her
daily experiences, secret hopes and bizarre fantasies. There is the same
mixture of earthy reality and contact with the supernatural as in the
journals of Wright and Bryan, but at much greater length. It is a genre of
popular biography comparable to the radical working men's and self-
help biographies of the nineteenth century, but centring on the search for
freedom to explore inner experiences. The account which follows is
based on this material, supplemented by the observations of her
followers. At times the exact chronological framework is difficult to
establish, since Joanna recorded only those events in her history which

she thought had some spiritual significance; and her habit of telling only part of her story at a time entails some collation and cross-referencing. Even so, the insight afforded into the mind of a Devonshire domestic servant in the time of the American and French Revolutions is a useful contribution to the study of popular mentalities. We catch a glimpse of the world as Joanna saw it – and it is a strange and unfamiliar view. It is not the view of the late eighteenth century that conventional historians have led us to expect. Yet it is one authentic aspect of the state of ideas at a popular level.

Joanna's first problem after her visitation was (like most prophets) to win credibility. When she told her sister about the 'voices' she heard, the reply was that Joanna was going out of her senses, and that none of her prophecies were likely to come true. Joanna predicted that a war was coming, that there would be a dearth of provisions, and that there would be great distress in the nation. Her employer, Mrs Lucy Taylor, was more impressed:

> there was scarce anything happened to the nation, or to particular families, or individuals, with whom she was acquainted, that she, Joanna, did not inform me would happen before it did, and all were fulfilled as Joanna predicted; and this continued for two or three years.[7]

At this level Joanna's claims were acceptable as those of a local wise woman, whose predictions, dreams and visions were part of a recognizable tradition. But Joanna could not be satisfied with such a role. She was convinced that God was speaking to her directly and specially; at the same time she was puzzled and uncertain. She needed guidance and reassurance, and so turned first to her new friends, the Methodists. At Easter 1793 she told her experiences to her class meeting, under the leadership of John Eastlake, one of the founding fathers of the Exeter society. This was not well received, and Joanna was greatly troubled. She withdrew from the society, despite Eastlake's attempts at conciliation. Her Spirit then ordered her to go to Henry Tanner, a lay preacher of the Calvinistic Methodist persuasion and an opponent of the Wesleyans. He listened favourably to her at first, but later decided that she was deluded. In the same year she approached the Reverend Mr Leach, a dissenting minister, who after hearing her in silence said: 'It comes from the Devil; for not one thing you have mentioned will come to pass.'[8] Nevertheless, she persisted in appealing to him until 1795, when he refused to pursue the matter further. So, rebuffed by the Methodists and Dissenters, Joanna turned to the clergy of the Church of

England. She had heard the Reverend Joseph Pomeroy, vicar of St Kew, Cornwall, preach in Exeter cathedral at Advent, 1793, and had been impressed. In 1796 she wrote to him, and he called on her at Mrs Taylor's shop. To her delight he said unequivocally that her communications were not from the devil, though he pressed her gently as to whether they might not be from herself, and considered privately that she was partly deranged. She wrote to him later (1804) that 'there is not one man upon earth hath strengthened my faith so much to prove clearly my visitation from the Lord as you have.'[9] Pomeroy paid dearly for his kindly tolerance, if not virtual encouragement, of Joanna; for she pursued him relentlessly for the rest of her days, and he particularly resented the unwelcome publicity of being mentioned in her pamphlets. Joanna could not rid herself of the idea that her fate was somehow destined to be linked with Pomeroy, and she was most reluctant to accept his angry attempts to shake her off. In the end she concluded that he was cast in the role of Judas. She wrote repeatedly to other clergy in Exeter, including the archdeacon and the chancellor of the diocese, asking them to examine her claims, but her letters were either ignored or returned with abusive comments. Her need for recognition remained unsatisfied and in 1800 she embarked on a new venture: she was ordered by the Spirit to put her writings in print.

It had been her custom to seal up many of her prophecies, with the intention that they should be opened later only by duly authorized ministers or judges. In addition she had accumulated since 1792 a stock of manuscripts, consisting of accounts of her dreams, their interpretation by a 'spirit invisible', and copies of letters to ministers. These she now drew on for her publications. With her savings and a loan totalling £100 in all she was able to print 1,000 copies of *The Strange Effects of Faith*. And although an unfriendly critic suggested that it was odd that the Spirit should have selected a printer who was a Deist (he was speedily replaced after Part I) the little pamphlets were truly bread cast upon the waters.[10]

The gathering of Joanna's disciples now began. Her first letter of support was from the Reverend Stanhope Bruce, followed by similar assurances from Webster and Foley. Four other followers of Brothers also came forward: Sharp, Turner, Morison, and John Wilson (a coach-maker of Kentish Town). These 'seven stars', as Joanna called them, accepted her invitation to visit Exeter in December 1801 to examine her writings. They invited five local clergymen, including the bishop and the archdeacon, to join them in order to make a jury of twelve as Joanna requested; but these clergy declined. The seven, however, were convinced. Before they returned home the writings were replaced in a sealed box, under the custody of Sharp. It was agreed that Joanna should move to London, and in May 1802 she went to stay with Mrs Basil Bruce in Jermyn Street, Foley and Sharp undertaking the financial responsibilities. The nucleus of Brothers' followers was crucial at this stage of the gathering process. Colonel William Tooke Harwood, Dr William R. Wetherell and William Bryan soon declared their belief in Joanna. Richard Law, a believer in Brothers, appealed to the prime minister to set an example by publicly supporting her.[11] Halhed was also prepared to believe in her mission, despite some conflict with his loyalty to Brothers. Colonel Basil Bruce, who had come out strongly for Brothers, to the extent of resigning his office rather than swear an oath, was enthusiastic for Joanna during the summer of 1801, but developed doubts before his sudden death a few months later.[12] His wife and father were stalwart believers. Joanna, naturally, did not think very highly of Brothers' claims. When Foley, in his first letter to her, offered to send her copies of Brothers' prophecies, she replied that she did not read any books but was guided solely by the Spirit. She felt compassion for Brothers in his confinement, but warned her followers that they should not believe all he told them. In one of her dreams she saw two heavy wagons descending a hill, but the first wagon broke down and blocked the path. The second wagon, with which she was travelling, therefore took another path and reached the bottom safely. Her Spirit informed her that this meant that she would go on, while Brothers was pulled down. Later her attitude to Brothers hardened, and she said that his writings were blasphemous and written under the influence of the devil.[13]

Following her removal to London the promotion of Joanna's mission by the seven went ahead rapidly. They circulated nearly 1,000 letters to members of parliament and took every opportunity to publicize her. Joanna's way of life changed outwardly in important respects. Instead of being a servant or working upholsteress she was now supported by wealthy believers like the Foleys and Bruces, who deferred to her and followed her instructions. She stayed with them in their homes, and was visited by disciples and newly made acquaintances. Her pamphlets sold well, and new ones appeared rapidly. During 1803 she toured various parts of the country, spending time with old friends in Exeter, with the Foleys at Oldswinford, and with George Turner in Leeds. Her Yorkshire tour drew large crowds, and left behind a residuum of believers in several northern towns. But it was obvious that she had little talent for public speaking and that her charismatic powers were best exercised through other channels. On her return to London in April 1804 she went to live with Jane Townley, a wealthy believer who provided a home for Joanna for the rest of her life. Miss Townley and her maid, Ann Underwood, acted as amanuenses to Joanna, and most of her communications from 1804 were taken down by Townley or Underwood directly from Joanna's dictation. Underwood was one of the few people who became adept at reading Joanna's nearly illegible handwriting.

Despite her success in attracting followers and in gaining acceptance among some respectable people, Joanna was at times unsure of herself and subject to depression. She attributed such doubts and perplexities to the temptations of Satan, and in August 1802 she had to argue her way to his defeat over a period of seven days. This she recorded in *A Dispute between the Woman and the Powers of Darkness* (London, 1802). But she still hankered after wider recognition, in particular from the clergy, and she was convinced that the way to achieve this was by means of a public trial. She and her writings were to be examined and 'proved' by twelve judges and twelve jurymen. How this notion originated with her is not obvious. In 1794 she had a vision of being in a room full of lighted candles and this was interpreted to mean that her writings must be proved by twelve men: 'Arise, shine; for thy light is come, and the glory of the Lord is risen upon thee.' Or the idea may have come from a suggestion by Pomeroy in 1796 that she should satisfy herself as to whether her visitation was from God by submitting her writings to the judgment of twelve ministers. According to believers there were three trials of Joanna. The first was in Exeter at Christmas 1801, when the seven visited her and examined some of her writings. The second was held at the High House, Paddington (rented by Foley for Joanna) in January 1803. Every effort was made to attract ministers and the public, but only her friends attended. A third, and more elaborate trial was therefore planned for December 1804. This took place at the Neckinger House, Bermondsey, the home of Elias Carpenter, who was an enthusiastic supporter and the owner of a prosperous papermill. Again the clergy were urged to come, and the event was widely advertised. The invitations met with the same rebuffs as before; Sharp, for instance, being told by a clergyman on whom he called that he had no opinion of a Holy Spirit that could not write grammar. So, although the trial was conducted according to legal forms, with an attorney in attendance, and with a solemnity which the believers likened to the trial of Jesus before Pilate, it was not the great public inquiry that Joanna had hoped for. It did, however, publicize the cause, and it served as a convention of the leading believers from all parts of the kingdom.[14]

Public interest was stirred not so much by Joanna's trials as by her seals.[15] We have already noted her predilection for sealing her writings. From 1802 she was ordered by her Spirit to begin the sealing of believers. 'Hurt not the earth, neither the sea, nor the trees, till we shall have sealed the servants of our God', cried the angel in Revelation 7:3. Believers were invited to sign a petition calling for the overthrow of Satan and the establishment of Christ's Kingdom on earth, and were given a seal with their name at the top and Joanna's signature below. The seal was a piece of paper on which was a circle and the inscription: 'The Sealed of the Lord, the Elect precious. Man's Redemption to inherit the Tree of Life. To be made Heirs of God and Joint-Heirs with Jesus Christ.'[16] It was then folded up and sealed with a seal which carried the letters I.C. (construed to stand for Jesus Christ) between two stars. Joanna explained that the Lord permitted her to find this seal, as if by accident, in sweeping out a house in Exeter; and that she had thought nothing of it until told by the Spirit to use it for sealing her writings. The sealing of the believers had meaning at several different levels. At its simplest it was an initiation ceremony, a symbol of good intentions and their acceptance by the prophetess. More deeply it was a protest against the presumed adequacy of formal religion (or 'gospel preaching' as Joanna described it) to bring in the kingdom of Christ, and a sign of personal commitment to guidance by the Spirit. It implied a sense of urgency, in that the time of the end was very near. But at a popular level the seals had a magical appeal. From Joanna's repeated injunction, 'Sign for Satan's destruction', it was but a short step to the belief that the seals were a protection against evil, in fact a talisman. This was apparent when a believer named Joachim was shot dead in June 1808 while walking home across the fields to Camden Town between eleven and twelve o'clock at night. Although he had previously had a dream which seemed to presage his murder, and his wife and daughters were 'great mockers of the Visitation and had been very warm with him for his belief', it was thought by the believers that he was protected by his seal. Joanna took the opportunity to warn them that the powers of evil were always active and the seals would not in themselves keep off all dangers.[17] Demand for the seals was brisk; 8,144 were issued by January 1804 and 14,000 by September 1807. Lists of people who signed their names and received seals were kept by leading followers in various places. The system was very vulnerable to abuse and misunderstanding. Joanna was constantly accused of selling the seals, and their supposed magical properties made them desirable objects for a black-market trade. In 1807, after admitting that 'there are thousands sealed who know not for what they are sealed', she gave orders for stricter tests of admission. Only those who were acquainted with her writings and had copies of the two pamphlets *Sound an Alarm in my Holy Mountain* and *A Caution and Instruction to the Sealed* were to be given seals. The Spirit informed Joanna that the sealing at first was like a net cast into the sea, gathering in good and bad; but henceforth only 'true believers in heart and mind' were to be sealed 'to be elect members of Christ'.

Joanna had no intention of forming a new sect. But like Wesley and others before her she discovered that when she was rejected by the established church her followers found it more congenial to meet separately. Three chapels were opened in the London area and Southcottian congregations were formed in the northern and midland towns and in the west country. Unlike Wesley, Joanna had no organizational talent, and the Southcottians were no more than a loose federation of local groups of believers, held together by their common belief in her mission. Nevertheless even such a simple organization entailed continuous supervision, and she alone was in a position to exercise authority over the believers. Disagreements among them, not to mention opposition from outside, occupied a good deal of her time. The influential Elias Carpenter, who had opened a chapel for her near the Elephant and Castle, withdrew after a protracted controversy in 1805. Mary Bateman, the Yorkshire witch who was hanged for poisoning in 1809, caused a flurry by her alleged associations with some of the believers. A variety of independent preachers engaged her in controversy; mocking letters in newspapers, passed on by indignant followers, had to be answered; and always there was the danger from 'false prophets' who threatened to mislead the faithful. Believers were, almost by definition, people prone to visions and dreams, and prepared to be guided by the Spirit wheresoever it should lead them. Well might Joanna have echoed the words of St Paul (II Corinthians 11:28) that in addition to her own sufferings and weakness she had to bear 'that which cometh upon me daily, the care of all the churches.'

Joanna maintained that of herself she was nothing, that she had neither knowledge nor authority. Everything she wrote and the decisions she made were ordered by the Spirit. How could a woman so humble and uneducated prophesy about the affairs of the nation and interpret deep mysteries of scripture except she who was guided by God?, she argued (and the argument was attractive to the more educated believers). Her decisions and injunctions were issued in the form of 'communications'. Some of these were 'ordered' to be printed. Many more circulated among believers in manuscript, and were copied by them and passed on to others. Southcottian families usually had manuscript collections of Joanna's communications and letters, copied into 'books of correspondence'. The communications were descriptions of her own or other people's dreams and visions, or passages of scripture, or items of contemporary news, followed by 'the answer of the Spirit'. She drew heavily on her past experiences in Devonshire, and frequently re-quoted her own earlier writings to interpret some fresh question or event. The writings were in both verse and prose, and at times heavily biblical in style. She explained that she used verse because 'verse gives an echo, and it is the voice of the Lord echoing back to man.'[18] Critics made fun of the doggerel with its forced rhymes. A typical example runs thus:

So now awake ye sons of Men,
And see your Bibles clear
The former things are come to pass
In all I told you here.
And now the new before your view
They all are hastening on;
My Law and Gospel I'll make clear,
To all the Sons of Men,

and so on for another three pages.[19] However, it is perhaps rather beside the point to condemn Joanna's effusions on poetic grounds, for this type of rhyme seems to belong to mystical utterance and is an indication of its automatic character. 'Expression, once it is divorced from the critical action of the surface intelligence', wrote Evelyn Underhill, 'always tends to assume a dithyrambic form.'[20]

The number of communications ran into many hundreds, perhaps thousands.[21] Joanna had difficulty in describing exactly the 'voices' which dictated these communications; 'but the words come to me as distinct to my hearing as though they were spoken in an audible voice.'[22] Towards the end of her life she recorded the delights of her visitation:

I have fresh things revealed to me every day. I am awakened every morning between three and four o'clock. I sit up in my bed till the day breaks; and have Communications given to me as soon as I awake. When the day breaks I rise and go down into the dining-room by myself; the moment I enter the room I feel as though I was surrounded with angels; feeling a heavenly joy which I cannot describe, and which has taken from me my natural appetite.[23]

The communications were then usually taken down by Underwood and witnessed by Townley. The faithful pair provided for all her material needs, submitted to her whims, and nursed her when she was sick. In addition to a home in London, Townley provided a house (Rock Cottage) in the Cotswold village of Blockley, where during her last years Joanna lived in seclusion, dictating communications from her Spirit.

In her first pamphlet, *The Strange Effects of Faith* (p. 16), she had made her claims clear:

> By types, shadows, dreams and visions, I have been led on from 1792 to the present day; whereby the mysteries of the Bible, with the future destinies of nations have been revealed to me, which will all terminate in the Second Coming of Christ, and the Day of Judgement, when the seven thousand years are ended.

She had also put forward her doctrine of the woman – and this was shortly to be given a new and momentous twist. Joanna identified herself with the 'woman clothed with the sun' of Revelation 12 and also with the bride of the Lamb in the nineteenth chapter. This had been revealed to her in a communication in 1796:

> Then now I'll tell thee what thou art –
> The true and faithful Bride,[24]

and was to be referred to many times subsequently. Her Spirit also informed her on another occasion that Christ was her spiritual husband. She noted particularly the important role of women in the Bible, how they had followed Christ faithfully to his crucifixion and were first at his tomb after the resurrection. The story of the Fall of man through Eve's disobedience and God's curse on the serpent ('I will put enmity between thee and the woman, and between thy seed and her seed: it shall bruise thy head, and thou shalt bruise his heel') Joanna took to be an indication that she was destined to vanquish Satan and deliver mankind from the thrall of evil. A Southcottian hymn put the matter simply:

> A woman Satan chose at first, to bring on man the fall;
> A woman God has chose at last, for to restore us all.
> As by a woman death did come, so life must come the same,
> And they that eat the fruit she gives, may bless God's holy name.[25]

Joanna spoke frequently of the 'promise' made to the 'woman', and her Spirit had assured her that she was the 'woman'. But what precisely did that mean? For some years she was content to leave it as one of those great mysteries which she could not understand but which would be revealed in God's good time. Then suddenly in 1814, she was informed by her Spirit: 'This year, in the sixty-fifth year of thy age, thou shalt have a Son, by the power of the Most High.'[26] Like Mary of old, she was to be God's chosen instrument for a second virgin birth.

Joanna was to give birth to Shiloh. The reference was to an obscure passage from Jacob's death-bed prophecy in Genesis 49:10 which in the Authorized Version was translated as: 'The sceptre shall not depart from Judah, nor a law-giver from between his feet, until Shiloh come.' Brothers had claimed to be Shiloh, and Southcottians later were to use the term in various ways. Joanna's Shiloh was identified with the man-child of Revelation 12:5, 'who is to rule all the nations with a rod of iron.' After the annunciation by her Spirit, Joanna prepared herself for pregnancy, the signs of which appeared to be unmistakable. She was examined by no less than twenty-one doctors in all (including Richard Reece, an eminent London surgeon) and seventeen of them said she was pregnant.[27] The leading believers greeted the news with delight, but also with caution, realizing the incredulity with which it would be received by the outside world. They gathered in London in August to investigate for themselves, and to make plans for the great event. Gifts for the expected baby were sent to Joanna: costly clothes, a silver cup and salver and a Bible elaborately decorated and bound in red morocco. A magnificent cradle of satin wood with gold ornamentation was made by Messrs Seddons of Aldersgate Street at a cost of over £200. It was hung with light blue and white satin; and a gold crown and the name Shiloh in Hebrew characters were embroidered at the head. The quilt was embroidered with an emblematical picture of Christ's reign on earth (the peaceable Kingdom) as in Isaiah 11. On Joanna's instructions a careful note was made of the names of the numerous donors, so 'that if there was a possibility of my being deceived, all persons should have their presents returned to them again.' As a final preparation, and after asking the advice of her friends, Joanna decided that she should take a husband in order to make Shiloh legitimate, though if no son were born the marriage was to be null and void. On 12 November 1814 she went through a private marriage ceremony with John Smith, 'a very respectable friend of about her own age' and steward to the Earl of Darnley.

The idea of a virgin birth by a woman of sixty-four seemed preposterous to non-believers and they reacted strongly. The papers were full of 'the most virulent and malicious abuse' (as Joanna said in her last pamphlet) and stories of the baby-smuggled-in-warming-pan variety were plentiful. One newspaper, the *Sunday Monitor*, however, treated the affair more seriously and opened its columns to correspondence and regular reporting of the Southcottian movement throughout the autumn of 1814. The demand for news of Joanna prompted the production of popular pamphlets about her: *Fairburn's Genuine Edition of the Life of Joanna Southcott, the Prophetess* (London, 1814) went through at least eleven editions in a few weeks. The cartoonists, too, had a field day, and the print shops displayed caricatures in which Joanna was depicted with full Regency coarseness. 'The Imposter, or Obstetric Dispute', by George Cruikshank, shows Joanna, very pregnant, attacking an opponent with a broom, while the surgeons stand by. In 'A Medical Inspection' by Thomas Rowlandson, Joanna, with large round buttocks, lifts up the front of her dress for the doctors to see. On 22 August a mob attacked Townley's house, and there were threatening incidents in the provinces. To avoid persecution the believers decided to lie low for a time. No distinctive dress was to be worn, the sealing was stopped, and preaching was suspended until after the birth of Shiloh.

The birth was expected some time in the autumn, but by November nothing had happened. Joanna had always been sensitive to the possibility that she was deceiving herself, but so far her communications had always reassured her. Now, however, she began to have doubts. Her signs of pregnancy diminished and according to Dr Reece (though denied by the believers) she declared, 'it all appears delusion'. She grew increasingly weak and died on 27 December 1814. Her body was wrapped in flannel and kept warm with hot-water bottles in the expectation that she would come to life on the fourth day. But dissolution of the body set in, and an autopsy was performed by Dr Reece on 30 December and attended by medical men chosen by both Reece and the believers. The dissection was performed on a table, with the doctors sitting around, and the believers standing behind, puffing their pipes to obliterate the smell of putrefaction. According to Reece, 'the believers were all on tiptoe to see Shiloh appear, and those who could not have a view themselves were most anxiously making inquiries of the others. No promised child, however, appeared.' The doctors certified that they found no evidence of organic disease sufficient to cause death, nor any evidence of pregnancy. On 1 January 1815 Joanna's remains were buried secretly in St John's Wood cemetery, where a gravestone and tablet were later placed. Disappointed as the believers were, they for the most part accepted the explanation that they had erred in expecting a temporal rather than a spiritual child. Several alternative accounts of what had happened were shortly put forward; but the most widely accepted view among the friends who had been close to Joanna was that Shiloh had indeed been born (perhaps spiritually) and immediately taken up to heaven, in fulfilment of Revelation 12:5: 'And she was delivered of a son, a man child ...; and her child was caught up unto God, and unto his throne.'

Such, in outline, was the career of Joanna Southcott. 'Religious imposter' was the verdict of the nineteenth century. But for today's historian there is more to be said than that. The details of her life suggest more interesting issues than whether or not her claims were 'true'. Consider first the social context. Joanna's life falls into three periods: 1750–91, the Devonshire farmer's daughter; 1792–1801, the Exeter prophetess; 1802–14, the head of a sect or cult on a national level. During the first period Joanna grew up in the culture of rural Devon. Her father was not a very successful farmer and, until she went into domestic service, she worked in the fields and in the dairy. Her writings are full of homely metaphors and descriptions of small incidents during her childhood and youth: a wasp's nest disturbed while her brother was ploughing, her terror at being sent late at night to inspect the cider in an out-house. She was always conscious, though not ashamed of her background: in her first reply to Foley, in July 1801, she told him plainly that she was a working woman, who had no time for reading, and that she was anxious he should not judge her to be of higher rank than she was.

In the culture of Devonshire labouring life belief in the supernatural was wide-spread. Visions, dreams and omens were accepted as clues to a world of spirits, both good and bad. Satanic forces had to be warded off. Providences demonstrated the hand of God intervening in everyday life. Folk-tales and superstitions enshrined these beliefs and passed them on to succeeding generations. Joanna absorbed this lore and her writings are permeated with it. Before she was fifteen the death of an atheist neighbour, at whose bedside she was watching, sank deeply into her mind. At midnight the room shook as if by thunder, and the dying man rose up and cried: 'there is a great black dog down in the window ... I tell you the devil is there.'[28] The black dog in English folklore was a sign of approaching death and also a form which Satan sometimes adopted. The story of the little flock of sheep, as told by Joanna, is worth repeating verbatim, as it conveys excellently both her style and the contemporary sense of the supernatural:

A man was tried in Exeter castle, for stealing sheep. He pleaded he did not steal them; for he was going to a fair, and the flock of sheep jumped over the hedge and ran before his horse. He rode as fast as his horse could run, to get before them; but still the sheep kept before the

horse. He turned his horse many ways to try to shun them, but the
sheep would immediately turn and get before him. He then turned his
horse, and thought to go home; but the sheep turned in an instant, and
came before him again. After his turning many times, trying every
way in his power to get before the sheep, and finding it impossible, he
thought he might as well go with them to the fair, as be found driving
them home to his own house; and in driving them to the fair he was
taken. And in this manner he pleaded in the castle to clear himself;
and the judge said he believed him innocent; but the jury said they
believed him guilty. The judge could not bear to give it up to the jury,
and said he would try another jury. He had another jury, and tried the
cause over again, and they found him guilty the same. When the judge
found he could not free him; but by the two juries had made the cause
more strong against him, the judge then addressed the prisoner – 'I
believe you innocent concerning stealing these sheep; but I believe you
are guilty of some fatal crime, for which the judgments of God
followed you, in the sheep, to punish you for a crime that you have
committed, in a crime that you have not; and as I have tried my
utmost to save you, and by that way brought it the harder against you,
it is impossible now for me to save your life, as you are found guilty
by both juries; therefore I shall thank you, as you must die, that you
will confess what crime you have committed.' The bloody wretch
then confessed, he lived a servant in the house with the mistress he
was then married to; but as she had got a husband when he went there
a servant, so to have the wife, whom he said he loved, he contrived,
one morning, when his master arose to go to a fair, to rise early and go
before him and meet him in a private place and murder him, which he
did. He then went home to bed as if composed, and happy in the
cruelty he had committed, and appeared easy and cheerful before the
wife. The night came, but no husband returned. She was alarmed; and
he pretended equal alarm the same; but would not go alone in pursuit
to find him. A miserable night was spent by the wife, and he appeared
to share her sorrows, as an angel of light, though he was the devil
himself. When the master was found murdered, he professed every
agony with the wife; and by his false and pretended love gained her
favour, and she afterwards married him. And at the time he was taken
he was going to the same fair that his master was going to when he
murdered him; and at the very place that he killed his master and
threw him in the ditch, the sheep that were in the field jumped over
the hedge and ran before him. So the innocent sheep brought the
guilty wretch to the end he deserved.[29]

This is not far from Bunyan. Indeed, in her *Dispute between the Woman and the Powers of Darkness* Joanna introduces a character, Apollyon, as Satan's friend. The language is strong and direct. 'Thou infamous bitch, thou poor, low bred bitch of a woman', roars Satan. To which Joanna can but reply, 'O! silly Satan – if thou casteth thyself out of heaven, do not think to pull me out also.'

Folk-tales provided a rich heritage on which Joanna could draw.[30] In 'The Hermit', Osmyn, who was 'an officer in the navy' gave Belinda, his beloved, a ring before he went to sea. His rival, Orlando, plotted to win Belinda by stealing the ring and to that end enlisted the aid of a hermit. But the hermit was in fact Osmyn in disguise, and so was able to frustrate 'the infamous and diabolical intentions of Orlando'. Another romance concerned a knight who learned from the stars that his wife would be a child recently born to a farmer, whom he had encountered in his travels. To prevent this low-born alliance he gave the farmer £3,000 for the child and then threw her into the sea. She was rescued by a fisherman, and when she had grown into a beautiful girl she was again seen by the knight, who bought her from the fisherman for £1,000. This time the knight determined to have her destroyed, but his plans were foiled, and he told her he would kill her himself:

'Ne'er tremble', said he, 'for this hour is your last,
So pull off your clothes, I command you in haste.'

She begged to be spared and he consented – provided that she never appeared in his sight again unless she could bring him his ring, which he threw into the sea. One day she was opening a fish and found the gold ring, and when the knight came to the house where she was serving, she showed it to him. He fell on his knees and said ' "Pardon, fair creature, I humbly pray, for thou hast a million of charms"; and then he married her, with raptures of joy and love.' Joanna was also familiar with the ballad of Lord Burnet and this too she was ordered by her Spirit to set down in her communications. While Burnet was out hunting his wife went to bed with the footman, Musgroves; a little page went and told Burnet and he returned to find the pair in bed together:

'Well, how dost thou like my bed?' he cri'd.
'And how dost thou like my sheets?
And how dost thou like my wedded lady,
That lies in thy arms asleep?'

Musgroves replied that he liked them well enough. Whereupon Burnet told the pair to dress (for it was a shame for a lord to kill a naked man or woman) and despatched them both with his sword – knowing that he himself would 'be hang'd tomorrow' for murder.

Foley found it a sore trial of his faith when he was ordered by Joanna to include this adulterous folk-tale in the pamphlet which he was publishing for her. But the reason for it, as for all the other stories, was that they were to be understood as 'types and shadows' prophetic to the nation at large. Theologically types are foreshadowings, as of the Christian dispensation in the historical events and persons of the Old Testament. Shadows can be allegorical rather than historical and are often synonymous with premonitions ('coming events cast their shadows before them'). Joanna used the terms loosely to denote spiritual meanings from everyday occurrences. In the case of folk-tales she took them as parables, in which God was speaking to the nation. Lord Burnet was Christ and his hanging was symbolic of the crucifixion; his wife stood for the Jews (an adulterous people) and Musgroves was Satan. When Burnet drew near to the hall on his return a friend of Musgroves sounded a horn to warn him, but Lady Burnet persuaded him to ignore it. This was a type of the second coming of Christ; and Joanna warned that if the nation behaved like the lady and the footman, then the nation would be destroyed for giving themselves into Satan's power. The story of the hermit was interpreted to mean that as Orlando had been caught in the very trap he had laid for Osmyn, so will Satan be caught in the trap he laid for others. The answer of the Spirit to the parable of the knight and the child was that this showed the impotence of man to fight against the decrees of God, for all is in the 'Womb of Providence'.

Pullen's *Index to the Divine and Spiritual Writings of Joanna Southcott* lists some seventy 'parables' of this sort, and over a hundred dreams. The Lord, said Joanna, 'warns by dreams and visions of the night'; and she recorded her own dreams and those of others for interpretation by the Spirit. From her grandmother she heard how one of her servant maids dreamt that in Caddy-fields, between Ottery and Fairmile, 'she met a cat, sitting upon a gate, which scratched her upon the right breast till she bled to death.' Her grandmother told the girl never to go that way alone, but she ignored the warning, and soon afterwards was found ravished and murdered at the same place she dreamt she met the cat. Another maid had a similar dream which she also told to Joanna's grandmother: she dreamed she was walking over Sidbury Hill and was stung to death by a serpent. The grandmother insisted that the girl should not go that way alone; but after some time she felt safe enough to go by herself – and she too was found ravished and murdered at the very spot that she dreamt the serpent met her. To a young apprentice maid who laughed at such things, the grandmother warned:

'Dreams are not always fables, Moll,
Though some wonders they do tell –
For 'tis in dreams the Lord doth warn
A way that men do not discern.'[31]

The dreams were not always on this level of folk wisdom, witness the following communication from Joanna:

'I dreamt that I had a large cloth full of eggs, and was going to put them up in a cart, without the cloth being tied, and as soon as I let go the cloth, the eggs began to tumble about the cart, and I began to pick them up, and put them into a very large jar; there was a woman on the other side of the cart, and I told her to pick them up also, which she did; but the eggs rolled so fast that ... we could not save the whole, and I was sorry to see so many broken in pieces.'

The 'Answer of the Lord' to this 'simple, foolish dream' was:

The eggs are the sealed people; those that were preserved whole, are those that keep their faith whole; but those that rolled off and were broken in pieces, are those that roll off through unbelief and fall away; and it is as much impossible to restore them as it is to put an egg together after it is broken in pieces.[32]

Joanna's belief that even the most trifling events of life had a spiritual significance was taken to extreme lengths. When Townley's two false teeth fell out, Joanna said they should not be put back, and used the incident to mark the day on which a letter about Pomeroy would be received. On another occasion she was walking with the Foleys and Bruces to visit Dr Wetherell, and complained that the gravel and small pebbles hurt her feet, so that Foley had to help her up Highgate Hill. To which the 'Answer of the Spirit' came with Bunyanesque directness: 'thy writings are the Hill of Difficulty, when thou dost not understand them. But as Foley assisted thee, so I [the Lord] will help thee and strengthen thee.'[33] Leaving aside its occasional trivialization, Joanna's doctrine was of the same order as could be found in the writings of more famous mystics. Few of her followers had read Boehme, but some were familiar with Swedenborg. When Joanna declared, 'everything on earth must bear a resemblance to what is in heaven'[34] she was, unknowingly perhaps, close to the doctrine of correspondences. In her simple, unsophisticated way she expressed the popular belief that there is a direct relationship between the visible and invisible worlds, and that certain people were favoured (or cursed) with special knowledge of this relationship. Joanna was favoured with communications direct from the Spirit, and she argued with Satan. She also prophesied.

The gift of prophesying was firmly established in the folk-culture of Britain, and when Joanna began to tell of her voices and to make prophecies there was a well-recognized role for her in Devonshire society. Lucy Taylor described the first intimations, in 1792, of Joanna's prophetic powers:

> She ... told me that there were troublesome times approaching; and though the necessaries of life were now cheap, everything would be dearer than ever was known in the memory of man; and advised Mr. Taylor to lay in a store; ... Mr. Taylor then said, 'Joanna, you are a prophetess?' to which she immediately replied with great spirit and apparent sincerity, 'So I am'; which was the first information I ever had that she assumed the character of a prophetess.[35]

Joanna's record of prognostication was impressive. She foretold the war with France, the poor harvests of 1794, 1795 and 1797, and the effects of the rain in 1799 and the sun in 1800 on the crops. She foretold the naval mutiny of 1797, and confounded Pomeroy by accurately predicting the death of the Bishop of Exeter. Occasionally she made mistakes, as when she predicted the Irish Rebellion (of 1798) would occur in 1795. This, she said, merely showed her error in judging the timing, as otherwise the information was correct. Some prophecies, which appeared to be nonsensical or pointless, she simply said she did not understand. But her position as a local oracle in Exeter was established in the 1790s. She was regarded as a wise woman, and by some as a witch. When she foretold a bad harvest she was 'cursed by buyer and seller. Both farmers and tradesman boasted of the plenty, and called me fool and old witch.'[36] On at least one occasion she was consulted by Mr Richard, a believer, who was losing his animals in a way that suggested witchcraft. Joanna, on the advice of her Spirit, told Richard to write 'Holiness to the Lord' on a piece of parchment and put it inside the horses' bridles and halters. This proved so effective that when Mrs Richard had a pain in her head she likewise wore the inscribed parchment round her head, with equal success.[37]

Joanna's role was accepted by labouring people as within the folk tradition. She was in the first instance – and, for some people, always remained – the Exeter prophetess, a local wise woman with a reputation that had happened to become known outside her own community. It therefore occasioned little surprise that a Yorkshire wise woman, Mary Bateman, had claimed to be one of the sealed and had used her association with believers for her own ends. When the demand for information about Joanna suddenly increased in 1814, following the announcement of the expected birth of Shiloh, a spate of chapbooks and cheap publications was produced.[38] Within the same folk tradition was the rough music that greeted the announcement of the expected birth in several parts of the country. At Horbury, near Wakefield, an effigy of Joanna was carried through the village, then shot at and burned head downwards.[39] This was repeated for three consecutive days. At Ilminster in Somerset the Reverend Edmund Baker, a believer, was the chief butt of the demonstration. He described what happened:

> Friday April 15 inst. was the day for all the clergy and gentry in the neighbourhood to meet and dine in the George Inn, Ilminster, and a bench of justices sit there the whole day. ... About ten o'clock in the morning [came] a horse and cart with a gallows in it and Buonaparte tied on one side, and an effigy of our Dear Mother on the other, big with child. Cider was given to the mob, etc. At eleven or after the cart with some of all sorts proceeded to my house. ... I tried to reason with them but all to no purpose. ... You did never see the Devil in men like the fellow in the cart who acted as Jack Catch [Ketch]. The abuse I received was beyond all thought and that of Poor Mother, though only an image.

After the hangman had stabbed the effigy in the belly, 'saying she was with child of a baboon' the procession went off to visit the houses of two other believers, and then returned to the Market House, where the justices and local gentry were meeting.

> Here I am told every obscene thing was done. The effigy ... was, by a doll put for the purpose, delivered before them all, [and] ... even some of their own vulgar women cried Shame. Then they were hung, shot for hours, and then burned.

The justices, far from stopping the demonstration, looked on from a window, 'with a smile of approbation'.

The context of the folk-culture, however, important as it is, does not provide a complete guide to Joanna's life. There is a personal dimension, operating within the framework of the culture to be sure, which can best be approached from a different angle. Her autobiographical writings suggest strongly that some type of psychological explanation, even at an elementary level, would be both possible and fruitful. Without making any claims for psycho-history a few observations may be ventured. Joanna had a strictly religious upbringing: 'the fear of the Lord was placed in me from a child, and I was fearfully made; I not only feared sin, but hated it.'[40] The death of her mother affected her deeply; and she had already been drawn towards the memory of her great aunt Sarah, who, said Joanna, was

> a very beautiful young woman. She was engaged to a young
> gentleman that had a great love for her, and she for him; but her
> father would not permit a union to take place between them, as he
> thought the young gentleman was not of a family grand enough for
> his daughter; so he compelled her to break it off. The disappointment
> made such an impression upon their minds that they were both
> determined to give up the world; and she gave herself entirely up to
> religion; and as she was very beautiful, she had many admirers, but
> refused them all. Her private meditations, and many hymns she
> composed, were afterwards printed; ... some of them I learnt when a
> child, as I greatly delighted in them.[41]

Sarah died of a broken heart when she was about thirty. Her verses impressed the young Joanna:

> Why should my passions mix with earth
> And thus debase my heavenly birth?
> Why should I cleave to things below,
> And let my God and saviour go?

The idea of religious consolation was implanted in Joanna's mind, and was soon linked to her tendency to melancholia, or conviction of moral unworthiness. Like some other prophetesses she had an abnormal, though not unusual attitude towards sex: attraction towards the loved one in her imagination, but repulsion from any physical contact when actually with him. Sex for Joanna became a category of sin, from which she escaped by means of fantasy. While denying herself any physical gratification of her desires, she ultimately achieved a purely imaginative satisfaction as the bride of the Almighty. Joanna was always attractive to men: as a young woman she was seldom without suitors, and in middle age still regularly received offers of marriage.[42] Yet she rejected them all. Her first lover was Noah Bishop, a farmer's son from Sidmouth, whom she alternately repelled and pursued, until he was maddened with passion for her: 'I ... was convinced his passion was love when he held me so strong by my hands that ... my hands and wrist [hurt] for many days'. Then there was John Thomas, an apprentice serge maker, who romantically assured her: 'I would rather have you without a farthing than any other woman with five hundred pounds.' Afterwards came a Mr Rigsby ('A handsome, genteel man', with an income of £60 a year), who fell in love at first sight when he saw her in Black Torrington church. She rejected him, to her father's disgust, on the grounds that he had an illegitimate child. Peter West was the next admirer ('a young man of remarkably good character, and one I thought remarkably handsome') but despite his ardour ('my brother said Peter's courtship was too hot to hold long'), which she encouraged and then repelled, Joanna rejected him too. These relationships both attracted and tormented her, and she sought an escape: 'all these ponderings in my heart drew my love almost to madness, that nothing but religion could keep me in my senses.' Her escape was into an interior world of her own imagination, a world of high born lovers (as in the folk-romances of Lord Burnet and the knight and the child) and, in middle age, spiritual husbands and brides.

It was a characteristic or condition of Joanna's neurosis that she was at the same time fascinated and repelled by sexual relationships. She longed for and yet rejected physical sex. Her writings are full of the imagery (mostly biblical) of brides, bridesmaids, bridegrooms, marriages, wedding feasts, wedding guests, as well as adultery, fornication and sodomy. Her dreams were frequently sexual, or even erotic. Townley described one such dream of Joanna in July 1804:

> She felt herself laying as it were in heaven, in the hand of the Lord, and was afraid to move, fearing she would remove his heavenly hand, which she felt as perfect as ever woman felt the hand of her husband.

Joanna then continued:

> In this happy manner I fell asleep, and in my sleep I was surprised with seeing a most beautiful and heavenly figure, that arose from the bed between Townley and me. ... His face was towards me, which appeared with beauty and majesty, but pale as death. His hair was a flaxen colour, all in disorder around his face. His face was covered with strong perspiration. ... His locks were wet like the dew of the night, as though they had been taken out of a river. The collar of his shirt appeared unbuttoned, and the skin of his bosom appeared white as the driven snow. Such was the beauty of the heavenly figure that appeared before me in a disordered state: but the robe he had on was like a surplice down to his knees. He put out one of his legs to me, that was perfectly like mine, no larger; but with purple spots at the top, as mine are with beating myself, which Townley, Underwood and

Taylor are witnesses of. Methought in my dream he got himself in that perspiration being pressed to sleep between Townley and me. I said to him, Are you my dear dying Saviour, that is come to destroy all the works of the devil? He answered me, Yes.[43]

Joanna's doctrine of the Woman becomes intelligible as a kind of theological feminism. She saw herself as destined to fulfil the promise made to Eve, that her seed [i.e. Joanna] should bruise the serpent's [i.e. Satan's] head. By struggling with Satan, and defeating him, she would redeem woman from the guilt incurred at the Fall, and make woman the 'true helpmate'. As woman tempted man at first, so at the last she is to bring his deliverance. Finally, woman is to be saved through child-bearing, her last and greatest glory. The object of this unorthodox theology was to support Joanna's claim to be the second Eve or bride of the Lamb, claims which can be interpreted as part of her fantasizing. She who could never bring herself to have an earthly husband found satisfaction in a spiritual marriage, decked out with all the erotic imagery of the bible. 'My beloved is mine, and I am his', she sighed, echoing the Song of Songs.

There is other evidence of her fantasizing. In her writings she refers to her father, and it is obvious that she was closely attached to him.[44] William Southcott could do little more than eke out a meagre living as a farmer, and in old age had to be supported by Joanna. But this peasant existence was transcended by legends of a more glorious family heritage, when the Southcotts had belonged to the landed gentry of Hertfordshire. Through a series of misadventures (including voyages to a rich uncle in Pennsylvania, shipwreck, and improbable promises of inheritable wealth) they had been reduced to their present state. From this romanticizing by William Southcott, Joanna found compensation and comfort in the belief in 'downstock'. Like the peasant girl in a folk-tale, she too was in reality high born.

To those who said that she was mad, Joanna gave a short answer: 'if the world judge that a firm belief in the Lord, relying on all the truths of the bible ... is madness, ... I was born mad and so was my mother before me.' And on another occasion she remarked that she was indeed 'out of my senses', for her writings came not from any sense or knowledge of her own but from a Spirit outside herself. Was she deranged?: 'I grant it; and so did all the prophets of old.'[45] This, of course, is the answer of a paranoiac, the lonely person with a complete and unshakable belief in herself and a logical answer (within her own premises) to all doubts and difficulties. Characteristic of the paranoid condition are the systems of delusion, erected to compensate for the refusal of the world to accept her special evaluation of herself. Joanna's conviction that every trivial happening in her life had a meaning capable of spiritual interpretation may be seen as a delusion of reference. And her final false pregnancy was but the last step along the road of hysteria. To say this, however, is probably not to say very much; and certainly not to reduce Joanna in any way. Paranoia, in varying degrees, is a common enough abnormality, and only in extreme cases is it categorized as madness. Joanna's doctrine of the woman arose out of her own need to assert her pre-eminence, and to this extent was part of her paranoia. But in another sense what she said was correct. Socially, the doctrine of the woman was a form of feminism: for she sought to redress the balance of guilt brought by the original Fall and make woman the 'perfect helpmate' of man. The dominant impression left by her writings is not of madness. Her neurosis is there all right: the infantilisms and ludicrous interpretations make that abundantly plain. But above all is the impression made by the strength of her faith. She was not always sure of herself; and Townley recorded periods of great depression. Yet always in the end came the triumph of her simple belief in herself as the instrument of God: 'for he that is mighty hath magnified me; and holy is his name.'

(ii) TRUE BELIEVERS

Once the gathering of the first 'true believers' (as Joanna designated them)[1] had taken place, the number of followers grew rapidly. Using the official Southcottian figures of those who were sealed, the numbers increased from 58 in 1803 to 8,144 in January 1804 and to about 14,000 in 1807.[2] The sealing was stopped in 1808, following the Mary Bateman scandal and also because of renewed accusations of the sale of seals; but by 1814 another 6,400 had been sealed, and the total in 1815 was about 20,000. This was considerably less than the 100,000 in the London area alone that was rumoured currently, and repeated many times later. It was also short of the target of 144,000 enjoined in Revelation 7:4. The sealed were the hard core of the believers; beyond them, as in other movements, was an unknown number of attenders and readers of her pamphlets – less committed people who were to some degree influenced by Joanna.

Fortunately we can go further than these overall figures of membership. From extant lists of believers it is possible to attempt a rough analysis by geographical location, occupation, family and sex.[3]

The material is far from complete; but the sample is reasonably large, and sufficiently remarkable in a popular movement of this kind to warrant attention. We have the names, and usually the addresses, of nearly 7,000 believers. From this information it is clear where the Southcottians were strongest.[4] London claimed 31 per cent of the total membership, and Yorkshire another 26 per cent. Devonshire, Lancashire and the Midlands were also strongholds. Apart from London, with over 2,000 believers, the largest single groups were at Sheffield (350), Crewkerne, Somerset (265), Gravesend in Kent (211) and Ashton-under-Lyne (200). In the Leeds–Bradford district there were at least 500 believers; and Halifax (56), Huddersfield (107), Pontefract (76) and Mexborough (62) were also represented. In Lancashire and Cheshire believers were sealed in Manchester (43), Stockport (121), Warrington (87) and Macclesfield (35). Stockton had 120 members. In the Midlands the main centres were Chesterfield (71), Leicester (45), Mansfield (84), Newark (81) and Nottingham (53). Devon had 13 per cent of the total number of believers, with strong centres in Exeter (145), Plymouth (169), Brixham (100), Bigbury (92), and sizeable (that is, over fifty) followings in Ashburton, Tiverton and Totnes. Also in the West Country were groups in Bristol (67) and Bath (77).

Information about the occupations of believers is less plentiful than about their location. For only a small fraction of the 7,000 names is it possible to identify, either from trade directories or from direct descriptions, their trade or calling. In Sheffield, Leeds and Bristol it would seem from small samples that the believers were artisans or small tradesmen. Among a group of thirty-four Southcottians in Birmingham in 1844 more than half were artisans or labouring men (powder-flask maker, tin-plate worker, wheelwright, silverer, tin-lamp worker) and the women were nurses, tailoresses, school teachers and servants. The majority of believers were also literate, at any rate to the extent of signing their names and reading the two required pamphlets on sealing.[5] Two further pieces of information can be gleaned from the membership lists: first, the preponderance of women, who outnumbered men 63 per cent to 36 per cent, among the believers; second, the apparently high proportion of single people (men and women), in the order of 67 per cent to only 32 per cent who are identifiable as members of a family.[6]

These statistics are confirmatory rather than surprising. They place the Southcottians squarely in the pattern of popular social and religious movements of the time. With a following made up of artisans, small tradesmen and servants, and a top leadership drawn from the more educated and affluent classes, the believers were socially parallel to the radical reformers or the Methodists. The geographical distribution, with strongholds in the northern and Midland industrial districts, and Devon substituted for Cornwall, is also reminiscent of Methodism. The preponderance of women and single people is characteristic of millennial sects elsewhere, and does not at this stage call for special explanation.

Somewhat more distinctive was the organization of the Southcottians. Joanna, as has been said, did nothing to create a structure for her movement. There were, therefore, no officers, no official hierarchy, and very few rules. The whole movement centred on herself, as the divinely inspired prophetess. All that was required of Southcottians was belief in the divine mission of Joanna and sealing to effect Satan's destruction. There was, of course, a fairly extensive canon of her writings, and familiarity with these was expected. At Teddington, Middlesex, the Reverend Edmund Baker kept a register which showed the number of Joanna's works owned by each member. Twenty-seven of the 125 believers had all, or nearly all of Joanna's fifty-four pamphlets which had been published up to 1811; some had only a few of the works; and everyone had the required *Sound an Alarm* and *A Caution and Instruction to the Sealed*.[7] The actual organization of the believers, such as it was, centred on the family and, in some places, on the chapel. Joanna relied heavily on the support of families such as the Taylors in Exeter, the Eyres in Bristol, the Foleys in Stourbridge and the Jowetts in Leeds and Bradford. They supervised the faithful in their areas, administered the sealing, and gave hospitality to Joanna (and to each other) on their travels. In some cases, as with Foley and Sharp, they undertook the heavy burden of editing and publishing Joanna's works. Where the believers were devoutly Anglican, or their leader was a Church of England clergyman, they were encouraged to attend their parish churches on Sundays and separate meetings during the week. Foley, for instance, held meetings at his house on Sunday and Thursday evenings, at which more than 100 attended.[8] But in other places, and particularly when there was no ordained minister to give guidance, separate Southcottian chapels were opened. In addition to three chapels in the London area, separate meetings were established in Exeter, Bath, Bristol, Leeds, Stockport and Ashton-under-Lyne. The services followed the liturgy of the established church, but the singing was from Philip Pullen's *Hymns, or Spiritual Songs, composed from the Prophetic Writings of Joanna Southcott*. A Southcottian ritual held at Joanna's trial in December 1804 suggests how the services might be conducted so as to be orthodox and yet adapted to the needs of the sect.[9] Wine was poured into a cup and handed round by the ministers, beginning with Joanna and the women, 'as I am come to redeem the Fall of women.' The men then drank in order of precedence – the ministers, the twelve, the jury, the elders, and finally the 'witnesses' at the trial. Each repeated the words: 'May I drink deep into the spirit of Christ; and may his blood cleanse me from all sin.' After everyone had drunk, Joanna pronounced the words: 'As we all have drunk in one cup, may we drink into one faith, and may that faith be in Christ.' This was not a sacrament, but a sign that the partakers desired 'a double portion of the Spirit' to be poured into their hearts. After this part of the ceremony was concluded Joanna gave an address, the writings were sealed up, and 'Joanna handed cakes to her female friends, which they broke among one another in token of love and friendship; and the men helped themselves for the same purpose.'

The weakness of the organization became apparent on the death of Joanna. Following the traumatic shock of the Shiloh tragedy came various conflicting claims to inherit Joanna's mantle, and at this point the institutional structure was not strong enough to prevent disintegration. Individual families kept in touch with each other, but differed in their interpretations and policies. In the 1840s attempts were made to unite the various groups of 'Old' Southcottians (i.e. those who had not followed the prophets John Wroe and Zion Ward), but by 1851 their numbers had shrunk to a mere 200, in four congregations.[10] They kept alive the Southcottian faith among themselves, and handed it on to their children. But there was little active proselytizing, and to avoid ridicule and hostility they lapsed into Nicodemism.[11] The movement also lacked other useful aids such as a periodical – always invaluable in a voluntary movement as an instrument of consolidation and policy direction. The *Edinburgh Review* opined that the failure of the Southcottians to become more numerous was because, first, they were not persecuted, and, second, they had no great preacher like Wesley or Whitefield.[12]

As with Brothers, the believers in Joanna seem to fall into certain fairly distinctive groups. First among the influential followers was a small number of Anglican clergymen. Thomas Philip Foley (1758?–1835) held the family living of Oldswinford, near Stourbridge, North Worcestershire, and also the nearby living of Wombourne. He was a kinsman of Lord Foley of Witley Court. But for his association with Joanna, he would have lived out his days in his quiet country rectory, unheard of and unimportant to all except local antiquarians who later happened to come upon his diary and accumulation of letters.[13] The handsome Foley, as he is reputed to have been known during his days at Jesus College, Cambridge, was apparently all set for a career as a typical hunting parson (surplice thrown over his hunting coat at hurried funerals, and so on), but at some point gave it all up for a more spiritual and inward religion – though according to local legend he still kept a fine white horse saddled in the rectory stables, ready to ride to the New Jerusalem when the Shiloh was born. Joanna was greatly strengthened and encouraged by the allegiance of Foley (and also of Bruce), especially after the disappointment with her first favourite clergyman, Pomeroy; and her Spirit soon ordered her to use Foley as one of the outlets for making her communications known to the world. He thus found himself, like Sharp and Townley, responsible for publishing some of Joanna's works, for which purpose he employed a Stourbridge printer, J. Heming. Foley maintained a voluminous correspondence with believers in various parts of the country. Oldswinford rectory served as a kind of clearing house for news of the movement and the dissemination of the latest communications from 'dear Mother'. All was on a very friendly family basis with inquiries about sick members and observations about the weather interspersed among theological speculations.

In the Stourbridge area Foley quickly built up a list of sealed believers. Details of them are sparse, but from oblique comments and the occasional fuller account we can gain a few impressions. 'Belles', the coachman on the Birmingham–Stourbridge coach, 'is a Sealed Brother and a firm believer', wrote Foley in 1807. At the time of Joanna's lying-in Thomas Child, a plane-maker of Stourbridge, wrote, 'The mockery is very great in our neighbourhood. It is hardly safe to go out.' Fears of a different kind are revealed in a letter from George and Elizabeth Rex of Lea Castle, dated 6 March 1813. Rex says that he has heard of Joanna for the past ten years. He read an account of her trial, lent to him by a friend, but thought nothing of it. During the last twelve months he has read several of Joanna's works and is now convinced that she is the woman of Revelation 12. Both he and his wife have had 'singular dreams and warnings', which have strengthened their faith, and they now wish to be admitted as believers and sign their names. They had intended 'to wait upon you personally'; but one of Foley's servants, who comes from Wolverley, 'knows us and would therefore recognise us', and it would be known all over the village. 'Mr. Knight, who I live with, might discharge me.' Rex adds that they are not ashamed of the faith, 'but we are ordered by Joanna to act with caution.' The bearer of the letter, James Lightbourne, is also a believer, 'and wishes to sign his name.'

Foley too had his troubles. When he announced his belief in Joanna his neighbours told him he must be going mad; and there were complaints to the bishop from some of his parishioners. Two local justices of the peace, Major Pidcock and Mr Homfray, challenged him to a duel in August 1806. They alleged that he had accepted a bet from Pidcock on the fulfilment of Joanna's prophecy that Bonaparte would be acknowledged as King by the British government, and that Foley had lost the bet and refused to pay up. His curate was unsympathetic to the cause; and even his wife, who had gone along with his enthusiasm for many years, finally revolted when no Shiloh was born: 'my wife and self had a violent breeze concerning our opinions of dear Joanna's divine writings and mission'; and they agreed to leave each other's opinions alone, 'as our ideas are as wide ... as the east is from the west.'

Joanna's death marked a crucial stage in the personal development of every believer. When prophecy fails a millenarian movement is put to a severe test. An explanation is called for, and may or may not be accepted by a majority of the believers. In the case of the Southcottians the failure mechanism operated quite smoothly, and a majority of the believers accepted the view that they had been mistaken in expecting a temporal birth. On re-reading Joanna's works they saw that the birth of Shiloh could be expected in a purely spiritual sense. After his visit to London in August 1814, Foley returned home to await the news of the birth of Shiloh, and was greatly perplexed by his non-arrival and Joanna's death. On December 30, three days after her death, he referred in his diary to her 'trance', and hoped for 'glad tidings that dear Joanna's spirit is returned to her body.' When he received news of the autopsy he advised the believers, who came to him for consolation, to sit still and remain quiet 'till further Divine light bursts forth upon us.' By 11 January 1815, after re-reading Joanna's last book, he was convinced that it was a spiritual, not a temporal child that should have been expected; and comforted himself with the reflection that God would clear up all mysteries in his own good time. The following Sunday, which was his first appearance in church after Joanna's death, he preached from II Corinthians 4:8 ('we are pressed on every side, yet not straitened; perplexed, yet not unto despair') to a large and curious congregation – 'many [of whom] I believe were much disappointed.' Foley weathered this crisis, and maintained his millennial faith. In 1817 he was expecting sudden and important happenings 'when our dear Mother returns to us from the wilderness where she now is.' At the time of Peterloo (August 1819) he assured an inquirer that 'the present disturbances in the north' were foretold by Joanna in 1803; but hastened to add that believers had nothing to do with them – 'we, the true followers of Joanna Southcott have nothing to do with politics in any shape or way whatsoever'; on the contrary, they did nothing but wait to welcome 'the millennium, the thousand years' rule, the Kingdom of Righteousness'.[14] In 1824 he was unable to dine with Lord Foley because of a vow he had made in 1810 that because of 'the persecution and great unkindness of many of my flock' he would not dine out in Stourbridge 'until after a certain event had taken place, and which has not yet been fulfilled.' Foley guarded the box of sealed writings until his death; and his son, the Reverend Richard Foley, of North Cadbury, continued in the same belief.

It is clear that Foley had what we can by now recognize as a millennial mentality. He was always prepared to investigate a report of some unusual happening, to give credence to supernatural claims however suspect their source, and to interpret trifling events as divinely inspired. Nothing was too odd or unlikely to attract his speculation that somewhere the hand of God was to be observed. Like most millenarians he constantly reminded himself of St Paul's dictum (I Corinthians 3:19) that 'the wisdom of this world is foolishness with God.' At times he was gullible for any quackery. In March 1804 he was ill with 'rheumatic gout in my chest' and a violent cough in his stomach. Joanna 'spread the case before the Lord', but no answer was forthcoming. She then accidentally scalded her hand while making some gruel, and she cured this by three applications of wet mud, soap and salt. Three days later she had a communication from her Spirit to the effect that as her hand had been cured by the application of three things, so Foley would similarly be cured by three things which would take the fire out of the boil in his stomach. The three things were: pills made of powdered rhubarb and 'best soap', a bottle of Daffey's Elixir; and a prescription from an apothecary. He also had to abstain from tea and take eggs. Foley followed these instructions, and was cured − 'blessed, blessed be God'. Again, in November 1805 he wrote to Robert Taylor in Exeter, repeating a story he had had from Morison and 'which you may depend upon.' A pregnant believer named Hadfield prayed to the Lord that 'if this work was from Him', a mark might be on her child's cheek when born. The Lord has given the mark requested: 'a red piece of flesh upon its cheek about the size of Joanna's seal and about twice the thickness, to the agreeable surprise of the Brethren.'[15] If these had been the beliefs of a labouring man they would have been ascribed by contemporaries to 'credulity' and ignorance. But in a beneficed clergyman who was a Cambridge MA and the cousin of a lord, this explanation would not do. The easiest way out was to put it down to madness in the form of religious delusion. But this was not felt to be entirely satisfactory: it was an excuse rather than an explanation. The millennial mind was altogether too common to be set aside quite so easily.

For the other clergymen who were believers we do not have as much documentation as for Foley. Nevertheless there are useful clues as to the sort of men they were. The Reverend Thomas Webster of the Borough, was prone to visions. He sent an account of his experiences when conducting a funeral service in Bermondsey churchyard first to Brothers, who offered his interpretation, and then to Joanna, who printed it in her *Strange Effects of Faith*, part IV. The vision, which appeared in the heavens, was of a great beast, standing on the continent and afterwards marching at the head of an immense army from out of a cloud, and then invading an island. Joanna's interpretation was that the beast was the devil, 'that is come at this last period to stir up all nations to war', and the land invaded was Turkey.[16] Webster published several works.[17] In his *Complete Anagogue* (1813), designed to answer the doubts of infidels, deists and Socinians, and to explain common problems in the biblical account of creation, he discussed the probability of the earth being inhabited by angels before the appearance of man.

The third clergyman among Joanna's original seven stars, Stanhope Bruce, was vicar of Inglesham, near Lechlade, Gloucestershire, and was similar to Foley in social position and influence. His son, Colonel Basil Bruce, was also a believer, and his sudden death at the beginning of her mission puzzled Joanna. At times she thought that perhaps Basil Bruce was the man-child of Revelation 12. During the summer of 1802 Joanna went to stay with Stanhope Bruce's married daughter, Mrs Beecraft, at Market Deeping in Lincolnshire. There she met the Reverend John Mossop, vicar of the neighbouring parish of Deeping St James, and he for a time was a believer. He had read Joanna's works the previous year, and although favourably disposed towards her claims felt that they were mixed up with a certain amount of 'rubbish' (as he complained to Stanhope Bruce). After meeting her at Market Deeping he wrote to Pomeroy to verify what she had told him. Mossop, however, had already been attracted to Swedenborg's teachings and this proved a cause of difficulty with Joanna.[18] As in the case of Brothers, Joanna had to define her relationship with Swedenborgianism, since other believers besides Mossop were interested in the New Church. She was of course no match for Swedenborg intellectually, and wisely eschewed doctrinal argument. Instead she suggested that Swedenborg's writings should be read 'as you would read the Arabian Nights Entertainments – then as a bee gathereth honey from every flower, we may gather something from them', but that they could not be relied on because they were not grounded in the Bible. Had Joanna read them 'some years back', she thought she would have been bowled over because she had insufficient anchor, and there were too many ideas to be coped with. But the Spirit directed that they should 'read no books but the bible'. Swedenborg's writings were in fact 'satan coming as an Angel of Light'.[19]

Ministers who espoused Joanna's cause had to be prepared for a fair measure of local opprobrium. The Reverend Robert Hoadley Ashe, vicar of Crewkerne, Somerset, was a biblical scholar who eagerly embraced Joanna's doctrines: 'I find that the Word of God out of your mouth is a clear burning light unto my feet, and a glorious light unto my path.' In 1814 Joanna was burnt in effigy in Crewkerne, and Ashe's parishioners forced him to promise 'never to do duty in Crewkerne church again unless Joanna Southcott [has] a child before January 12th.' (However, he continued to hold the living until his death in 1826.) In the neighbouring village of Dowlish, Edmund Baker suffered similar experiences and also had troubles of a different order. Baker was minister of a Southcottian chapel in Teddington, Middlesex, from about 1809 to 1811; and then moved to Dowlish, Somerset, where he had a chapel which served believers in the Ilminster area. He closed the chapel some months before the expected birth of Shiloh, in accordance with Southcottian policy, and refused to re-open it for some time after Joanna's death. Some of the believers, including the two ladies who had given Baker the house which was used as the chapel, objected, and wished him to allow other (probably Methodist) preachers to use it. Baker fought this backsliding, and declared his intention to hold the chapel 'in trust for the Friends who stand faithfully by the Woman', and not surrender it to any other preacher. His 'little flock' was still in his care in 1851.[20]

In the Bristol area the believers were organized by the Reverend Samuel Eyre, a clergyman of the same cast of mind as Foley and Stanhope Bruce. His son, Major Robert Eyre, was also a believer, and worked closely with Sharp and Wilson in London. Samuel Eyre is notable chiefly for the tenacity of his millennial beliefs and his unshakable devotion to Joanna's cause. In 1828 he was still confidently expecting that she would return to this world, 'in union with Mrs. Townley and Miss Underwood', and speculated that she would probably appear where the sealed writings were deposited, namely at Foley's. Throughout the 1830s he recalled the events of Joanna's life, and tried to apply them as types and shadows of contemporary happenings. Visions in the sky at night, the state of the harvests, the 'intrusion of the papal beast' in 1820, some 'rather singular manifestations in dreams' – all were called in to substantiate his belief that the times were hastening to their end, and that Joanna's prophecies would shortly be fulfilled.[21] In the late 1830s and early 1840s he became involved in disputes with Lavinia

Elizabeth Chapman Jones, who annoyed many of the Old Southcottians by her zeal in collecting Joanna's communications and assumptions of a leadership role. Lavinia was a niece of Mrs Lucy Taylor of Exeter, Joanna's friend and former employer; and she (Lavinia) and her husband, David Jones, a printer of Bradford-on-Avon, undertook the re-publication of Joanna's works in the 1850s, and tried (unsuccessfully) to get possession of the famous box.

It would be unwise to build any elaborate generalization on the basis of half a dozen Anglican clergymen. At the same time they cannot be dismissed out of hand. The sample is small; but one wonders how many clergy might, like Pomeroy, have been prepared to be Nicodemian, or secret, followers. To evangelical Protestants and for partial sympathizers with Wesley the side track which led to Southcottianism was always open, even though most did not pursue it very far. Certain intellectual currents and seventeenth-century religious traditions, which we normally associate exclusively with nonconformity, may have had a hold among a small number of the established clergy. The clergy may also have been much closer to the popular religion of the supernatural and magic of their parishioners than has been commonly recognized. Perhaps not many of them read Boehme; but were they all completely innocent of neo-Platonic influences? The young S. T. Coleridge, who was brought up in the vicarage of Joanna's own parish, Ottery St Mary, imbibed sufficient of Devon folk-lore and regard for the starry universe to feed his later zest for the marvellous and the relation between substance, shadow and symbol:

> For all that meets the bodily sense I deem
> Symbolical, one mighty alphabet
> For infant minds; and we in this low world
> Placed with our backs to bright Reality,
> That we may learn with young unwounded ken
> The substance from its shadow.[22]

The frequency with which almanacs, old prophecies and chapbooks are found among the papers of believers (including the clergy), and their consuming interest in signs and wonders, suggest a type of belief in the supernatural which could comfortably include elements of the magical and demonic. An instinctive, inarticulate neo-Platonism facilitated the acceptance of doctrines of correspondences, analogy, and types and shadows. If we find it hard to understand why educated clergy of the Church of England should have accepted Joanna and her writings it may be useful to look backwards from the late eighteenth century rather than

1 Richard Brothers
(William Sharp, 1795)

2 Joanna Southcott
(William Sharp, 1812)

3 The Great Red Dragon and the Woman Clothed with the Sun
(William Blake, *c.* 1800–5)

4   The Wise and Foolish Virgins [The Midnight Cry] (William Blake, *c.* 1826)

5 The Last Judgement (John Martin, 1853)

6   The Great Day of his Wrath (John Martin, 1852)

7 Credulity, Superstition and Fanaticism
(William Hogarth, 1762)

8 *below* The Prophet of the Hebrews
(James Gillray, 1795)

Pub.d March 5.th 1795 by H. Humphrey N.o 37 New Bond St.

The PROPHET of the HEBREWS.— the PRINCE of PEACE,—conducting the JEWS to the PROMIS'D-LAND.

9 A Medical Inspection (Thomas Rowlandson, 1814)

forwards to our own day; for we then realize that Foley, Bruce, and the others were nearer to the seventeenth century than to us. The world of Bunyan, even without the innumerable reprints of *The Pilgrim's Progress*, was not far removed. A work such as *The Certainty of the Worlds of Spirits* (London, 1691) by the Puritan divine, Richard Baxter, illustrates the point. Here we have a collection of accounts of apparitions, visions and witchcraft, drawn from Worcestershire, Devon and other parts of the country, which is very similar to parts of Joanna's writings. The stories are homely, concerning maids and farmers and labouring people: the detail is vivid and compelling; and the supernatural is unquestioningly assumed in connection with sickness, accident and the fortunes of everyday life. If Baxter was acceptable, Joanna could well be too. By means of their belief in her mission, Joanna's clerical followers combined a respect for the authority of scripture with a desire for an inward religion of the world of spirits.

Nevertheless, the clergy who believed in Joanna were a highly respectable and conservative element among the Southcottians. Like the leaders of Wesleyan Methodism, they strongly protested their loyalty to the state, and were opposed to involvement in political affairs. After Joanna's death they refused to acknowledge any of the various aspirants to her succession, preferring to remain 'fireside' believers.[23] In this they were followed by most of Joanna's Old Guard – Sharp, Owen Pughe, Townley, Underwood and the Taylors. But others among the believers were of a different cast of mind. In the north, where there were no clergymen among the believers, and where the movement was strongly based, other millenarian characteristics were observable among the faithful. George Turner, a merchant of Leeds and the acknowledged leader in the area, was not so much a follower as a prophet in his own right. In some respects he resembled Brothers.

Not much is known about Turner's early life.[24] For many years he was guided by an inner voice, and published several books of his communications. He was one of the seven stars who visited Joanna at Exeter in December 1801, and had previously been a disciple of Brothers. Joanna stayed at Turner's house during her Yorkshire tour, and she accepted the divine nature of his visitation – though when his voice told him that he was to be the husband whom Joanna should take before the birth of Shiloh, she told him that his communication must have come from Satan. Turner's ascendancy in the movement was greatly strengthened by Joanna's death, as his voice now ordered him to assume the role of her successor. His message was that Shiloh would shortly appear, and that preparations must be made for this great event. He came to London in May 1816 and advertised in the newspapers. A strident, and increasingly apocalyptic note appeared in his pronouncements. The events of Revelation 6:12-17 would begin on 28 January 1817: 'and there was a great earthquake; and the sun became black ... and the whole moon became as blood; and the stars of the heaven fell unto the earth.' He issued a proclamation, dated 18 January 1817, announcing his programme:

> I am ordered on the 28th to go to the Palace Yard and declare the Word of the Lord against the Treasury, Horse Guards, Carlton House, the Playhouses, Churches, and Chapels, the Tower, Somerset House, and other public places. The Angel of the Lord shall sink all by earthquake. The whole United Kingdom is to be divided to the People in the Roll [i.e. the believers].

This was strongly reminiscent of Brothers: and the government responded by re-enacting the Brothers case. As in 1794-5, the administration was alarmed by the rising tide of popular radicalism and protest during the winter of 1816-17. In the spring of 1817 Habeas Corpus was suspended, a Seditious Meetings Act was passed, and Cobbett fled to America. Turner's proclamation had included radical demands for an overturning of the social order, free postage, abolition of taxes, and cheap ale. On his return to Leeds he was arrested and charged with high treason. But as with Brothers, Turner was declared insane, and was committed to an asylum in York. He remained there for three years, busily writing out the commands of his voice. His plans for the arrival of Shiloh have all the crazy detail of Brothers' schemes for the building of Jerusalem: Shiloh's palace will be 50 miles square, and will have walls of gold set with precious stones; there will be 70,000 male musicians and 70,000 singing women, 500,000 servants, carriages of gold, and so on. He also revived Brothers' doctrine of the lost tribes of Israel, and assigned the believers to their appropriate tribes.

Nevertheless, Turner's adroit running of the Southcottian movement through a central committee showed considerable acumen. Under the guise of divine commands he dispensed sound advice to the faithful. He advised 'P.' against separating from his wife, and told him not to rely on dreams and visions ('Visions are ordered to remain with those that see them, and not for my children to rely upon them'). The strains imposed by living with a non-believing spouse, the problems of sons who are 'violent opposers', and the wisdom of allowing children to be catechized by the minister every Sunday – all were dealt with as they arose. He told one inquirer not to worry about reading Swedenborg; another not to be tempted into adultery. The believers were not to wear black, which signifies mourning and the powers of darkness, but blue, which is an emblem of faith. In his pastoral care Turner was (as his voice proclaimed), 'like to my servant Moses'.

In 1820 he was released from the asylum, and immediately resumed his prophetic leadership. He initiated new ceremonies of marrying the female believers to the Lord (to be brides of Christ), and announced that his voice had told him that he was to have 15,050 wives. During a period of five weeks in July and August 1820 he travelled many hundreds of miles to perform his peculiar marriage ceremony, in which he kissed each woman and she kissed him. Turner next put his hand on the woman's knee to signify that 'she will bow unto the Lord, to his word and command.' She was then declared to be married to the Lord, and her name was entered in the marriage book. The climax of these ceremonies was on 30 August 1820, when 600 of the believers sat down to the Marriage Supper of the Lamb in Westminster. This was intended to be part of the preparations for the coming of Shiloh, and Turner incautiously fixed the date for the second advent. First it was to be 14 October 1820, then when nothing happened, 10 April 1821. The believers survived the usual disappointment; but Turner himself was crushed, and in September 1821 he died. His legacy to the Southcottian movement – authoritarian rule, bizarre ceremonies, and Christian Israelism – was picked up by John Wroe, whose career and teachings will be considered below.

Not all the believers in the north were of Turner's kind; and in any case during Joanna's life time his idiosyncrasies were somewhat muted. Samuel Jowett of Leeds belonged to the Old Southcottian rather than the Turner–Brothers type of millenarianism. In a pamphlet written thirty years later he recalled the mood of 1814 when Shiloh was expected:

> Our eyes were so dazzled with the glorious prospect set before us, of those things taking place immediately, that were then made known; we became like the man taken out of a dark room, and placed in the radiant beams of the sparkling sun, the light so overpowering him that he could not see: – so it was with us – the idea of having one of the GODHEAD to reign over us was overwhelming, after being so long tyrannized over by man, under evil influence; that we could not calmly and deliberately consider what was delivered unto us, because of the bright shining picture of the illustrious era which was presented to our view.[25]

Here spoke the religious romantic: 'bliss was it in that dawn to be alive.'

Jowett was then about thirty; as an old man in his eighties he still retained his faith, and was guardian of the box of sealed writings. Another facet of the millenarian mind appears in Samuel Hirst, a watchmaker of Leeds, to whom Joanna took a special fancy ('Hirst and his family are chosen servants of mine'). He and his wife and daughter made a journey to Herefordshire in 1804 to visit Mrs Hughes, a wise woman who claimed powers of divine healing. But their daughter received no benefit, and Hirst concluded that Mrs Hughes 'is not visited by a Good Spirit.'[26]

The believers in Yorkshire attracted a fair amount of publicity.[27] Joanna's missionary tour in 1803 had drawn large numbers – perhaps as many as 6,000 at Halifax – and the local newspapers had given coverage of her visit. Thereafter the interest was maintained by charges and counter-charges in pamphlets and broadsheets. That Joanna took these exchanges seriously is shown by the number of references to them in her works published between 1804 and 1806. At Halifax she had a strong defender in John Crossley, who debated her claims with the local Baptist, Independent and Methodist ministers. The social respectability of these believers, however, was not matched by a corresponding degree of intellectual respectability. Not only did their ideas lack the weight of religious orthodoxy, they were also at times dangerously close to popular views of magic and the supernatural. This could be an embarrassment, as the case of Mary Bateman demonstrated.

In March 1809 Mary Bateman (née Harker) was hanged at York for poisoning.[28] Joanna and the believers were therefore naturally anxious to repudiate any connection with her; but to some extent this was a display of wisdom after the event. Mary Bateman's background was similar to Joanna's and her early career was quite parallel. She was born at Asenby, near Thirsk, Yorkshire in 1768, the daughter of a small farmer. She was taught to read and write, and at thirteen entered domestic service in Thirsk. About 1787 she went to York, still as a domestic servant, but shortly learned the trade of a mantua-maker from her employer. The following year she went to Leeds, where she worked as a mantua-maker, and in 1792 married John Bateman, a wheelwright. Later accounts of Mary Bateman emphasize her thievish and vicious disposition from childhood; but at the same time admit that she was neat in her person and dress, spoke softly and modestly, and was a good housewife. Her husband was sober and industrious, and in constant employment. Sometime in the 1790s she began to practise as a wise or cunning woman, specializing in fortune-telling and the provision of charms. Her clients were mainly love-sick girls and women who were faced with medical and family problems. She claimed to be able to 'screw down' or neutralize the evil (and usually anonymous) persons who had put an 'evil wish' or spell on her clients which was the cause of their misfortunes. Normally a wise woman charged a small fee for such services, but Mary Bateman apparently found this insufficient and went on to exploit to the full the unhappy circumstances in which her clients found themselves. Fraud, blackmail and intimidation followed. Finally, in the case of Rebecca Perigo, the wife of a Leeds clothier, who had gone to her for a cure for a pain in her breast and whom she embroiled in a series of exactions, Mary Bateman resorted to poisoning with arsenic. She was indicted for murder and fraud, and found guilty.

Mary Bateman's association with the Southcottians was, on her part, almost certainly fraudulent. It is nevertheless a significant comment on certain aspects of the movement. She, like other contemporaries, judged that some of the believers in Joanna were likely to be the same sort of people who would be vulnerable to, or interested in her (Mary Bateman's) own claims to supernatural powers. She and her husband therefore became sealed as believers and made some inroads among sections of the Southcottians in Leeds and York. In 1806 she displayed a miraculous hen which laid millennial eggs marked 'Crist [sic] is Coming', and collected fees from visitors to her home in Black Dog Yard. Joanna's reaction to this was by no means as unequivocal as might have been supposed. Later she condemned Mary Bateman as a false prophet and denied that the Yorkshire witch had ever been a believer even though she had 'falsely' obtained a seal.[29] But on first hearing of the eggs she treated the report with caution rather than immediate repudiation. The phenomenon was not inherently impossible, she argued, and instanced the case of a woman being with child by her master, who wanted to swear the child to a servant. But the woman refused, and when the child was born it had the names of the master on its thigh, 'which was the wondrous working of the Lord to confound the unjust master.'[30] On the other hand the eggs might be a mockery and forgery. From her Spirit she could get no clear answer; and she concluded, somewhat lamely, that whether true or false the episode was intended as 'a warning to the nation'. For the *York Herald* and similar critics the Mary Bateman affair was an excellent opportunity to discredit Joanna by bracketing the two women, and ignoring the difference between millenarian belief and thaumaturgy. For Joanna it was vital that she should distinguish herself from wise women, even when (unlike Mary Bateman) they were harmless; and this was one reason why she was so adamant that no payment should ever be received for the seals.

There is no evidence that Mary Bateman claimed to be a prophetess, though perhaps she hardly needed to do so. For as an old Thirsk woman, who was a believer in Joanna, declared twenty years later, 'She [Mary Bateman] will come again; she mun come again, Sir, 'afore all will be right.'[31]

In other parts of the country the same mixture of merchants, tradesmen, professional and popular elements is found among the believers; though in each area there were also individual factors and problems which made the local Southcottian community unique. South London is a particularly instructive example. Here the believers were at first organized by Elias Carpenter, a philanthropist and churchman, who lived in Bermondsey.[32] He had begun his successful career 'in trade and science' at the age of fourteen in a merchant's counting-house in Antigua, West Indies. Subsequently he acquired a paper mill in Bermondsey, where he established a night school for his employees. He met Joanna in 1802 and became a believer. For the next three years he was one of her most ardent disciples, and her third public trial was held at his home, Neckinger House. It is possible that Carpenter was introduced to the Southcottians by the Reverend Thomas Webster, who was a neighbour, though he (Carpenter) had been unimpressed earlier by his reading of Brothers, in whom Webster had believed. Carpenter held meetings for the study of Joanna's works, undertook the sealing of believers, and opened a chapel (near the Elephant and Castle) which he called the House of God. In January 1804 he was arrested and examined on suspicion that the Southcottians were plotting to rescue Brothers and overthrow the government, but was released.[33] The fears of the magistrates were ungrounded, but their nervousness is understandable. To an outsider the apocalyptic language of the millenarian seemed to threaten social and political upset, and the peculiarities of some of the believers did nothing to lessen such fears. Carpenter himself was respectable enough; but he gathered round him others of more questionable background. How he came to do this he does not make clear. But in his first pamphlet, *Nocturnal Alarm* (London, 1803), he sounds like a fairly typical evangelical Christian, earnestly searching the scriptures for signs of the times. Having convinced himself that the second coming is nigh, he has little difficulty in accepting Joanna's claims, and urges all devout Christians to do likewise. He dissociates himself from such seventeenth-century millenarians as Thomas Venner and the Fifth Monarchy Men, but concludes that Christopher Love's prophecies of the last days being due in the 1790s must have been inspired. Carpenter was not exclusive in his acceptance of the evidence of divine guidance, and was prepared to believe that God spoke directly through other 'instruments' as well as through Joanna. It was a sign of the last days that 'very many persons' were being 'spiritually visited'. This belief led to disruption among the Southcottians; but at first Joanna was not antagonistic to the 'false prophets' whom Carpenter patronized.

Foremost among these was Henry Prescott, commonly called Joseph. He was rescued from Christchurch workhouse, and taken to live with Carpenter in 1803, because of the visions he (Joseph) had been receiving ever since 1793 when he was a child of eight. Joseph made drawings of his visions, which were then taken to Joanna for interpretation.[34] The subjects were usually apocalyptic, portrayed with a plethora of angels, crowns, stars, clouds and celestial figures in flowing robes. Although without much artistic quality, these water-colours have a certain appeal as primitives. Joseph was apparently quite untaught: Carpenter found him 'to all appearance a truly artless, simple-minded youth'. Joanna's Spirit declared that Joseph's visions 'confirm the Bible and my prophecies', thus annexing his testimony to her own greater mission. But the precarious stability of this arrangement was upset when Carpenter took the visions as direct communications to himself and disputed the need for Joanna's interpretation. A long and wordy wrangle ensued, with Carpenter resisting Joanna's claim to be the sole channel of divine guidance, and Joseph urging his patron to independent action.[35]

Carpenter received similar encouragement from another of his protégés, Thomas Dowland. He was a reputed sorcerer and necromancer, and had been a disciple of Ebenezer Sibly, the astrologer.[36] By the time Carpenter came to know him, in January 1804, Dowland was a poor old man, about sixty-three years old and totally deaf in one ear. Carpenter persuaded him to give up astrology and the black arts, and he became a sealed believer in Joanna. He had long been prone to visions and dreams, and in 1804 he received communications for Carpenter from the Spirit. That he was but 'a very timid, weak and ignorant man', who did not always understand the communications, only strengthened Carpenter's belief in their divine origin. The results were similar to Joanna's communications, in rhymed couplets but printed as prose. The following is a fair specimen:

Each of their labour is now made clear, And God hath shew'd you how to steer, You should oft-times in prayer be, To know if God hath a message to send by thee. Now Carpenter, thy God again doth show, Is that thou must call on men below, And tell them they must hear thy voice; If they reject they'll soon repent their choice.[37]

Dowland died in December 1804 – though he appeared to Joseph in a vision later. As with Joseph, Joanna attempted to integrate Dowland's visitation (some of which she admitted was from the Lord) into her own, but was only too relieved that his death came as 'a caution to you all'. She tried to resolve the conflict with Carpenter by suggesting appeal to a meeting of believers representative of the two sides; but the schismatical currents proved too strong, and in 1805 Carpenter parted company with the majority of believers who remained faithful to Joanna. Thirty years later he was still preaching in his chapel, 'to a very well-dressed congregation'. He called himself 'Elias, who was to come', the herald of the messiah, who was shortly to make his appearance to the faithful.[38]

The loss of Carpenter's chapel was countered by the opening of a new one in Duke Street, Southwark, in the spring of 1805. This was under the superintendence of William Tozer. He had come from Exeter, where he was a lath render, and had joined Carpenter at the House of God but then switched his allegiance to Joanna. Observers commented on his uncouthness and thick Devonshire accent:

> vehemence is the characteristic of his harangues. There is wildness in his looks, as well as thunder in his voice ... Prodigies are the burden of his charge; and the millennium and the judgements preparatory to it are the stated topics on which he expatiates.[39]

In contemporary accounts by outsiders he is usually presented as the 'high priest' of Southcottianism – perhaps because his image accorded with what it was felt a millenarian ought to be like. He impressed Dr Reece, the surgeon who conducted the autopsy on Joanna, as a fanatical believer: 'on the subject of the prophetess his conversation was so *outré*, as to border on insanity.' In conversation with Reece he related 'what he termed a remarkable circumstance,' namely,

> that when on a journey into Devonshire he accidently met with a copy of Moore's *Almanack* for the year in which Joanna was born, and the frontispiece of it was a representation of angels rejoicing for the birth of the Prophetess.[40]

Tozer was by no means alone among the believers in his ambition to assert himself as a sectarian preacher.[41] His chapel in Duke Street was acquired mainly through the efforts of Peter Morison of Liverpool, who had come up to London after receiving visions about the quarrel with Carpenter. Morison was one of Joanna's original seven stars, though when he first visited her at Exeter in August 1801 she thought him mad and entertained him at a friend's house. Later, when she realized that he had been sent by the Lord, she regretted that she had been so off-hand. Little is known about Morison, but from some of Joanna's letters to him it is apparent that she feared he might become another Carpenter. He preached widely in the North, and his message was sufficiently radical to invite persecution and arrest. He claimed to be visited by a Spirit, and warned that

> by the end of this year [1806] there would be no hedge, nor even a brick standing, and by that time all persons of every description who did not take the seals would be cut off by the judgements of God; [and] the clergy would be lost for ever, and would be like dung – for they were dumb dogs that would not bark – and all the property and land belonging to the rich would be taken away and given to the sealed people.[42]

This was not to Joanna's liking, and she told him she did not wonder he was persecuted if he preached such erroneous doctrine: 'why should you expect the rich to be cut off for enjoying the things that you are teaching the others to long for?' Unlike Carpenter, however, Morison was always contrite after Joanna's reproofs, and promised (vainly) to amend his ways. He remained a believer for many years after her death and was preaching until about 1836.

Morison was not a central figure among the London believers; and after his brief intervention at the time of the Carpenter dispute, he went back to the north. In the metropolis the leadership of the main Southcottian body was in the hands of a few disciples close to Joanna. Jane Townley occupied a special position. The prophetess lived with her; and Townley and her maid, Ann Underwood, took down Joanna's communications and issued them to the world. Townley was a central correspondent for the movement as a whole. Like most of the believers she expected that the Shiloh announced in 1814 would be a temporal child, but realized later that she was mistaken and should have looked for a spiritual birth. After Joanna's death she defended the true Southcottian faith against both unbelievers and rival prophets, being guided in this by communications from the Spirit. Right up to the time of her death in 1825 she believed that she would live to see the millennium.[43] In her later years she was assisted by William Owen Pughe, the Welsh druidical scholar, whom we have noted earlier for his combination of millenarian belief with mythological theory. He acted as her secretary and executor. In December 1804 he had been one of the jury at Joanna's trial and was subsequently consulted by Joanna on matters of folk-lore and magic.

The second leading figure in London, upon whom Joanna relied heavily, was William Sharp. He, like Foley, was ordered by Joanna's Spirit to print parables and communications which he could not understand, and which indeed were incomprehensible since the explanations of Sharp's parables were printed in the pamphlets published by Foley, and vice versa. This mix up of the Spirit's instructions was explained by Joanna as intended to try the faith of the two disciples.[44] Sharp emerged from such trials with flying colours. His steadfast faith enabled him to withstand the mockery of his friends:

> I have the natural pride of man, and have no desire to be an object of ridicule; but whatever pain or mortification the pride of character, or of reputation, may produce in me, it is my superior duty to adhere to Truth. The mockery of the world I must endure; the pity of my friends, who would promote every worldly advantage for my interest, I must feel; and many, I know, are sorry for me, believing me to be a deluded man.[45]

Dr Reece thought Sharp was 'a plain honest man, of deep thought and great research', who was convinced that Joanna would give birth to a child and that the millennium would then begin. Even after her death Sharp did not give up hope, and asked Reece whether he would believe in Joanna's mission should she be resuscitated and produce a boy. To which Reece replied that such an event would certainly be the work of the Lord, but that it was 'as reasonable to expect the building of St Paul's to ascend into the air.' Sharp told him: 'Ah, Sir, you take only a *professional* view of it, but I take a *spiritual* one.' When the autopsy finally destroyed the last hopes of the believers who were watching, Sharp was the only one who held out to the rest any balm of consolation. Life, he observed, was involved in mystery. Though overwhelmed by their disappointment the disciples should not give up their search to know God's ways.[46]

In his devotion to Joanna's cause Sharp was prepared to risk his worldly goods and to abandon such natural business acumen as he may have possessed. He and Wilson and Major Eyre decided to borrow money for the promotion of her mission, and thereby fell into the hands of an unscrupulous Jewish money-lender, John King. They signed bills of exchange totalling over £2,000 but received only a fraction of this sum in cash, and when they refused to repay the full amount of the bills at the end of a year, King took them to court. Apparently King at first professed sympathy with the believers and discussed problems of prophecy with them.[47] But in the Court of King's Bench it was insinuated that the Southcottians calculated on the arrival of the millennium before the repayment of the bills was due. The business dragged on through 1806–7, and Sharp was distressed by the unwelcome publicity which it brought. Yet his faith was unshaken. Persecution was to be expected, and was in fact a corroboration that Joanna fulfilled the promises and warnings of scripture.

Sharp was a man who believed that the world, as hitherto known, was about to come to an end. 'The whole tendency of [Joanna's] writings proves that the Millennium, or Kingdom of Christ, is at hand,' he wrote in 1804. Two years later he was more than ever convinced that things could not go on in their old way for much longer: 'The present awful state of the world has been increasing in calamities ever since the year 1792, the very year when the Spirit of Prophecy was given to Joanna.'[48] War, inflation and taxation have laid unprecedented burdens on the people. 'When the mind of man reflects upon what has happened within the period of the last thirteen years, [he] must conclude that some great and mighty change is about to take place.' To comprehend these vast changes we have to search the scriptures for God's promises and plans, and when we do so, argues Sharp, we see that Joanna is the fulfilment of them. Before the dawn the earth is in darkness, and only the moon sheds a little reflected or borrowed light; all objects are imperfectly seen, and the real truth cannot be discovered. At present mankind is under the governance of the moon, which in Joanna's writings is used as a type of Satan. But Joanna is the 'woman clothed with the sun and the moon under her feet'; and the rising sun is a type or emblem of Christ. Sharp marvels at the simplicity of this imagery, purposely drawn from nature so that it can be understood by the most ignorant of men, without 'the aid of what is called learning.'

It is apparent that Sharp, like many another artisan seeker before and since, was much occupied by the problems of theodicy.

> It is certainly every man's duty to enquire why he is not both wise and happy; or for what end he was created. ... These reflections must surely lead men to know what they ought to be, by reflecting what they are.

As he argued his way forward from the origins of evil and the nature and destiny of man, Sharp's logic led him inexorably to the acceptance of Joanna's claims: 'there is a chain of evidence composed of a variety of parts, or links, from the beginning of Genesis to the end of the Revelation.' The great and eternal questions about man's being would be answered through dreams, visions and the interpretation of scripture; and Joanna was the key to unlock these hitherto unfathomable mysteries.

The deists and infidels, by their denial of everything supernatural, were precluded from answering these most fundamental questions, thought Sharp; and he dissociated himself totally from the views of some of his acquaintances of the 1790s. Even so, deism and 'naturalism' were 'alarmingly increased' – 'the days are now arrived, when there is scarce faith upon the earth' – and the dire warnings of the last days in Mark 13 were now entirely apposite.

The leadership of the London believers included other members of Joanna's old guard. Some of these, like Colonel Harwood and Dr Wetherell, have already been noticed; others, like John Hows ('a very sensible man,' said Dr Reece) and Elias Jameson Field (Joanna's main book agent, and a central correspondent with the provinces), escape detailed delineation. A younger generation of active believers also begins to appear after about 1805. And of these, John Pye (1782–1874), is particularly interesting, for like Sharp and Blake he was an engraver. Born in Birmingham, of a family of engravers, Pye specialized in landscape engraving and became a favourite of J. M. W. Turner, whose paintings he lucratively made into prints. He was for long a critic of the Royal Academy and campaigned ceaselessly for reform of the system of art patronage. His other enthusiasm was Joanna's mission. He became a believer some time in his twenties, and was a member of Tozer's congregation.[49] His name appears on most of the publications concerned with reunification of the various Southcottian congregations in the 1840s, and he seems to have been the leader of a Southcottian chapel in Gray's Inn Lane. By this time the Southcottians had reached the stage of sect development when internal divisions seemed to hinder further growth of the cause as a whole; but conflicting views on the precise nature of the birth of Shiloh in 1814, and on the policy of opening chapels proved remarkably intractable.[50] The believers were only too conscious of the futility of 'sitting tamely by ... and quarrelling one with another', but were hard-pressed to find some form of action on which to unite. Pye and his friends then proposed that Satan should be brought to public trial. The believers had already 'signed for Satan's destruction'. Now they were called upon to follow this up with appropriate action. The same means that had been used to get rid of Jesus in his day must be used to get rid of Satan. A formal indictment, trial and condemnation were called for, and in December 1846, before a jury of believers, Satan was found guilty of the murder of Jesus and Joanna.[51]

This episode belongs to the more bizarre aspects of Southcottianism, and is perhaps in line with Brothers' vision of Satan walking through London and Joanna's seven-day dispute with the devil in 1802. It presents very real problems of comprehension; for unless we simply dismiss it as madness we have to recognize facets of the millenarian mind which today are almost totally unfamiliar. It is one thing to say that people believed in the devil as a person; but quite another to appreciate how the trial of Satan (or indeed petitioning for Satan's destruction) could be regarded as an effective programme of action. There is an extreme literalness in this type of millenarianism which, as Joanna would have said, 'stumbles' us. Our sensibility to the problems of the millennium is so reduced, and our acceptance of the premises from which the millenarians started so minimal, that with the best will in the world we find it extremely difficult to see things as they did. We can follow the logic of their arguments but we miss the vital spark that makes them compelling. For our comfort we may remark that many contemporaries of the Southcottians had a similar problem, though they were more likely to be aware of other manifestations of millennialism than we are. Our danger is to see Pye, Sharp and the others as more or less isolated figures, or at the most set against some 'background' of political and social events. In fact it is more fruitful to consider the believers as part of a wider millennial culture which extended beyond specific sects or institutions. This will not in itself explain why individual Southcottians held the beliefs that they did; but it will help to provide reference points from which those beliefs can be approached. The context of belief is for the historian an important factor in accounting for its form and rationale at a particular time.

The sub-culture of millennialism and millenarianism can be charted in several ways: through the apocalyptic sermons of respectable preachers, by the records of millenarian sects, in the works of artists and poets. For Pye and Sharp we can establish our point by reference to romantic painting. Whereas Sharp's pamphlets sold in their hundreds, John Martin's apocalyptic scenes were viewed by thousands when exhibited in London and by many more when reproduced as engravings in the annuals, *Forget Me Not, Friendship's Offering, The Keepsake*, and in illustrated editions of the Bible.[52] Martin (1789–1854) was a painter and engraver who made a name for himself with large canvases depicting 'The Fall of Babylon', 'Joshua commanding the Sun to stand still', 'The Deluge', 'The Last Judgment', 'The Great Day of His Wrath', and 'The Plains of Heaven'. He depicted vast landscapes and cataclysms on a cosmic scale with great buildings toppling down and man reduced to ant-like proportions. Francis Danby (1793–1861) painted in the same style, with subjects like 'The Opening of the Sixth Seal' and 'The Israelites crossing the Red Sea'. In America Washington Allston's paintings similarly echoed the warnings of millenarian writers. It is difficult to estimate the impact that such pictures made. But by 1861, when Mrs Henry Wood published her best-selling *East Lynne*, Martin's genre was sufficiently well-known to be quoted in the novel as a type.[53] Martin was probably a deist, though in his later years he may have been associated with British Israelism.[54] He lived in the shadow of insanity; for his brother Jonathan was confined in a lunatic asylum after setting fire to York Minster, his brother William was harmlessly mad, and he (John) was known as 'Mad Martin'. Sharp admired Martin's work, and characteristically assured him that his 'Belshazzar's Feast' was 'a divine work, an emanation immediately from the Almighty'.[55] When considered in relation to the heroic, romantic imagination of Martin and his friends, Sharp begins to appear somewhat less isolated and peculiar. In the context of this millennial imagination the believers seem altogether more comprehensible. Instead of being *sui generis*, they take their place on a continuum stretching from mild concern with prophecy to extreme second adventism. Our focus now sharpens. We perceive that the Southcottians were not simply millenarians, but a particular group within a larger millenarian world. We are led to ask not only why did the believers hold millenarian beliefs, but why did they hold a particular type of millenarian belief?

No simple, cut-and-dried answer to these questions is adequate; but from the composite experiences of the believers we can glean a number of useful clues. It is clear that most of Joanna's followers were sincere, earnest Christians, dependant for guidance on a literal interpretation of the Bible. They had pondered long over the scriptures, especially the prophecies and promises of the coming of Christ's kingdom, and were committed members of existing churches and sects. Nevertheless, they were deeply dissatisfied − with themselves, with their religious institutions, and with society. The causes and occasions of their dissatisfaction were complex; but their concern and unhappiness resolved itself into a deep yearning for a New Heaven and a New Earth. Not content merely to listen to sermons, they wanted an active, 'vital' form of Christian involvement. Many of the believers had already had some form of inner-light experience, and all were ready to be influenced by visions and dreams. They longed for some authority who would confirm and sanctify these experiences, and who would also cut through the conflicting claims of all the churches. Only the Saviour himself, or at the least his directly appointed messenger, could fulfil such longings. And so the believers were led to the great hope of the second coming. They were already familiar, through their study of scripture, with the terms and conditions of that event. Their distinctive role as millenarians was to announce its timing and incarnation.

The imminence of some great change lies at the root of Southcottian belief. During Joanna's lifetime, and especially in the 1790s, this was directly related to the events of the French Revolution. But the same sentiments were being uttered fifty years later by a second generation of believers who had never known Joanna personally. 'We live in an age when the whole civilised world appears to be on the eve of some great and important change', declared W. B. Harrison, a Manchester believer, in 1842.[56] He argued that this would be admitted by thousands who nevertheless had no idea of the direction and result of the change but who, like the mistaken Chartists and Owenites, were looking for some great 'deliverance'. Harrison's belief in this great change, however, was not derived from the economic and social distress of the late 1830s and 1840s so much as confirmed by it. He had been a believer for thirty years. The change he contemplated was beyond the scale of most contemporary social reformers (with the exception of Robert Owen):

> We are on the eve of the most important event that ever occurred within the limits of creation, the destruction of Satan from the face of the earth, and the restoration of man to a state of purity and happiness equal to the one from which he fell ... a change of vast and transcendent importance.

To the believers it seemed that there was so much wrong with society, so much evil in the world, that it was impossible to conceive how it could be changed except by divine intervention. The crucial judgment the Southcottians had to make was as to the timing of the change. After the disappointment of 1814 they were reluctant to name a date for the return of Shiloh or some other miraculous manifestation of the second advent; but most believers expected that the millennium would begin during their lifetimes.

The agency by which the great change would come about was of course the final and defining characteristic of the Southcottians. Belief in 'dear Joanna's mission', as Foley usually put it, was the bond uniting the otherwise disparate elements among the believers. They had come to acknowledge the validity of her claims after reading her works in the first instance. So clear and compelling did her case seem to them that they were puzzled that others did not see likewise. 'I am astonished that everyone who has access to her books is not instantly convinced that they are written by inspiration', declared Daniel Roberts.[57] If the world was not convinced, thought the believers, it must be in part at least because the matter had not been presented with sufficient cogency. And so in pamphlet after pamphlet they set down their testimony to the force of Joanna's claims. Given the normal starting point of Protestant evangelical orthodoxy, they had no doubt of their ability to present a logical, step-by-step argument showing first the possibility and then the inescapable conclusion that Joanna was the prophetess fulfilling the promises of scripture. Whether or not they were able to convince others, they convinced themselves. Satisfied that the signs of the times indicated the proximity of the millennium, they were only too ready to accept Joanna as the agency by which it would be effected. Not all Southcottians needed to ratiocinate their belief, and even for some who did it was probably no more than auxiliary to other grounds of conviction. Direct communication from the Spirit, by means of voices, visions or dreams, was vouchsafed to many of the believers, and provided an impregnable (if at times erratic) basis of faith in the prophetess. Belief in a supernatural agency of change, though usually supported or defended by reasoned argument from scripture, was not in the last resort dependent upon it. In the last days it was to be expected that abnormal and 'impossible' channels of communication would be used, as the believers awaited 'the second coming of our beloved Lord, in might, majesty and glory'.

CHAPTER SIX

FALSE PROPHETS

The problem of rivals is very troublesome for most millenarian prophets and prophetesses. All social and religious movements have to face challenges to the leadership, especially at times of succession, and usually mechanisms are devised for handling such matters. In millenarian movements these problems assume a rather special – and sometimes intractable – form. The prophetess's claims are based on personal revelation, and her charisma provides the authority for her leadership. She also draws round herself followers who similarly claim to receive direct messages from the Spirit, and these are usually sanctioned by her. This could be hazardous, as Joanna discovered in the case of Carpenter and Prescott. When believers were led into disobedience by following their Spirit it had to be argued that this could be only because the Spirit was an evil spirit, and any claims made thence were false. Even more dangerous for the cause was the problem of a successor on the death of the prophetess. Among millenarians who believed that they were living at the end of time questions of succession could hardly arise, since the messiah (or Shiloh) would shortly arrive to reign over the faithful. They were therefore bound to be taken by surprise, and unprepared, when the prophetess died before the coming of the kingdom. Joanna had designated no successor. The believers relied on direct communications from the Spirit for guidance; not surprisingly there was some confusion and conflict. As various claimants came forward to inherit Joanna's mantle, the believers remembered the words of Jesus (Matthew 7:15): 'Beware of false prophets, which come to you in sheep's clothing, but inwardly are ravening wolves.'

The decision to accept or reject a particular claimant depended to some extent on the view taken of what happened in December 1814. Three main interpretations were available to believers. First was the view that the birth had been postponed and that Joanna would return to life in due course. An alternative theory was that the child had been born and immediately 'caught up unto God' in accordance with Relevation 12:5, so that he had not been seen, but would return 'to rule all the nations with a rod of iron'. Third was the belief that the birth was intended to be spiritual, not temporal, and that the 'child' would be some individual who would be identified as the spiritual child of Joanna. Jane Townley and Owen Pughe thought for a time that this person might be Pomeroy. Whichever version he accepted, the believer was committed to the expectation of some great event in the future, usually described as the coming of Shiloh. The claimants played on this theme, purporting to be either the herald of Shiloh (like George Turner) or (as with Zion Ward) Shiloh himself. Turner secured the allegiance of many believers in the north and also won the support of some Southcottian meetings elsewhere. William Shaw, whose communications are dated 1819 and who died in 1822, was recognized as a true Southcottian prophet; but little is known about him and his writings appear to have circulated only in manuscript. Jane Townley, Foley, Sharp and their friends were suspicious of all later prophets, and refused to acknowledge their claims. But the Southcottian movement could not be contained within the bounds of the old guard's orthodoxy. False prophets sprang up on all sides, elaborating new plans for the millennium, and giving new commandments to the believers. Records of most of these developments are sparse, but enough remain to show what was happening.

In London Samuel Charles Woodward Sibley organized a group of believers who called themselves the Household of Faith.[1] He was a watchman who had been permitted by Joanna to hold meetings in his house, and he accepted the interpretation that Shiloh was caught up to God immediately after his birth and would return to conquer Satan and prepare the way for the second advent. Men are bewildered by the multiplicity of interpretations of scripture, he argued. But God would raise up a lowly voice to confound 'the wise and learned who live by preaching', as He did in Christ's day. The congregation made a (perhaps untypical) appearance in the streets in January 1819. Led by Sibley blowing a trumpet, the believers paraded through the City, proclaiming the coming of Shiloh. Each wore a white cockade and a star of yellow ribbon. Sibley's wife cried out: 'Woe! woe! to the inhabitants of the earth because of the coming of Shiloh', and this was repeated by others. A hostile crowd soon collected and fighting broke out. Sibley and his wife were brought before the magistrates and required to refrain from causing similar breaches of the peace in the future. Normally the Household of Faith was a peaceable enough body which met in a chapel in Smithfield to listen to Sibley. In 1825 a visitor reported five hundred in his congregation, but by 1834 'old Sibley' was described as a harmless old gentleman 'who preaches to a chosen few on Sunday evenings.'

Another believer whose voice commanded him to prophesy and preach was Joseph Allman (or Almond) who adopted the more scriptural name of Zebulun.[2] He divided his followers into twelve tribes. For a long time he was hampered by poverty, but then was enabled to live more comfortably by the support of a wealthy convert, Captain William Woodley, RN. Zebulun had a small following in London, and also in other old Southcottian centres such as Stourbridge, until his death in the late 1840s. His communications were mainly grandiose pronouncements with very little content. 'Song XXXV' of his *Songs of Royal Sion* is typical:

I'm Jah, Christ Jesus, Shiloh, here,
The man child, now for all is clear,
Because the twain are joined as one,
The we-man, Christ, the Father's Son.

I'm Shiloh, King, with iron rod
And here I'll reign, as we-man God;
In Union bow before my throne,
I'm Christ that did for all atone.

A third claimant to the succession in London came from outside the ranks of the old believers. Alexander Lindsay, a member of the Scottish aristocracy, opened a chapel in Southwark in 1825. He won over Tozer to his cause, and secured the support of many believers from Tozer's chapel in Duke Street.

Elsewhere in the country similar situations developed. Foley complained in 1821 that he had recently received 'seven or eight blasphemous letters from a Mary Joanna' who lived at Staverton in Devon.[3] She had requested an invitation to Oldswinford rectory, claiming that she was to fulfil the mission of Joanna. She also said that she was the wife of Shiloh and that Christ dwelt within her human form. Mary Joanna was in fact Mary Boon, the wife of a shoemaker. Her chief disciple was John Field, a stonemason who took down her communications and corresponded with believers in other parts of the country. Prophecies and general fulminations against Satan, uttered amid a froth of millenarian rhetoric ('I who speak through my handmaid am the holy, holy Almighty and merciful God, Jesus Christ and Shiloh. And I say to my handmaid ...'[4]), formed the staple of her writings. She enjoined her followers to observe the Mosaic law; with the result that they incurred local hostility by working on Sundays and keeping the sabbath on Saturdays. Mary Boon was illiterate, and appears to have originally been a local wise woman who latched on to the success of her more famous predecessor. She visited London and had followers in Walworth.

The Judaism which Mary Boon emphasized in her interpretation of Southcottianism was taken much further by the most successful of all the false prophets, John Wroe (1782–1863).[5] In northern towns the 'beardies' or 'Johannas', as Wroe's followers were called, provided the popular image of Southcottians[6] – although they were vigorously repudiated by the old believers. Wroe had not known Joanna during her lifetime nor, as far as is known, had he any contact with millenarians before 1819, when he suffered a severe illness. He recovered his bodily health, but remained disturbed in his mind, and 'wrestled with God both day and night, for several months.' Sometimes he wandered about the fields and sat under the hedges to try to read easy passages from his Bible.

> Soon after this, he was visited with what are called trances or visions; at the commencement of most of which he was struck blind and dumb, his eyelids became as firmly united as if they had naturally grown together: and his tongue fastened in his mouth, in which state he remained during the whole period of their continuance, which was sometimes seven, twelve, twenty-four, or thirty-six hours: after one of the trances he continued blind for six days, but not dumb. Many remarkable events were revealed to him.

He then became an attender at the Southcottians' meetings in Bradford, but did not join the society, as he thought from his visions that he was commanded to become a Jew. So he went to the synagogue in Liverpool but, after a vain argument with the rabbi, returned home. His voice now told him 'Go thou to the Jews at London, and declare the words which I shall give thee.' Again rebuffed, he nevertheless nurtured his Judaic dream, which in a short time he was to transmute into a new type of movement. Back in Bradford, he continued with the Southcottians, and after George Turner's death Wroe's Spirit informed him in August 1822 that he was to be Turner's successor.

Wroe now made a determined bid for the leadership, using the system of elected local committees which Turner had set up to consolidate the movement. At first the Bradford committee was reluctant to acknowledge him, but after he had gained the support of a bare majority, he forced the issue by dramatically using two men with drawn swords to divide the congregation. 'The service being concluded the two men having the swords ... again held them up, when the greater part of the Bradford society were convinced of his mission and walked under them.' The Bradford committee, 'in conformity with directions from the Spirit through John', invited the committees in Ashton-under-Lyne, Stockport, Sheffield and Colne each to send two delegates to investigate Wroe's claims. He also visited other meetings in the north to win support. Instead of consolidating his position throughout the movement, however, he left England in April 1823 for a missionary tour in Gibraltar and Spain, and extended this later in the year to a second tour in France, Austria and Italy. Accompanied by a travelling companion on each expedition, Wroe visited synagogues and cathedrals; but to most of the rabbis and priests with whom he talked he appeared to be no more than an eccentric or slightly mad traveller to be either humoured or indignantly expelled. In December his voice told him to return to England; and on his way back to the north he visited Chatham and Gravesend, where the believers decided to accept his leadership. From Ashton-under-Lyne, which he made his headquarters, Wroe travelled extensively to other Southcottian meetings during 1824 and 1825. In London he made little headway. Jane Townley refused to see him when he called on her; and although he confronted Lindsay and Sibley in their respective chapels he could not win the allegiance of their congregations. Similarly in the south and west he failed to win many of the old believers. Edmund Baker at Ilminster told Wroe that he was 'going a wild-goose errand'; and visits to Dr Ashe at Crewkerne and to believers at Bigbury were equally fruitless. But in Lancashire, Cheshire and the West Riding of Yorkshire (i.e., in Turner's territory) he won over many of the meetings.

Wroe was a highly controversial figure. He had the capacity to arouse strong hostility not only in non-believers (which was to be expected) but also among Southcottians themselves. This was more than antipathy to a false prophet – many old believers refused to accept Turner, but they did not vilify him. Wroe is 'the personification of ignorance and vulgarity ... a most vile and immoral character', wrote W. B. Harrison, adding for good measure that he had a notoriously bad character as a tradesman 'before he commenced prophet', and was 'wholly ignorant of Joanna Southcott's writings and ... mission'.[7] This hostility was probably rooted more in objection to Wroe's personal behaviour than to his mission as such, though the two became closely interlinked. He does not seem to have made any specifically antinomian claims, though he was prepared to quote the First Epistle of John 3:9 on sinlessness. Wroe's non-respectability (not to say ignorance and debauchery) may have offended some middle-class believers, but was not in itself any bar to millenarian acceptability. Indeed, a certain John-the-Baptist-like roughness was not out of place in a true prophet. Edward Lees reported Wroe's first visit to the Ashton meeting on Christmas Day, 1822:

> His appearance at the time was not very prepossessing. He came into the meeting with his hat upon his head – was very poorly attired – spoke very indifferently, and made many mistakes and blunders, which, coupled with the reports of his former conduct, had at first an unfavourable impression.[8]

Nevertheless, he was listened to patiently, and a majority of the society accepted his leadership.

From his *Life and Journal* it is apparent that Wroe's way of life was very different from Joanna's, and that he emphasized different aspects of the millenarian tradition. He had few physical advantages: he was poor, hunchbacked, and constantly ill. His father, a small farmer and 'worsted stuff manufacturer', of Bowling, near Bradford, treated him harshly, according to John Wroe, and they quarrelled. Because of a scanty schooling, Wroe could read only imperfectly. Before preaching he would have his text read to him, and he marked his hand with letters to remind him of it. Wroe was a wool-comber by trade, but had difficulty in supporting his wife and family. She, like John Wright's wife earlier, dreaded the commands of her husband's 'voice', and was opposed to his setting out on his travels. As in all such cases, this merely strengthened his resolve to go, for it confirmed the scriptural warning (Luke 14:26) that to follow the Lord a man must forsake all, including his family. After he became accepted as the prophet Wroe was supported by his wealthier disciples. For many years he took nothing from them except hospitality, clothing, and his coach fares when travelling; but after he left Ashton in 1831 he changed, and accepted larger gifts from the faithful. Some of his habits were odd, though not without biblical precedent. In September 1824 he was ordered by the Spirit to leave Ashton and wander in the fields for fourteen days, feeding only on nuts and berries – which was intended as a sign against eating 'unclean meat'. He was also partial to public baptism, and on several occasions was rebaptized in the rivers Medlock (near Ashton) and Aire (near Apperly Bridge) in the presence of large crowds. This was a cleansing rite, 'to wash off the filthiness that the world has given thee.' In April 1824 he was publicly circumcised in the presence of the Ashton meeting, and during his wanderings later in the year he himself circumcised a young man at Barnsley. Sexual temptation was never far from Wroe, and his obsession with cleansing may have been related to his feelings of remorse and need for penance. Be that as it may, it was his sexual weaknesses which were ultimately his undoing. He was charged before the Bradford magistrates with an offence against his twelve-year-old servant-girl, but was acquitted. Subsequently the Ashton society had to set up an inquiry into Wroe's sexual indecencies with three young women of the congregation, and it was concluded that he 'had shown a laxity of right principles.'

The most distinctive element in Wroe's teaching was his Judaism. References to the role of the Jews in the last days occur in the writings of most millenarian leaders, but with Wroe the matter was made central. He did not put forward any elaborate theories about Israel, like the speculative mythologists; nor did he plan to lead the Hebrews back to the Holy Land, like Brothers. In one of his 'divine communications' he referred to the visible and invisible Hebrews, but his mission was to both alike, 'that they shall be circumcised both in heart and flesh.'[9] He divided his followers into the twelve tribes of Israel. His Christian Israelism was essentially practical: the observance of the whole of the Mosaic law together with additional rules commanded by the Lord through Wroe. These 'Laws of God' were revealed to Wroe piecemeal between 1822 and 1832, and resulted in a code of conduct governing dietary habits, sexual behaviour, family relations, dress, Sabbath observance, and the treatment of animals. Enforcement of these laws was a severe test of faith. To grow a beard when it was the fashion to be clean-shaven, to wear odd-looking clothes, and to eat only kosher meat was to set oneself apart from other people. It was an invitation to ridicule, if not persecution. Nothing is more remarkable than Wroe's success in imposing such sectarian extremes on blunt Yorkshiremen and shrewd Lancashire industrialists. The rigours of the regime were well described by one who experienced them at first hand:

In 1823 the law was reimposed; in 1824 circumcision was revived; the beard was ordered to be worn; swine's flesh and shellfish and other unclean food were forbidden; flannel was ordered to be cast off by all the believers, old and young, a severe trial, faithfully endured, it is said, without unpleasant results; black clothing of every description was denounced; cotton also was interdicted to all who could afford linen, which alone was considered worthy to be worn next the skin. A severe moral law was promulgated – spirits and tobacco were absolutely forbidden; they were not even to be tasted; and moderation in all things was enforced by severe penalties, and these penalties were sometimes immersion seven times in water, sometimes corporal punishment, inflicted by the women, with rods, and the women were commanded to strike without fear on the bare shoulders, or be themselves subjected to their own peculiar penalties, which were still more trying to the feelings.[10] In time Wroe became a tyrant, severe and austere; and his person was dreaded by all who followed him. But though they feared him, they confessed that his law was good, and made them better men.[11]

We are fortunate in having the testimony of one Wroeite who was both literate and of an original turn of mind. James Elishama ('Shepherd') Smith (1801–57) was destined by his father for the Presbyterian ministry, and after obtaining his degree from Glasgow University in 1818 spent several years as a private tutor and visiting preacher.[12] He was not satisfied by the orthodoxies of the Church of Scotland and began a restless search for a more acceptable faith. His millennial yearnings were for a time satisfied by the teachings and inspiration of Edward Irving; but after several visits to Ashton he was convinced that Wroe was a man of God, and in 1830 he joined the Southcottians there. During his thirteen months with them he preached, ran a school and taught Hebrew. After leaving them he associated with the socialists and radicals in London, and later in the pages of his journal, *The Shepherd*, elaborated a combination of religious millennialism and social radicalism which he termed universalism. His account of Wroe and other Southcottians is in a work entitled *The Coming Man*, parts of which are autobiographical. The book was finished in 1848 but only published posthumously (1873). It is in the form (popular among reformers in the first half of the nineteenth century) of a novel, the characters being vehicles for the exposition of universalist doctrines and millenarian experiences.

In the following passage Benjamin (i.e. Smith) is introduced to Wroe:

It was a fine May morning when Benjamin first made his appearance in Salem, [i.e. Ashton], and presented himself before John the Jew. The prophet was a stern, elderly man, of forbidding aspect, by no means like Moses, nor much in the habit of controlling his feelings. His beard was full-grown, and his mouth was covered with strong, grizzled moustaches; he had a white or undyed broad-rimmed hat upon his head, a Quaker's coat without collar, of a sort of wine colour, and a silk velvet waistcoat. He was in the vestry belonging to the Sanctuary, and he held a rod of iron in his hand. Several of his chief men, some of them gentlemen to appearance, others rather clownish-looking, sat or stood around him.

'Well, young man,' said the prophet to Benjamin, 'what has brought a man like you amongst a people like we?'

'I come,' said Benjamin, 'to learn what I do not know.'

'Well, if you come with an honest heart you shall be welcome, but you must not expect to come here without bearing a burden like the rest of your brethren.'

'I expect to carry my share of the burden.'

'Are you willing to obey?'

'I hope so. I think obedience the first duty a man ought to learn.'

'Well said, young man. Are you willing to hold your tongue when commanded to be silent?'

'That is a part of the duty of obedience.'

'It is; "He learned obedience by the things that He suffered." "When He was reviled He reviled not again." Can you bear to be abused? Can you bear to be robbed? Should the Lord desire your silver or your gold, would you give it up? Will you cast all your jewels into the treasury? I see a ring on your little finger, will you give up that?'

'Oh, willingly.'

' 'Tis enough; I do not want it; I want the heart, but the heart must be tried. "Obedience is better than sacrifice, and to hearken than the fat of rams." Are you willing to submit to the baptism of blood – the rite that was imposed upon Abraham and all the males of his house? for without this you can only come into the outer court, and not into the inner court of the sanctuary; neither can you hold office amongst us.'

'I am willing.'

' 'Tis well, then; we accept thee as a brother, and if thou prove a false one, the evil lie at thine own door. I say thee and thou to thee now, for so we speak to one another, but we "you" the world.'

Smith then described what it felt like to be a Wroeite:

Benjamin was now a member of one of the most disreputable and outcast of all the sects in England – a sect that had no communion or fellowship of feeling with any other sect, but was cut off from the main body of the Church like the Jews themselves, whose better name of Israelite it had adopted. He began now to feel that he must be despised by gentlemen and ladies, by people of fashion and men of the world; that he must appear in a dress that would expose him to the contempt of the Christian sects and the infidel wanderers, to the sneer

143

of the well-dressed passenger in the street, the scoff of the profane, and the jest of the young and the thoughtless. He must now know what it is to be reckoned vile. Yet so far from being disheartened he felt unusually cheerful, and seemed to say with David, 'I will yet be more vile than thee, and will be base in mine own sight.'

He very cheerfully submitted to all that was enjoined. He suffered his beard to grow. He gave away his black hat and his black clothing, and faithfully removed every thread of cotton from his attire. Even his worsted stockings he gave away to a poor man, and substituted linen in their stead. Nothing but linen clothing touched his person. This was the law, and he scrupulously obeyed it. During the first month he looked rather an odd figure with the stubble of his growing beard, his white broad-rimmed, low-crowned hat, his Quaker claret-coloured coat with large buttons, and waistcoat of similar colour; and he was advised by his Israelitish brethren to keep frequently rubbing the upper lip, from the middle outwards, in order to give the hair a set, for they who neglected this had a most uncomely moustache, which hung over the mouth and dipped into liquor whenever they attempted to drink. As he particularly disliked this falling moustache, which he was told was occasioned by the set which was given to the hair in shaving downwards, he for several weeks was most assiduously employed in using means to prevent the evil – means which he was happy to find at last were crowned with success, for he had a free clean mouth when the beard was grown.

He was now a Jew or Israelite bodily and spiritually. Who could say that he was not? He had gone back further than the Middle Ages; he had gone back to the First Ages, and was just such another Jew as St Peter himself. And he kept the law of Moses as faithfully as any modern Jew. He abandoned the use of pork, of shell-fish, of eels, or fish without scales. He abandoned even the occasional use of spirits, of tobacco or snuff, and adopted all the cleanly, chaste, and orderly habits which were enjoined, namely, washing hands and beard before going to bed; and numerous other little domestic and personal customs which, though not perhaps entitled to the name of moral virtues, were at least emblematical of them, and poetically related to them; for so very minute was the law in some particulars, that if one sex should even interfere with the office of another sex – such as a man presuming even to pour out a cup of tea for himself when a woman was at the table – the offender was punished by undergoing an act of ablution, or perhaps the infliction of personal punishment. ... A sort of espionage was ordained throughout the whole society; for every one who was witness to a breach of the law in another was commanded to inform, or himself be subject to the penalty of the transgression. This was indispensable to insure the keeping of the law in the private intercourses of life. It was a new sort of life for Benjamin. He was now a spy and an informer.

Smith's superior education gave him a position of influence among the Ashton Wroeites. He hoped to succeed Wroe in 1831, but it is obvious that Smith's qualities were of an order very different from Wroe's. Smith was a preacher, not a prophet. He was altogether much more intellectual and cultivated than most of the believers, and at times he gives the impression that he was pursuing a philosophical rather than a religious quest. The gap between him and the ordinary Wroeites is well brought out in his account of his landlady, whom he called Mrs Riddle. She had been a believer in Joanna; then had followed Turner; and now had come to Ashton by command of the Spirit to join Wroe. The law against the use of wigs or false curls or false teeth – or indeed anything false whatever – was a great trial to her. Previously she had worn false hair and jet black ringlets ('heart-breakers'), but Wroe commanded her and all other grey-headed ladies to strip themselves of such lies. 'La!,' said the old lady when relating the incident, 'do you know, I thought I should have fainted on the spot.' The command to wear only one skirt (usually of 12 to 16 yards of coarse linen) occasioned rebellious thoughts:

'Do you know I have my doubts sometimes; he [Wroe] has such strange ways. I don't think the Lord concerns himself about such trifles as the number of petticoats that women wear. I thought the old fellow meant to kill us when Wroe ordered only one to be worn; and, do you know, I would not obey the last order – I wore my two. Well, one day in the Sanctuary, Yaacov [i.e. Wroe] got up with his hat on his head and his poker in his hand – ha, ha, ha! – and began arailing against some who had disobeyed the commands, like the old Israelites, and who reasoned and judged and followed their own judgement; but all such should be cut off, and their bodies should die in the wilderness. And then he came to the point, and specified among other things the wearing of two petticoats – oh, criminy! how I did tremble. I thought the old fellow just looked at me, so I hung down my head, for I could not look him in the face, for I know I was guilty; but la! the Lord ain't angry for that, eh?'

The element of caricature or gentle satire in this description is obvious. But it was not Smith's intention to make fun of the Wroeites, and he maintained always that Wroe was a true prophet whose thought had mystery and depth despite his ignorance and want of education. Smith, who had spent his time teaching Hebrew to Ashton cotton-spinners, was well aware of the limitations and potentialities of the faithful. Mrs Riddle serves to remind us of yet another layer in the millenarian mould.

In contrast to Mrs Riddle was one of Smith's characters named Seafield. He was a young man whom Wroe had sent out as a preacher, and who had suffered innumerable hardships in the exercise of his mission — to such an extent that he was now 'in the last stage of a decline'. He was rapidly dying, though with little pain, and took pleasure in talking of the world of spirits, the idea of which he had borrowed, in a simplified way, from Swedenborg's writings. Benjamin (or Smith) was at first oppressed by the pleasure which Seafield took in conversing about his own death, but then realized that Seafield was one of the happiest men he had ever met because of his faith in the millennium. The Christian-Israelite doctrine, explained Smith, is like that of Moses, a doctrine of terrestrial redemption, and does not say anything about the world beyond the grave. But it teaches this peculiar doctrine: that when the millennial kingdom is established the dead will become ministering angels to the church of the redeemed on earth, and will attain immortality. 'I shall see it all, therefore', said Seafield, 'though worms destroy this body, yet still I shall see it.' Which, if any, of the Israelite preachers 'Seafield' was modelled on, we do not know. He was included in Smith's pantheon as a representative or significant figure, perhaps to show the strength and comfort to be derived from millenarian belief.

Wroe's following was strongest in the two towns, Bradford and Ashton-under-Lyne, and in the later nineteenth century the 'Johannas' were incorporated into local folk-history. In Bradford, it is said, crowds used to gather on Sundays to see Prophet Wroe walk in procession along Tyrell Street and Bridge Street to hold a service in the old cock-pit. He was accompanied by twelve virgins, dressed in white and wearing long white veils.[13] In Ashton the impact was greater still.[14] There the believers included, in addition to the usual shopkeepers, artisans and labouring people, several rich and influential townsmen: Samuel Swire, a coal owner and later mayor; the Lees brothers, Henry, Samuel and William, who owned mills; and John Stanley, a one-time mechanic who had risen into the ranks of the property owners. These men were able and willing to finance Wroe's plans for transforming Ashton into the New Jerusalem. A magnificent sanctuary was built in Church Street in 1825 by Stanley at a cost of £9,500; and a mansion fronted with Doric pillars was provided for Wroe on the banks of the river Tame. The boundaries of the town were redrawn, and four 'Gates of the Temple' erected at the four cardinal points on the outskirts of Ashton, to be inhabited by the high priests of the temple. It was intended to link the gates with walls, like a medieval city, but these were never built. However, enough was done in Ashton to indicate the shape of the coming millennial kingdom.

Within the sanctuary, secret and secluded from the world, the Wroeites tasted the joys promised to the Israel of God. The building had thick walls and no windows, being lighted by two glass domes in the roof. It was sumptuously finished, with floors of polished oak and galleries and seating in St Domingo mahogany. All the fittings were of silver and bronze. Two large pulpits, one on each side, reached up to the height of the gallery. At the door two 'office bearers' with drawn swords admitted only those who were dressed in a white linen surplice, called the ephod. The service included much singing, and a band of thirty or forty musicians provided the accompaniment. A hierarchy of high priest, priests and levites, wearing distinctive robes, conducted the services. Wroe took no part in this, but stood or sat in his ordinary clothing in the outer court in the gallery. He was not the minister of the sect, but a prophet. With his hat on his head and his iron rod in his hand he addressed the people from time to time: 'This morning the angel of the Lord appeared unto me and said. ...'[15]

Wroe faded out of the Ashton picture following the charges laid against him in 1831. Public prejudice against him had always been strong – supported by such incidents as the death of an infant a few days after it was circumcised. But in 1830 Wroe said that he was commanded to take seven virgins to cherish and comfort him, and his immoral behaviour with some of them caused dissension among the believers. An inquiry or trial ended in a riot, and Wroe decided to leave town. Even so, his sense of style did not desert him, and he left at the head of a procession, singing chants and hymns in Hebrew, with the society's printing press on a wagon 'drawn by four beautiful horses with uncut manes and tails'. From time to time Wroe returned to Ashton, but his activities were mainly in Yorkshire, and he transferred his headquarters to Wakefield, where the disciples contributed lavishly to his support. He made missionary tours to America and Australia, and died in Melbourne in 1863.[16] The Ashton society continued after his departure but on a reduced scale, and in 1842 the Sanctuary was given up. Elsewhere the Christian Israelites flourished, and in 1853 had fifty societies organized in England, thirteen in Ireland, and a few in Scotland and Wales.[17]

Wroeism invites comparison with other religious movements. William Cooke Taylor was informed in 1842 that many of the Christian

Israelites had been absorbed into Mormonism, and it is not difficult to see points of similarity between the two sects that might make this attractive.[18] Wroe was in many respects a lesser Joseph Smith. The mob violence against Wroe and the attempts on his life were mild presages of the events in Illinois in 1844.[19] The teaching of both men was a vestigial Christianity, heavily overlaid with a new revelation. Both sects were committed to a type of this-worldly redemption; and the building of Zion in Salt Lake City would be no bad exchange for the establishment of the New Jerusalem in Ashton. The same authoritarian rule by the prophet (whose private life was not above reproach), the insistence on observing outward rules and codes of conduct, and the resultant high standards of ethical behaviour (noted by most fair-minded observers) characterized the two cases.

More immediate were questions of the relation of Wroeism to the nonconformist sects in England, particularly the Methodists. Like Joanna, Wroe's first reaction when seeking spiritual comfort was to turn to the Methodists. During his crucial illness in 1819 his wife requested four Methodist preachers to visit him and pray with him, but they all refused. Evidently the leaders of Bradford Methodism, for whatever reasons, had no wish to become compromised by association with the likes of Wroe. On his part Wroe continued to expect some sympathy from their membership: 'a remnant shall come forth from the Methodists and other sects.' He commissioned itinerant field preachers and sent them forth 'without scrip or purse', very much in the manner of Wesley's early preachers. It is plain from their reports that these Israelite preachers were sometimes looked upon by outsiders as a species of enthusiast akin to the Methodists. When Wroe himself was on a preaching tour in the north in 1827 he applied to the mayor of Berwick for permission to preach in the streets and was told to apply to the Methodists first to see if they would lend him their chapel. Only when they refused was he allowed to speak from the steps of the town hall.[20] But though the Methodist leadership was hostile to the Wroeite preachers, the membership was frequently prepared to listen and to provide hospitality. Wroe's prophecies and attempts at healing were not likely to offend many humble Methodists – quite the contrary. And if Mrs Riddle was put out by Wroe's prohibition of false curls, she would have fared no better with Wesley.[21]

The state of Methodism and of sectarian religion in general provides one part of the context of Wroeism: the other part comes from the social and economic changes wrought by the newly emergent industrialism. This context is seen most clearly in the two strongholds of Wroeism,

Bradford and Ashton. In Bradford, the centre of the worsted industry, the change from domestic to factory production with all the classic social ills endemic in the first Industrial Revolution, went on rapidly during the first two decades of the nineteenth century and culminated in a burst of new mills in the 1830s. The town grew at an exceptional rate: from 16,000 in 1811 to 44,000 in 1831, and 67,000 in 1841. The area had for long been strongly nonconformist: originally Baptists and Independents, but later strengthened by Methodists (Wesleyans, Primitives, and other connections). In 1841 there were only two Anglican churches as against eighteen chapels in the town; and in Bradford parish, which included the out-lying townships, the figures were 16 and 70. Ashton, though smaller, was much the same. There the dominant industries of coal and cotton-spinning were producing another rapidly expanding factory town, with accelerating growth in the 1820s and 1830s. But in Ashton opposition to economic and social change from the church and lord of the manor (the Earl of Stamford) hampered the development of a full industrial society until after the ending of the Napoleonic Wars. Nonconformists had difficulty in establishing themselves in the town as they were frequently unable to acquire land or premises for their chapels. Nevertheless, such opposition served only to strengthen feeling against the establishment; and the Methodists and Independents made headway. In 1841 Ashton had seven churches and twenty-nine chapels. Wroeism flourished in a situation in which, first, there was unparalleled social disruption, resulting from the destruction of a traditional way of life and the emergence of new classes and relationships; and in which, second, the established church (led by 'blind guides' and 'dumb dogs that do not bark') failed to 'preach the Word', thus leaving the way clear for Methodists and independent sectarians.[22]

Given this context, it is possible to see Wroeism as a search for order and authority in a period of social and religious chaos. Such an analysis is not new; and an interesting version of it was in fact put forward by Shepherd Smith in *The Coming Man*.[23] He drew a comparison between the old domestic industry of the country and what he called the 'social system' of production in large factories. The latter system was 'subduing' the former, and as the change progressed the character of the population was undergoing 'an evident and corresponding revolution'. The domestic system was 'timid, and ignorant, rude, superstitious, credulous', but also basically 'sober and orderly', except on festal occasions when all classes ran to excess. By comparison the social system was 'bold, intellectual, and argumentative, crammed with one-sided facts, irreverent and suspicious of all instruction that did not come from its own class or from those who flattered its own tastes.' The authority of rulers, clergymen and parents was questioned; the rising generation was determined to find truth for itself and to be humbugged by no one. Wroeism, argued Shepherd Smith, was a response of people who were worried and confused by the social and moral changes of their time. It was a reaction to the 'chaos in which authority was destroyed in the heart.' Wroe provided the authority for which men yearned by setting up a spiritual despotism. And by a strange paradox 'he gathered his flock out of the very midst of the children of liberalism.'

This type of explanation is satisfactory as far as it goes; but it tends to be vague and open-ended. The context of social disruption through industrial change plus a seed-bed of Methodism and sectarian religion is general rather than particular. Can we sharpen the focus of our lens on the Christian Israelites? Unfortunately we do not have any lists of the Wroeite membership nor any records to show fluctuations in numbers. Questions of social class, response to specific economic and social changes, and relation to contemporary political and religious institutions are therefore difficult to answer. It would be extremely useful in analysing the social role of millenarianism if we knew, for instance, how many Wroeites were depressed hand-loom weavers, how many were tradesmen or mill owners, and what were their religious experiences before and after their membership of the Christian Israelites. Information on such points, however, is at best fragmentary and inconclusive, and has to be deduced obliquely from reference to other matters. For example, Shepherd Smith nowhere says explicitly that working men formed part of the membership at Ashton. But in discussing the problem of enforcing religious discipline on the faithful he remarks:

> The most riotous were the working men. They were most
> independent. Many of them were bold impudent, and defied the
> prophet to his teeth, and were thrust out of the society; and some of
> them returned over and over again, penitent and in tears, petitioning
> for readmission, and promising obedience and submission thereafter.
> They were generally allowed to give another trial of their patience.[24]

This not only establishes the presence of working men, but implies much else, such as the kind of men they were, the nature of Wroe's charisma, and the internal problems of the sect. A tantalizing picture of millenarian cotton-spinners or hand-loom weavers is conjured up, but alas is doomed to fade for lack of historical sustenance. Yet the picture once glimpsed cannot be entirely forgotten.

Wroe's prophecies and communications contain a number of social references, but the interpretation of some of them is obscure. Clearly he was not concerned to elaborate a programme of social and political reform like an Owenite or Chartist; but he was concerned with a this-worldly regime for his followers, who were not totally withdrawn from society and who needed guidance in their relations with it. In general he advocated non-involvement in social and political issues:

> Let not my children interfere with the concerns of the nations ...; the manufacturers of all branches shall be against the land-owners, and the land-owners against them; and they that are of Israel will not interfere with them.[25]

In 1831 he prophesied the delays which would be encountered in passing the Reform Bill, the building of the York and Whitby railway, and the cholera epidemic. Like Joanna he had little difficulty in foretelling poor harvests and periods of commercial distress such as 1825–6. He condemned the new Poor Law of 1834 because it separated husbands and wives in the workhouse, and saw in it the fulfilment of Daniel 12:11 ('the abomination that maketh desolate').

At times Wroe was brought into more direct contact with social conflict. He was by trade a wool-comber, and although he had presumably given up wool-combing when he became a full-time prophet, he would know and be known by the wool-combers in Bradford. Wool-combing was a skilled handicraft, crucial to the whole worsted trade, and the wool-combers were organized in a powerful union. In 1825 they called a calamitous strike (the Bradford Turn-Out) which lasted for five months and involved a total of 20,000 to 30,000 wool-combers and weavers in the West Riding.[26] The wool-combers were forced back to work on the employers' terms, after suffering great hardships; and their defeat was followed by an employers' ban on the union and the introduction of machine-combing. With their trade virtually extinguished and their union existing only in secret, the wool-combers were in a sorry plight. The following year there were riots in Bradford against the introduction of power looms for worsted weaving; and the hand-loom weavers soon found themselves in the same distressed condition as the wool-combers. These traumatic experiences of workers in the worsted industry coincided with Wroe's hegemony in the Christian–Israelite movement, and it is tempting to look for some relationship between the two phenomena. Were there Wroeites among the striking wool-combers? Is there any evidence of a turning to millenarian sects in this time of hardship and despair? We cannot answer these questions with any degree of assurance. That Wroe was in some way involved in the Bradford Turn-Out seems probable, but his exact role, if any, is obscure. The accounts given in his *Life and Travels* and in the *Preachers' Letters, 1825* seem designed to conceal as much as they reveal.[27] On Sunday, 18 July 1825, he addressed a large meeting in Bradford, at which he said that the striking wool-combers would fail to get their advance in wages, 'for their attempt was a work of evil.' This enraged his hearers, who threatened to pull his house down when the strike was ended. The employers sarcastically commented: 'We may as well give up, for Wroe has prophesied that we shall overcome them, and anything that he prophesies is sure to turn out contrary.' On the following day Wroe was visited at home by four men from the Wakefield district, who 'pretended they were come to ask how the turn-out combers would succeed.' Who they were and what their real purpose was remains a mystery. Perhaps they were in some way connected with the union, or maybe they wished to consult him in his capacity as a wise man. Wroe repeated his prophecy that the wool-combers would be defeated, but added that the Lord would also afflict the employers and that the banks would fail. This in fact happened during the commercial crisis at the end of 1825; and his forecast of the wool-combers' defeat was grimly accurate: 'many [wool-combers] of the town and neighbourhood of Bradford were seen in the fields, getting blackberries, nettles, etc., for very hunger, and went to the public houses to beg grains, from the same cause.' One could speculate endlessly about what Wroe was up to at this time: why his prophecies of failure (hardly likely to be popular) should have been listened to and taken seriously; whether he was trying to distance himself from the struggle by calling a plague on both your houses; what were the motives of the four mysterious men who visited him. But, like so much of the story of Yorkshire trade unionism in this period, we can in the end catch only glimpses through the mists of obscurity which enshroud the subject. Whatever part Wroe played in the Bradford Turn-Out, he took care that the official version of it should be made innocuous to the point of fatuity. We can sharpen our focus on the Wroeites, but only certain arbitrarily selected aspects are visible.

Shortly after the Bradford Turn-Out, Wroe heard for the first time of John (Zion) Ward (1781–1837), the last of the false prophets to be mentioned here. At that time Ward was living in Walworth, a hotbed of millenarianism. He was a labouring man and a seeker, whose spiritual autobiography is a notable addition to our collection of this genre.[28] As a child in Ireland he was frightened by the scriptural accounts of the torments of hell, and developed a strong awareness of sin. In 1790 he came to Bristol with his parents and was apprenticed as a shipwright, but soon fell into bad company (obscenity, swearing and cursing). This, he said, 'increased my sense of guilt.' Before three years of the apprenticeship had passed he removed to London with his father, and learned shoemaking from his brother. He then entered the navy as a shipwright, and fell in with evil company once more. His sense of guilt lay on him like a heavy burden, and he feared to read his Bible because of the mockery of his companions. At the battle of Copenhagen, serving on the man-of-war, *Blanche*, he was terrified and resolved to leave the navy. After being paid off at Sheerness in 1803, he married and settled down to the business of a shoemaker. His wife was fond of listening to preachers, and their family life was dominated by evangelical religion. However, he was restless, in both body and spirit, and the family moved to Carmarthen in Wales for three years. There he joined the Methodists and sought earnestly for salvation, but in vain. He returned to London, recommenced shoemaking, and resolved to give up all religion. One day he wandered into Sion Chapel in Lant Street, Southwark, and after listening to the minister, the Reverend Jeremiah Learnoult Garrett, became a Baptist.[29] He was convinced of sin; and yet, he says, 'I found no peace.' Following dissensions in the Lant Street chapel, he left and joined another set of Calvinists, but then moved on to the Sandemanians, for whom he became a preacher in 1813.

Ward first became acquainted with Joanna's mission at the time of her death in 1814. He read her *Fifth Book of Wonders*, received it as the word of God, and became, he says, greatly comforted by her message. However, he was not welcomed by the Southcottians, who probably suspected him of unorthodox views and an over-eagerness to preach. He therefore went back to the Methodists and became a local preacher for them, but was dismissed (he claims) because of his Southcottian beliefs. Ward became a follower of Turner, and was present at the Marriage Supper in London in 1820 when Turner announced the coming of Shiloh. For ten years (1815–25) Ward remained a seeker, reading his Bible and searching for a new revelation. In his own words he explained his millennial hopes:

> I was earnestly looking out for some one to be visited by the Spirit, to revive the work, and raise up the cause of God, that was so trodden under foot by the persecuting spirit in the religious sects and parties, who with one united voice cried down the visitation of the Spirit to Joanna, and all visitations of the kind. ... I went everywhere that I heard of any one being visited by the Spirit of God to prophesy, in hopes of finding the truth, in the Lord's appearing, according to the word.

In this mood in 1825 he encountered Mary Boon. 'I read her prophecies with great attention, for the command in Scripture was upon my mind, "despise not prophesyings".' He concluded that her communications were from God and that in her was manifested the return of Joanna's spirit. Accordingly he 'united with her visitation', and was shortly chosen as 'the reader of the word to the people'. He also acted as her secretary, and adopted the observances of Judaism which she enjoined. For Ward's long-suffering wife this was the last straw. She had always opposed his belief in Joanna, and resented his seeking and preaching to the detriment of his shoemaking and the support of his large family. Now he appeared to have taken up with another woman, and insisted on keeping the Jewish sabbath and observing strange dietary habits. 'I was ordered by the word,' he said, 'through the Prophetess, to become a eunuch for the kingdom of heaven's sake, and ... to separate from my wife.' Presumably he interpreted this text from Matthew 19:12 metaphorically rather than literally, and explained that it was revealed to him that the eunuch represents God's elect servant.

For the next three years (until 1828) Ward suffered 'the invisible work of regeneration'. He was visited with dreams and visions, and tormented as to his true identity. Finally he realized that he was Shiloh. Had he not been present at Turner's celebration for the arrival of Shiloh?: the believers had been mistaken in looking for a heavenly visitor: the promised Shiloh (in the person of Ward) had indeed been there, but they had not recognized him. As the implications of this claim were gradually borne in on him, and as he devoted more and more time to working out his doctrinal position, his shoemaking was neglected. At last his voice told him to stop working altogether. His wife in desperation appealed to the local magistrate, who committed Ward to Newington workhouse. He still refused to work, however, and in November 1828 escaped and went to Charles William Twort's house in Walworth. Twort was a 'visited' character and in touch with some of the believers. He immediately accepted Ward's claims and became his constant companion and chief supporter. Ward said that he was now 'a new man, spiritually named Zion'; and his followers, who shortly began to gather, dated the new dispensation from his visitation in 1825.

Southcottianism was given yet another twist as Ward proclaimed that he was not only Shiloh, but also God and Christ and Satan. He arrived at this apparently blasphemous position from the doctrines which he had worked out during the three year period of his visitation.[30] The scriptures were intended only to baffle human skill and reason, and the self-wisdom of the learned. Many happenings described in the Bible never occurred literally: the first chapter of Genesis, for example, is not an account of the creation of the material world (which has no beginning or end), but a description of the new creation of man through the mysterious wisdom of God. The prophecies describe, in figurative language, the creation of a new mind and heart in man (the incarnation of the divine nature) in these latter days. Jesus Christ is not an actual person who lived 1800 years ago, but is the principle of divine light, love and wisdom, now come to redeem mankind. Ward denied the historical Jesus – his birth, miracles, death, resurrection and ascension. There is no such place as heaven above the sky, he assured his followers: 'Heaven must be in man, and in man is the Judgement Seat of Christ.' Whether Ward was talking of a type of mystical deification open to all believers is not very clear. In 1831–2 he told his congregations that every person was (or could be) Christ and in a state of sinlessness. But in his previous formulations on the question of the millennium and the second coming he reserved a special place for himself. As a good Southcottian he believed that the last days had already begun; but he spiritualized the second coming to mean his own revelation of the true nature of scripture and divine wisdom. Before this revelation he was in a fallen state because of his reliance on human reason and the false religion of the churches: he was in fact Satan. After his revelation he was Jesus Christ – and he remembered, appropriately enough, that his birthday was 25 December and that his mother's name was Mary. 'This', he said, 'is the great mystery of the scriptures, that Satan became Christ.'

Shocking as these doctrines seemed to orthodox Christians, they were not original to Ward. Apart from their similarity to ancient heresies in the church, they flourished among small groups of radicals and seekers, especially in the late 1820s and early 1830s. Richard Carlile, the radical republican, had worked his way from deism via atheism to an allegorical Christianity. He championed the Ashton Wroeite, Henry Lees, who in 1824 was charged with manslaughter following the death of a child whom he had circumcised. Carlile was also in touch with the Muggletonians in Nottingham and London, and knew about the case of Joseph Dylks, the American Leatherwood God, who is discussed in chapter 7.[31] Carlile was joined at the Rotunda in Blackfriars Road by the Reverend Robert Taylor, 'the Devil's Chaplain'. Taylor's deism was based on his own esoteric blend of comparative religion, mythology and astronomy. He traced the gospel story to astronomical beliefs held in antiquity, and argued that Jesus Christ was not an historical figure but a personification of general wishes or principles. It seems probable that Ward was influenced by Carlile and Taylor, for he was unlikely to have arrived at his doctrine of the allegory of scripture entirely unaided.[32] Certainly he knew them by September 1831, when he lectured in the Rotunda.

Shepherd Smith's doctrine of universalism also contained similar elements. He was acquainted with Ward – 'who is very estimable as a man, also his doctrine, much of which I admire as a principle.'[33] At the centre of Smith's universalism were the three ideas of polarity, analogy and the spiritual millennium.[34] The concept of polarity, or apparent contradictions, was based on the discovery that God and the devil were one and the same. It may have been that Smith developed this view out of a need to preserve his faith at the time of Wroe's departure from Ashton; for it enabled him to recognize that Wroe was evil even though he was a genuine prophet of God. The problem of evil in a world created by a benevolent God, Smith solved by declaring that what was called evil was in fact part of the divine plan for the ultimate realization of the millennium. This was the basic polarity. It was only an apparent contradiction, and likewise other contradictions were susceptible to the same interpretation. All philosophies and beliefs and movements contained some truth – and also falsehood – for all were part of God's plan, though none was final or complete in itself. The unity of God and the devil, good and evil, virtue and vice gave Smith a broad tolerance and sympathy towards any doctrine or movement in which he could find an element of truth. In his journal, *The Shepherd*, his emphasis was on unity, the reconciliation of opposites, and demonstration of the need for contradictions to arrive at truth.

Closely connected with his doctrine of polarity was Smith's 'science of analogy'. The eighteenth century had been fond of the analogies of scripture with nature; and we have already noted the attraction of Swedenborgianism for some artisan seekers. Somewhat in this tradition Smith argued that

> a perfect analogy subsists between the physical and the metaphysical, or moral, world. The same laws are at work in each, for both belong to the universal nature which is one grand unity throughout.[35]

A belief in the 'religion of progress' followed from this doctrine: as man developed through successive stages of his history, so God revealed himself in new and appropriate ways. This led to Smith's third idea – universalism or the millennium – since orthodox Christianity, which had earlier superseded Judaism, was now in its turn no longer adequate to the stage which man's development had reached. The millennium which Smith anticipated was defined in a spiritual sense. His early belief in a personal second coming of Christ was superseded by the discovery that:

> the true Messiah was a divine principle, or in other words, the spirit of
> God manifested in the adoption of a beneficent ruling principle by
> human society; and that, whenever the fundamental character of
> Christianity, namely social love and equality, was received as the basis
> of political government, then it might be positively asserted that
> Christ was come, and that the Messiah had begun to reign.[36]

When the millennium was begun all men would become Christ in a
spiritual sense: the messiah was the spirit of truth. (At the same time,
Smith did not rule out entirely the possibility of a physical second
coming, for he had the millenarian's strong sense of crisis and longing to
participate in the battle of the last days.)

Within this framework Smith was able to accommodate other doctrines
familiar to Ward. Smith accepted the Bible as historically true, but was
also prepared to use it allegorically. The second coming, for instance,
while taking a spiritual form would repeat the pattern of the first: it
would be effected by a minority of reformers and iconoclasts, who would
be rejected by the chosen people, persecuted and finally triumphant. The
existing Christian churches were Antichrist, and would therefore be
destroyed, so that the millennium could begin. At the same time the
restoration of the Jews would take place, in the sense that the 'truths' of
Judaism would be incorporated in the third dispensation, which would
thus be the new Israel, or Christ's kingdom on earth. From the principle
of analogy it was reasonable to expect that the millennium, which was
'the period of the Lord's coming in spirit', would come not to professing
Christians, but to infidels. 'The Jews rejected Christ; and from analogy
we may conclude that the Christians will oppose the introduction of the
Millennium by the spirit of liberty.'[37]

Shepherd Smith's arguments were of course more sophisticated than
Ward's. Whereas Smith relied on intellectual, rational processes, Ward
was guided by the Spirit. Nevertheless, Smith's position is relevant for
placing Ward in context and also for demonstrating some of the
possibilities of millenarian development inherent in Southcottianism
once false prophets were unchecked. 'He [Ward] is not a man possessed
of much information, but he has contrived to gather around him many
possessed of more learning and knowledge than himself', commented
Smith.[38] Most of those who gathered around him at first had been
believers in Joanna and Turner. Ward regarded himself as Joanna's
successor, in his role of Shiloh and (later) Christ, and his first book, *The
Vision of Judgement* (1829) was subtitled *or the Return of Joanna from her*

Trance. During and immediately after his confinement in the workhouse Ward wrote to various groups of Southcottians and attempted to win their recognition for his claims.[39] The Old Guard completely rejected him; and Foley condemned his book as 'a Satanic deceit'. Ward tried to woo John Finlayson, who still carried the flag for Brothers, by admitting that Brothers was a true prophet; but without much success. He also failed to convince Carpenter and his followers at the House of God. It therefore seemed prudent to leave his home base in Walworth and visit the believers elsewhere. Accompanied by the faithful Twort, Ward set out on a provincial tour in 1829 and continued his travels throughout 1830. At Nottingham, Chesterfield, Worksop, Blyth, Barnsley, Sheffield and Birmingham he made converts, and also encountered 'extreme opposition and persecution from the religious of all sects, more especially the professed Christians.'[40] He seems to have had most success in the Midlands; and Birmingham and Nottingham became his chief strongholds. Believers opened chapels for him; and according to Shepherd Smith he gained nearly 2,000 followers in two years.[41]

Ward reached the height of his influence in 1831. Most of the year he remained in London (apart from a short visit to Ashton, where he hoped, vainly, to be accepted as Wroe's successor). An advertisement in the *Judgement Seat of Christ* announced his weekly programme: 'the Borough Chapel, High Street, Borough is open for preaching of the Everlasting Gospel on Sunday mornings at half past ten o'clock, afternoons at three, and in the evenings at half past six.' He also preached at chapels in Finsbury Square and Hackney. But he met with opposition, especially from rival Southcottians in the Southwark area, such as Elizabeth Fairlight Vaughan.[42] She was an old (and orthodox) believer in Joanna, and something of a prophetess in her own right; and she set herself firmly against all false prophets, including Carpenter and his House of God, Wroe and his Israelites, and Ward and his Shilohites.

An increasing radicalism in Ward's teaching alienated still further the orthodox Southcottians. On his tour the previous year he had begun to attack the establishment, and had found that this was well received. 'Priestcraft detected! Its overthrow projected! How this can be effected', screamed one of his handbills. Back in London he began to associate with Richard Carlile's radical circle at the Rotunda, and delivered a series of discourses there. The government, as with Brothers in 1795 and Turner in 1817, became alarmed at the radical implications of the millenarian message. The rising of the agricultural labourers (Captain Swing) and the struggle for parliamentary reform produced an atmosphere of nervousness in government circles comparable to the earlier periods of repression in the 1790s and 1817–19. In January 1831 Carlile was indicted for sedition and sentenced to two years' imprisonment; and in July the Reverend Robert Taylor was given a similar sentence for blasphemy. The government kept an eye on Ward, as also did the Society for the Suppression of Vice. The Borough Chapel, as well as the Rotunda, were kept under surveillance.[43] It was not long before Ward overstepped the bounds of legal propriety, and the government was quick to pounce. He and Twort went to the Midlands on a preaching tour, and at Derby were brought to book for their attacks on the established church.[44] 'The Bishops and Clergy are Religious Impostors, and as such by the Laws of England liable to Corporal Punishment', proclaimed one of Ward's handbills. Ward and Twort were prosecuted for blasphemy in August 1832 and each was sentenced to eighteen months' imprisonment in Derby gaol. Ward made good use of his enforced leisure by studying hard and by issuing frequent 'epistles' to the faithful.[45] After his release in February 1834 he continued his preaching tours, as there had been some falling away among the believers while he was in prison.

In October 1834 Ward began a brief association with James Pierrepont Greaves, the 'Sacred Socialist' (1777–1842). Greaves was a rich merchant turned philanthropist and educational reformer, who had acquired something of a reputation as a sage and mystic.[46] He was an admirer of Thomas Taylor, the Platonist, and had studied Boehme, William Law and neo-Platonism. Greaves was a devotee of vegetarianism, celibacy and general asceticism as a means of attaining spiritual ends; and thought for a time that Ward could be similarly persuaded. Accordingly he was 'very liberal in helping the cause', and would have been more so (to the extent of providing a chapel) if Ward had been more co-operative. At his first meeting with Greaves, Ward had been on his guard against 'philosophy and learning'; but then became more impressed – and tempted. However, he rejected the temptation: first, he said, because Greaves' attempt to attain divinity by a self-imposed regimen of 'bread and water' was erroneous; and, second, because he wished to remain independent of Greaves and his rich friends – 'I will never run after anyone for their money, nor for their favours.' So, to his credit, Ward refused to be seduced from the truth of his visitation as he saw it, and concluded that Greaves was guilty of pride and self-love although he appeared to be very pious. Ward made his home at Bristol, and later at Leeds, where he died in 1837 following a series of strokes which had partly incapacitated him for two years previously. His congregations melted away after his death, but in

Birmingham and Nottingham a faithful remnant kept his memory alive and republished his works.[47]

The false prophets were false only in that they were not acceptable to the majority of Southcottians, more especially those who had been closest to Joanna during her lifetime and those who subsequently thought of themselves as the orthodox or old believers. But the false prophets were successful in winning acceptance by a minority of Southcottians. Their strength was local or regional, particularly in the industrial north and Midlands, and in parts of London such as Southwark. Each prophet was anxious to claim the exclusive inheritance of Joanna as a powerful aid to his legitimation; but his authority was derived from the direct power of the Spirit. New doctrines and observances were commanded by the Spirit through the prophet, and usually represented an extension or distortion of some aspect of Joanna's teachings. From the usual millenarian speculation about the return of the Jews in the last days could develop Wroe's Christian Israelism; from Joanna's emphasis on types and shadows one could lead on to Ward's doctrine of the scriptures as allegorical. With the false prophets the tendency towards the formation of separate sects was greatly strengthened. Joanna had recommended the believers to be loyal members of the Church of England, but she had also sanctioned the use of Southcottian chapels with their own preachers. Like the Methodists after the death of Wesley, the Southcottians found that the logic of their position after 1814 impelled them to independent sectarianism. For Joanna it was just tolerable that she should attend Anglican services to receive the sacrament: for Wroe and Ward the notion was unthinkable. This change partly represented the altered social context in which the false prophets were operating. In the 1820s and 1830s the social and psychic needs of those who were attracted to millenarianism were different in form, and possibly to some extent in content, from the needs of millenarians in Joanna's day. The day-by-day impressions of the French Revolution and the struggle against Napoleon had faded; the pressures of the new industrial society had increased enormously; the strengthening of the Nonconformists relative to the established church was plain for all to see. The false prophets were keen to wear Joanna's mantle, but they had to give a new interpretation to her message.

PART III

THE MILLENNIAL DAWN

CHAPTER SEVEN

PECULIAR PEOPLES

So far millenarian belief has been presented in the context of popular life and thought in Britain. But this is not entirely adequate for a full appreciation of millenarianism. Some questions – such as the uniqueness or otherwise of British millenarianism – can only be answered by going outside the British context. In other cases, for example the Shakers, the story is incomplete if it is limited chronologically and geographically. A comparative approach, using material from two different but not too dissimilar societies, therefore seems prima facie likely to be useful. No elaborate methodology of comparison is proposed here: simply the use of one society to suggest areas and approaches in the other. From this could come hypotheses which may or may not be confirmed. It is a method for alerting us to points which we might otherwise miss through taking them for granted, for extending the range of our hypotheses. An Anglo-American comparison is an obvious, though by no means the only possibility for such an approach.[1]

The millenarians of the late eighteenth and early nineteenth centuries assumed a universal validity for their claims. They felt that, despite the great differences between British and American society, millennial beliefs were interchangeable or perhaps supranational. After all, the events of the last days were to be played out on a cosmic scale. In practice the cultural similarities between the two societies facilitated exchanges of ideas and personnel. The common background of Protestant evangelicalism and the tradition of dissent from the seventeenth century eased the task of itinerant millenarians. Some sects, like the Shakers and Mormons, were for a time virtually Anglo-American. Others, notably the Southcottians and Millerites, made little headway outside their country of origin.

We do not, however, always have to take contemporaries at their face value. Millennial beliefs were not necessarily identical in Britain and

America just because they had the same origin or bore the same labels. There were some subtle differences, and also (unexpected) similarities. To illustrate this we shall consider three American religious movements which in their different ways were millenarian: the Shakers, Mormons and Millerites. An extended treatment of the historical problems posed by these three sects, fascinating as it would be, is beyond the scope of this study. We are concerned with millenarianism as a constituent of popular belief, and only secondarily with religious institutions. We shall therefore select only those aspects of Shakerism, Mormonism and Millerism that are directly relevant to our purpose, trusting that this may nevertheless be sufficient to shake some of our cruder notions of British uniqueness and American exceptionalism.

The little band of Shakers who, as described in chapter 2, followed Ann Lee to New York in 1774, did not immediately meet with much success in spreading their gospel.[2] Their fate might well have been to disappear from sight as completely as the Buchanites who followed them to America sixteen years later. On arrival the Shakers had to split up, some members finding employment in Albany, while the prophetess worked in New York as a laundress. John Hocknell, the only affluent member of the group, enabled the society to purchase a tract of land at Niskeyuna, near Albany, NY, and there in 1776 the members were reunited and began the hard manual toil of earning a living and creating a community in the wilderness. After four years they began to attract converts, thanks to the New Light revival among the Baptists in New Lebanon, NY, and neighbouring towns in Massachusetts. Among these new adherents was Joseph Meacham, a lay preacher from Enfield, Connecticut, who was later to become leader of the sect. As with other millenarian movements, the recruitment to the Shakers came in the first instance largely from those who were already religiously awakened. Seekers after salvation who could not find spiritual rest in the churches created out of the doctrines of 'the great awakening' came to investigate the claims of the Shakers, and some remained to stay. Ann Lee died in 1784, by which time there were perhaps a thousand believers in New England and New York state. Two decades later another revival enabled the Shakers to repeat the 'gathering' process. The Kentucky Revival of 1799–1806 proved to be a fertile ground for Shaker missionaries. The New Lights, 'Schismatics', and other seceders from the orthodox Baptist, Presbyterian and Methodist congregations were precisely the people likely to be attracted by the challenging demands and far-reaching claims of the Shakers. Richard McNemar, a Presbyterian minister and leader of the New Lights, repeated the role of Joseph

Meacham earlier and became an influential Shaker elder. From their base in the north-east the Shakers expanded westward into Ohio, Kentucky, and Indiana. At the end of the eighteenth century there were eleven communities, and in 1803 the membership was between 1,300 and 1,400. By 1823 the numbers had risen to 4,100; and in the decade 1840–50 a peak of 5,500 to 6,000 in eighteen separate communities was reached. After the Civil War the numbers declined steadily, and by 1910 had fallen to about 1,000. The early period of Shakerism, up to c. 1806, was essentially the time of gathering, master-minded by Joseph Meacham. Thereafter, until the mid years of the nineteenth century, Shakerism in most respects reached its apogee.

Converts to Shakerism found that they had opted for a kind of lay monasticism. They became members of a small community, based on celibacy and common ownership of goods. Each society was subdivided into several 'families', consisting of between thirty and a hundred persons who functioned as an independent economic unit. Men and women lived side by side but were organized in strict separation. The family was governed by two elders and two eldresses, who in turn were subject to the central ministry of the society. The New Lebanon society enjoyed a primacy over the other societies who looked to it for a 'lead'. This structure was rigid and hierarchical, and the central ministry at New Lebanon (where ultimate authority was vested in the chief elder) was self-perpetuating. A further organizational refinement was the classification of members into orders or classes (sometimes, confusingly, called families) according to their degree of commitment. Thus newcomers were members of the novitiate order and retained their own property and natural family life; in the junior order the convert still owned his own property but dedicated its use to the community; and in the highest or church order all worldly goods were given to the society and a covenant was signed to this effect.

The Shaker communal system ('Gospel Order') attracted wide-spread attention from travellers and social reformers in the first half of the nineteenth century, who seldom failed to admire the Shakers' Puritan simplicity and prosperity while ridiculing their celibacy and religious 'absurdities'.[3] To many utopian reformers Shakerism demonstrated the practicability of communitarianism. But the Shakers had no original theory of collectivism, and owned no debt to earlier communitarian movements. Gospel Order emerged from pragmatic experience. The social and economic implications of life on the frontier, and the problems posed by celibacy and withdrawal from the world, led the Shakers to formulate their communitarian system, which could later be equated with apostolic Christianity. This element in Shakerism was given prominence later, notably during the leadership of Frederick W. Evans, an English immigrant who was converted from Owenism. In Ann Lee's original revelations there was little attention paid to such matters, which only became urgent when the number of followers increased. It was the working out of the logic of Shaker beliefs that created the need for communism. Other millenarians faced this same problem of how to give practical effect to their beliefs; but few solved it so completely as the Shakers. Ann Lee's revelations and contacts were not superior to Joanna Southcott's; yet the institutional strength of the Shakers was far greater than the Southcottians. It is an interesting speculation to consider what might have been the future of Southcottianism had Joanna been succeeded, not by Turner and Wroe, but by leaders of the calibre of the early Shaker elders and eldresses, James Whittaker, Joseph Meacham, and Lucy Wright. The millenarian beliefs of Shakers and Southcottians had much in common – and also some important differences – and this prompts comparative questions about the functional role of the two sets of beliefs. Did people become Shakers for the same kind of reasons as they became Southcottians? How were these beliefs related to social and intellectual life at the popular level on both sides of the Atlantic? Did statements of apparently the same belief have the same meaning in the two cultures?

Mother Ann (or, simply, Mother), as Ann Lee was known to believers, was a figure very similar to Joanna or Mrs Buchan. In each case there was the humble background of labouring life in the eighteenth century, the search for religious experience, the escape from sexual reality, the signs and revelations, and the final, stupendous claim to divine authority and the announcement of the millennium. 'It is not I that speak', Mother Ann told her followers when describing her 'grand vision' while imprisoned in Manchester, 'it is Christ who dwells in me.' She said that she walked with Christ, 'as with a lover ... I am married to the Lord Jesus Christ. He is my head and my husband, and I have no other.'[4] In later Shaker theology (as developed, for instance, by Frederick [Shaker] Evans), this appearance of Christ to Mother Ann in 1770 was the second advent.[5] The millennium (or Kingdom) began in 1792, when Gospel Order was fully established. This marked the ending of the 1,260 days ('the reign of the beast'); the cleansing of the sanctuary (i.e. the foundation of the Shaker church) then took place, and sin was finally conquered. Continuing his interpretation of the Book of Revelation, Evans equated Mother Ann with the woman in the wilderness, who escaped from the dragon, which (with a fine Americanization of prophetic chronology) he identified with the English church and state. Prophecy had been fulfilled in that Ann was Christ in his second appearing, this time in female form.

Refinements and variants of Shaker millennial doctrine are found at different periods in the history of the church. The 1848 edition of *A Summary View of the Millennial Church* inclined to a spiritual interpretation of the second coming ('Christ as the elemental spirit of eternal life'), and rejected any literal arrival of the Son of Man 'coming in the clouds of heaven'.[6] These clouds, it was argued, were clouds of faithful witnesses of God. No sudden, cataclysmic change was to be looked for, but rather a gradual and steady advance of mankind towards 'the light of the millennial day'. A dispensational theory in support of Shaker millennial claims was first elaborated by Joseph Meacham, using the prophet Ezekiel's vision of the holy waters (chapter 47) and the 'four living creatures' of Revelation 4. Four periods or dispensations of human history were distinguished, during which there had been a progressive unfolding of God's purpose, culminating in the Shaker millennial 'church of the Last Dispensation'.[7] The intricacies and ingenuities of Shaker millennial theology were fully up to the standard of other millenarian sects, and to that extent were likely to satisfy the inquiring seeker after millenarian truth. Further millenarian satisfactions of a different kind also derived from Shaker beliefs.

Central to Shakerism, and distinguishing its believers from the world, was what Henri Desroche has called ascetic feminism. The roots of this belief about the nature of sin, sex and marriage are traceable to Mother Ann's experiences. According to official Shaker sources, 'It is remarkable, that, in early youth, she had a great abhorrence of the fleshy cohabitation of the sexes, and so great was her sense of its impurity, that she often admonished her mother against it', for which her father, a blacksmith, tried to whip her.[8] She was the second eldest of eight children, and her mother died (perhaps in childbirth) while Ann was still young. When Ann in her turn came to be married, she bore four children, all of whom died in infancy. This turned her against her husband, Abraham Standerin (or Stanley), also a blacksmith, and confirmed her distaste for sexual relations.

By the immediate revelation of Christ, she henceforth bore an open testimony against the lustful gratifications of the flesh, as the source and foundation of human corruption; and testified ... that no soul could follow Christ ... while living in the works of natural generation, or in any of the gratifications of lust.[9]

Abraham Standerin accompanied his wife to America, and she nursed him through a long illness in New York; but she 'refused to live in the flesh with him', and he finally left her for another woman.

Mother Ann's revelation made it clear that the source of all evil was ultimately sex. In the usual manner of millenarians she and her followers had little difficulty in appropriating biblical texts in support of their doctrine. Original sin was the sexual act into which Adam and Eve were tempted by the serpent, and the forbidden fruit of which they partook was lust.[10] From this came the institution of marriage, which thus had its origin in the fall of man. Marriage, in fact, is no more than legitimized or institutionalized lust. Or, as Mother Ann expressed it, 'marriage of the flesh is a covenant with death and an agreement with Hell.'[11] Celibacy is therefore enjoined on all who would enter the kingdom of heaven. Only by giving up the 'lusts of the flesh' and 'filthy gratifications', and by overcoming the passions could salvation be attained. In the words of a Shaker song of 1838:

My carnal life I will lay down
Because it is depraved.
I'm sure on any other ground
I never can be saved.[12]

The Shakers never underestimated the difficulties and personal suffering that this doctrine could entail. In Shaker language 'to take up one's cross' meant embracing celibacy. Married converts gave up cohabitation and went through a form of de-marrying. Single converts, after making a full confession of their sins, found themselves surrounded by regulations designed to reduce to a minimum the risk of sexual passion. Life in a Shaker family was elaborately organized on monastic principles. The very architecture, with its separate accommodation for men and women, wide or dual staircases to avoid physical contact between the sexes, and spartan simplicity to discourage romantic affections, reflected the same values. Detailed rules (later known as Separation Acts) were laid down for daily behaviour. It was 'contrary to order' for brethren and sisters to milk together; for a brother and sister to eat at one table, unless there was some company; for a sister to go to the barn, wood-house or road alone; for the brethren to go into the room when the sisters were making the beds. It was also forbidden 'to look at beasts when they copulate' and 'to allow any copulation productive of mongrelism.'[13] The apostate Thomas Brown has a story about three young women at Niskeyuna who 'amused themselves by attending to the amour of two flies in the window'. They were observed by one of the eldresses, who ordered them, 'for thus gratifying their carnal inclinations' to strip themselves naked and whip each other.[14]

This was the negative side of Shaker belief about sex, the crucifixion of lust. Against it could be set the positive conviction that the Shaker family was superior to the marriage familism of the world, and afforded the means to salvation. In a small community, withdrawn from the world, and with a flourishing economy based on farming, gardening and handicrafts, Shaker beliefs about the family appeared practicable and attractive. So it seemed to many visitors who came away from Shaker societies impressed. The Shakers were not the only people in the early nineteenth century who felt the need for some form of social organization other than the private family. Owenites and others saw in community life the alternative they were seeking — alternative to the assumptions, attitudes and values of the family in existing society.[15] Frederick Evans is the best known of those who actually made the transition from Owenism to Shakerism. Relatively few social reformers, of course, followed his example. But the point to be made is that Shaker belief and practice in this respect was in harmony with the aspirations of other contemporaries who were seeking for personal and social salvation.

Also on the positive side was the Shaker emphasis on equality of the sexes. Theologically this was derived from an interpretation of the first chapter of Genesis: 'God created man in his own image ...; male and female created he them'; from which, it was argued, men and women are equally of God. Throughout scripture there are instances of God revealing his mind and will to prophetesses, witness Miriam, Esther, and Deborah. Finally, in Mother Ann has come 'the manifestation of Christ in the female'.[16] As Jesus was the second Adam, so Ann is the second Eve, destined to redeem mankind from the thraldom to sin caused by the first Eve's 'violation of the temple of chastity'. The sexual duality of God was mirrored in the Shaker duality of elders and eldresses. Father Joseph Meacham and Mother Lucy Wright had together instituted Gospel Order, on the basis of sexual equality; and throughout all Shaker organizations this duality was maintained. A new and radical role for women was here proclaimed. To refuse to be married, to bear children, to have sexual relations; to be treated as the equal of men in status and authority was a reversal of the role of women in contemporary society. Such a thoroughgoing feminism was the logical outcome of the doctrine of male and female messiahship. We are reminded of Joanna Southcott's and Mrs Buchan's sturdy but less coherent feminisms. There are the same or similar claims by the prophetess, with theological under-pinnings. But the institutional structures necessary for the practical

169

embodiment of religious feminism – notably a viable communitarianism – are either lacking or much weaker. Nevertheless the appeal of millenarianism as an alternative to, or solution of the problems of sexual relationships is comparable. A total of some 20,000 people became Shakers between 1770 and 1900, and a majority of them were women. Whatever the motives, personal or social, of these converts to Shakerism, its feminist appeal seems likely to have been strong. Viewed from this angle the feminism of British millenarian movements appears as a plant which in a more favourable soil and climate might have blossomed more abundantly.

The reaction of the world to Shaker celibacy and what were thought to be Shaker teachings and practice concerning sexual relationships was hostile. Persecution of the little group began in Manchester, when violence was used against the brethren and Ann was imprisoned; and the same treatment continued after the settlement at New Lebanon. During the revolutionary war the Shakers were suspected of disloyalty, and their firm testimony against taking oaths and bearing arms contributed further to their unpopularity. As with the Buchanites and Wroeites in Britain, the most extravagant charges of sexual aberration were levelled against the Shakers, often by ex-converts. Thomas Brown denied that the Shakers danced naked, 'men and women together', but he pursued at considerable length his investigation of the rumour that Mother Ann and some of the old believers had danced naked in the woods as a mortification of the flesh.[17] Again, to those who did not believe it possible to live celibately in the conditions of a Shaker family, it seemed inescapable that there must be some 'fruits of their unlawful embraces', and that to conceal such offspring infanticide was resorted to. Hostility to the Shakers, sometimes to the extent of burning and destroying property and assaulting believers, usually arose out of disputes concerning the custody of children or young women. Difficult problems ensued when one partner of a marriage joined the Shakers but the other refused;[18] or when a convert wished to leave the family and recover his property. When such cases were made public, and sometimes legal actions were brought, feeling against the Shakers could run high.

Shaker worship was also so unusual as to arouse suspicion. In essence it had much in common with the religious behaviour of other inner-light sects, especially of course the French prophets, but also with the Schismatics of the Kentucky Revival. At first the believers were moved to ecstasy in any way that occurred to them, without any set form. The earliest eyewitness account is by Valentine Rathbun, Sr, a Baptist minister in Pittsfield, Massachusetts, who had been temporarily attracted to the Shakers but then became their bitter critic. Describing a Shaker meeting at Niskeyuna in May 1780, he wrote:

> In the best part of their worship every one acts for himself, and almost every one different from the other: one will stand with his arms extended, acting over odd postures, which they call signs; another will be dancing, and some times hopping on one leg about the floor; another will fall to turning around, so swift, that if it be a woman, her clothes will be so filled with the wind, as though they were kept out by a hoop; another will be prostrate on the floor; another will be talking with somebody; and some sitting by, smoking their pipes; some groaning most dismally; some trembling extremely; others acting as though all their nerves were convulsed; others swinging their arms, with all vigor, as though they were turning a wheel, etc. Then all break off, and have a spell of smoking, and sometimes great fits of laughter ... They have several such exercises in a day, especially on the Sabbath.[19]

One of the functions of these 'spiritual labours' was mortification of the lusts of the flesh, the crucifixion of pride and self, and debasing of the body. Hence the bizarre and sometimes ludicrous antics noted by observers: grovelling in the dust, stamping on the devil, following an outstretched arm. But the Shaker love of order ensured that these 'gifts' were soon brought under control:[20] the involuntary convulsions and frenzied 'signs' were given a ritual form in the dance, which became the most distinctive aspect of Shaker worship. 'Dancing is the gift of God to the church', Brown was informed in 1798; and plenty of precedents were found in the Old Testament.

> We dance each like a living spark
> As David danced before the Ark

proclaimed a Shaker song. From the first 'square order shuffle' the dances developed through the marching and 'ring' dances to complex rituals during the period of spiritualism, 1837–47.[21] A visitor to New Lebanon in 1832, Professor Benjamin Silliman, left this impression:

> The worship commenced by the men arranging themselves in line at one end of the room, and the women on the other, and after a few words were addressed to them by the Elder they all kneeled down in opposite lines, facing each other, and after a period of profound silence, they commenced singing hymns from a book, the words of which were unintelligible to the auditors. After this they rose and marched backwards and forwards, facing each other, to a tune which

they all sang; then they faced the wall, with their backs to the audience, and marched in the same manner, backwards and forwards towards the wall.

When this exercise ended they formed two circles, a smaller and larger one, and marched to the tunes sung by the inner circle, which composed the principal singers; their hands also keeping time, either by the alternate motion of swinging backwards and forwards, or by clapping them together as they became animated by the tunes which were sung. This exercise continued about half an hour, when they retired to their seats.[22]

Edward Deming Andrews makes the important point that Shaker ritualism, no less than the more famous Shaker furniture and artifacts, was a true folk-art.

Though the tunes, songs, marches, ring dances and other forms of devotional 'exercises' were composed by individuals, they were intended for communal use. Their character and form were particularly social: the songs reflected in content the thought and aspiration of the whole group; their tempo was adapted to prescribed parts of the service and dance techniques which the eighteen societies had all adopted in common. The same songs spread through the scattered branches of the order. They were perfected in the week-day singing meetings of the families and bequeathed to the community in the united sabbath worship. They were exchanged among different families. Hundreds were composed as gifts to particular elders or eldresses, or to beloved brothers or sisters. Popular pieces such as 'Come life Shaker life', ''Tis the Gift to be Simple' and 'My Carnal Life I Will Lay Down' became authentic symbols of a distinct folk culture.[23]

A new emphasis in Shaker beliefs appeared during the decade of revival known as 'Mother Ann's work'. Beginning in 1837 among a group of adolescent girls, a wave of spiritualism spread throughout the Shaker societies, and was welcomed and carefully controlled by the leaders. Communications from the spirit world were received by individuals (in Shaker terminology, 'instruments') through visions, trances and ecstatic states. Mother Ann, the early Shaker leaders, departed members and others sent messages, directing the activities of the believers and urging renewed efforts towards salvation. During 1841–2 the revival reached a climax, with revelations from Holy Mother Wisdom (the co-equal of God the Father in the Shaker concept of the duality of the deity). New rituals were introduced as a consequence: the

Midnight Cry, in which lamps were carried through the rooms of every building; and the Sweeping Gift, a rite of spiritual and physical cleansing. Spiritual communications took several forms: new hymns and songs; beautifully inscribed papers with symbolic crowns, doves, trumpets and other emblems; and drawings and paintings dictated by the Spirit. These visionary drawings were similar to those of Joseph Prescott and some of the other Southcottians.[24] In each case there was the same careful penmanship, the highly stylized apocalyptic symbols, and heavenly adornments of angels, stars, clouds, chariots, and thrones. Likewise the communications had much in common: a similar down-to-earth touch of reality, a concern for the details of daily living, and an ability to discern spiritual significance in the most ordinary and unlikely happenings. Clearly the Shaker appeal was to a type of mind similar in many, though not all respects to that of the British millenarians.

This becomes manifest when we ask the question, why did people become Shakers and what sort of people were they? Of the original group in Manchester three (James Wardley, John Hocknell and John Partington) were not labouring people, but only Hocknell accompanied the sect to America. Most of the early converts in the New World were probably working farmers and their sons and daughters, but from the New Light revivals came ministers and preachers who provided an essential body of more educated leaders. The insistence on celibacy and obedience to the elders would presumably tend to attract or discourage people according to their type of personality. Thomas Brown, for example, could not bring himself to accept the authoritarian leadership, and so left the Shakers. On the other hand observers noted that the total security provided by membership in a Shaker family was likely to appeal to the uncompetitive, unadventurous, or socially inadequate elements of the population. Women in particular – single, widowed or unhappily married – were likely to find a refuge in Shakerism. To all who wished, for whatever reason, to withdraw from the world and lead an ordered and peaceful life, the Shakers had much to commend them. If this hypothesis of differential recruitment is correct, it may be that the societies, once they were established and economically prosperous, increasingly attracted seekers after security, whereas in the early days the converts were seekers after religious truth.[25] The emphasis shifted from millenarian hopes to communitarian satisfactions. Mother Ann's work was perhaps an attempt to check this drift towards accommodation with worldly values and reassert the ascetic disciplines and spirituality of the early days.

It would be hazardous to generalize the reasons why people became

Shakers. Questions of personal psychology, religious development, and social situation and expectations entered into the convert's decision. The mix was different for each individual. Essentially Shakerism gave a very definite answer to the old question, what shall I do to be saved?; and in a broad sense all who came to the Shakers did so because they were seeking salvation. But why seek salvation through Shakerism rather than in some other sect? Again, there is no single answer to fit all cases. But we can observe certain common personality traits and social characteristics among many of the believers, and these may be related to specific Shaker doctrines. Shakerism created a very distinctive culture of its own. Contemporary observers remarked that a Shaker village looked different from an ordinary village (it was neater, cleaner, better planned), and Shaker farmers were not the same as other farmers (they worked more methodically, and to greater effect).[26] Yet in other respects the Shakers were very typical American frontiersmen, with many of the same interests and concerns as their worldly neighbours. Like other millenarian sects they were never able to escape the paradox of withdrawal from and involvement in the world, of rejecting and yet reflecting (albeit negatively) the dominant society.

Manual labour was obligatory for all members of a Shaker community, including the elders and ministers. 'Hands to work and hearts to God' was a slogan learned from Mother Ann, and the sacredness of all labour was constantly reiterated. No work was ever considered degrading, and the simplest domestic job was imbued with a spiritual significance. More expediently, hard work was an antidote to lust, and the basis of those Puritan virtues which produced the ordered prosperity so much admired by visitors. Agriculture was primary. 'Every commune, to prosper, must be founded, so far as its industry goes, on agriculture. Only the simple labors and manners of a farming people can hold a community together,' declared Frederick Evans.[27] The Shakers were farmers and gardeners – and also handcraftsmen. Their skill as woodworkers, basketmakers, spinners and weavers was widely recognized, and their products were valued for the high quality of their workmanship and the utility of their design. Shakerism was grounded in the traditions of agriculture and handcrafts, and was close to the lore of the countryside. Shaker artisans displayed great ingenuity in inventing labour-saving devices; and the sisters were expert in the collection and use of medicinal herbs. From such activities emerges a picture of a simple people, working steadily but not excessively, conservative-minded and guided by leaders who strictly interpreted their traditions.

It is not surprising that Nordhoff discovered that the Shakers 'are not a reading people.'[28] The early believers, 'being chiefly of the laboring classes and generally in low circumstances of life', were not expected to have had much formal education; though their leaders who had been ministers in other sects brought with them their skill in biblical exegesis. Shaker emphasis on usefulness and self-help did not encourage literary study, and in Shaker schools the children were made literate but not encouraged in higher or classical learning, which was 'mere lumber of the brain'. Nordhoff noted the 'extremely limited range' of Evans's library, and quoted a Swedish brother who had been a student but soon weaned himself 'from the habit of books'. For, as the *Testimony* put it, 'Though a man should gain all the natural knowledge in the universe, he could not thereby gain either the knowledge or power of salvation from sin, nor redemption from a sinful nature.' No books, pamphlets or almanacs were allowed in the family without the consent of the elders, nor was it permitted to read books 'when out among the world, that are not allowed of among Believers.' Those who teach in school 'shall devote their time to teaching their scholars, and not to studying themselves, further than is necessary to enable them to do their duty in teaching.'

This tendency to anti-intellectualism was confirmed, and perhaps strengthened by other characteristics of Shaker 'internal order'. The passion for neatness and cleanliness, derived originally from Mother Ann, was carried to extremes. The minutest details of daily living were regulated:[29] how to eat at meals ('when you take a piece of bread, take a whole piece ... and when you cut meat, cut it square and equal, fat and lean, and take an equal proportion of bones'); how to sit in meeting ('none should sit crosslegged nor in any awkward posture in the time of any meeting for worship'); how to walk on the stairs ('when brethren and sisters go up and down stairs, they should not slip their feet on the carpet or floor, but lift them up and set them down plumb, so as not to wear out the carpets or floor unnecessarily'). And everywhere was the insistence on order: 'good order', 'Gospel order', 'united order', 'order of the day', 'contrary to order'. Order meant uniformity, obedience to strict rules and regulations, and subordination of self. The 'work of mortification' was intended to dissolve a convert's natural affections and render him dependent on communal 'leads'.[30] Hatred of normal appetites and desires led to debasing acts to mortify carnal nature, for example creeping on the floor like an animal. Reason was to be abandoned in favour of direct revelation from God and the commands of the elders. Such an atmosphere was not congenial to independent thinking or decision-making. Things of the mind could take only a low order of priority, for they were not deemed necessary, or even helpful, for salvation. If we apply the hypothesis of differential recruitment to this situation, we have another factor in assessing the kind of people likely to be attracted to Shakerism.

Unintellectualism was also charged against the second of our American millenarian movements, the Mormons. Contemporary critics waxed eloquent about the ignorance and illiteracy of Joseph Smith, condemned Mormon converts as deluded, and denounced Mormon beliefs as 'subversive of human reason'.[31] All revealed religion is inherently open to the charge that it does not set a pre-eminently high regard on reason, and all the millenarian sects led by latter-day prophets in the eighteenth and nineteenth centuries were so attacked (to which they blandly replied, in the words of St Paul (I Corinthians 1:20), 'hath not God made foolish the wisdom of the World?'). But in introducing the Mormons as a millenarian sect a distinction has to be made between them and other millenarians like the Shakers. Alone of all the millenarians surveyed in this book, the Mormons became a large and flourishing church which still continues. There is therefore a whole literature of Mormon theology and history on a scale which does not exist for the other millenarians. Moreover controversies and issues from the early days have a more than scholarly significance, for in some cases they touch upon matters of Mormon faith. Any estimate of Joseph Smith, for example, is almost bound to be received differently by Mormons and non-Mormons. It is no part of this study to get involved in the (admittedly fascinating) details of Mormon history and historiography, but simply to present certain aspects of early Mormonism for comparison. For this purpose we need an outline sketch of Joseph Smith and the development of the Mormon church up to 1847; an examination of certain millenarian themes in Mormonism; and a brief mention of Mormonism in England. What follows is not a balanced and comprehensive account of early Mormon history: it is a selection of material which seems relevant to the millenarian experiences hitherto described.[32]

We cannot do better than begin with Joseph Smith's own account of his first visions and prophetic mission:

I was born in the town of Sharon, Windsor county, Vermont, on the 23d of December, AD 1805. When ten years old, my parents removed to Palmyra, New York, where we resided about four years, and from thence we removed to the town of Manchester, a distance of six miles.

My father was a farmer, and taught me the art of husbandry. When about fourteen years of age, I began to reflect upon the importance of being prepared for a future place; and, upon inquiring the state of salvation, I found that there was a great clash in religious sentiment. If I went to one society, they referred me to one place, and another to another – each one pointing to his own particular creed as the *summum bonum* of perfection. Considering that all could not be right, and that God could not be the author of so much confusion, I determined to investigate the subject more fully, believing that if God had a church, it would not be split up into factions, and that if he taught one society to worship one way, and administer in one set of ordinances, he would not teach another principles which were diametrically opposed. Believing the Word of God, I had confidence in the declaration of James – 'If any man lack wisdom let him ask of God, who giveth to all men liberally and upbraideth not, and it shall be given him.'

I retired to a secret place in a grove, and began to call upon the Lord. While fervently engaged in supplication, my mind was taken away from the objects with which I was surrounded, and I was enrapt in a heavenly vision, and saw two glorious personages, who exactly resembled each other in features and likeness, surrounded with a brilliant light, which eclipsed the sun at noon-day. They told me that all the religious denominations were believing in incorrect doctrines, and that none of them was acknowledged of God as his church and kingdom. And I was expressly commanded to 'go not after them,' at the same time receiving a promise that the fulness of the Gospel should at some future time be made known unto me.

On the evening of the 21st September, AD 1823, while I was praying unto God, and endeavouring to exercise faith in the precious promises of Scripture, on a sudden a light like that of day, only of a far purer and more glorious appearance and brightness, burst into the room; indeed, the first sight was as though the house was filled with consuming fire. The appearance produced a shock that affected the whole body. In a moment a personage stood before me, surrounded with a glory yet greater than that with which I was already surrounded. This messenger proclaimed himself to be an angel of God, sent to bring the joyful tidings, that the covenant which God made with ancient Israel was at hand to be fulfilled; that the preparatory work for the second coming of the Messiah was speedily to commence; that the time was at hand, for the Gospel in all its fulness to be preached in power, unto all nations, that a people might be prepared for the millennial reign.

I was informed that I was chosen to be an instrument in the hands of God, to bring about some of his purposes in this glorious dispensation. ... I was also told where there was deposited some plates, on which was engraven an abridgment of the records of the ancient prophets that had existed on this continent. The angel appeared to me three times the same night, and unfolded the same things. After having received many visits from the angels of God, unfolding the majesty and glory of the events that should transpire in the last days, on the morning of the 22nd of September, AD 1827, the angel of the Lord delivered the records into my hands.

These records were engraven on plates which had the appearance of gold; each plate was six inches wide and eight inches long, and not quite so thick as common tin. They were filled with engravings in Egyptian characters, and bound together in a volume, as the leaves of a book, with three rings running through the whole. The volume was something near six inches in thickness, a part of which was sealed. The characters on the unsealed part were small, and beautifully engraved. The whole book exhibited many marks of antiquity in its construction, and much skill in the art of engraving. With the records was found a curious instrument, which the ancients called 'Urim and Thummin', which consisted of two transparent stones, set in the rim on a bow fastened to a breast-plate.

Through the medium of the Urim and Thummin I translated the record by the gift and power of God.[33]

The *Book of Mormon* was published early in 1830, and shortly thereafter the gathering of the saints began. In the words of Joseph Smith:

On the 6th April, 1830, the 'Church of Jesus Christ of Latter-day Saints,' was first organized in the town of Manchester, Ontario county, state of New York. Some few were called and ordained by the Spirit of revelation and prophecy, and began to preach as the Spirit gave them utterance, and though weak, yet were they strengthened by the power of God; and many were brought to repentance, were immersed in the water, and were filled with the Holy Ghost by the laying on of hands. They saw visions, and prophesied – devils were cast out, and the sick healed by the laying on of hands. From that time the work rolled forth with astonishing rapidity, and churches were soon formed in the states of New York, Pennsylvania, Ohio, Indiana, Illinois, and Missouri.[34]

Joseph's first converts were members of his own family and friends in the neighbourhood. He attracted some support in southern New York, but the crucial success was the conversion of members of the sect of

Campbellites (Disciples of Christ) in Kirtland, Ohio. The centre of the new church moved to Kirtland, and missionaries were then sent to the Indians in Missouri, which was soon declared to be 'the land of promise and the place for the city of Zion' (July 1831).[35] A settlement was established at Independence but the Mormons, who now numbered about 1,200, were attacked and driven out, and so they moved on into neighbouring counties in Missouri. At first they were welcomed by the local people, but soon they were asked to leave. They established themselves at Far West, Missouri, but here they encountered more violent opposition, and after a massacre of Mormons at Haun's Mill in October 1838, they decided to move out of Missouri. In the spring of 1839 some 5,000 Mormons arrived in Illinois, and commenced to build yet another settlement on a bend in the Mississippi river. It was called Nauvoo which, said Joseph, 'means in Hebrew a beautiful plantation.' The saints, as the Mormons called themselves, were welcomed in Illinois, where the two political parties, Whigs and Democrats, each hoped for their support. The state legislature granted an unusually favourable charter to the new city of Nauvoo, making it independent in many respects and sanctioning a local militia, the Nauvoo Legion. As with their previous efforts, the Mormons proved themselves to be remarkably effective settlers, and by 1842 the town had been planned and the population had risen to between 14,000 and 15,000. Yet their very success was the Mormons' undoing, and the pattern of persecution and violence was shortly repeated. In addition to antagonism from non-Mormons, Joseph was also faced with opposition from some of his church leaders who, in retaliation for his attempt to suppress their newspaper, brought a court action against him. The governor and state authorities took this as an opportunity to intervene, and Joseph, his brother and some others were imprisoned in Carthage gaol. On 27 June 1844 a crowd of armed men attacked the gaol and shot Joseph and his brother, Hyrum, dead. There were fears that the saints, mobilized in their Legion, would seek to avenge the murder of the prophet; but they decided against this, and instead determined to move on yet again. This time their destination was far beyond the most westward limits of settlement, deep in the Rocky Mountains. Beginning in February 1846, under the leadership of Brigham Young, the great exodus set out, and in July 1847 the Mormons reached their new home in the Great Salt Lake Valley, Utah.

The gathering of the saints was attended by an unusual degree of bitter opposition. Tarring and feathering, imprisonment, assault, and burning of their homes and crops were the lot of Joseph Smith and his followers wherever they went – Ohio, Missouri, or Illinois. Other millenarian sects met with ridicule, opposition and sometimes violence; but none was subjected to the repeated and prolonged persecution of the Mormons. America was used to sectarian unorthodoxy, and individual Mormons were not regarded by contemporaries as very different from other 'deluded' enthusiasts. They were good neighbours, hard-working, and peaceable. But they were a 'peculiar people', and their separateness from Gentile society was increasingly emphasized by their actions, all of which were ultimately directed to building an earthly kingdom of God. At Kirtland, Independence, Far West, Nauvoo – wherever the church was currently gathering – plans for the speedy building of Zion were put into effect. Streets were laid out, a large temple begun, and the centralized, directing authority of the church was everywhere apparent. This frightened non-Mormons, and their first welcoming of the saints gave way to unease and then hostility. In the frontier society of Missouri in the 1830s Mormon insistence on separateness and superiority was almost bound to cause antagonism, and Mormon doctrine on the special place of the Indians in America aroused suspicion and resentment. In Nauvoo the independent power of the town leadership, the military strength of the Legion, and Mormon views on polygamy again appeared as a threat to non-Mormons. Mormonism, it was argued, was an American Islam, and Joseph Smith was the New Mahomet.[36] After fourteen years of trying to build the New Jerusalem in the bosom of America the Mormons found their millennial hopes frustrated. They intended to reject existing society and its values, but they found that society rejected them even more powerfully. Only in the isolated and unsettled wilderness of Utah were they able to build the city of Zion and establish the kingdom of the saints, as foretold in Isaiah 40:9, 'O Zion, that bringest good tidings, get thee up into the high mountain.'[37]

The millenarian content of early Mormonism was pronounced. In the articles of faith which Joseph drew up, he declared:

> We believe in the literal gathering of Israel, and in the restoration of
> the Ten Tribes; that Zion will be built upon this continent; that
> Christ will reign personally upon the earth, and that the earth will be
> renewed, and receive its paradisiacal glory.[38]

From time to time Joseph assured some of his closest followers that they would live to see the second coming; and many of his revelations in 1831 indicated that 'the great day of the Lord is nigh.'[39] However, he did not try to calculate the date of the second advent from the biblical time prophecies, but contented himself with texts from Isaiah and Revelation to show that the last days were come. Like most millenarians, the

Mormons made full use of the 'signs of the times' to prove that the millennium was approaching[40] – an irrefutable argument since virtually any event can be so interpreted.[41] Parley P. Pratt, one of the twelve apostles appointed by Joseph to assist in ruling the church, explained the Mormon doctrine of the millennium and the second advent:

> There are three general resurrections revealed to man on the earth; one of these is past, and the other two are future.
>
> The first general resurrection took place in connection with the resurrection of Jesus Christ. ...
>
> The second will take place in a few years from the present time, and will be immediately succeeded by the coming of Jesus Christ, in power and great glory, with all His Saints and angels. This resurrection will include the Former and Latter-day Saints, all those who have received the Gospel since the former resurrection.
>
> The third and last resurrection will take place more than a thousand years afterwards, and will embrace all the human family not included in the former resurrections or translations.[42]

This would appear to be a fairly orthodox premillennialist statement. But in fact Mormonism does not fit easily into a neat millenarian category. Parley Pratt's 'few years' before the second advent had to be extended, during which time the Mormons exhibited a truly postmillennialist zeal for progressive improvement and optimism in extending Christian agencies. Mormonism was 'a uniquely *American* form of millenarianism'.[43] Zion was to be built in the American West, and that in the near future. It was a kingdom of this world, and it offered practical, material benefits here and now. No man could know the time of the second coming; but, Joseph told his followers, Christ would not come until the saints had created conditions worthy of a divine ruler.

The peculiarly American quality of Joseph's revelations is brought out in the *Book of Mormon*. He wrote:

> In this important and interesting book the history of ancient America is unfolded, from its first settlement by a colony that came from the tower of Babel at the confusion of languages, to the beginning of the fifth century of the Christian era.
>
> We are informed by these records, that America in ancient times, has been inhabited by two distinct races of people. The first were called Jaredites, and came directly from the tower of Babel. The second race came directly from the city of Jerusalem, about six hundred years before Christ. They were principally Israelites, of the descendants of Joseph. The Jaredites were destroyed about the time

that the Israelites came from Jerusalem, who succeeded them in the
inheritance of the country. The principal nation of the second race fell
in battle towards the close of the fourth century. The remnant are the
Indians who now inhabit this country. This book also tells us that our
Saviour made his appearance upon this continent after his
resurrection; that he planted the Gospel here in all its fulness, and
richness, and power, and blessing; that they had apostles, prophets,
pastors, teachers, and evangelists – the same order, the same
priesthood, the same ordinances, gifts, powers, and blessing, as was
enjoyed on the eastern continent; that the people were cut off in
consequence of their transgressions; that the last of their prophets who
existed among them was commanded to write an abridgment of their
prophecies, history, etc., and to hide it up in the earth, and that it
should come forth, and be united with the Bible, for the
accomplishment of the purposes of God in the last days.[44]

The central character in the book is a Hebrew prophet, Lehi, who, to
escape the Babylonian captivity, led his family from Jerusalem to the
promised land, America, about 600 BC. Two of his sons rebelled against
him, for which they and their people (the Lamanites) were punished by
the curse of a dark skin, and the American Indians were their
descendants. The Nephites, descended from Lehi's faithful son, warred
with the Lamanites; and the story of their adventures, together with
those of Mormon, the Jaredites, and Moroni, is recounted in the manner
of the Old Testament. The *Book of Mormon* provided an explanation of
the origins of the American Indians, at a time when there was
speculation in America and Britain about primitive peoples. It also
showed the special favour in which God had viewed America when he
led the Israelites to their new home. Joseph's interpretation of the lost
tribes of Israel supported his millenarian claim 'that Zion will be built
upon this [the American] continent.'

Historians have noted how, in this way, Mormonism identified with
the old American conviction that the New World was exceptional, that
America was a promised land, for which God had reserved a special
destiny.[45] The *Book of Mormon* was also an expression of the American
search for 'a usable past', part of a growing patriotic consciousness of the
need for a native ideology. But from a millenarian perspective early
Mormonism looks somewhat different. If Joseph taught that Adam had
dwelt in the Mississippi Valley[46] and that Christ had visited the
Nephites,[47] William Blake believed that Noah and the patriarchs had
lived in Britain and that the Holy Lamb of God had walked upon

England's mountains. Richard Brothers' theory of British Israel linked the Anglo-Saxons with forgotten Israelite ancestors; and the Southcottians were assured that in God's providence a special place had been given to the British people. It was a characteristic of millenarians to pronounce God's wrath upon the society around them, but at the same time to assure their compatriots that a special role in the coming millennium was assigned to their nation. In this respect Joseph was no more (and no less) exceptionalist than his British counterparts. It almost seemed as if the more they emphasized their separateness or withdrawal from the nation at large, the more millenarians felt it necessary to assert that theirs was a higher patriotism and that they were the saving remnant (or new Israel) of the whole nation.

Just as Brothers' doctrines of British Israelism were given credibility by the contemporary concern with speculative mythology, so Joseph's account of American Hebrew origins found support in popular scholarship and speculation about the Indians. Elias Boudinot's *A Star in the West: or a Humble Attempt to Discover the Long Lost Tribes of Israel* (Trenton, 1816) was but one of a number of works speculating on the subject.[48] Ethan Smith's *View of the Hebrews; or the Ten Tribes of Israel in America* (Poultney, Vermont, 1823; 2nd edition, 1825) was possibly known by Joseph. It contained 'all the items of three generations of specious scholarship and piecemeal observation on this subject'.[49] Western New York and Ohio were rich in Indian burial mounds and other relics, and curiosity about them was rife. Digging for buried treasure, the use of crystals, and the rituals of folk-magic were well known in rural communities, and there is some evidence that Joseph had a local reputation as a scryer. These roots in folk-lore and popular occultism would seem to be parallel to those we have observed in other millenarian movements; and for the prophet or prophetess there is a familiar progress 'from necromancy into revelation, from revelation to prophecy, and from prophecy to leadership of a ... religious movement.'[50]

If, however, the *Book of Mormon* had been no more than another speculative account of American Israelism it would not have made the impact that it did. Its themes were essentially the age-old problems that have perplexed men in all generations: the nature of God's revelations, good and evil, personal salvation. These were the problems which agitated many people in western New York (the Burned-over District)[51] in the second quarter of the nineteenth century, and the *Book of Mormon* can be seen as a projection of the beliefs and attitudes of post-revival, sectarian religion. 'As such, it is an almost completely neglected primary source for the intellectual history of the common man.'[52] One of the problems of popular millenarian religion is that it has to handle complex theological and philosophical issues at a level which can be generally understood; but the level must not be too simple or it will not satisfy those seekers after salvation whose rejection of their earlier beliefs is the motive for their turning to the new prophet. Joseph's solution to this problem was extremely well tuned to the needs of labouring people in America and England in the 1830s and 1840s. He did not offer an allegorical or abstract interpretation of the Bible in place of earlier and now unacceptable formulations, but added his own scripture which was to be taken literally. He rejected the harshness of Calvinism and the emotionalism of revivalism, while retaining the Puritan work ethic and direction by the inner light of the Spirit. He was as Arminian as Wesley (salvation was offered freely to all who would respond to Christ's call): but he spoke with the authority of God's prophet.[53] The provision of answers to perplexing questions of theology combined with the assurance of divine authority was recognized by contemporaries as likely to have a powerful appeal. 'This prophet Smith', wrote Alexander Campbell, 'through his stone spectacles, wrote on the plates of Nephi, in his book of Mormon, every error and almost every truth discussed in New York for the last ten years. He decides all the great controversies – infant baptism, ordination, the trinity, regeneration, repentance, justification, the fall of man, the atonement, transubstantiation, fasting, penance, church government, religious experience, the call to the ministry, the general resurrection, eternal punishment, who may baptize, and even the question of free masonry, republican government and the rights of man.'[54]

The Reverend Alexander Campbell was understandably hostile to the prophet as he had recently lost some of his leading followers to the Mormons. Campbell, a Scottish immigrant, had left the Baptists in 1827 and founded a congregation known as the Disciples of Christ, or Campbellites, who believed in the imminence of the second coming. Three Campbellite preachers – Sidney Rigdon, Parley Pratt and Orson Hyde – were converted to Mormonism, and Rigdon brought over his whole congregation at Kirtland, Ohio, who were organized in a community and held all things in common.[55] From this stemmed the early Mormon experiment with communitarianism in the form of the United Order of Enoch, under which property was held by the church and the producer retained only sufficient for himself and his family. The communitarian element, which was frequently associated with millenarian movements, was thus present in early Mormonism, and provided the basis for an ethic of work and property, and a social structure in the millennial kingdom.

The accession of the ex-Campbellites was the crucial point in the initial gathering of the Latter-day Saints. Rigdon was a well-known and able preacher in Ohio. He was also a millenarian and had recently quarrelled with Campbell over the communitarian issue at Kirtland. When Rigdon read the *Book of Mormon* he was well prepared to see in it the fulfilment of his millenarian hopes and, after meeting Joseph, to accept him as the prophet for whom he had been waiting. The same was true, with individual modifications of the pattern, for other converts who came from the Campbellites, Baptists, Methodists and revivalist sects.[56] As with the followers of Richard Brothers in Britain, they were already seekers – and sometimes millenarians – who were on the look-out for a new prophet, and for the signs of the times. 'He who sets out to find signs and omens will soon find enough of them', observed Alexander Campbell. 'He that expects visits from angels will find them.'[57]

How true this was can be shown by the experience of countless millenarians. For Mormonism Parley Pratt provides as good an example as any. He describes how, in the autumn of 1830, shortly after his baptism as a Mormon, he was returning from an (unsuccessful) missionary visit to the Shakers:

> I had been on a visit to a singular people called Shakers, at New Lebanon, about seven miles from my aunt Van Cott's, and was returning that distance, on foot, on a beautiful evening of September. The sky was without a cloud; the stars shone out beautifully, and all nature seemed reposing in quiet, as I pursued my solitary way, wrapt in deep meditations on the predictions of the holy prophets; the signs of the times; the approaching advent of the Messiah, to reign on the earth, and the important revelations of the Book of Mormon; my heart filled with gratitude to God that He had opened the eyes of my understanding to receive the truth, and with sorrow for the blindness of those who lightly rejected the same, when my attention was aroused by a sudden appearance of a brilliant light which shone around me, above the brightness of the sun. I cast my eyes upward to inquire from whence the light came, when I perceived a long chain of light extended in the heavens, very bright, and of a deep fiery red. It at first stood stationary in a horizontal position; at length bending in the centre, the two ends approached each other with a rapid movement, so as to form an exact square. In this position it again remained stationary for some time, perhaps a minute, and then again the ends

approached each other with the same rapidity, and again ceased to
move, remaining stationary, for perhaps a minute, in the form of a
compass; it then commenced a third movement in the same manner,
and closed like the closing of a compass, the whole forming a straight
line like a chain doubled. It again remained stationary for a minute,
and then faded away.

   I fell upon my knees in the street, and thanked the Lord for so
marvellous a sign of the coming of the Son of Man.[58]

Here is the typical millenarian sensibility; and Pratt's autobiography
provides an equally typical thumb-nail sketch of a first generation
American Mormon. He was born in 1807 in Burlington, New York, of
old New England Puritan stock. His father was a farmer and part-time
school master. Parley attended common school until the age of fifteen
and was fully literate, though he later thought his opportunities for
education had been very limited. He worked on farms as a hired man to
raise money, and then went west to buy his own farm on the frontier,
some thirty miles west of Cleveland, Ohio. In 1827 he married; and his
wife kept school while he cleared the land and planted crops. He had
joined the Baptists when he was eighteen, but after hearing Rigdon
preach he became a Campbellite. Beginning in 1830, he says, he felt a
need 'to search the prophets'; and he decided to sell his farm and become
a full-time preacher. Despite financial hardship, he drew upon the bank
of faith – 'true bills and founded on capital that will never fail, though
heaven and earth should pass away.'[59] While travelling in western New
York he heard of the *Book of Mormon* and visited the Smith family.
Joseph was away in Pennsylvania, but Pratt met Hyrum Smith and was
baptized into the church by Oliver Cowdery who had been Joseph's
secretary during the translation of the *Book of Mormon* from the golden
plates. In due course Parley Pratt became an apostle ('The Archer of
Paradise', Joseph called him) and proselytizer in England. But always
there shone through his works the millenarian vision of his early days. In
language reminiscent of Washington Allston's painting, 'The Deluge',
Pratt described the creation:

   darkness fled, the veil was lifted, light pierced the gloom, and chaos
   was made visible. O what a scene! A world without landscape,
   without vegetation, without animal life, without man or animated
   beings. No sound broke on the stillness, save the voice of the moaning
   winds and of dashing, foaming waters. Again, a voice comes booming
   over the abyss, and echoing amid the wastes, the mass of matter hears
   and trembles, and lo! the sea retires, the muddy, shapeless mass lifts its

head above the waters. Molehills to mountains grow. Huge islands next appear, and continents at length expand to view, with hill and vale, in one wide, dreary waste, unmeasured and untrodden.[60]

The memoirs of Lucy Mack Smith, the prophet's mother, are a mine of information about millenarian origins and the rural culture in which they were nurtured.[61] In a general setting of the fortunes of the Mack and Smith families, she recounts the stories of recovery from sickness (especially when despaired of by the doctors), deaths and near-deaths, loves and marriages, failure of crops, debts and mortgages, court cases, and hopes of provision for old age. Almost every major event in the family history is related to a dream or vision by some member of the family; miracles and providences abound; and prayer is answered directly. As a young girl she was distressed by the death of her sister, Lovina, and determined to seek 'a change of heart'. She read her Bible and prayed; but was frustrated by a recurring problem:

> If I remain a member of no church, all religious people will say I am of
> the world; and if I join some one of the different denominations, all
> the rest will say I am in error. No church will admit that I am right,
> except the one with which I am associated. This makes them witnesses
> against each other; and how can I decide in such a case as this, seeing
> they are all unlike the Church of Christ, as it existed in former days?

After she was married her doubts continued. She decided to be baptized, but did not join a church: 'my mind was considerably disquieted. It was wholly occupied upon the subject of religion.' Her oldest brother, Jason Mack, was also a seeker and, from the age of twenty, 'a preacher of the gospel'. She records that when she thought of attending religious meetings, her son Joseph refused to accompany her, saying:

> Mother I do not wish to prevent your going to meeting ... but do not
> ask me to join ... I can take my bible, and go into the woods, and
> learn more in two hours than you can learn at meeting in two years.

In an atmosphere so thoroughly antinominian, Joseph's claims to divine revelation (and indeed the claims of anyone else) were bound to be taken seriously. For seekers growing weary of their search he offered a spiritual rest and authoritative answers to many of those problems which plagued ordinary people like his mother.

The enemies of Mormonism were convinced that 'practical antinomianism and the enthusiastic views of spiritual agency' were responsible for the success of the Latter-day Saints. Mormonism, argued Henry Caswall, somewhat prematurely in 1843, could not have arisen in

England, where more mature religious institutions 'would have opposed a bulwark against ... fanaticism', and where 'the names of its prophets and teachers would have ranked with those of Southcote [sic] or of Muggleton.' [62] Another critic also interpreted Mormonism as a type of aberration found in all churches and ages, and classified it with 'similar fanaticisms' such as Joanna Southcott, Brothers, and Swedenborg. In particular he noted that Mormonism pandered to the popular craving for the 'comforts of religion', by which was meant religious excitement, novelty, and 'internal revelations, visions, raptures and ecstacies of all sorts', ascribed to the direct influence of the Holy Spirit. The people who became Mormons were those who 'have never sought much else in religion but to get periodical happy feelings.' And he added scornfully that 'every Mormon knows that Smith's book is true because he sought in agonizing prayer and God, by his Spirit, revealed it to him.'[63] In fact, the antinomian tendencies in early Mormonism were soon curbed. When others began to have their own revelations Joseph warned that these could be from the devil, and insisted that all revelations must come through him.[64] The antinomianism which led seekers to embrace Mormonism in the first instance was thus channelled and directed once they had joined the church. Antinomianism in the sense of freedom from the restraints of the moral law, with its concomitant claims to sexual freedom, was handled carefully by the Mormon leadership. There was never any suggestion that saints were permitted to indulge in sexual promiscuity or commit adultery. But polygamy, or plural marriage was approved for some of the leadership, and the 'sealing' of more than one wife to Joseph and certain elders was practised in Nauvoo. The doctrine of polygamy, though publicly denied until 1852, was recorded secretly in Joseph's revelation of 12 July 1843, in which temple marriage, for 'time and eternity', was permitted with more than one wife when commanded by the Lord.[65] This new doctrine – for it had not been part of the original revelation and was, indeed, denounced in the *Book of Mormon* – caused dissension within the church, and aroused Gentile hostility to the Mormons. Polygamy, more than any other Mormon doctrine, set the saints apart from the world and made them a peculiar people, just as celibacy isolated the Shakers. The Mormon doctrine of marriage exalted sexuality as much as Shaker beliefs degraded it.

In June 1837 a Mormon mission to Britain was established.[66] Led by successive apostles and elders sent from America, the missionaries met with an encouraging response. Within eight months of the first preaching of Mormonism in Preston a conference of 700 members met in the town. By 1840 the number of saints in England was 4,000; and by the end of 1842 there were 7,500. A peak membership of nearly 33,000 was reached in 1851. Thereafter the numbers declined, as emigration outpaced recruitment, and the rate of conversions declined. The church was highly organized into conferences and branches throughout the United Kingdom, numbering forty-two and 602 respectively in 1851, with a full complement of high priests, elders, priests, teachers and deacons. But the hopes of the converts were set ultimately on a Zion 5,000 miles away, not on building the kingdom of the saints in Britain. During the fourteen years 1837–51 nearly 17,000 of the 50,000 who had been baptized in Britain emigrated to America. The flow of emigrants was uneven, with peak years followed by periods of lesser activity. Thus 1,600 British Mormons sailed in 1842, more than 2,000 in 1849, and (the largest number of all) 11,000 in the years 1853–6. In the fifty years 1840–90 some 55,000 British converts emigrated. These are relatively large numbers in comparison with other contemporary millenarian groups, and suggest the need to look a little more closely at some of their implications.

The initial successes of the mission were in Lancashire, Yorkshire, the Staffordshire Potteries, the Black Country, Herefordshire and Gloucestershire; with extensions into Scotland, Wales and 'the great Babylon', London ('the hardest place I ever visited for establishing the gospel', wrote Wilford Woodruff, one of the apostles, in 1840);[67] and these seem to have remained the strongholds of Mormonism during the next decade.[68] Without an analysis of the 50,000 converts up to 1851 it would be hazardous to generalize confidently about the geographical, religious, and social origins of British Mormons. Some of their areas of recruitment (the industrial north and Midlands – and also London) were already millenarian territory; but they also made headway in rural parts of the west Midlands. We would expect to find the Mormons gathering converts from other sects, and there is some evidence to this effect. At Doncaster about twenty-five members of an Aitkenite congregation became Mormons;[69] and in the Ledbury district of Herefordshire, Wilford Woodruff converted the superintendent and most of the members of the United Brethren, who were seceders from Primitive Methodism.[70] At Ashton-under-Lyne there were cases of ex-Wroeites joining the Mormons, who had a church in the town.[71] A random sampling of Mormon converts in the early 1840s includes:

John Needham, a draper who had been searching for religious conviction but was unable to find it in Methodism and finally joined the Mormons in 1838; Paul Harris, shoemaker of Manchester, who opened his basement shop to the Mormons in 1838; John Bourne, a potter and a Methodist, who was baptized by Alfred Cordon in 1839; Richard Steele, a potter who had become interested in the Methodists as well as the Socialists, and who was already on a religious quest when he heard of the Latter-day Saints in 1839 and was baptized in January 1840; William Barton, son of a printer but working in a Manchester factory when he and his parents were converted to Mormonism in November 1841; John Freeman, whose efforts at employment took him into shoemaking, brickmaking, reaping, and itinerant singing in markets and fairs, and whose religious quest led him from the Baptists to the 'Independents' and to the Christian Chartists before his conversion to Mormonism in 1844; Sarah B. Layton, whose parents belonged to the laboring classes and who moved from the Methodist church to the Church of England and then, after her sister had joined the Mormons, was baptized on 1 January 1842; and John Martin, a chimney sweep who was baptized in 1842.[72]

Observers remarked upon the 'respectable' nature of Mormon converts. On 3 April 1841 the *Athenaeum* reported that

Mormonism is making rapid progress particularly in the manufacturing districts, and it is also spreading in Wales. Furthermore, its converts are not made from the lowest ranks; those sought and obtained by the Mormonite apostles are mechanics and tradesmen who have saved a little money, who are remarkable for their moral character, but who are exposed to the delusion from having, as Archbishop Sharpe expressed it, 'studied the Bible with an ill-balanced mind'.[73]

This verdict was confirmed by a Liverpool shipping manager a decade later:

With regard to Mormon emigration, and the class of persons of which it is composed, they are principally farmers and mechanics, with some few clerks, surgeons, etc. They are generally intelligent and well-behaved, and many of them are highly respectable.[74]

The success of the mission to Britain poses some interesting questions in the historical interpretation of Mormonism. In particular, if Mormonism was as strongly and particularly American as has been suggested, why did it appeal to people in Britain? What meaning did the *Book of Mormon* have for readers without much knowledge of America or the Indians? Were there other elements in the Mormon message, such as the hope of emigration and the gathering of the millennial kingdom, which made a strong appeal? For each convert there were individual motivations and we cannot know the inner logic of each man's decision. But some factors were assumed to be of common concern, and these are reflected in Mormon literature designed to interest believers and potential converts. In the pages of *The Latter-day Saints Millennial Star*, published first in Manchester and then in Liverpool from 1840 onwards, we have some indication of the topics which were deemed to be of interest and the attitudes and assumptions in Mormon thinking. News from America, reports of conferences, the comings and goings of missionaries, sermons and letters from elders occupy a good deal of space. But there are also accounts of miraculous healing (in Rumford, Bury, Merthyr and Edinburgh), the casting out of devils (Leamington Spa), and speculation as to whether angels have to eat.[75] Dreams, visions and signs of the times are plentifully recorded. The *Star* in the 1840s was completely Anglo-American. It assumed that society was basically similar in the two countries, and that on a practical level there were no problems beyond those of pioneer living and frontiersmanship. The enemies and difficulties were the same in both countries. Environment was virtually ignored: so also was time. Life in Old Testament days was treated as similar to modern times, with prophets, miracles and God's commandments as plain now as then. For to the true millenarian past and present were fused together, and place had little significance.

The likelihood is that in Mormonism a certain type of seeker found satisfactions for which he was looking, and the message of Joseph Smith appeared equally credible to him whether in America or Britain. John Greenleaf Whittier visited a Mormon meeting in 1847 and described his impressions. The meeting happened to be in Lowell, Massachusetts, but it might equally well have been in Preston, Lancashire:

> In listening to these modern prophets, I discovered as I think, the great secret of their success in making converts. They speak to a common feeling: they minister to a universal want. They contrast strongly the miraculous power of the gospel in the apostolic time with the present state of our nominal Christianity. They ask for the signs of divine power; the faith, overcoming all things, which opened the prison doors of the apostles, gave them power over the elements, which rebuked disease and death itself, and made visible to all the presence of the living God. They ask for any declaration in the Scriptures that this miraculous power of faith was to be confined to the first confessors of Christianity. They speak a language of hope and promise to weak, weary hearts, tossed and troubled, who have wandered from sect to

sect, seeking in vain for the primal manifestations of the divine power.[76]

The last of the three movements to be considered – Millerism – was the most openly and obviously millenarian.[77] The Millerites fixed a precise date for the commencement of the millennium and geared all their efforts to preparing for it. Compared with Shakerism and Mormonism, Millerism was short-lived (1831–44), but it reached an unprecedented crescendo of intensity in 1843 and 1844. Many stories intended to discredit millenarians by reducing them to figures of fun can be traced to the Millerite period. In popular imagination the Millerites have become the people who wore white ascension robes, who gathered on mountain tops to await their Lord's second coming in the clouds, and who appeared as cases of 'religious delusion' in the state asylums. Whatever the factual basis of such stories, they are now part of the folk-lore of nineteenth-century American millenarianism.

The eponymous William Miller (1782–1849) was a farmer from Vermont. Self-educated, an omnivorous reader, member of the local literary society and freemasons – he for a time abandoned the Christian beliefs of his youth, and became a deist. As a prosperous citizen he served as local constable, justice of the peace and sheriff; and during the war of 1812 was a volunteer captain of infantry. After his discharge he returned to farming, and in 1816 regained his Christian faith and joined the Baptists. For two years (1816–18) he studied the Bible intensively, using only the marginal notes and Cruden's *Concordance*, and formulated his views on the prophecies, which especially fascinated him. 'The Bible was now to me a new book', he wrote. 'It was indeed a feast of reason.'[78] But as he continued his study of the prophecies in his spare time from farming he came to startling conclusions:

> I commenced their study with no expectation of finding the time of the Saviour's coming, and I could at first hardly believe the result to which I had arrived; but the evidence struck me with such force that I could not resist my convictions. I became nearly settled in my conclusions, and began to wait, and watch, and pray for my Saviour's coming.[79]

He did not, however, feel any compunction at this time to go out and proclaim these conclusions to the world at large. During the next thirteen years he was content to go on studying and playing his part as a prominent citizen and lay member of the Baptist church in Hampton, New York, whither he had moved after the death of his father. Not until

1831, when he was in his fiftieth year, did Miller preach his first sermon – and then only because the regular minister of the nearby Baptist church in Dresden was away one Sunday. Miller preached on Daniel 7 and 8, and was persuaded to continue with a series of lectures on the second advent. His message was enthusiastically received, and he was soon invited to speak at other places in the western Vermont – northern New York area. Rapidly his travelling, preaching and correspondence increased. In 1833 he was licensed to preach by the Baptists; and in 1834, convinced that God was calling him to a special mission, Miller became a full-time preacher.

Until 1838 he bore a 'solitary witness' (as later Adventists said) in the small towns and villages of northern New England and New York state, preaching wherever he was invited to go. But in the second phase of the Millerite movement, from 1838 to 1840, he made an entry into the cities and was joined by a number of ministers from different churches, notably Josiah Litch (Methodist Episcopal), Charles Fitch (Congregational), Henry Jones (Congregational), Henry Dana Ward (Episcopal), and Joshua V. Himes (pastor of the Chardon Street Chapel of the Second Christian Church of Boston), who quickly became the chief promoter and publicist of the movement. Miller had been content to preach only where invited, and his aim was to work within existing churches, warning them of Christ's speedy return. Under Himes's direction Millerism became more expansionist and aggressive. Lecture tours were organized for Miller, halls were hired, and the first Millerite periodical, *Signs of the Times*, was launched in Boston. Beginning in the autumn of 1840 a series of general conferences was convened which helped to unify the movement and give it a simple institutional form. This was followed in 1842–3 by large camp meetings on the Methodist model – thirty-one during the summer of 1843 and more than 124 in the two years 1842–3. Over a score of adventist periodicals appeared, and Himes published a steady stream of books and pamphlets in his *Second Advent Library*. From the summer of 1843 opposition to Millerism mounted in the churches, and members and ministers were expelled for adherence to the adventist cause. For their part, the Millerites identified the Babylon of Revelation 18 with Antichrist, interpreted to mean not only the Roman Catholic church but also the Protestant churches. And in a well-publicized sermon in July 1843, Charles Fitch proclaimed the old sectarian message: 'Come out of her, my people.'

Miller's teachings had in fact reached a stage at which compromise was impossible, for he had finally set a date (1843) for Christ's return. The implications of this were so vast that they completely overshadowed all other issues. Using the 2,300 days prophecy of Daniel 8:14 and the seventy weeks of Daniel 9:24, Miller concluded that prophetic time would end during the Jewish year 1843, which was between the equinoxes of 21 March 1843 and 21 March 1844. The 'cleansing of the sanctuary' was interpreted to mean that the earth would be purged of evil 2,300 years after the time of Daniel's prophecy, which Miller calculated was made in 457 BC. He arrived at this date by interpreting Daniel's seventy weeks (i.e. 490 days) as meaning 490 years, on the principle that a 'day' means a year of time. From the 490 years he subtracted AD 33, the date of the crucifixion (on the premise that Christ's death marks the end of the seventy weeks or 490 year-days), leaving 457. By subtracting this date from 2,300 he was left with 1843 as the date of the second advent.[80] A slightly different Millerite formula arrived at the same result, thus:

$$70 \times 7 = 490 - 2300 = 1810.$$
1810 added to AD 33 makes 1843.[81]

This method of calculation was, of course, not original to the Millerites. Most prophetic expositors before them had used similar techniques, and the dates were the standard Bible marginal ones. The Millerites, however, pushed the argument to its logical conclusions, and finally settled on an exact date when Christ would appear. With the expiration of the Jewish year in the spring of 1844, Miller rallied his followers by recalling the command to the prophet Habakkuk that though the vision 'tarry, wait for it' (Habakkuk 2:3). The 'tarrying time' lasted from April to July 1844, when a new interpretation was adopted. It was agreed that the date of the crucifixion should be revised, and that the true ending of the 2,300 years would be the tenth day of the autumnal Jewish 'seventh month'. The second advent could therefore be expected on 22 October 1844. Miller had earlier interpreted the Midnight Cry as the general advent awakening of the nineteenth century: the wise virgins were the believers, the foolish the unbelievers, their lamps were the Bible, and so on. But now the Millerites argued that this had been only a preliminary alarm: the true Midnight Cry was now sounding: 'Behold, the Bridegroom cometh, go ye out to meet Him.'

From mid-August the movement swept forward to its climax. Some 200 ordained ministers and nearly 2,000 lay preachers conducted an intense campaign of preparation for the events of 22 October, supported by a swelling tide of periodicals, books, pamphlets and broadsides. Between 50,000 and 100,000 persons withdrew from their churches and awaited the second coming.[82] As the time of the end drew nearer the faithful were admonished to set their temporal affairs in order and search their hearts. During the final week Millerites closed their stores, abandoned their crops and animals, and resigned from their posts. Some gave away their goods to the poor, and Millerite periodicals were distributed free. The *Advent Herald* of 16 October informed its readers: 'as the date of the present number of the *Herald* is our last day of publication before the tenth day of the seventh month, we shall make no provision for issuing a paper for the week following'; and the 'final' issue of *The Midnight Cry* (19 October) headed its editorial with St Paul's valediction: 'Finally, Brethren, Farewell'.

On the Last Day (22 October) the Millerites met quietly in their homes and meeting-houses, to pray and wait for their Lord. They had long meditated on this awesome event, and were thoroughly familiar with its biblical descriptions. But after a day and night vigil, the expected signs did not appear. Their saviour did not come on clouds of glory, the earth was not rent by earthquakes, there were no lightnings or trumpets or eclipses or lakes of fire and brimstone: only a day as other days. Great was the disappointment. 'Our fondest hopes and expectations were blasted', wrote Hiram Edson later, 'and such a spirit of weeping came over us I never experienced before. It seemed that the loss of all earthly friends could have been no comparison. We wept, and wept, till the day dawn.'[83]

As with other movements in which prophecy failed, Millerism was not long in producing explanations of the failure – though in its original form the Millerite movement did not survive. But the disappointment was especially acute for Millerites because of the very literal nature of their expectations. No gap could be wider than between the reality of 22 October and Miller's description of the Last Day, in which he depicted the supposed reflections of a sinner:

Ah! what means that noise? Can that be thunder? Too long, too loud and shrill; more like a thousand trumpets sounding an onset. It shakes the earth. ... See, see, it reels! How dreadful! How strange! ...
Another phenomenon to frighten poor, ignorant fanatics. I will not be afraid. Let Nature play her fantastic gambols. My soul's too brave to shake, too big to be afraid. ...
    There was a time when superstition reigned ... but now the world has become more wise; they are not fools and cowards, as our forefathers. ... Hark! another sound, more long, more loud, more dreadful still! Rock, rock! the world is rocking men, like babes, to sleep. I will not yet be scared. ... I am not shaken yet. Nature will

work her own cure; and, while these Christian fools are trembling under their vain imaginations of these sights and signs of the great last day, I stand un. ... A third great blast – a shout, a cry! What means this wild roar? I'll go and see. ...

The mountains shake and tremble on their base; the hills move to and fro; the compass-needle has forsaken the pole, and leaps towards the zenith point. The sea has fled its bounds, and rivers backward in their channels run. What can this mean? Is nature in a fit? ... The light! the light! it still approaches nearer to the earth – and brighter too; it dazzles my weak sight. Is it a comet, or some other orb, that has strayed from its track, and, by the laws of gravitation, is approaching to our earth? ... Another sound! A dreadful blast, a hundred-fold more loud than former trumpets! This shakes my soul; my courage, too, has fled ... What but a Gabriel's trump could give such sounds – so loud, so long, so clear? ... Look! the sun has veiled his face; all nature heaves a groan, one deep-drawn sigh, and all is still as death. ...

The clouds – those vivid clouds, so full of fire – are driven apart by this last blast, and, rolling up themselves, stand back aghast. And, O, my soul, what do I see? A great white throne, and One upon it. His garment is whiter than the driven snow, and the hair on his head is like the pure wool. See fiery flames issuing from his throne, rolling down the vault of heaven like wheels of burning fire. Before him are thousands and thousands of thousands of winged seraphim, ready to obey his will. See Gabriel, the great archangel, raising his golden trump to his mouth. The last great trumpet sounds, – one heavenly shout, – and in a moment every angel flies, each different ways, in rays of light, to this affrighted globe. The earth now heaves a throb for the last time, and in this last great throe her bowels burst, and from her spring a thousand thousand, and ten thousand times ten thousand immortal beings into active life. And then those few who had looked on the scene with patient hope, were suddenly transformed, from age to youth, from mortal to immortal; and thus they stood, a bright and shining band, all clothed in white, like the bright throne which yet appeared in heaven.[84]

This is reminiscent of the paintings of John Martin and Washington Allston, referred to earlier. It is an aspect of the sub-culture of millenarianism which was especially prominent in Millerism, and which presents a peculiar psychological problem: how to prepare for the Last Day? Familiar as one might become with scenes from romantic painting and with the imagery of the Book of Revelation, it is difficult to take in such a stupendous idea as the sudden appearance of the Divine Being and the complete ending of the world in its present form. Just how to act and speak in the presence of the Lord, whom one is expecting shortly to meet face to face, presents thoughts which could (or should) have enormous implications for each believer. From accounts of the Millerites one is left with the impression that they struggled hard to comprehend their situation and made the appropriate responses in words, but that they were so bogged down by the literalness of their interpretation as to be incapable of grasping the full meanings of the End of Time. The language of Millerite leaders when describing their great disappointment and renewed hopes seems somehow quite inadequate to the nature of the occasion. For example, Luther Boutelle, a shoemaker from Groton, Massachusetts, recorded:

> the 22nd of October passed, making unspeakably sad the faithful and longing ones; but causing the unbelieving and wicked to rejoice. All was still. No *Advent Herald*; no meetings as formerly. Every one felt lonely, with hardly a desire to speak to any one. Still in the cold world! No deliverance – the Lord not come! No words can express the feelings of disappointment of a true Adventist then.

But he soon recovered, and commented cheerfully: 'it was not long after our disappointment before the light began to break in upon us, and we saw there was to be a waiting time, a midnight before the Lord would come.'[85] The hope of the millennium was not easily extinguished – even though in the long term the reaction to Millerism strengthened those postmillennial doctrines which were part of orthodox evangelical Protestantism.[86]

Inadequate as they were bound to be, individual Millerites made valiant efforts to come to terms with the idea of apocalyptic time. A particularly well-documented case is Ezekiel Hale, Jr, a business man in Haverhill, Massachusetts.[87] He became a follower of Miller after listening to his lectures in Haverhill during 1839 and 1840, and from 1841 to 1844 Hale was completely obsessed by thoughts of the second advent. He concluded that it would be sinful to be found in possession of any considerable amount of property at the Lord's coming, and therefore deeded his mills to his oldest son, Ezekiel J. M. Hale. After the great disappointment, the elder Hale brought a suit in equity for the recovery of his properties, alleging fraud and deception in the transaction. The case is interesting because of the evidence (on oath) produced as to Hale's state of mind in the period of Millerite enthusiasm. Witnesses for the plaintiff sought to show that he was mentally unfit, because of his erroneous belief that the second advent was due in 1843–4, to dispose of his property at that time. The defendant of course produced evidence that his father was in every way normal and so competent to transfer the estate. From this testimony Hale emerges as a man already known to his neighbours as a supporter of 'ultraisms': temperance, anti-slavery, Grahamism (diet reform). He had been a Baptist, then seceded to form a separate church, returned to the Baptists, and in 1838–9 left them to organize a Union Evangelical Church (in Winter Street, Haverhill) which favoured liberal, evangelical causes. When Millerism came along no one was surprised that he espoused that too. 'He talked much about the Second Advent of Christ, and the coming end of the world', said his daughter. 'It was almost his whole topic of discourse. He attended meetings of those holding these views as often as there was one.' Ladd Haselton, a mason by trade and an old acquaintance, recalled a conversation outside Hale's house in the rain. 'The Lord is coming, Mr. Haselton, the Lord is coming ... depend upon it, be prepared to meet him', said Hale; whereupon Haselton made a mental note to himself: 'that man's crazy.' Several witnesses deposed that Hale in 1842 was 'very credulous', that he readily believed stories of remarkable visions, and that he travelled long distances to see people who had had unusual dreams and visions.

His son-in-law, Augustus M. Coburn, who kept a store in Haverhill, gave a convincing description of the family meeting at which the disposal of the property was discussed:

When I entered the room, the plaintiff was engaged in conversation with the family, all of whom were present. He said he had called a meeting of the family for the purpose of consulting with them in reference to his property. He said, 'You know my views on the advent question; I expect Christ will shortly appear; and I wish to make some disposition of my worldly affairs. I dare not be found with the property in my possession when the Lord comes, as he shortly will.' He said he had called the meeting for the purpose of seeing if the family could not unite with him in some plan by which he could get rid of it. It was a solemn matter, he said, and he wished to ask God's direction. He knelt down and prayed. He prayed that the matter under consideration might not withdraw their minds from the coming of Christ, so soon to take place; that their affections might be weaned from the world; and that all might be ready to meet the Saviour when he came, as he shortly would. ... He said, what he proposed was, that he himself should take a portion of the property, such as might be agreed upon, that he should feel free to spend in the advent cause. As they differed in opinion from him, he wished to regard their rights, and would be satisfied with what they were willing he should take; not that he believed the property would do them any good. He then proposed asking the members of the family what course he had best pursue.

Some of the family advised a sale, others not. Coburn said: 'If you wish for money to spend in the advent cause take the income and spend that. You will regret it, if you ever, in this state of feeling, dispose of your property.' But his brother-in-law, Ezekiel, who wished to take over the property, interrupted him, saying: 'Well, Gus, you don't know but what the world will end. Father has a right to do as he pleases.' A wrangle over the value of the property then followed, with the defendant suggesting a low figure and the others a higher sum. Some days later Ezekiel Hale settled the mill upon his oldest son, and made provision for his other children. What he did on 22 October 1844 we are not told, nor how he adjusted his beliefs subsequently. The suit was settled mutually in 1851, and the property mostly returned to him. Hale was not a national figure in the Millerite movement, and his case is the more significant in that it shows us the effects of millenarian belief among the followers. Not least it highlights the great difficulty (perhaps near impossibility) of escaping from the trammels of earthly existence even in the face of divine cataclysm. To have to haggle about the market price of property when one believed that 'the Lord is coming ... depend upon it' was inconsequential in the extreme. There was here a psychological equation which millenarians simply could not balance.

In their expositions of prophecy and preparations for the last days, the Millerites elaborated certain aspects of millenarian sub-culture to a high degree. Millerism was essentially a literate movement. William Miller was not a prophet with charisma, like Joseph Smith, but a preacher. Occasionally he was addressed as Father Miller, but more usually he was referred to simply as 'Bro. Miller'. His message, like that of the other Millerite leaders was 'search the scriptures.' The basis of this millenarianism was not direct revelation (though visions and dreams provided powerful confirmation) but a literal interpretation of the Bible. This accorded well with the dominant Protestant orthodoxy of the time, and Millerism was in this respect only a rather unusual version of evangelical and revivalist religion. Topics discussed in the pamplets of the *Second Advent Library*, for instance, were not confined to the second coming but included problems of immortality and resurrection, the nature of the fall, the promise to Abraham, entire consecration, and the Israel of God. Nevertheless it was the emphasis on adventism which distinguished the Millerite movement and gave it a special appeal.

Miller's long and solitary study of the Bible was by no means unique. The image of 'the old farmer' (as he called himself) puzzling his way through the intricacies of prophetic revelation and finally attaining that certainty which had eluded the learned divines was attractive to men similarly stationed in life and with similar interests and hopes. Millerism appeared as a form of religious or theological self-help, which encouraged a do-it-yourself interpretation of scripture. To guide seekers Miller formulated fourteen rules of interpretation, which were widely printed in the movement:

I   Every word must have its proper bearing on the subject presented in the Bible.

II   All Scripture is necessary, and may be understood by a diligent application and study.

III   Nothing revealed in Scriptures can or will be hid from those who ask in faith, not wavering.

IV   To understand doctrine, bring all the Scriptures together on the subject you wish to know; then let every word have its proper influence; and if you can form your theory without a contradiction, you cannot be in error.

V   Scripture must be its own expositor, since it is a rule of itself. If I depend on a teacher to expound to me, and he should guess at its meaning, or desire to have it so on account of his sectarian creed, or to be thought wise, then his guessing, desire, creed or wisdom, is my rule, and not the Bible.

VI   God has revealed things to come, by visions, in figures and parables; and in this way the same things are oftentime revealed again and again, by different visions, or in different figures and parables. If you wish to understand them, you must combine them all in one.

VII   Visions are always mentioned as such.

VIII   Figures always have a figurative meaning, and are used much in prophecy to represent future things, times and events – such as mountains, meaning governments, Dan. 2:35, 44; beasts, meaning kingdoms, Dan. 7:8, 17; waters, meaning people, Rev. 17:1, 15; day, meaning year, &c. Ezk. 4:6.

IX   Parables are used as comparisons to illustrate subjects, and must be explained in the same way as figures, by the subject and Bible.

X   Figures sometimes have two or more different significations, as day is used in a figurative sense to represent three different periods of time, namely first, indefinite, Eccles. 7:14; second, definite, a day for a year, Ezk. 4:6; and third, a day for a thousand years, 2 Pet. 3:8. The right construction will harmonize with the Bible, and make good sense; other constructions will not.

XI   If a word makes good sense as it stands, and does no violence to the simple laws of nature, it is to be understood literally; if not, figuratively.

XII   To learn the meaning of a figure, trace the word through your Bible, and when you find it explained, substitute the explanation for the word used; and if it make good sense, you need not look further; if not, look again.

XIII   To know whether we have the true historical event for the fulfilment of a prophecy: If you find every word of the prophecy (after the figures are understood) is literally fulfilled, then you may know that your history is the true event; but if one word lacks a fulfilment, then you must look for another event, or wait its future development; for God takes care that history and prophecy shall agree, so that the true believing children of God may never be ashamed.

XIV   The most important rule of all is, that you must have *faith*. It must be a faith that requires a sacrifice, and, if tried, would give up the dearest object on earth, the world and all its desires.[88]

Armed with this methodology, and assured that God will guide those who sincerely trust him, the 'wayfaring man', argued Miller, need not fear that he will err far from the truth. Following Miller's lead, it was open to anyone to convince himself (or otherwise) by his own efforts that the second coming was imminent.

A perusal of *Signs of the Times* confirms the intellectual level and type of mind for which Millerism was catering. The paper was made up of articles on prophecy, news of the movement, and the usual snippets of information about extraordinary events in various parts of the world. But its most original features were the charts and diagrams illustrating the prophecies and biblical chronology. Woodcuts of apocalyptical seals, trumpets and vials; fantastic beasts with wings and horns; and the great image of Daniel 2:31 portrayed vividly the millenarian message. Large lithograph copies of a composite chart on the prophecies of Daniel and Revelation were also made for publicity in 1843 and became one of the identifying marks of the movement. Millerites were pioneers in the use of visual aids. The general level of writing was such as could be followed by any careful student. It was not esoteric. There were no hidden meanings or occult references – indeed, Miller attributed his years of deism to an incorrect (i.e. mystical) interpretation of the Bible. A thorough acquaintance with the scriptures was held to be essential, though this did not necessarily imply very deep study of them. Significantly, 'study' was equated with reading and re-reading the Bible. The bible-centredness of Millerism was well calculated to appeal to followers who were intelligent but not highly educated. Like other millenarians, Millerites often seem to have been self-educated men with a thirst for knowledge. For such men the study of the Bible in the way the Millerites prescribed was very attractive. It was an exercise which combined skills in calculation, detective work and bibliography – yet could be begun without any previous expertise and without the resources of a library. There was the delight of making new discoveries, and the overwhelming sense of the urgent relevance of the task. The whole of human history was made plain in a series of phases leading up to the present, and knotty intellectual problems could be set aside as of no account in these last days when time itself would shortly end. That much of this intellectual fare was second rate, that at times it amounted to a kind of pseudo-learning, may indicate one of the needs that Millerism was tuned to meet.

In considering the functional role of Millerism it is also pertinent that a number of its leaders were associated with reform causes. How many of Miller's followers were 'ultraists' it is impossible to say; but it is clear from evidence such as the Hale case that Millerism was associated in the public mind with the general reform ethos. Himes's Chardon Street Chapel in Boston was a notable centre for abolitionism, non-resistance, temperance, and Grahamism; and the same causes were espoused by Josiah Litch, Charles Fitch, George Storrs, Henry Jones, Joseph Bates and other prominent Millerites. The appeal of Millerism was to men who already favoured social change, and who were happy to see their former causes subsumed under one great and final movement. 'I will overturn, overturn, overturn it', they quoted from Ezekiel 21:27, 'and it shall be no more, until he come whose right it is; and I will give it him.' They had (for the time being) given up hope of gradual reform leading to a Jacksonian millennium, and had withdrawn from politics. Joseph Bates explained the position to his temperance and abolitionist friends who reproached him for no longer attending their meetings:

My reply was, that in embracing the doctrine of the second coming of the Saviour, I found enough to engage my whole time in getting ready for such an event ... so much more could be accomplished in working at the fountainhead.[89]

The Millerite movement had some repercussions in Britain, though not on anything like the same scale as the Mormons. From 1841 to 1846 Millerite preachers visited various parts of the country, chapels and halls were hired, and several short-lived periodicals were published.[90] The preachers were often British emigrants to the USA who returned to proclaim their new-found faith: such were Robert Winter from Vermont and Charles Dealtry of New York. In 1846 Himes himself, accompanied by two other preachers, arrived on an adventist mission. The strongest centres of Millerism seem to have been Nottingham and the West Country; though individual congregations were also established at Uckfield (Sussex), Liverpool, London, Leeds and elsewhere. The total number of converts was not large: perhaps 2,000 to 3,000 at most; and their social composition was mainly small tradesmen, artisans and shopkeepers, with usually one wealthier member in each congregation. To respectable 'students of prophecy' Miller's exegesis was of considerable interest; but to outsiders the Millerites seemed little different from other millenarian sects, and they were often confused with the Mormons. In fact the Millerites' closest links were with the Campbellites, Irvingites and the small independent congregations listed in the 1851 Census of Religious Worship under such names as 'Christians', 'Christ's Disciples' and 'Primitive Christians'. Himes studied the Southcottians in London and was also in touch with the Wroeites of Ashton-under-Lyne. And, as a final link between the two movements, when Wroe died in 1863 his successor at Wakefield was Daniel Milton, who had been a Millerite in New Hampshire until 1844.

Millenarian prophecy among the Millerites, Mormons and Shakers can be seen from one angle as part of the generally accepted belief of evangelical Protestantism. But viewed from the other end of the continuum the three movements appear to have a less respectable, and more folk character. Local prophets and millenarian movements abounded in America in the late eighteenth and early nineteenth centuries, and it was to these that the Shakers and Mormons were usually related by hostile observers. Beyond the nationally known figures was another layer of millenarian characters. Jemima Wilkinson's experiences, doctrines and community resembled the Shakers'.[91] The daughter of a Quaker farmer from Rhode Island, she was drawn to the New Light enthusiasts while in her teens. In 1776 she had a severe illness, and she subsequently believed that the visions which she saw in the delirium of her fever were revelations from God. After recovery she claimed that her old body (or tabernacle) had died, and that the 'spirit of life from God' had resurrected her as a new person with a divine commission to preach. She now assumed the name of Public Universal Friend. Disciples were soon attracted, including several wealthy patrons; and in 1788 the community of New Jerusalem was founded in western New York state. The followers were not numerous: about 150 in New Jerusalem, and perhaps another 200 in New England. After Jemima's death in 1819 the community slowly declined; but the society did not finally end until 1863 with the death of James Brown, the last recognized leader of the Universal Friends. Jemima did not claim to be the messiah (contrary to what some of her followers implied), but simply that she was divinely inspired. She strongly advocated celibacy (her mother had twelve children in twenty-five years and died soon after the birth of the last child) but did not insist on it as rigidly as Mother Ann Lee.

More extreme were the claims of Joseph C. Dylks, 'the Leatherwood God', who appeared in eastern Ohio in 1828. The story of his sudden appearance in Salesville and the conversion of local worthies in the church and community to his views is a remarkable example of millenarian enthusiasm.[92] 'I am God, and there is none else', he proclaimed.

> I am God and the Christ united. ... There is now no salvation for
> men except by faith in me. All who put their trust in me shall never
> taste death, but shall be translated into the New Jerusalem, which I am
> about to bring down from Heaven.[93]

As he came down from the pulpit in the Salesville 'temple' his disciples cried 'Behold our God!', and the congregation fell on their knees and worshipped him. On other occasions he showed believers the stigmata in his hands. Who Dylks really was and where he came from remains a mystery. He first appeared at a camp meeting in the area; and his subsequent mission divided the community into supporters and opponents. Twice he was brought before magistrates, who were unable to convict him of any legal offence; and he was then forced to flee for his life. He told his followers that he had decided to establish the New Jerusalem in Philadelphia, and set out for that city with his three chief apostles. But they lost track of him in Philadelphia and never saw him again. Faith in Dylks, however, continued in the valley of the Leatherwood creek for many years, and in 1870 there were still believers who looked for his reappearance to establish the New Jerusalem.

Within the established millenarian movements there was always danger from false prophets. The Campbellite *Millennial Harbinger* for 1831 reported the activities of Prophet Davidson, a disciple of Dylks, who appeared in Vermont.[94] He announced that the millennium would begin in 1832, and gained support in the towns of Bakersfield, Fairfax and Fairfield.[95] In Hartford, Connecticut, Giles, the Prophet of God, declared in 1840 that the millennium had begun with him; and in 1844 the Millerites were warned against Michael Hull Barton who, it was said, pretended to extraordinary spiritual gifts in order to seduce religious married women into spiritual wifery.[96] Obviously no single interpretation can fit these varied millenarian prophets and movements. But their very numbers and variety attest the strength of their popular roots.

What, however, comes from this exercise in Anglo–American comparison? The first impression is of the similarities and parallels between millenarians in the two countries. There is the same pre-occupation with the great millennial themes of the time: prophecies, the signs of the last days, the midnight cry, Antichrist and the binding of Satan, and the restoration of the Jews. Everywhere the symbolism and imagery of the Book of Revelation keeps appearing; everywhere there is the discussion of dreams, signs and visions. Between specific movements and revelations the echoes are unmistakable: Mother Ann and the Shakers have much in common with the Buchanites and the Southcottians; Joseph Smith's teachings about the American Indians are paralleled by Brothers' theories of British Israel; the Millerites' come-outer stance is matched by the Wroeites' withdrawal from gentile society: Joanna and Joseph Smith each drew upon a strong heritage of folk-culture. The followers fall into familiar patterns: an inner group of educated and wealthier disciples and a wider following of farmers, artisans, women and labouring folk, gathered from among seekers in other sects and churches, and from certain readily identifiable geographical areas. Communitarian solutions to problems of separateness from the world and individual familism appeal to Buchanites, Shakers and early Mormons. A forthright feminism and unorthodox sexual relationships arouse suspicion or enmity among unbelievers. A recurrent anti-intellectualism breaks through the crust of scriptural learning so beloved by millenarians on both sides of the Atlantic.

Yet our second impression is to modify the similarities and take notice of the differences. In some cases it would appear that a movement in one country developed further or more intensely than its analogue in the other. Thus Millerism demonstrated the dangers of a too literal interpretation of the time prophecies, and raised in acute form the

205

dilemma of what happens when prophecy fails. Again, the range of possible alternatives that might have been open to a movement are suggested by what happened in another sect. Who can say whether the believers in Joanna might not have been more successful had they followed more closely the methods of Ann Lee's followers?; and why could not John Wroe have equalled the achievements of Joseph Smith? But of course these things did not happen and so speculation about them beyond a certain point is idle. 'Success' and 'failure' in such cases are notoriously inappropriate concepts for the historian.

The comparative dimension shows us groups of seekers in both countries, sharing elements of a common millenarian culture. But the search for personal and social salvation had to be worked out in different contexts; and the more closely these contexts are examined the more clearly does it appear that millenarianism was a prescription for the cure of many different ills and a recipe for the realization of many types of aspiration. Although millenarians in Britain and America drew upon a common fund of symbols, imagery and vocabulary, they did not necessarily use them in the same way or for the same purposes. The doctrine of the Woman, the restoration of the Jews, or the coming of Shiloh were given twists of meaning peculiar to each millenarian sect. Within these contextual limitations, however, there remained a core of millenarian belief whose central purpose was to give meaning to the experiences of labouring people in both countries.

CHAPTER EIGHT

THROUGH A GLASS, DARKLY

Having assembled our millenarian materials we have now to return to the point from which we started and try to assess the contribution of millenarianism to popular understanding. It will be obvious that under the general term millenarian we have uncovered persons and movements differing widely from each other in a great variety of ways. Some of our millenarians would have indignantly repudiated any association with their so-called fellows. There were profound differences about what was meant by the millennium, the ways in which scripture should be used, the validity of inner voices, and the claims of prophets and prophetesses. Critical contemporaries, however, were more inclined to discern points of similarity and to classify together people who held such views; for they recognized a common core of belief, attitudes and values: Joanna Southcott seemed but a later version of Mrs Buchan or Mother Ann Lee, the Mormons only a repetition of earlier antinomian sects. Instead of always considering how the world looked to the millenarians it is sometimes useful to see how the world looked back at them. And a main problem for the world was to distinguish the popular millenarians from earlier prototypes or other contemporary religionists. Academic speculation about the nearness of the millennium, and a spate of sermons and pamphlets on Daniel and Revelation poured forth in the 1790s;[1] and the general religious ethos of bible-centred, Protestant evangelicalism was favourable to an apocalyptic interpretation of events in Europe. All this was entirely orthodox and respectable.

But respectable millennialists were anxious to dissociate themselves from what Joseph Priestley called 'Brothers and other curiosities'. Anglican parsons with a penchant for the study of prophecy, and Dissenting preachers full of eschatological learning were largely immune from the ridicule which fell on the Southcottians in 1814 or the revulsion occasioned by reports of the Wroeites at Ashton-under-Lyne. The world recognized certain marks of popular millenarianism which were distinctive: the revelatory claims of prophets and prophetesses, the attempt to relive the conditions of the Gospels, the interpretation of scripture by the light of the Spirit, and the sense of apocalyptic urgency appropriate to belief in imminent and sudden changes on a cosmic scale. It was not so much the content of their beliefs that distinguished the millenarians as the way in which they held those beliefs and the purposes to which they were applied. To this extent our distinction between respectable millennialists and popular millenarians is valid and useful. But the dichotomy cannot be applied rigidly, for there were some people who partook of the characteristics of both types. Respectability or scholarliness were not always on one side; nor was adventist enthusiasm always limited to shopkeepers and artisans. This is evident in the case of the Irvingites, who developed from a highly fashionable London congregation of the Reverend Edward Irving into a notorious hotbed of millenarianism.[2] Irving, a minister of the Church of Scotland and friend of Thomas Carlyle, established himself as a popular preacher in London, and then, about 1825, became absorbed in the study of prophecy. He believed that the 1,260 years were the period 533–1792, ending with the French Revolution. During the next thirty years (1793–1823) the first six vials of wrath were poured out upon the Beast, and the seventh was about to be poured. Irving's preaching on the second advent was reinforced by his contact with millenarian movements in the west of Scotland in 1828–30. Revivals at Rosneath, Row, and Port Glasgow were accompanied by prophesyings, healing, speaking with tongues, and 'extraordinary manifestations' of supernatural power. In 1831 Irving's preaching in his Regent Square church was interrupted by an outbreak of 'utterances'; and Irvingism rapidly developed gifts of prophesyings, glossalalia, spiritual healing, automatic writing, and telepathy. Irving was promptly removed from his church and expelled from the ministry of the Church of Scotland. For a short time in 1832 his followers met in the Owenite socialist headquarters in Gray's Inn Road – which perhaps provided the ultimate confirmation in the eyes of the world that the Irvingites were no longer acceptable. Irving and his congregation – and the Catholic Apostolic Church which they subsequently formed – came from the middle classes, and some of them were very wealthy. But to study and preach on Daniel and Revelation was one thing: to act as though the last days were actually here was quite another. The former could be a mainly intellectual exercise, a matter of complexity and debate; the latter reduced all questions to a few basic simplicities before the compelling urgency of the imminent arrival of the Messiah and the Last Judgment.

So the world looked back at the millenarians and declined to accept them at their face value. The religiously orthodox recoiled with horror and indignation: rival sectarians challenged them and disputed points of interpretation: educationists and other reformers were confirmed in their worst fears of the credulity, ignorance and superstition of the lower orders: men of the world affected an amused tolerance. These responses came from different perceptions of millenarianism, reflecting both the predilections of the observers and the variations among millenarians. Each observer had his own (partial) explanation of aspects of popular millenarian belief and behaviour: none was able to encompass the whole. Each saw, as it were, through a glass, darkly. In trying to account for millenarianism the world directed its attention to certain specific aspects of the phenomenon and neglected others. With the historian's advantage of hindsight, however, we may be able to probe a little further into the problems of explanation. At least three levels of analysis would seem to be relevant: first, a psychological explanation of the motives of the prophets and their followers, and the relations between them; second, an analysis of the social context in which millenarianism appeared; and third, some intellectual explanation of why millenarian beliefs were attractive.[3]

The commonest explanation, then as now, was that millenarians were mentally deranged. 'Every age indulges in the conceit that nervous disorders are on the increase because of the complexity of its civilization with its discontents.'[4] Melancholy and hysteria did duty in the eighteenth and nineteenth centuries; schizophrenia in our own times. It is an attractive and convenient theory to see millenarian prophets as psychotics, and their followers as neurotically inclined people who could not cope. Add to this their frequently deviant sexual behaviour and apparently obvious delusions, and there seems little need to look further for an explanation. Brothers and Turner were confined in asylums and Joanna had to refute allegations of madness. The psychological histories of Mother Ann Lee, Mrs Buchan and Joanna relate directly to their doctrines of sex and the Woman. Visions, voices and dreams are to be accounted for by some unusual psychological condition of the individual concerned. The world of the late eighteenth and early nineteenth centuries did not use this language. Contemporaries seldom spoke of authority, guilt and conscience; but the problems they wrestled with were often personal problems, and modern behavioural science may provide useful hypotheses for some of these. The Shakers' and Wroeites' regulation of the minutest details of daily living suggests a psychological need for order, authority and rules of behaviour. A personal need for security and reassurance may well have been a prime motivation among some millenarians: in the words of a Mormon hymn: 'A Church without a Prophet is not the Church for me; It has no head to guide it; in it I would not be.'

Contemporary concern, however, was usually expressed in a more fundamental way. It took the form of an attempt to relate religious enthusiasm to insanity: millenarianism was a form of madness. The eighteenth century inherited from the seventeenth the idea of melancholia and developed it into the English Malady — that peculiar susceptibility of the English (aided by their climate and the stress of urban life) to depression, loneliness and suicide, and from which it was but a short step to delirium and madness.[5] The inner voices and visions of seekers, the communications, commands and ecstacies of prophets and prophetesses were but 'distempers of the brain' and the first stage of lunacy. What more natural then, than to seek confirmation of such a theory among the inmates of a madhouse, or (in the more fashionable phraseology of the 1830s) the patients of a lunatic asylum? Confined in Bethlem (the oldest, and for long the only, national hospital for the care of the insane) was Margaret Nicholson, who attempted to stab George III in 1786. She was a domestic servant from Stokesley in Yorkshire, and suffered from the delusion that she was related to the royal family and was the rightful heir to the throne. According to the chapbooks of the time she received a vision from an angel who told her to prophesy: the sun and moon would be eclipsed; cold foggy weather, floods and thunderstorms would afflict the country; and there would be 'tumults and insurrections among the lower class of people'.[6]

Also in Bethlem was James Hadfield, who attempted to assassinate the king at Drury Lane Theatre in 1800. He was a silver-spoon maker by trade, and had served in a dragoon regiment in Flanders, where he was badly wounded in the head during the fighting in 1793. He was discharged from the army on grounds of insanity: 'when mad he would call himself Jesus Christ and God.'[7] Hadfield was persuaded to kill the king by a more sinister character, Bannister Truelock, who was also admitted to Bethlem in 1800. Truelock, an Islington shoemaker and contemporary of Brothers, claimed to be a prophet. Like Brothers, Truelock was on intimate terms with the Almighty: 'he was a good looking man and very kind to me.'[8] The messiah, said Truelock, is to come 'from my mouth, in spirit, not in fleshy substance'; and he declared that he had been pregnant with the messiah in this way for over twenty-five years. The time 'is fast approaching when all things are to be fulfilled'; and he told Hadfield that the assassination of the king would remove the last obstacles to the great changes in the world which were now due. It is possible that Truelock had connections with political radicalism. He derided the Bible as an absurdity ('vulgar and indecent history') and was labelled as 'embracing all the profane and anti-Christian tenets of the Carlilean-school of theology'. In Bethlem he was kept away from other patients lest he should convert them to his views and instigate a 'general mutiny'. In December 1821 he escaped, in order to get his writings published, and went to William Hone, the radical bookseller and publisher of Ludgate Hill. Hone would not risk publication without an advance payment of £100, and declined to put Truelock up for the night; and Truelock returned to Bethlem with his manuscript the next evening. It was admitted that in his ordinary conversation he 'betrays not the smallest symptoms of a disordered intellect.' He was extremely dissatisfied with his confinement in Bethlem, 'despite many privileges allowed him'; and one can sense the frustration that made him, in the eyes of the authorities, a 'radical malcontent'. In the name of madness the prophet was caged and rendered impotent.

The next generation saw a notable addition to Bethlem's patients in the person of Jonathan Martin, who was confined for setting fire to York Minster in 1829. After serving six years at sea, he had returned in 1810 to his native locality of Durham and Northumberland and worked as a tanner. He underwent conversion and joined the Methodists; but in 1818 was confined in an asylum in West Auckland, having talked of shooting the bishop. He absconded, was put in Gateshead Asylum, and again escaped. From 1821 until 1829 he worked intermittently as a tanner, and wandered about the north of England, hawking copies of his *Life*, preaching, prophesying, and writing letters denouncing the clergy as imposters.[9] Dressed in his glazed, low-crowned hat and short black-leather cape, he appeared to be yet another religious eccentric who claimed to have visions and the power to prophesy. At his trial for arson he explained that he had had 'two remarkable dreams', by which he understood that God commanded him to burn the Minster. Before lighting the fire he knelt down in the choir and thanked God for helping him in his task: 'I had had a hard night's work, but the Lord Helped me.' Had he not been so helped in his diabolic task, Martin might have been tolerated as a harmless eccentric, like his brothers William ('the natural philosopher'), Richard and John (the painter, mentioned in chapter 5), all of whom were thought to be distinctly odd. As it was, Jonathan Martin confirmed the fears of those who suspected a connection between enthusiastic religion and madness.

This hypothesis was put forward and evidence adduced for it, from various quarters. It appears in Hogarth's print, 'Credulity, Superstition and Fanaticism: A Medley', in which an enthusiastic preacher declaims from the pulpit to a congregation which includes Mary Toft, the rabbit woman. A thermometer, in place of the usual hour-glass, registers degrees from prophecy to madness, and the text of the address is from II Corinthians 11:23, 'I speak as a fool.' The *Gentleman's Magazine* in 1815 purported to give cases of maniacal delusion among followers of Joanna.[10] A phrenological doctor at Montrose Lunatic Asylum compared patients suffering from religious delusions and an excessively developed organ of veneration, with noted religious enthusiasts of the past.[11] And Dr George Man Burrows, the owner of a private asylum in London, pronounced authoritatively:

> Enthusiasm and insanity bear such close affinity, that the shades are often too indistinct to define which is one and which the other.
> Exuberance of zeal on any subject, in some constitutions, soon ripens into madness: but excess of religious enthusiasm ... usually and readily degenerates into fanaticism; ... and permanent delirium too often closes the scene.[12]

Religious madness, of one sort or another, appears almost everywhere in the nineteenth century when once one starts looking for it, hidden away in the corners of family histories or floating on the fringes of millenarian groups. How many more cases were there like Beatrice Webb's grandmother, Mary Seddon, who was obsessed with the mania of leading the Jews back to Jerusalem and was confined in an asylum for fifty years?[13] We do not know. In the best documented account by a patient of his psychosis the millenarian element is strong. John Thomas Perceval was an officer in the Guards, and the fifth son of Spencer Perceval, the prime minister who was assassinated in the House of Commons in 1812. With a strong evangelical background, John Perceval was attracted to Irvingism, and in 1830 visited Scotland to investigate the supernatural manifestations at Row and Port Glasgow. 'I was ... strongly persuaded that the time of the end was at hand', he recalled later, and he became convinced that he was 'to proceed through the world as an angel, under the immediate guidance of the Lord, to proclaim the tidings of his second coming.'[14] He had visions while praying and was guided by voices. When the power of the Spirit came upon him, he explained, he opened his mouth and sang spontaneously. 'This voice was given me, but I was not the master of it; I was but the instrument. I could not use it at my own command, but solely at the command of the Spirit that guided me.' By December 1830 he was clearly schizophrenic and was confined in private asylums until 1834. After his release he wrote a *Narrative* of his mental and religious state. It is a remarkable document. At first glance it appears simply to corroborate George Man Burrows; but on closer reading, Perceval's testimony suggests the limitations of an explanation of his beliefs in terms of sanity and madness. Perceval was able to make a recovery, to return to the normal world; and he then looked back on his psychosis and saw where and when he had lost touch with reality. But he still believed that his voices had been real; he had just not understood them correctly. As he put it, 'the spirit speaks poetically but the man understands it literally.' He concluded that lunacy was only a matter of degree, since most of his experiences were familiar to all men; that the prophets of the Old Testament and the apostles of the New would undoubtedly have been judged insane by the standards of the 1830s; and that for a Protestant country to allow a mad doctor to decide whether his patients' voices and visions were from the Holy Spirit was to substitute lunatic asylums for the inquisition.

In the same year that the first volume of Perceval's *Narrative* appeared, a contemporary psychotic, John Nichols Tom, posed an altogether more dangerous millenarian challenge. Tom was a wine merchant and maltster from Truro, who in 1832 suddenly appeared in Canterbury, claiming to be Sir William Percy Honeywood Courtenay, Knight of Malta and heir to the earldom of Devon.[15] In the excitement following the First Reform Act, Courtenay stood for parliament at Canterbury, but was defeated. However, he became well known in the area, and impressed many by his handsome figure, eccentric but colourful dress, and populist rhetoric. In an ill-judged attempt to champion the local fishermen, Courtenay gratuitously interfered in the trial of some smugglers at Rochester, and was indicted for perjury. He was found guilty and sentenced, but was then confined in the county lunatic asylum. There he remained from 1833 to 1837, when he was released. He immediately sought out his former followers and rallied them behind a millenarian programme in which he, as the messiah, would put down the mighty from their seat and exalt the humble and meek. In May 1838 the local magistrates, fearing that Courtenay was enticing labourers from their work and inciting them to violence, issued a warrant for his arrest. When the constables attempted to serve the warrant Courtenay shot one of the party and mangled the dying man with his sword. A detachment of infantry was then sent from Canterbury to arrest Courtenay, who was found with some of his followers in Bossenden

Wood in the neighbourhood of Dunkirk and Hernhill. In the desperate fight which ensued eleven people, including Courtenay, were killed, and seven more wounded.

Courtenay's story has most of the familiar elements of a popular millenarian movement: a charismatic leader, a radical social programme, a following of labouring men and better-off farmers, and a small circle of adoring female disciples. But at this point our concern is with the relation between millenarian belief and madness. Courtenay's delusions were quite definite. He said that he was the messiah and that the day of judgment and the millennium were close at hand. A charcoal burner described the effect that Courtenay had on his followers:

> A man as I knows well, heard Sir William preach, and then he giv'
> 'em all the sacrament, and after that he anoints himself and all of 'em
> with oil, and tells 'em that then no bullet nor nothing could harm
> 'em; – and Sir William, he sat upon the ground with his back against
> a tree like, and there was all the women a crying and praying to him,
> – and they says to him, 'Now do tell us if you be our blessed Saviour,
> the Lord Jesus Christ!' and says he, 'I am he'; – and then he shows
> 'em the mark of the nails in his hands which was made when he was
> put on the cross. – Now that's no lie, and I knows him well as see it.[16]

It was remarked at the time that Courtenay bore a striking resemblance to the traditional likeness of Christ; and when he appeared upon his white mare it seemed as if the promise of Revelation 6 was being fulfilled: 'And I saw, and behold a white horse; and he that sat on him had a bow; and a crown was given unto him; and he went forth conquering, and to conquer.' How this affected a farmer's wife is described in an account of an interview with a Mrs Wraight, whose husband at the time was in Maidstone gaol awaiting trial (Edward Wraight Jr took part in the battle of Bossenden Wood, and his father was killed there):

> We began to talk immediately of the late disasters, and I soon found an
> opportunity of asking her if she had really believed that Tom was our
> Saviour. I wrote down her answer as nearly as possible, in her own
> words. 'Oh yes, Sir, certain sure I did believe him; and good warrant I
> thought I had. William Wills, you see, Sir, came one day to our
> cottage, and we had some ale; and, says he, "Have you heard the great
> news, and what's going to happen?" – "No," says we, "William
> Wills, what be it?" – and he said the great Day of Judgement was
> close at hand, and that our Saviour had come back again; and that we

must all follow him. And he showed us in the Bible, in the Revelations, that he should come upon a white horse; and go forth to conquer. And sure enough, Sir, the day after, as we were coming in our cart from market, we met the groom leading Sir William's white horse; and he told us that all the country would be up, for the great jubilee was to come, and we must be with 'em. And so, Sir, you see, next day poor Edward certainly did go to join 'em, little thinking what was to happen. And the day after, as they were all passing by the house, I looked out, and Master Foad was just at the tail of them. And I said, "Do you, Master Foad, believe he is our Blessed Saviour?" "Oh yes," he says, "Mrs. Wraight, for certain sure he is, and I'll follow him to the world's end!"'[17]

After Courtenay's death his followers did not immediately give up their belief in him, for he had promised that he would rise again. They did not see anything inherently unlikely in this: they believed what he said, namely that he was divine. As one of his female disciples said, after inviting him to a tea party, 'You may be sure he isn't one of us; he isn't like to us. To hear him talk, and see him, it's not at all like talking to a man.' Another believer, the wife of a bailiff, refused to admit to the interviewer that Courtenay was an imposter:

She persisted in affirming that, even if Sir William (for, not withstanding his celestial dignities, she always gave him his earthly one) had been deceived in some respects, he was nevertheless a holy man inspired by God, and that if he had even gone astray himself, he had led her (to use her own expression) into heavenly paths.

The one thing that none of the believers mentioned was that Courtenay might have been mad, even though his leading supporters were fully aware that he had been in the county asylum. Whatever the verdict of the respectable world, madness was not part of the popular understanding of millenarianism – or rather, charges of madness did not diminish but only confirmed the truth of the claims of Courtenay and other millenarian prophets. The gap between polite and popular culture was here very great. Millenarians did not accept the culturally dominant conception of reality, but inhabited a distinctive world of their own. In this (largely traditional) world madness was explained in terms of supernatural intervention, not as due to natural psycho-medical causes. Divine madness did not have much to commend it to respectable, orthodox religionists of the 1830s. But the embarrassing – and exciting – idea was deeply embedded in the Christian (and Platonic) tradition. The prophets of the Old Testament and the saints later were often portrayed as mad. Had not Isaiah walked naked and barefoot as a sign and a portent? And was not Christ himself the supreme exemplar of the foolishness of God? Christ by his folly, his mad love, redeemed mankind from wisdom and sanity.[18] The divine madness results from a profound inner disturbance of spirit, a destruction and recreation of man, through which comes the knowledge of God. If the Christian experience has much in common with madness, if vision and madness are not far apart, then sanity, or normality, is the enemy of true religion; for it stifles vision and denies the voice of the Spirit. Blake believed that inspired and visionary people would always be called mad by the world, and that the so-called insane were, ironically, the truly healthy.[19] He recorded, about 1819, that the poet William Cowper (who was for a time confined in an asylum) came to him and said:

> O that I were insane always. I will never rest. Can you not make me truly insane? I will never rest till I am so. O that in the bosom of God I was hid. You retain health and yet are as mad as any of us all – over us all – mad as a refuge from unbelief – from Bacon, Newton and Locke.[20]

Blake of course was not insane in the way that Cowper or still less Courtenay were. But what Blake was rejecting was the rationalism, order and propriety (always symbolized for him by the unholy trinity of Bacon, Newton and Locke) which dominated polite culture. He rejoiced in his madness as a challenge to the world of orthodoxy. In his rejection of 'the outward creation' he was not far from the world of the millenarians:

> 'What', it will be Questioned, 'When the Sun rises, do you not see a round disk of fire somewhat like a Guinea?' 'O no, no, I see an Innumerable company of the Heavenly host crying, "Holy, Holy, Holy is the Lord God Almighty." '[21]

Blake's biographer, Alexander Gilchrist, writing in the 1860s, regretted that attitudes to insanity had changed: 'it is *only* within the last century and a half [that] the faculty of seeing visions could have been one to bring a man's sanity into question.'[22] Today it seems more obvious that madness is culturally defined; that society has certain norms of behaviour from which deviance is penalized in obvious or subtle ways. Eccentricity is usually tolerated, and may even be socially or intellectually institutionalized, as was the idea of divine madness in Old Testament times or the Middle Ages. Some cultures make it possible for messiahs, prophets and visionaries to function in an acceptable manner: others have no room for such people, who have therefore to be denigrated and (if potentially disruptive) put away. To respectable middle-class thinkers in the first half of the nineteenth century it seemed that if millenarians could be labelled insane that would be sufficient to discredit them. But this assumption was not apparent to many ordinary men and women whose ideas about madness were much more traditional. The rational and scientific view of the universe had not penetrated as far into society as some of the exponents of that view supposed. Millenarians were people who were either unaware of these intellectual trends or who, being aware, were, like Blake, repelled by them. For people susceptible to a millenarian appeal the attempt to explain away millenarianism by ascribing it to mental derangement was beside the point. Like later psychological explanations it did little more than put a new label on a familiar phenomenon. Carlyle, as usual, grasped the heart of the matter:

> Witchcraft, and all manner of Spectre-work, and Demonology, we have now named Madness and Diseases of the Nerves. Seldom reflecting that still the new question comes upon us: What is Madness, what are Nerves? Ever, as before, does Madness remain a mysterious-terrific altogether *infernal* boiling up of the Nether Chaotic Deep, through this fair-painted Vision of Creation, which swims thereon, which we name the Real. Was Luther's picture of the Devil less a Reality, whether it were formed within the bodily eye, or without it? In every the wisest Soul lies a whole world of internal Madness, an authentic Demon-Empire; out of which, indeed, his world of Wisdom has been creatively built together, and now rests there, as on its dark foundations does a habitable flowery Earth-rind.[23]

The danger of psychological explanations of millenarianism is that they usually tend to reduce the millenarians in some way. If a person's beliefs and behaviour are to be accounted for by mental upset or physical defect, he ceases to be a responsible agent. He is stripped of his dignity of making a choice and becomes the victim of forces beyond his control. This makes it difficult for us to take his beliefs seriously, and does not help towards that understanding of the popular mentality for which we are looking. Moreover there is the danger of assuming that an analysis of individual behaviour can be used to explain group phenomena. Even if we are willing to agree with contemporary critics that Courtenay and Brothers were madmen we have still not explained why their followers were prepared to believe in them and accept millenarian doctrines.

Instead of worrying whether millenarians were mad or sane, diseased or healthy, we should be asking how they perceived themselves and their needs and why millenarian beliefs provided an acceptable ideology. But for this we need to turn to our second level of analysis and consider more closely the social context.

Most social interpretations of millenarianism relate it to three factors: a period of crisis and upheaval; feelings of anxiety and insecurity; and a deprived or oppressed class. It will be useful to see how far our millenarians fit into this frame, and whether their beliefs can be accounted for in these terms. If, as has been suggested, millenarian ideas were not confined to cranks and oddities, what is the social significance of millenarian beliefs, what gives them credibility, and why were they nevertheless confined to certain sections of the population?

Beginning with the circumstances favourable to millenarianism, it is not difficult to show that 1780–1850, and the 1790s in particular, was a period of great political, economic and social upset, both in Britain and Europe. Contemporaries were well aware that they were living in unusual times and the connection with millenarian beliefs was soon made. 'It has always been observed that times of calamity are peculiarly fertile in visions and prognostications, predictions and prophecies', observed Halhed in 1795. 'When the minds of men are softened by the pressure or the apprehension of accumulating evils, then is the moment for the salutary warnings of the internal monitor and the cautionary voice of the spiritual guide.' Nothing was more natural, he argued, than to expect at such a time the arrival of Brothers the prophet. 'The present moment teems with these anticipations of futurity, beyond the example of every former period.'[24] The Quaker merchant, James Jenkins, confirmed such impressions: 'this [1789] seems to have been a time of strange delusions in which Friends were too much concerned – I was myself one of very many who resorted to Richard Brothers, the Prophet'; and the 1793 yearly meeting was visited by Job Scott (from Providence, Rhode Island), who prophesied that Revelation 12 and 14 was being fulfilled, and advised Friends 'to be quiet and silent spectators of the awful scene' – which, said Jenkins, impressed him at the time, though later he had some doubts.[25] The sense of the extraordinariness of the times was continued throughout the years of the Napoleonic wars – the period in which Joanna's mission was at its height. And the grim years of the 1830s and the Hungry Forties saw the proliferation of the later Southcottian sects, who similarly believed that they were living in a time of crisis.

The question we have to consider, however, is not only whether millenarians and others thought they were living in an age of crisis, but whether they actually were. In a broad sense the position is clear enough. Between 1780 and 1850 (that is, within one man's lifetime) Britain changed more than she had done for many hundreds of years previously. At the beginning of this short time span the country was still basically agricultural, traditional, and with a small population; by the end it had been transformed into the world's first industrial civilization, committed to change, improvement, and a rapidly increasing number of people. In the course of this transformation the political system was rebuilt, the economy vastly expanded, and the social structure subjected to enormous pressures. Old institutions had to adapt or go under; the 'fury of innovation' which Dr Johnson had foreseen earlier in the eighteenth century set the tone of the new society. Living in such a time of acute social change was for many people uncomfortable, bewildering, traumatic. Familiar social landmarks disappeared, assumptions about stability and normality were no longer unquestioned, the sources of authority to which men looked for guidance were not convincing as they once had been. A new ideology to take account of the disruption or weakening of the old social order and to sanction new aspirations was needed. Millenarianism was that ideology. Although at first it may appear bizarre, in context it has a rationale which makes it intelligible. Millennial beliefs were a response to this period of crisis.

So runs our general interpretation of millenarianism. As far as it goes it is fairly unexceptionable; but it suffers from the weakness of dealing in generalities. What, for instance, did living in an age of crisis actually mean for the humble follower of Brothers or Joanna? For one person it may have meant being out of work or having to work excessively long hours because of technological changes in the textile industry; for another, reading about the French Revolution and Napoleon in the newspapers and wondering where it would all end; for a third, supporting radical political movements – or it may have been any one of a thousand other experiences. Again, the period 1780–1850 was not one of unrelieved depression or crisis. Periods of economic slump and prosperity, and peaks of social tension can be easily identified; but evidence which would correlate these directly with millenarianism is hard to find. The most we can say is that some millenarian sects, such as the Southcottians and Wroeites, were strong in certain areas and periods which were also characterized by economic distress and social protest.

As an alternative – or perhaps an auxiliary – to theories of a period of general crisis, we can posit the notion of wide-spread feelings of anxiety and insecurity arising out of the stresses and strains of the time. Sudden, unexpected social change (amounting sometimes to a disaster), we may argue, induces personal disorganization and, in some cases mental upset.[26] The individual's sense of society and his identity in it is destroyed, and old beliefs do not provide a convincing explanation of what is happening to him. Anxiety and feelings of meaninglessness result; and millenarian beliefs provide both an explanation of the present state of things and an indication of how it will be resolved. This hypothesis has the advantage that it can deal with specific case histories of millenarians (provided the documentation can be found); and reminds us moreover that personal and social factors are closely intertwined, for although the causes of millenarian movements lie in social disruption, personal psychopathologies may be mobilized in such movements – just as revolutionary movements mobilize men at odds with their societies for many reasons other than an abstract passion for social justice.[27] Millenarians pointed to contemporary evils, both national and personal, and looked for salvation from them. Like Brothers, the believers understood international events as the fulfilment of prophecies of the last days; like Foley, they expected psychic millenarian benefits to help them in their daily chores and troubles. But whereas the former evils were remote and experienced through reading the newspapers, the latter were immediate, intimate and experienced directly. Illness, bereavement, family disagreements, financial difficulties, local persecution: these fill the correspondence of the Southcottians. The millennium was the ultimate salvation from all these ills; in the meantime daily life with all its anxieties was to be lived – and perhaps made more bearable – in the light of the assurance that a new heaven and a new earth were not far off.

The anxiety hypothesis, however, is not without its difficulties. Stress and strain are present in all societies at all times, and we have no way of knowing (as opposed to suspecting) that the period 1780–1850 was more stressful and strained than other periods. There is a danger of projecting our modern obsession with anxiety and insecurity into interpretations of the past. Longing for the millennium may equally well spring from joyousness as from anxiety. At present it would seem that the precise relationship between social change and psychological disorder (despite common assumptions to the contrary) is insufficiently understood to warrant using it for any but the most casual of historical interpretations. To see popular millenarian beliefs as simply defences against anxiety or compensations for inadequacies would be to subscribe to a very crude functionalism. But we should also beware of over-intellectualizing the explanatory functions of millenarianism. The desire to make sense of their world was undoubtedly present in many believers, but it was seldom expressed as a detached, intellectual inquiry. Rather were they looking for more limited and emotional satisfactions. Systems of popular belief are essentially practical, and are concerned with common and continuing problems. As long as the old beliefs appear to be successful they are unlikely to be abandoned. For this reason popular millenarianism contained many traditional elements, and seemed to its critics to be out of date – while paradoxically it was at the same time condemned as a dangerous innovation.

The third factor in a social interpretation of millenarianism is the theory of deprivation, either absolute or relative. Where a class or group suffers a lowering of its standards of living in terms of wealth and status, where the poor get poorer, or where oppression of various kinds increases, social discontent may be channelled into millenarian movements. One who suffers, hopes; and one who hopes, believes, as the old folk saying has it. Hence the chiliasm of despair; millenarianism is the religion of the oppressed. Deprivation may also be not absolute, but relative, as when an individual or group has socially legitimate expectations which, because of certain changes, are not fulfilled. Domestic workers overtaken by technological shifts in the textile industry might be cited as examples of this – as indeed might many similar cases produced by the Industrial Revolution. In all such instances of deprivation there is the possibility (to put it no higher) that individual and social discontent may find expression in millenarianism. Did it in fact do so?

None of the millenarian movements we have looked at had any substantial following among the very poor. There is little to suggest that the disinherited and outcastes of society found solace or hope in millenarian belief. Such evidence as we have points to support from artisans, small farmers, shopkeepers, tradesmen, domestic servants and women, together with an important minority of merchants, businessmen, clergy and members of the professions. Middle-class observers repeatedly expressed surprise that the followers of millenarian prophets were not the poorest and most ignorant members of the community, but on the contrary were people of modest social standing, people 'who ought to have known better.' F. Liardet, the investigator of the Courtenay affair, found that the messiah's main supporter was a prosperous farmer, and that the village schoolmistress was also a believer. The followers who fought in the battle of Bossenden Wood were not riff-raff: 'of the sixteen persons now in gaol at Maidstone, and eleven others discharged on their own recognizances, nearly the whole were men of steady, reputable characters.'[28]

The combination of artisans and other labouring people with lower middle-class elements is a prime factor in Weber's classic theory of the origins of religious radicalism. These classes, it is argued, are the most likely to be alienated in some way from the established order, and therefore may be sensitive to prophetic appeals. Changes in their status or occupation may make it difficult for them to identify with the traditional institutions of society and may thus increase their predilection for radicalism. Allied to them are the proletarian (pariah) intellectuals – self-taught artisans and lower middle-class seekers – whose search for salvation is transposed from an inner, personal quest to a wider critique of society and its meaning. If this thesis is to be used to explain early nineteenth-century millenarianism, however, we have to show more than that Southcottians and Wroeites were drawn largely from certain social groups. We have to show how those groups were alienated or relatively deprived to such an extent that some of their members became millenarians. Granted that some distressed hand-loom weavers in the West Riding became followers of Joanna, and that in the Wroeites' ranks were hard-pressed Bradford wool-combers, what was there in the social condition of domestic servants or engravers or small shopkeepers that should have made them susceptible to millenarianism? Perhaps if we had more detailed biographical information about more millenarians we could answer this question with some confidence. As it is, the theory of relative deprivation (like the theory of stress and strain) is in danger of accounting for everything and nothing. Almost every millenarian, one suspects, might be shown to be relatively deprived in some way. But why he or she should react to deprivation by becoming a millenarian, and not something else, remains obscure.

Nevertheless the commitment of millenarians to social change in some form seems to be a recurrent theme of the movements and personalities we have been examining. Basically millenarianism was an ideology of change: it focused attention on the great changes which were currently taking place in these last days, and promised a vast transformation of the social order when all things would be made new. Men and women who were looking eagerly for a new heaven and a new earth could not but be consciously aware that the future would be utterly different from the present, and their thinking thus became attuned to the idea of change. This in itself was an achievement: it was the beginning of 'a new dawn of social consciousness'.[29] But progress to this position was gradual and incomplete for some millenarians, whose concept of salvation was at first personal (deliverance from daily ills) rather than concerned with changing the social order. We may envision a progression from personal needs and suffering to a community or sectarian sentiment extending to the believers, and thence to a social eschatology embracing the whole world. Some forms of millenarianism did not lay out a programme of social change to which believers subscribed; the millennium was a vision, acceptance of which implied assent to change. Other millenarians, like the Shakers, Buchanites, Mormons or Wroeites, formed communities or quasi-communities which changed drastically the social norms of their members.

For the most part this social change was in a radical direction. In a society dominated by an aristocratic and Anglican establishment any movement outside its paternalistic control was a radical departure, a potential threat to that deference, respect and subordination which was held to be necessary for social stability. The very existence of ideas and voluntary associations independent of traditional institutions and leaders was suspect. It was not necessary to profess liberal political opinions to be branded as a subversive: the suspicion of being tainted with enthusiasm – or indeed any form of religious deviance – was taken to imply sympathy with upsetting the status quo. Millenarians, by the very fact that they were drawn from the lower orders and were outside the established church, were a challenge to authority. The Church of England was expected to function as an agent of social control; and millenarians, like all religious dissidents, seemed only to weaken that function. In vain might the Reverend Thomas Foley dissociate himself from the events of Peterloo: the heinousness of his offence (in the eyes of his bishop and of his cousin, Lord Foley) was that he of all people, a Church of England rector, should countenance the claims of a popular 'imposter' like Joanna Southcott. For by so doing he subverted both sound doctrine and his expected social role. Joanna herself of course was no political radical, and always protested her loyalty to the Church of England. But that did not prevent her condemnation as an undesirable influence; how else could the establishment view her gloomy prophecies and warnings about the state of the nation, her theological feminism of the Bride of the Lamb, and her sealing of thousands of believers for the overthrow of Satan?

All millenarians were liable to find themselves regarded as radicals, simply because they were dissident. But for some millenarians the charge had more substance. The links between some of Brothers' followers and political radicalism in the 1790s have already been indicated and could be further strengthened. For instance the printers and publishers of radical tracts frequently performed the same service for the millenarians. Brothers' publisher, George Riebau, was a member of the London Corresponding Society. H. D. Symonds, Arthur Seale and B. Crosby were other radicals who published Brothers' and Joanna's works along with Paine, Spence and Volney.[30] In the next generation the same pattern was repeated in the connection between Richard Carlile's Rotunda radicalism and the millenarians who followed Zion Ward. By the 1830s and 1840s millenarian and radical beliefs frequently overlapped. Courtenay may have been a member of the Spencean Philanthropists, who advocated the doctrines of land reform propounded by Thomas Spence.[31] Certainly in his addresses the Kentish messiah often hinted at a more equitable distribution of property, and promised that when he inherited his kingdom 'no man should have less than fifty acres of land.'[32]

Dig into the history of popular radicalism almost anywhere before 1850 and the chances are good that a millenarian reference will be unearthed. The Owenites in the 1830s drew heavily upon millenarian ideas and vocabulary; and early historians of socialism compared the utopian socialists with millenarian sects.[33] Two examples must suffice to illustrate the way in which Owenites and Chartists and millenarians could move back and forth between their respective worlds. Thomas Dudgeon, a Scots farmer, emigrated to the USA about 1831. He had previously been president of a society of some 700 evicted crofters, and in 1820 joined the Owenites in Edinburgh. In America he was drawn towards William Miller, but had some reservations about the 'second personal coming of our Lord'.[34] Dudgeon worked out his own philosophy, blended from Owenite doctrines of community and character formation plus millenarian expectations and prophetic chronology. He concluded that he was living in the last days and that the messiah's kingdom would be hastened by the adoption of small communities, phrenology, and 'modern science', especially 'hydrostatics'.

Our second example is William Loveless, brother of George and James Loveless, the Tolpuddle martyrs, who in 1834 were sentenced to transportation after they had organized a trade union for agricultural labourers. Following a great public agitation for their release, George and James returned from Van Dieman's Land, but found that they could not settle down in England, and in 1844 emigrated to Canada. In a series of letters to his brother George, William Loveless revealed himself as a millenarian.[35] The study of prophecy and speculation about the date of the second coming was for William 'my absorbing subject'. He advised George to consider carefully the signs of the last days, in particular the return of the Jews to Palestine; he discussed the interpretation of Nebuchadnezzar's dream in Daniel and related it to the beasts in

Revelation: 'ah, George, with me it is frequently an anxious question, when will the great event [i.e. the second coming] be accomplished?; doubtless it will be in our time.' In 1847 he joined the Chartist National Land Plan and looked forward to the day when he would be located on a four-acre smallholding. Of course, he wrote, this 'will sound small in the ears of you Canadian farmers who possess 100 acres.' But 'we seek not to be rich in this world's goods – we wish only to work for ourselves so that we may enjoy the fruit of our toil, without being subject to a tyrant master.' He did not (as might have been expected) equate the Land Plan with the millennium ('Mr. O'Connor ... anticipates locating 30 thousand in 7 years from the commencement'), but saw it only as an opportunity for a brief sojourn in this world before passing on to 'a better land'. From this sketchy correspondence it is not possible to reconstruct William Loveless' views in detail. We can, however, catch glimpses into the mind of an agricultural worker and note the combination of deeply radical convictions with millenarian speculation.

Given the evidence that some millenarians were also radicals, it is natural for the historian to look for a pattern in this relationship. How and when were millenarian and radical beliefs held; and can we say that at a certain point the one set of beliefs replaced the other, or were they held simultaneously? In the relatively few cases (such as that of William Sharp) in which there is sufficient documentation to answer such questions, no clear pattern of switching from millenarianism to political radicalism and vice versa emerges. We cannot say, from the evidence, that men turned to millenarian prophets when their efforts at political and social change were frustrated, that the millennial hope waxed as political ideals waned.[36] It may have been so with some men; but it was not necessarily so with all or most. In so far as we are considering beliefs rather than membership of movements, it is possible that, for the individual concerned, the function of millenarianism and radicalism was the same. We do not have to suppose a polarity between (religious) millenarianism and (political) radicalism, with peaks of intensity in different years. The need was for an ideology of change, for salvation from a variety of social and individual ills, and that need remained fairly constant. As the seeker pursued his quest through this evil world, inspired by his vision of a new heaven and a new earth, he might find expression of his beliefs first in one and then another form. He did not consciously have to abandon the one to accept the other, for the core of his beliefs remained constant. He could be both a millenarian and a radical at the same time.

But although some millenarians involved themselves with radicalism, and all millenarians were inevitably conscious of great and impending change, millenarian life was not for the most part centred on devising specific ways to change society. Social change and the social context, important as they are in explaining millenarianism, are not the whole story. To complete our analysis of millenarianism we have to look at a third category of explanation and consider the intellectual and spiritual appeal of millenarian beliefs. The setting of these beliefs was evangelical Protestantism and it was from this wider milieu that millenarianism took its bearings. Familiarity with millennial doctrines, vocabulary and imagery was part and parcel of everyday evangelical religion. Isaac Watts' vision of the New Jerusalem was typical:

There is a Land of pure Delight
Where Saints Immortal reign;
Infinite Day excludes the Night,
And Pleasures banish Pain.[37]

And millennial hymns abounded:

Great God! what do I see and hear!
The end of things created:
The judge of mankind doth appear,
On clouds of glory seated!
The trumpet sounds! the graves restore
The dead which they contained before!
Prepare, my soul, to meet Him.[38]

The popular millenarian was distinctive not because of his beliefs but because for him the millennium was more than a matter of hymn singing. His belief in prophecies, providences, Satan, and the literal truth of the scriptures was shared by the majority of his fellow Christians. When the (evangelical) world looked back at the millenarians it found much to object to, but its difficulties were not the same as ours today. The cultural matrix of evangelical Protestantism made the claims of the millenarians seem more formidable than they do now. For instance, if Abraham's command from God to kill his only son, Isaac, as a sacrifice could be accepted as God's word, how could the voices and claims of prophets and even madmen be refuted? Perceval in his *Narrative* makes the point that he never contemplated anything, even when mad, as horrible as that.

Given certain common premises, the claims of millenarian prophets were not easy to refute on logical grounds. An examination of the opponents of Richard Brothers and Joanna Southcott shows the difficulty the critics had in constructing a convincing case.[39] Few were prepared to deny absolutely that God might still speak to men through prophecy, so prophets and prophetesses could not be dismissed *a priori*. The argument was then as to whether a particular prophet was genuinely sent from God – a matter about which there was room for endless debate. Again, visions and voices were validated by a great weight of Christian testimony, and could not be simply put down to hallucination. The strength of the tradition of the inward witness of the Spirit (inconvenient as it always was for orthodox or majority denominations) meant that millenarian claims were assured at least of a hearing in certain quarters. If millenarian visions and visitations were to be discredited they had to be shown to be from the devil ('demonocracy detected') rather than flatly denied as having any existence at all. Christians of all persuasions knew that Satan was a real and personal danger: 'your adversary the devil, as a roaring lion, walketh about, seeking whom he may devour' (I Peter 5:8). Arguments based on the theological unsoundness of particular millenarian doctrines, or on error in calculating the time prophecies were inconclusive, to say the least. In a religious culture which had debated such issues for many generations without arriving at a consensus the millenarians could hardly be ruled out of court for holding beliefs which were by no means new and for which they adduced scriptural support. Even the failure of specific millenarian prophecies about the second coming did not conclusively refute millenarianism: for those who wanted them there were always convincing explanations from scripture and revelation as to why the promised events had not materialized.[40]

Further strengthening of the millenarian appeal came from the tremendous visual impact of passages in Daniel and Revelation. The millenarian message was communicated through powerful images, conjured up in the mind and portrayed by artists. The Book of Revelation has an exhilarating effect beyond reason alone:

> The crowns, the thrones, the gold, the jewels, the colours, the trumpets, the violence of action and the impact of incredible numbers and awe-inspiring size – all these images stir that threshold of the brain where monsters lurk and supernatural glories blaze. John is stirring with a kind of surrealistic artistry the vastness of our unconscious minds.[41]

There is a feeling of being caught up in a vast drama involving the whole human race. Angels and demons and monsters appear before our eyes on a scale which dwarfs all earthly experience. Moreover, all complexities are reduced to a simple dualism of good and evil. The redeemed and the damned are plain to see. And as if this were not enough to capture the heart and imagination of the earnest seeker, he is assured that the persecuted minority like himself will now be on top. He will live for ever in the New Jerusalem, amid jewels and gold and beautiful gardens, and there will be no night.

The assurance of being identified with this cosmic drama was one of the psychic benefits of millenarian belief. At the other extreme millenarianism provided assurance that the minutiae of daily life were also part of God's providence. When Joanna spoke of her homely experiences as types and shadows of national happenings she showed how meaning and significance could be given to the most ordinary incidents in the life of a labouring woman:

> From Types and Shadows, Lord, how clear,
> Thou shew'st thy heavenly Kingdom's near,
> Which all the learned now despise,
> This proves the blindness of the wise,
> Who on their knowledge now depend, –
> God will confound them in the end.[42]

Other millenarians, like Zion Ward, used the Bible allegorically as a preshadowing of their own struggles and the circumstances of their own time. The effect of this was to reinforce a kind of spiritual levelling: the experiences of simple, unlearned people were imbued with divine meaning: the events of the great world could be interpreted through every man's reading of the scriptures. Ancient Christian teachings that the poor receive and understand the wisdom of God more fully than the rich and learned were given a new emphasis; and the fashionable Romantic regard for the 'passions and thoughts and feelings' of common men found (perhaps unlooked for) confirmation.[43] By the use of everyday events of life to interpret national, world and cosmic happenings, the millenarians reduced the scale and complexity of those happenings to the level of an ordinary person's understanding. Public history became simply individual histories on a grand scale.

The search for meaning, in both personal experience and the world at large, usually found expression in some form of eschatology. The millenarians, as we have seen, were by no means agreed on chiliastic doctrine: whether the millennium is in the future or has already begun; whether it is physical and literal, or inward and spiritual; Christ as an historical figure in the past versus Christ indwelling in man. Two types of eschatology resulted from these varieties of interpretation: apocalyptic and existential. The former belief was that the second coming and the last judgment lay in the future: such was Millerism and the main body of Southcottianism. The latter, or existential eschatology, was that the second coming and the last judgment were here and now. For Zion Ward and Shepherd Smith the new life had already begun: they had been born again.[44] In the words of St Paul, 'if any man be in Christ, he is a new creature: old things are passed away; behold, all things are become new.' (II Corinthians 5:17). Thus some seekers, who had not been able to find rest in the established church or mainline dissent, discovered through millenarian prophets a religion which suited their existential needs. When Blake wrote of divine humanity and Ward of heaven in man they were voicing more than a personal idiosyncracy. They were speaking to a tradition with roots in the seventeenth century and earlier, and which still found adherents in the nineteenth century because it provided an explanation of the mysteries of life to men who were dissatisfied with both the orthodoxies of evangelical religion and the claims of Enlightenment reason.

Millenarianism was attractive not only for the intellectual and spiritual content of its beliefs, but also for the way in which those beliefs could be discovered. Although a majority of millenarians were not highly educated people, many of them seem to have had a thirst for knowledge and were in a real sense self-educated. In their autobiographies they refer to their efforts for educational self-improvement, and their personalities frequently display the traits of auto-didacticism. There is a certain narrowness of outlook, a limitation of the imaginative qualities, and an unawareness of the true perspective of knowledge. We have seen how in the case of the Millerites the study of the Bible in the way the millenarians prescribed was very appealing to certain types of believer, and how the vast amount of annotating, indexing, correlating and cross-referencing provided a form of pseudo-learning. Joanna's followers spent a huge amount of time copying, recopying and indexing her communications in manuscript for circulation among themselves.[45] Self-help in the interpretation of scripture appealed strongly to men like William Loveless. For the small farmer or artisan who had neither access to a library nor time for extended study this concentrated searching for texts and calculating the time prophecies was well suited. It provided an attractive mixture of intellectual discovery, mystification and ultimate authority.

At the same time an anti-intellectual element assured a continuing populist appeal. Virtually all millenarian sects and prophets were at pains to disavow the need for any advanced learning. They took pride in being 'people of one Book', of receiving 'truths hidden from the wise', and remembered that God had always preferred to speak through humble men. As Zion Ward put it, 'Scripture is not explained at the Universities; no, God don't go there, he comes to the humble dwelling of the lowly, who seek him sincerely.'[46] Joanna protested to Foley soon after she met him that she never read any books: 'I should not like to read any books to mix my senses with any works but those of the Spirit by whom I write.'[47] When they read their bibles, millenarians did so in a non-intellectual way (though in this respect they were no different from many of their Methodist and Evangelical contemporaries). In fact, to repudiate the orthodoxy of the churches (including respectable millennialism) which was supported by an elaborate array of scholarship, and to assert their independence from such 'human learning', millenarians had to adopt a non- if not an anti-intellectual stance. Perhaps this was what Blake had in mind when he wrote: 'The Beauty of the Bible is that the most Ignorant and Simple Minds Understand it Best.'[48] We may also see this anti-intellectualism as part of the repudiation of rationalism, and connect it with Muggletonianism (the devil is human reason) and Blake's Urizen. It then becomes one more part of the struggle to assert values which are alternative to the dominant culture of the Enlightenment.

But here our evidence runs out. We are in the realm of possibilities and hypotheses, not conclusive data. As so often in this investigation of popular beliefs we are left at the point where fascinating vistas begin to appear, but they remain in shadow. We see only as through a glass, darkly. At the end of this book it is apparent how little we really know about what ordinary people 'think and feel'; and until further studies have been made and perhaps new historical techniques devised we are not likely to know much more. By concentrating on millenarianism we have nibbled at one corner of a very large theme, and we have impinged on many topics that could not be followed up. There are therefore no neat conclusions to be drawn, only the record of an exploration into largely unknown territory. Like travellers of old we have come back with tales of strange people with strange ideas. Not every reader will believe the traveller's tales; but some may be excited enough to go and look for themselves.

NOTES
AND REFERENCES

INTRODUCTION

1 Joseph Lawson, *Letters to the Young on Progress in Pudsey during the Last Sixty Years* (Stanningley, 1887), pp. 37–8.
2 *Minutes of the Committee of Council on Education*, 1845, vol. 1, pp. 266–7, quoted in Richard Johnson, 'Educational Policy and Social Control in Early Victorian England', *Past and Present*, no. 49 (November 1970), p. 104.

3 Milton Rokeach, *Beliefs, Attitudes and Values: a Theory of Organization and Change* (San Francisco, 1970), p. 2.

CHAPTER ONE   THE HOPE OF THE MILLENNIUM

1 Cf. J. M. Roberts' stimulating discussion of nonsense beliefs in chapter 1 of his *The Mythology of the Secret Societies* (London, 1972).
2 The so-called synoptic apocalypse is contained principally in Matthew 24 and 25; Mark 13; and Luke 21.
3 Details of this type of millennialism are given in LeRoy Edwin Froom, *The Prophetic Faith of Our Fathers*, 4 vols (Washington, DC, 1946–54). Also useful are Ernest R. Sandeen, *The Roots of Fundamentalism: British and American Millenarianism, 1800–1930* (Chicago, 1970); and James W. Davidson, 'Searching for the Millennium: Problems for the 1790's and the 1970's', *New England Quarterly*, vol. XLV, no. 2 (June 1972).
4 Following the distinction suggested by Ernest Lee Tuveson, *Redeemer Nation: the Idea of America's Millennial Role* (Chicago, 1968), pp. 33–4. Tuveson gives the name millenarian to those who expected the imminent physical return of Christ, and millennialist to the believers in a gradual triumph of Christian principles, culminating in a

holy utopia or millennium. The former were usually premillennialists, and the latter postmillennialists. Contemporaries used the terms millenarian, millenary, and millennialist as synonyms; and this usage has been followed by some later writers and historians.
5 The distinction was also made in the late eighteenth and early nineteenth centuries. Thus Joseph Priestley, while studying carefully the prophecies and writings on the millennium in the 1790s, identified himself entirely with the scholarly tradition, and brushed aside '[Richard] Brothers, and other curiosities' (Clarke Garrett, 'Joseph Priestley, the Millennium, and the French Revolution', *Journal of the History of Ideas*, vol. 34 (1973), p. 63). From the other side, Ebenezer Aldred, an eccentric prophet from Derbyshire, took issue with the learned Henry Kett's *History the Interpreter of Prophecy*, 2 vols (Oxford, 1799) in which Kett related the beast of Revelation 13 to infidelity and Jacobinism (Eben-Ezer, *The Little Book* (London, 1811), p. 3).

6 See W. H. Oliver, 'Owen in 1817: the Millennialist Moment' in Sidney Pollard and John Salt (eds), *Robert Owen: Prophet of the Poor* (London, 1971), pp. 182–3.

7 See David Brion Davis, *The Problem of Slavery in the Age of Revolution, 1770–1823* (Ithaca, NY, 1975), pp. 288–9.

8 Ernest Lee Tuveson, *Millennium and Utopia: a Study in the Background of the Idea of Progress* (New York, 1964), pp. 139–40 and *passim*.

9 Dixon Ryan Fox, *Ideas in Motion* (New York, 1935), 'Refuse Ideas and their Disposal', p. 102.

10 Norman Cohn, 'Medieval Millenarism: its bearing on the Comparative Study of Millenarian Movements' in Sylvia L. Thrupp (ed.), *Millennial Dreams in Action* (The Hague, 1962), p. 31. Also useful is Norman Cohn, *The Pursuit of the Millennium* (New York, 1961).

11 Bryan R. Wilson, *Magic and the Millennium: a Sociological Study of Religious Movements of Protest among Tribal and Third-World Peoples* (London, 1973). As the subtitle indicates, the book is not directly concerned with British and American millenarianism in our period, but chapter 1 especially is most useful methodologically. The brief summary in this paragraph does not do justice to the complexities and mutations in Dr Wilson's valuable book.

12 George Shepperson, 'The Comparative Study of Millenarian Movements' in Thrupp (ed.), *Millennial Dreams*, p. 45.

13 See E. J. Hobsbawm, *Primitive Rebels* (Manchester, 1959), p. 65 for examples.

14 E.g. the concept of the secularization of adventism in Richard Hofstadter, *The Paranoid Style in American Politics* (New York, 1965), pp. 29–30.

CHAPTER TWO PROPHETS AND PROPHESYINGS

1 Max Weber, *The Sociology of Religion*, trans. Ephraim Fischoff, intro. Talcott Parsons (Boston, Mass., 1963), p. 46. This paragraph follows closely the Weberian approach.

2 Bryan R. Wilson, *Magic and the Millennium: a Sociological Study of Religious Movements of Protest among Tribal and Third-World Peoples* (London, 1973), p. 499.

3 Weber, *The Sociology of Religion*, p. 59.

4 Among the large body of recent literature on millenarianism in the seventeenth century, the following are the most useful for our purposes: William M. Lamont, *Godly Rule* (London, 1969); B. S. Capp, *The Fifth Monarchy Men* (London, 1972); William Haller, *Foxe's Book of Martyrs and the Elect Nation* (London, 1963); C. Hill, *Antichrist in Seventeenth-Century England* (London, 1971) and *The World Turned Upside Down* (London, 1972); P. Toon (ed.), *Puritans, the Millennium and the Future of Israel* (Cambridge, 1970).

5 R. A. Knox, *Enthusiasm* (Oxford, 1950), p. 388.

6 See the cases of William Bryan and Daniel Roberts dealt with on pp. 69, 133, 252. The official records of the Society of Friends do not always make clear the reasons for disownment, only that the member concerned was visited

by certain 'weighty Friends', on whose advice the Meeting acted.

7 Robert Hindmarsh, *Rise and Progress of the New Jerusalem Church in England, America and Other Parts*, ed. the Reverend Edward Madeley (London, 1861), p. 44 and quoted in Clarke Garrett, *Respectable Folly: Millenarians and the French Revolution in France and England* (Baltimore and London, 1975), p. 151. For the Ranters in the seventeenth century see A. L. Morton, *The World of the Ranters* (London, 1970); and Cohn, *The Pursuit of the Millennium* (New York, 1961), appendix: 'The "Free Spirit" in Cromwell's England: the Ranters and their literature'.

8 John Wesley, *The Journal of John Wesley*, ed. Nehemiah Curnock, 8 vols (London, 1909–16), vol. III, pp. 237–8.

9 *Ibid*, p. 238.

10 See Bernard Semmel, *The Methodist Revolution* (London, 1974), ch. 2.

11 Wesley, vol. III, p. 237.

12 Quoted in Knox, p. 450.

13 George Lavington, *The Enthusiasm of Methodists and Papists Compared* (London, 1749 and 1751). References from Polwhele's edition (see note 14), pp. 145–6; and Semmel, *Methodist Revolution*, p. 16.

14 R. Polwhele, preface to Lavington's

Enthusiasm (London, 1833), p. cxiv. Richard Polwhele (1760–1838) was an Anglican clergyman who wrote on the history and traditions of Devon and Cornwall (Joanna Southcott's home-ground). See entry in *Dictionary of National Biography* (*DNB*). The relation of Joanna to Methodism was noted, but misunderstood, by Robert Southey in his *Letters from England*, 3 vols (London, 1808), vol. III, p. 238; and the theme is developed further by E. P. Thompson in *The Making of the English Working Class* (London, 1963), pp. 382–8.

15 John Locke, *An Essay Concerning Human Understanding* (London, 4th edn, 1700), bk. IV, ch. 19.

16 George Fox, *Journal* (London, Everyman edn, 1962), p. 28.

17 William Blake, *Poetry and Prose*, ed. Geoffrey Keynes (London, 1967), 'Marginalia to Berkeley', p. 820.

18 See D. P. Walker, *The Decline of Hell* (London, 1964), p. 226; and A. L. Morton, *The Everlasting Gospel: A Study in the Sources of William Blake* (London, 1958), p. 37.

19 W. B. Harrison, *A Letter* [on] *the Divine Mission of the late Joanna Southcott* (Leeds, 1842), p. 94.

20 Alexander Gilchrist, *Life of William Blake*, 2 vols (London, 1880), vol. 1, p. 112; and Morton, *Everlasting Gospel*, pp. 52–3.

21 Robert Southey, 'The Works of the Reverend William Huntington', *Quarterly Review*, vol. XXIV (October–January 1820–1), p. 472.

22 Joanna Southcott, *What Manner of Communications are These?* (Stourbridge, 1804), pp. 97, 99.

23 See Rufus M. Jones, *Studies in Mystical Religion* (London, 1909); and *Spiritual Reformers in the 16th and 17th Centuries* (London, 1914).

24 Jacob Boehme, *Apology to Balthazar Tilken* (1621), pt II, p. 298, quoted in Jones, *Spiritual Reformers*, p. 170.

25 Jacob Boehme, *The Epistles*, repr. from 1649 edn (Glasgow, 1886), pp. 29–30.

26 Jacob Boehme, *The Signature of All Things* (London, Everyman edn, n.d.), p. 91.

27 *Ibid.*, p. 6.

28 *Epistles*, p. 176.

29 *Signature*, p. 10.

30 Blake, *Poetry and Prose*, p. 118.

31 *Signature*, p. 155.

32 The survey is titled 'Ralph Mather's account of spiritual persons, to Henry Brooke', and is in 'The Correspondence of Henry Brooke; Copies by his Son-in-Law [Holcroft]', Walton Collection, Dr Williams's Library, London, MSS. I(i)43. Also reprinted in Christopher Walton, *Notes and Materials for an adequate Biography of ... William Law* (London, 1854), pp. 595–6; and extracts in Désiré Hirst, *Hidden Riches: Traditional Symbolism from the Renaissance to Blake* (London, 1964), pp. 238–46. Mather was a Swedenborgian field preacher. He came from Bolton, and was said to have been an 'advocate [in London] for the Spinners and Weavers about Bolton, many of whom were imprisoned for rioting and destroying cotton mills' in 1779 ('Correspondence of Henry Brooke': note on letter from Mather to Brooke). Mather had joined the Methodists and worked closely with Wesley, who described him in 1774 as 'a devoted young man, but almost driven out of his senses by Mystic Divinity' (Wesley, *Journal*, vol. VI, p. 10). He was for a time a Quaker; and was then attracted to the writings of Swedenborg. Together with Joseph Salmon he served as a Swedenborgian missionary, beginning his preaching and organizing tours in 1786. Subsequently he became minister of the Swedenborgian church in Liverpool; and then emigrated to the United States, where he continued as a pastor of the New Church at Germantown, near Philadelphia, and at Baltimore. His fellow-missionary, Joseph Salmon, had been a Methodist local preacher, and had been introduced to Swedenborg's works by the Reverend John Fletcher, vicar of Madeley, Shropshire, about 1785. See Hindmarsh, *Rise and Progress of the New Jerusalem Church*, pp. 64–6; and Garrett, *Respectable Folly*, pp. 159–60. I am also indebted to Clarke Garrett for his unpublished paper 'Mystics and Millenarians in Eighteenth Century London' (1976).

33 Letter dated 30 September 1755. Walton, *Notes and Materials*, p. 597.

34 'Correspondence of Henry Brooke'. Letter from Mather to Brooke, undated, but apparently 1779. For Mrs Lead, see Walker, *Decline of Hell*, pp. 218–30; and Jones, *Spiritual Reformers*, pp. 227–31. Mrs Lead's works are listed in the *DNB* entry.

35 The BL copies of Jane Lead, *A Fountain of Gardens*, 3 vols (London, 1696–1701) [4412.1.25]; and *The Signs of the Times* (London, 1699) [3185.e. 22(i)] are inscribed by the painter, Philip James Louterbourg, who became a follower of Brothers.

36 There has been little recent study of the Muggletonians and the most useful work is still that by Alexander Gordon. His researches are set out in two articles, 'The Origin of the Muggletonians', and 'Ancient and Modern Muggletonians', in *Proceedings of the Literary and Philosophical Society of Liverpool*, vols XXIII (1868–9) and XXIV (1869–70) (London, 1869, 1870); and in entries for Muggleton, Reeve, Birch and Tomkinson, in the *DNB*. The 'six principles' are quoted from 'Ancient and Modern Muggletonians', pp. 186–7. The following two items add little to Gordon's account: George Charles Williamson, *Lodowick Muggleton*, Sette of Odd Volumes no. LXXI (London, 1919); Augustus Jessopp, 'The Prophet of Walnut-Tree Yard', in *The Nineteenth Century*, vol. XVI (July–December, 1884). Muggleton's autobiography (to 1677) is told in *The Acts of the Witnesses* (London, 1699).

37 E.g. *A Volume of Spiritual Epistles* ([London], 1755); *A Transcendent Spiritual Treatise* ([London], 1756); *A Stream from the Tree of Life*, ed. John Peat ([London], 1758); *A Divine Looking-Glass* ([London], 1760); *The Acts of the Witnesses* (London, 1764); *Collected Works*, 3 vols (London, 1820), another edn, 1832; Joseph and Isaac Frost (eds), *Divine Songs of the Muggletonians* (London, 1829). Peat, in his introduction to *A Stream from the Tree of Life* says that the believers are now (1758) only 'a handful', but that nevertheless in the last seven years they have reprinted many of the prophets' works, and he lists eleven titles.

38 William Hamilton Reid, *The Rise and Dissolution of the Infidel Societies in this Metropolis* (London, 1800), p. 53, noted the similarity between some Muggletonian doctrines and the teachings of Swedenborg.

39 And E. P. Thompson has suggested (letter in *The Times Literary Supplement*, 7 March 1975) a further fascinating possibility: 'It [Muggletonianism] became an esoteric tradition capable of nourishing a highly intellectual anti-intellectualism: and in a century which made excessive claims for Reason this may have offered some minds an alternative resource'; and he hints at some such connection with William Blake.

40 Useful secondary accounts of the French prophets are given in Henri Desroche, *The American Shakers*, trans. and ed. John K. Savacool (Amherst, Mass., 1971); Knox, *Enthusiasm*; and John Symonds, *Thomas Brown and the Angels* (London, 1961), which also has a bibliography of the French and English prophets.

41 Samuel Keimer, *A Brand Pluck'd from the Burning* (London, 1718), p. 54. The references to this work in the following paragraphs are from pp. 30, 34, 39, 52, 54, 58, 74. See also *Journal of the Friends Historical Society*, vol. XXII, nos 1–4 (1925), pp. 1–9; and C. Lennart Carlson, 'Samuel Keimer', *The Pennsylvania Magazine of History and Biography*, vol. LXI (Philadelphia, 1937), pp. 357–86.

42 Keimer, *A Brand Pluck'd from the Burning*, p. 80, referred to Dorothy Harling,

she that called herself the Permanent Spring … who would lift up her clothes before a company of men and women believers, crying out, 'Come in Christ, come in; Come in Christ, come in.' This woman was disowned after some time, by the Spirit, through John Potter.

43 Abraham Whitrow, *Warnings of the Eternal Spirit* (London, 1709). Preface by Sir Richard Bulkeley.

44 Walker, *Decline of Hell*, p. 256.

45 See Richard Roach, *The Great Crisis* (London, 1725–7).

46 E.g. John Lacy, *The Scene of Delusions* (London, 1723).

47 Wesley, *Journal*, vol. II, pp. 136–7. Entry for 28 January 1739.

48 Calvin Green and Seth Y. Wells, *A Summary View of the Millennial Church* (Albany, NY, 2nd edn, 1848), pp. 10–11.

49 In addition to Desroche, *Shakers*, see also Edward Deming Andrews, *The People Called Shakers* (New York, 1953), ch. 1.

50 Among others, *An Impartial Account of the Prophets* (London, 1708) was reprinted in *The World's Doom*, 2 vols

(London, 1795), a collection of Brothers' pamphlets. Keimer's account was reprinted in part in D. Hughson, *A Copious Account of the French and English Prophets* (London, 1814); and again in M. Aikin, *Memoirs of Religious Imposters* (London, 1823). *The Prophetical Mirror* (London, 179?) included prophecies by Jurieu and Lacy. John Maximilian Daut (author of *The Approaching Judgements of God*, London, 1710) was quoted frequently in the 1790s. Lacy's *The General Delusion of Christians* (London, 1713) was reprinted in 1832 with a preface by Edward Irving.

51 'After this blessing and pageantry was over, Nicholas Facio, who sat at a table as a writer, gave to each of us a little piece of parchment, about two inches diameter, on which was writing. What was on mine was as follows: "Jonathan, of the tribe of Aser, keep this as a precious pearl." ' Keimer, *A Brand Pluck'd from the Burning*, p. 47.

52 *A Brand Pluck'd from the Burning*, pp. 59–70, prints 'An hymn set to musick upon the occasion of John Lacy's leaving his lawful wife by the command of the Spirit and taking Elizabeth Gray, a prophetess', by Richard Roach, and in the footnotes gives details of the prophets and their followers. This list and brief description of some sixty persons is reprinted in Aikin, *Religious Imposters*, pp. 77–81.

53 A succession of prophets and messiahs in the sixteenth and seventeenth centuries is listed in Capp, *Fifth Monarchy Men*, pp. 32–3, 42–3; and in Keith Thomas, *Religion and the Decline of Magic* (London, 1971), pp. 133–8. Virtually all the claims, experiences and projects of millenarian prophets in the late eighteenth and early nineteenth centuries can be paralleled in the earlier period.

54 Vols II, pp. 214–15; III, pp. 148, 239.

55 Mather referred to Bell as 'a man of an illuminated soul'. Letter to Brooke [n.d.], Walton Collection, Dr Williams's Library, MSS. I(i)43. See also Knox, *Enthusiasm*, pp. 505, 543–7; and Robert Southey, *Life of Wesley*, 2 vols (London, 1820), ch. 24.

56 Semmel, *Methodist Revolution*, p. 17.

57 Accounts of Best are given in the *DNB*; and in Garrett, *Respectable Folly*, pp. 151–2. Visits to him are described in a letter from Thomas Langcake to

Henry Brooke, 30 November 1782, in Walton Collection, Dr Williams's Library, MSS. I(i)43; and in James Jenkins, 'Records and Recollections, 1761–1821', MS., 4 vols, pp. 830–1, Friends Library, London. The suggestion that Best may have been a Swedenborgian is made in M. L. Danilewicz, ' "The King of the New Israel": Thaddeus Grabianka (1740–1807)', *Oxford Slavonic Papers*, n.s. 1 (1968), p. 63.

58 Polwhele, preface to Lavington's *Enthusiasm*, p. cxiv. Another case of a prophetess in 1788 is given in the Rainsford Papers, BL Add. MSS. 23, 675. f. 28, 30, 31. Ralph Hodgson of West Auckland described how an angel had appeared to a young woman named Margaret who was living with him, and whose parents were in Darlington. She had previously frequented Methodist meetings, against the wishes of her parents. She was a very patient, self-denying person. The purpose of the angel's visits was 'to make known that the Lord was shortly about to destroy the wicked from the face of the earth, both root and branch, as fire doth stubble.' The angel said that the Lord would give warning of the coming destruction in a day of thunder and lightning. Margaret knows that the day is near, but is not at liberty to make the exact date known, because the angel has instructed her to say only that the time is at hand. She 'spoke with Mr Westley at Darlington, 16th June (if I mistake not).' Margaret was 'afflicted in the body by Evil Spirits', and Hodgson described an incident in a lonely wood when he 'and another preacher' saw two evil spirits attempting to destroy her. In another letter from Hodgson to Elhanan Winchester (an American millenarian), 15 December 1788, Hodgson opined that the story of Margaret is intended as a warning that the Lord will shortly destroy the wicked; but adds 'as to the Millennium, from what I can understand from the Angel, it is to be considered in a spiritual sense – that is, Christ's reigning in the hearts of those that believe in him.' The Reverend Richard Clarke (a theosophist in the seventeenth-century tradition, and a friend and correspondent of Henry Brooke) commented (20 January 1789): 'For my

own part I regard it as a delusion, a
second Mrs Buchan.' For Clarke and
Winchester, see Hirst, *Hidden Riches*,
pp. 246–67.

59 Sarah Flaxmer, *Satan Revealed; or, The
Dragon Overcome* (London, [1795]), from
which the quotations in this paragraph
are taken. For Mrs Flaxmer and Mrs
Eyre, see also Garrett, *Respectable Folly*,
pp. 175, 187, 195–6.

60 Details of Wright and the Avignon
society are given on pp. 69–72.

61 I am indebted to Mr Dafydd Guto Ifan
of Talsarnau for information about Mari
y fantell wen, and for transcripts and
translations of the following Welsh
sources: John Lloyd, 'Llanfihangel y
traethau', *Journal of the Merioneth
Historical and Record Society*, vol. 3, pt. 2
(1958); D. Tecwyn Jones, *Atgofion
Cynnar* [Early Memoirs] (1950), p. 19;
R. T. Jenkins, 'Mary Evans ("Mari y
Fantell Wen")', *Dictionary of Welsh
Biography down to 1940* (London, 1959);
R. Owen, *Hanes Methodistiaeth Gorllewin
Meirionnydd* [History of Methodism in
West Merioneth], (Pennal, Merioneth,
1890) vol. 2, p. 13; Robert Jones, *Drych
yr Amseroedd* [Mirror of the Times]
(1820); *Cymru*, vol. VII, no. 39 (1894),
pp. 157–8.

62 See *Ardudwy: Catalogue of an Exhibition
at Coleg Harlech Arts Centre, 24th
March–26th April* [1975] (Coleg Harlech,
1975), p. 63, describing a figure of Mari
created by schoolchildren of Ysgol
Ardudwy, Harlech.

63 The main source is Joseph Train, *The
Buchanites from First to Last* (Edinburgh
and London, 1846). Train (1779–1852)
was a local Scottish antiquary who
corresponded with, and collected
materials for Sir Walter Scott; and his
book was based on manuscripts in the
possession of, and interviews with
Andrew Innes (1757–1846), the last
surviving Buchanite. There is an entry
for Mrs Buchan, by T. F. Henderson,
in the *DNB*; a chapter on the
Buchanites in John Montgomery, *Abodes
of Love* (London, 1962); and a fictional
account in F. L. Lucas, *The Woman
clothed with the Sun* (London, 1937). The
main Buchanite publications are [Hugh
White], *The Divine Dictionary; or, A
Treatise indicted by Holy Inspiration*
(Dumfries, 1785); and *Eight Letters
between the People called Buchanites and a
Teacher near Edinburgh* (Edinburgh, 1785).

See also *Satan's Delusions: A Poem on
the Buchanites* [n.p., Kilmarnock printed]
(1784).

64 *Eight Letters*, p. 38; and (for the next
quotation), p. 41.

65 Innes' account in Train, *Buchanites*, p.
42.

66 A typical outsider's view of the
Buchanites is given in a letter from the
poet, Robert Burns, to his cousin, James
Burns, dated 3 August 1784 (*The Letters
of Robert Burns*, ed. J. De Lancey
Ferguson, 2 vols (Oxford, 1931), vol. 1,
pp. 18–19):

We have been surprized with one of
the most extraordinary Phenomena in
the moral world, which, I dare say,
has happened in the course of this
last Century. – We have had a party
of the Presbytry Relief as they call
themselves, for some time in this
country. A pretty thriving society of
them has been in the Burgh of Irvine
for some years past, till about two
years ago, a Mrs Buchan from
Glasgow came among them, & began
to spread some fanatical notions of
religion among them, & in a short
time, made many converts among
them, & among others their Preacher,
one Mr Whyte, who upon that
account has been suspended and
formally deposed by his brethren; he
continued however, to preach in
private to his party, & was supported,
both he, & their spiritual Mother as
they affect to call old Buchan, by the
contributions of the rest, several of
whom were in good circumstances;
till in spring last the Populace rose &
mobbed the old leader Buchan, & put
her out of the town; on which, all
her followers voluntarily quitted the
place likewise, and with such
precipitation, that many of them
never shut their doors behind them;
one left a washing on the green,
another a cow bellowing at the crib
without meat or anybody to mind
her, & after several stages, they are
fixed at present in the neighbourhood
of Dumfries. – Their tenets are a
strange jumble of enthusiastic jargon,
among others, she pretends to give
them the Holy Ghost by breathing on
them, which she does with postures
& practices that are scandalously
indecent; they have likewise disposed
of all their effects & hold a

community of goods, & live nearly an idle life, carrying on a great farce of pretended devotion in barns, & woods, where they lodge & lye all together, & hold likewise a community of women, as it is another of their tenets that they can commit no moral sin. – I am personally acquainted with most of them, & I can assure you the above mentioned are facts.

67 Train, *Buchanites*, p. 128.
68 White, *Divine Dictionary*, quoted in Train, *Buchanites*, pp. 58–9.
69 Train, *Buchanites*, p. 222. Train's

account of his correspondence and interviews with Innes (pp. 198–237) is valuable first-hand material on millennialism.

70 Hugh White, *A Small Performance entitled Philotheos* (Richmond, 1806); and 'Cosmogenia', *Intellectual Repository for the New Church*, vols II–III (1815–16). I am indebted to Mr Robert W. Fulks Jr for information on White's Swedenborgianism in America, and for his unpublished paper 'Swedenborgian Subculture: the Church of the New Jerusalem in Jeffersonian Virginia'.

CHAPTER THREE SIGNS AND WONDERS

1 Keith Thomas, *Religion and the Decline of Magic* (London, 1971), p. 223.
2 John Heydon, a seventeenth-century astrologer and writer on Rosicrucian mysticism, quoted in [Richard Alford Davenport], *Sketches of Imposture, Deception and Credulity* (London, 1837), p. 300.
3 For some useful thoughts on this theme see N. Abercrombie, J. Baker, S. Brett and J. Foster, 'Superstition and Religion: the God of the Gaps', in David Martin and Michael Hill (eds), *A Sociological Yearbook of Religion in Britain* (London, 1970), vol. 3.
4 William Blake, *Poetry and Prose*, ed. Geoffrey Keynes (London, 1967), p. 862 (Letter to Butts, 22 November 1802).
5 E. Peacock in *Notes and Queries*, 2nd ser. i (1856), p. 415, quoted in Thomas, *Religion and the Decline*, p. 666. A useful corrective to the possibly misleading impression that magic, astrology and wise men and women disappeared after the end of the seventeenth century is E. P. Thompson's review article, 'Anthropology and the Discipline of Historical Context', *Midland History*, vol. 1 (1972), pp. 51–3. Thompson suggests that the 'ignorance' and 'scepticism' of the lower classes (about which their more educated contemporaries complained) was really the expression of an alternative, coherent system of religious symbolism. From the huge amount of material documenting the survival of folk-lore in the nineteenth century the following may be taken as a random sample which has come my way while searching for evidence of millenarianism: the Reverend J. C.

Atkinson, *Forty Years in a Moorland Parish* (London, 1891); Joseph Lawson, *Letters to the Young on Progress in Pudsey during the Last Sixty Years* (Stanningley, 1887); William Howitt, *The Rural Life of England*, 2 vols (London, 1838); Flora Thompson, *Lark Rise to Candleford* (London, 1945); Thomas Hardy, *The Return of the Native* (London, 1878); John Harland and T. T. Wilkinson, *Lancashire Folk-Lore* (London, 1867); Richard Blakeborough, *Wit, Character, Folklore and Customs of the North Riding of Yorkshire* (London, 1898); Christina Hole, *English Folklore* (London, 1940). There is a useful note on 'Popular Religion' by A. W. Smith in *Past and Present*, no. 40 (July 1968). See also, James Obelkevich, *Religion and Rural Society: South Lindsey, 1825–1875* (Oxford, 1976), 'Popular Religion', ch. VI.
6 The following quotations are from Thomas Cooper, *Life, Written by Himself* (London, 1872), pp. 18–19, 34–5; William Lovett, *Life and Struggles* (London, 1876), p. 18; Joseph Barker, *Life, Written by Himself*, ed. John Thomas Barker (London, 1880), pp. 19–22; Samuel Bamford, *Passages in the Life of a Radical*, 2 vols (London and Manchester, 1841–3), pp. 130–1 and chs 20, 21, 22.
7 John Wesley, *The Journal of John Wesley*, ed. Nehemiah Curnock, 8 vols (London, 1909–16), vol. VIII, pp. 90–1, 95 (entries for 31 August, 16 September 1790).
8 See entry in *DNB* (which lists the main pamphlets in the controversy); and *A Short Narrative of an Extraordinary Delivery of Rabbits, performed by Mr John*

Howard, Surgeon, at Guildford. Published by Mr St André, Surgeon and Anatomist to His Majesty (London, 1727). Hogarth satirized the affair in his two prints, *Cunicularii or the Wise men of Godliman in Consultation* (c. 1726); and *Credulity, Superstition, and Fanaticism. A Medley* (1762).

9 See Richard Reece, *A Correct Statement* ... (London, 1815), repr. in Alice Seymour, *The Express*, 2 vols (London, 1909), vol. II, p. 364.

10 Again, the best account is in the *DNB*. [Davenport], *Sketches of Imposture*, pp. 160–2 adds little.

11 Foley's account and 'the answer of the Spirit' is in Joanna Southcott, *The True Explanations of the Bible. Part VII ... With an Account of Ann Moore* (London, 1810), pp. 608–13. See also Handbill, in Greater London Record Office collection, GLRO 1040/61–3.

12 Communication, 12 May 1813. BL Add. MSS. 47, 800. f. 162.

13 See Sigmund Freud, *The Interpretation of Dreams*, trans. A. A. Brill (New York, 1932), pp. 4–12, 43.

14 Harland and Wilkinson, *Lancashire Folklore*, p. 145.

15 See below, p. 95.

16 Robert Southey, *Letters from England*, 3 vols (London, 1807), vol. II, pp. 283–4.

17 E.g. the full account of Wrightson, 'the Wise man of Stokesley' (Yorkshire) in Atkinson, *Forty Years*, pp. 110–25, and Blakeborough, *Customs of the North Riding*, pp. 187–92. Also accounts of 'Witch Pickles', who lived near Leeds, and Hannah Green, 'the Ling Bob witch' (West Riding) in John Timbs, *English Eccentrics and Eccentricities* (London, 1898), pp. 136–7, 139–41, and *The World's Doom*, 2 vols (London, 1795), p. 72. For crystal gazing and conjurors see James E. Smith, *The Coming Man*, 2 vols (London, 1873), vol. II, pp. 330–62, referred to below, p. 142.

18 Robert Burton, *The Anatomy of Melancholy* (London, 1924), p. 294.

19 Wesley, *Journal*, vol. VI, p. 109. The other quotations are from vol. V, pp. 265–6, where Wesley describes the case of Elizabeth Hobson. Further references to witchcraft are in vol. V, pp. 374–5, and vol. III, p. 251.

20 For a general account of astrology see the excellent chapters 10–12 in Thomas, *Religion and the Decline*.

21 Zadkiel [Lieutenant Richard James Morrison], *The Grammar of Astrology* (London, 1852), p. 355.

22 E.g. Zadkiel's *Grammar* was often reprinted with Lilly's *An Introduction to Astrology* (London, 1647; and many subsequent editions). At a more popular level were the chapbooks such as *Lilly's new Erra Pater; or a prognostication for ever whereby a man may learn to give certain judgement of the weather ... may prophesy of peace or war, sickness, want or plenty, or dearth of corn or cattle* (London, [n.d.]).

23 P. 1. The following quotations are from pp. 42, 43, 54, 71, 192.

24 Nicholas Culpepper, *Astrological Judgement of Diseases* [n.p., n.d.]. See also his *Medicaments for the Poor; or Physick for the Common People* (London, 1670). Culpeper's famous *Complete Herbal* was frequently bound with his *English Physician* (e.g. Ebenezer Sibly's edition, London, 1805).

25 Harland and Wilkinson, *Lancashire Folklore*, p. 10.

26 Ebenezer Sibly (1751–1800), son of a mechanic, was a physician (MD King's College, Aberdeen, 1792) and studied surgery in London. His *Astrology* went through twelve editions before 1817, and was frequently quoted as a favourite text-book of wise men. Sibly was a freemason and a student of occult traditions and contemporary theosophy. He was a brother of Manoah Sibly (1757–1840), a prominent Swedenborgian and minister of the New Jerusalem chapel in Friars Street, Ludgate Hill, London. Originally a shoemaker, Manoah later opened a bookshop and ran a school. He was a self-taught scholar of Hebrew, Greek, Latin, Syriac, and like his brother was also attracted to occult studies. The Sibly brothers were part of the mystical-occult circle in London which took seriously the claims of millenarians like Richard Brothers. They also seem to have had radical sympathies (e.g. Ebenezer's enthusiastic endorsement of the American Revolution in his *Astrology*; and Manoah's editions of the trials of the radicals Thomas Hardy and I. Gillham in 1795). See entries in *DNB*; and Marsha Keith Manatt Schuchard, 'Freemasonry, Secret Societies, and the Continuity of the Occult Traditions in English Literature' (unpublished PhD

thesis, University of Texas, Austin, 1975), pp. 380–91.

27 E.g. in his dispute with Bartholomew Prescott, a Liverpool astrologer, and one-time believer (*DNB* entry for Brothers). See also the satirical pamphlet, *Further Testimonies of the Authenticity of the Prophecies of Mr Richard Brothers, Astrologically accounted for ...* (London, 1795).

28 BL Add. MSS. 47, 800. f. 124 (communication dated 11 June 1808). See also Joanna Southcott, *Astrology and Witchcraft* (Bradford on Avon, 1853); and the Reverend G. Beaumont, *Fixed Stars; or, an Analyzation and Refutation of Astrology ...* (Leeds, 1803). Joanna was always very curious about witchcraft; e.g. she asked one of her leading disciples, William Owen Pughe, for a full account of witchcraft practices in Wales (GLRO 1040/193: copy of letter from Joanna to Fox, 5 September 1810).

29 William Scruton, *Pen and Pencil Pictures of Old Bradford* (Bradford, 1889), p. 244.

30 Bryan R. Wilson, *Magic and the Millennium: A Sociological study of Religious Movements of Protest among Tribal and Third-World Peoples* (London, 1973), p. 101, and ch. 3 *passim*.

31 Eustace F. Bosanquet, *English Printed Almanacs and Prognostications* (London, 1917), pp. 1–12.

32 *The Stranger in Reading* (Reading, 1810), p. 117, quoted in Stephen Yeo, *Religion and Voluntary Organisations in Crisis* (London, 1976), p. 299.

33 Thomas, *Religion and the Decline*, p. 294.

34 *Athenaeum*, 2 and 16 January 1828. See also R. K. Webb, *The British Working Class Reader, 1790–1848* (London, 1955), pp. 28–9. *The Poor Man's Guardian*, 11 October, 8 November 1834 advertised eighteen different (unstamped?) almanacs for sale at Hetherington's and Watson's Repository in the Strand. M. K. Ashby, *Joseph Ashby of Tysoe, 1859–1919* (Cambridge, 1961), p. 283, records a collection of Raphael's and Zadkiel's astrological almanacs that a cottager had lent her father.

35 *Athenaeum*, 2 January 1828. See also *The British Almanac and Companion to the Almanac* (London, 1828), pp. 21–30; and *ibid* (1829), pp. 7–12, for further attacks on the almanacs by the Society for the Diffusion of Useful Knowledge. A later example of the continuing need to discredit popular superstition is 'Confessions of a Fortune Teller', *The British Workwoman*, nos 9–15 (1864–5).

36 Typical examples, among many, are: *The Charter Almanack for the Year 1841* (Leeds); Joseph Barker's *The Reformer's Almanac and Companion to the Almanacs for 1848* (Wortley, 1848); *Anti-Corn Law Almanack* (Manchester, 1841); *The Phrenological Almanac* (Glasgow, 1842); *The Cooperator's Family Almanack* (Halifax, 1879).

37 In his autobiography John Clare describes an old wheelwright who used Napier's *Key to the Revelations* and Moore's *Almanack* indiscriminately in his interpretations of contemporary happenings. *The Prose of John Clare*, eds J. W. and Anne Tibble (London, 1951), pp. 45–6. The association between almanacs and millenarianism is also made in the Harvard University Library copy of Moore's *Vox Stellarum; or a Loyal Almanack for ... 1814* (London, 1813), p. 25 [call number Br. 3700.22], where the former owner of the almanac has noted in the margin of the page for December: '27 at 4 o'clock in the morning died Joanna Southcott, a Prophetess for upwards of 26 years and had her thousands and tens of thousands of Followers.'

38 'If you have not got the Prophetical Almanac by Moore, you must get one. It is a 3/6 Book – and may be had of any bookseller', wrote the Reverend Thomas Foley to his fellow-Southcottian, Charles Taylor, on 16 March 1821 (BL Add. MSS. 47, 795. f. 94). Almanacs are commonly found in collections of Southcottians' papers; e.g. *The Royal Prophetic Almanack*, 1842, in GLRO 1040/170; and *The Prophetic Almanack*, 1831, in GLRO 1040/186.

39 See p. 126 below.

40 The full title indicates the object of the work, 1750 being the date of Joanna Southcott's birth and 1792 the date of her visitation: *Scriptural and Hieroglyphic Observations which were foretold in the Years of 1750 and 1792 by Francis Moore alluding to the Present Times. To which is added a singular account of the Emigration of the Jews in 1812* (London [1812]). A similar production, but with a more pronounced British–Israel slant, was Ralph Wedgwood's *The Book of Remembrance: the Outline of an Almanack, constructed on the ancient cycles of time, and proving, by an Harmony of Prophetic*

Numbers, that this is the predicted Era of New Things, the Final Restitution of all Things: the fullness of the Gentiles, the accomplishment of Israel's Warfare ... (London, 1814).

41 Victor E. Neuburg, *Chapbooks: A Bibliography of References to English and American Chapbook Literature of the Eighteenth and Nineteenth Centuries* (London, 1964); and Neuburg, *The Penny Histories* (London, 1968). A useful classification of chapbooks is used in *Catalogue of English and American Chap-Books and Broadside Ballads in Harvard College Library* (Cambridge, Mass., 1905). An older work, containing many reprints of chapbooks, is John Ashton, *Chapbooks of the Eighteenth Century* (London, 1882; repr. New York, 1966).

42 Bamford's childhood experiences are recalled in his *Early Days* (London, 1849), p. 90.

43. In addition to chapbooks proper there was a proliferation of small, cheap volumes, reprinted and sold in chapbook style. Milner's 'Cottage Library', published in Halifax, was only one of several such ventures. See J. F. C. Harrison, *Learning and Living, 1790–1960* (London, 1961), pp. 34–6.

44 See Leslie Shepard, *The History of Street Literature* (Newton Abbot, 1973); Robert Collison, *The Story of Street Literature* (London, 1973); Victor E. Neuburg, 'The Literature of the Streets' in H. J. Dyos and Michael Wolff (eds), *The Victorian City*, 2 vols (London, 1973). Henry Mayhew, *London Labour and the London Poor*, 4 vols (London, 1861–4), vol. I, pp. 293–335 has much on street literature and street art. Also Charles Hindley, *Curiosities of Street Literature* (London, 1871) and *The Life and Times of James Catnach (late of Seven Dials), Ballad Monger* (London, 1878); and James Catnach, *A Collection of the Books and Woodcuts of James Catnach* (London [1869]).

45 See chapter 5(i), note 38.

46 Printed by Tregortha at Burslem, 1813. Another edition was published in parts by J. Nicholson, Halifax, 1829 (copy among Southcottian papers in GLRO 1040/286). It was perhaps this edition to which Lawson, *Pudsey*, p. 42, refers in describing typical family reading in

the 1820s and 1830s. A similar collection was *The Compleat Wizzard; being a collection of authentic and entertaining narratives of the real existence and appearance of Ghosts, Demons, and Spectres ...* (London, 1770).

47 A good example of the connection between this type of case and the world of occultism, freemasonry and millenarianism is a letter to General Charles Rainsford from a friend ['C.M.'], dated 24 September 1789, in which C.M. says he has not heard of Lukins' case and would be glad to learn more. He also refers to 'the ideas of your friend Behmen', and mentions Peter Woulfe (Rainsford Papers, BL Add. MSS. 23,669. f. 102). Woulfe was a member of the Avignon society and later a follower of Richard Brothers. See below, pp. 72, 243, n. 25

48. E.g. *The Surprising Wonder of Doctor Watts, who lay in a trance three days, to which is added a sermon preached at his intended funeral ...* (London [n.d.]); and 'Strange and Wonderful Account of the Rev. John Miller, Minister, of the City of Bath, who remained in a Trance for Four Days and Nights ...', in Hindley, *Curiosities*, p. 29.

49 Cf. *Prophetic Conjectures on the French Revolution* (London, 1793), discussed in Clarke Garrett, *Respectable Folly: Millenarians and the French Revolution in France and England* (Baltimore and London, 1975), pp. 170–2.

50 There were many editions of Wesley's little book, often bound with 'The General Receipt Book; or Oracle of Knowledge', and 'published for the booksellers'. In this connection it is also relevant to mention another chapbook-style production, *Aristotle's Masterpiece*, a collection of sex lore and manual of sex practice, which went through innumerable editions in the eighteenth and nineteenth centuries. This provides an interesting parallel example, from the field of medicine, of the gap between popular and intellectual knowledge. See Janet Blackman, 'Popular Theories of Generation: the Evolution of *Aristotle's Works*. The Study of an Anachronism' in John Woodward and David Richards (eds), *Health Care and Popular Medicine in Nineteenth-Century England* (London, 1977).

CHAPTER FOUR   NEPHEW OF THE ALMIGHTY

1 *The World's Doom; or the Cabinet of Fate unlocked*, 2 vols (London, 1795). Quotations in this and the following paragraph are from the introduction, pp. ix–xxiii.

2 The main secondary accounts are Clarke Garrett, *Respectable Folly: Millenarians and the French Revolution in France and England* (Baltimore and London, 1975); Cecil Roth, *The Nephew of the Almighty* (London, 1933); Ronald Matthews, *English Messiahs* (London, 1936), ch. 3; and G. R. Balleine, *Past Finding Out* (London, 1956), ch. 4. There is also an entry in the *DNB* by the Reverend Alexander Gordon.

3 R. Brothers, *A Revealed Knowledge of the Prophecies and Times*, bk II (London, 1794), in *World's Doom*, vol. I, pp. 277–8.

4 Joseph Moser, *Anecdotes of Richard Brothers* (London, 1795), in *World's Doom*, vol. II, p. 316. Moser was a justice of the peace and governor of the poor for the united parishes of St Margaret and St John the Evangelist.

5 R. Brothers, *An Exposition of the Trinity* (London, [1795]), pp. 34–5.

6 Vol. 65(1), 1795, p. 250.

7 E.g. William Huntington, *The Lying Prophet Examined, and his False Predictions discovered* … (London, 1795); *A Crumb of Comfort for the People; or a Pill for the Prophets … A tract … explanatory of the tragi-comedy of the Brassy Head* (London, 1795).

8 The full titles of the two parts convey accurately the millennial tone of the work: *A Revealed Knowledge of the Prophecies and Times. Book the First. Wrote under the direction of the Lord God, and published by his sacred command; it being the first sign of warning, for the benefit of all nations. Containing, with other great and remarkable things, not revealed to any other person on earth, the Restoration of the Hebrews to Jerusalem, by the year of 1798, under their revealed Prince and Prophet, Richard Brothers; and, A Revealed Knowledge of the Prophecies and Times. Particularly of the present time, the present war, and the prophecy now fulfilling. The year of the World 5913. Book the Second. Containing, with other great and remarkable things, not revealed to any other person on earth, the sudden and perpetual fall of the Turkish, German and Russian Empires. Wrote under the direction of the Lord God, and published by his sacred command; it being a second sign of warning, for the benefit of all nations. By the man that will be revealed to the Hebrews, as their Prince and Prophet.* Bibliographical details of the work are confusing. Passages in pt I are dated variously 3 January, 10 July and 20 September 1794; and in pt II, there are five different dates between 11 April 1794 and 20 February 1795. It is not clear whether successive editions throughout 1794 added new material, or whether the two parts were compilations of material written on the dates shown. The original and 'official' publisher was George Riebau of London, but some editions do not show the publisher. The *World's Doom* edition of 1795 was published by B. Crosby, London, and is in a smaller format and repaginated. A Dublin edition of 1795 is recorded. In America editions were published in Philadelphia (several, 1795), Albany (1796), and West Springfield, Mass. (1797). A French edition was published in Paris in 'An. IVᵉ'.

9 Nathaniel Brassey Halhed, *A Calculation on the Commencement of the Millennium* (London, 1795), in *World's Doom*, vol. II, p. 69.

10 *A Revealed Knowledge*, in *World's Doom*, vol. I, p. 152. The quotations in this and the following paragraphs are from the same source, unless otherwise stated.

11 R. Brothers, *A Letter to Philip Stephens* (London, 1795), pp. 20–2.

12 S. Green, *A Letter to the Publisher of Brothers's Prophecies* (London, 1795), in *World's Doom*, vol. I, p. 633.

13 Nathaniel Brassey Halhed, *Second Speech in the House of Commons*, in *World's Doom*, vol. II, p. 108.

14 Nathaniel Brassey Halhed, *The Whole of the Testimonies to the Authenticity of the Prophecies and Mission of Richard Brothers* (London, 1795) in *World's Doom*, vol. II.

15 These impressions are drawn from Halhed's *Testimonies* and his other pamphlets in the *World's Doom*. The entry in the *DNB* suggests that Halhed was 'probably captivated by some resemblance between the teaching of Brothers and the oriental mysticism with which he was familiar.' Quotations in this and the next paragraph are from Halhed's *Testimonies* and *Calculation*.

16 J. Finlayson, *The Last Trumpet and the Flying Angel* (London, 1849), p. 15. A list of Finlayson's publications is given in the *DNB* entry by the Reverend Alexander Gordon.

17 H. F. Offley, *Richard Brothers, neither a Madman nor an Imposter; with a few observations on the possibility of his being the*

Prophet of God (London, 1795).

18 *Recital of an Open Vision, seen by Thomas Webster, while he was speaking over a corpse at the grave side in Bermondsey Church Yard*, in *World's Doom*, vol. II, p. 518.

19 George Coggan, *A Testimony of Richard Brothers in an Epistolary Address to the People of England* (London, 1795), in *World's Doom*, vol. I, p. 563. Information and quotations are from this source.

20 Thomas Taylor, *An Additional Testimony given to vindicate the Truth of the Prophecies of Richard Brothers* (London, 1795), in *World's Doom*, vol. I, pp. 521–52.

21 William Wetherall, *An Additional Testimony in favour of Richard Brothers* (London, 1795); Samuel Whitchurch, *Another Witness! or Further Testimony in favour of Richard Brothers* (London, 1795); J. Crease, *Prophecies Fulfilling; or, the Dawn of the Perfect Day* (London, 1795); *Look Before you Leap, or, the Fate of the Jews a warning to the People of other Nations, in the case of Richard Brothers, the Prophet. By one who readeth and revereth the Scriptures* (London, 1795).

22 John Wright, *A Revealed Knowledge of Some Things that will speedily be fulfilled in the World. Communicated to a Number of Christians, brought together at Avignon ...* (London, 1794) in *World's Doom*, vol. I, consists of two main parts: a 'narrative and journal' by Wright; and collections of prophecies, quotations, questions and answers of the Avignon society. William Bryan's *A Testimony of the Spirit of Truth, concerning Richard Brothers ...* (London, 1794) in *World's Doom*, vol. I, is 'a brief account of the manner of the Lord's gracious dealings with me', interspersed with homilies on British Israelism and the prophecies. Robert Southey used these two works for his account of Wright and Bryan (whom he knew) in his *Letters from England*, 3 vols (London, 1807). There are also references to Bryan in James Jenkins, 'Records and Recollections, 1761–1821', 4 vols (MS.; also typed transcript); and a [MS.] account of his journey to Avignon, dated 9 December 1791, in John Thompson, MSS. 35. Details of his disownment and references to his wife, Elizabeth, and his five children are given in the [MS.] Minutes, Westminster Monthly Meeting, vols 10, 11 (1782–96). These items are in the Friends Library, London. The later history of Wright and Bryan is not known in detail. Wright became a bookseller for a time. According to Elijah Waring, *Recollections*

and Anecdotes of Edward Williams, the Bard of Glamorgan; or Iolo Morganwg, B.B.D. (London, 1850), p. 92, Bryan 'afterwards emigrated to America, where he had several sons respectably settled, and where he died at a great age, only a few years ago.' Waring accepted Southey's view that Bryan was an 'unconscious agent' in a deep political plot for the subversion of all the governments of Europe by the Avignon society. Similarly, Edward Williams (Iolo) believed that Brothers, whom he visited, was deceived by two French 'ventriloquists' who imposed on him to further the designs of revolutionary France; and after Brothers' confinement Williams wrote to Pitt accordingly (p. 85).

23 In exploring the complicated relations between the Avignon society, early Swedenborgianism and Brothers' followers, it is best to start with Clarke Garrett, *Respectable Folly: Millenarians and the French Revolution in France and England* (Baltimore and London, 1975). Reference can then usefully be made to the following: M. L. Danilewicz, ' "The King of the New Israel": Thaddeus Grabianka (1740–1807)', *Oxford Slavonic Papers*, n.s., 1 (1968); W. R. Ward, 'Swedenborgianism: Heresy, Schism or Religious Protest?', in D. Baker (ed.), *Schism, Heresy and Religious Protest*, Studies in Church History, vol. 9 (Cambridge, 1972); Hindmarsh, *Rise and Progress of the New Jerusalem Church in England, America and Other Parts*, ed. the Reverend Edward Madeley (London, 1861). There are also important references in the Rainsford Papers, BL, Add. MSS. 23,675, f. 24, 26; and 23,670, f. 75; and in the Walton Collection, Dr Williams's Library, London, MSS. I(i)43, pp. 199–208, 315–18. On the Avignon society see Auguste Viatte, *Les Sources Occultes du Romantisme*, 2 vols (Paris, 1965), vol. I, pp. 89–103; Claude Mesliand, 'Franc-maçonnerie et religion à Avignon au XVIIIᵉ siècle', *Annales historiques de la Révolution française* (Paris, 1969), no. 197, pp. 447–67; and Claude Mesliand, 'Renaissance de la franc-maçonnerie avignonnaise à la fin de l'ancien régime (1774–1789)', *Bulletin d'histoire économique et sociale de la Révolution française*. Année 1970 (Paris, 1972), pp. 23–82. M. K. M. Schuchard, 'Freemasonry, Secret Societies and the Continuity of the Occult Traditions in English Literature' (unpublished PhD thesis, University of Texas, Austin, 1975), in chapter IX, attempts to integrate Brothers and some of his followers (notably Wright and Bryan) into the history of freemasonry

and occultism, and assumes a close connection with the Avignon society and Swedenborgianism.

24 *The New Jerusalem Magazine* (London, 1790), p. 175.

25 See his reference to 'Peter Woulfe, one of the Avignon Society', in *A Revealed Knowledge*, in *World's Doom*, vol. I, p. 341.

26 Bryan, *A Testimony*, in *World's Doom*, vol. I, p. 503.

27 J. Duché, *Discourses on Various Subjects*, 2 vols (London, 1779), vol. I, pp. viii–ix. There is an outline of Duché's life in the *DAB*, but little about his period in England (1777–92). The most useful study is Clarke Garrett, 'The Spiritual Odyssey of Jacob Duché', *Proceedings of the American Philosophical Society*, vol. 119 (1975), pp. 143–55.

28 See the question which Wright put to the 'Holy Word' at Avignon as to whether his wife should come to the society 'with Duché'. Wright, *A Revealed Knowledge*, in *World's Doom*, vol. I, p. 454. This reference may be to Jacob Duché's son, Thomas Spence Duché, an artist, who visited the south of France.

29 Sharp engraved the frontispiece by Benjamin West to Duché's *Discourses*, and was also involved in the publishing details. David V. Erdman, *Blake: Prophet against Empire* (New York, 1969), pp. 12, 290.

30 E. Swedenborg, *The True Christian Religion* (London, 1771; 1883 edn), para. 779.

31 E. Swedenborg, *Heaven and its Wonders and Hell* (London, 1905 edn), para. 89.

32 E. Swedenborg, *The True Christian Religion*, para. 193.

33 E. Swedenborg, *Divine Love and Wisdom* (Amsterdam, 1763; London, 1875 edn), para. 184.

34 See J. G. Davies, *The Theology of William Blake* (Oxford, 1948), ch. 3.

35 Erdman, *Blake*, pp. 36, 175 notes a shadowy parallel between the careers of Sharp and Blake.

36 W. S. Baker, *William Sharp* (Philadelphia, 1875); *DNB* entry by E. Irving Carlyle.

37 In 1780 Sharp 'painted and engraved a political picture of George Washington with liberty cap and don't-tread-on-me rattlesnake'; and made other engravings for the Society in 1782. Erdman, *Blake*, p. 36.

38 Privy Council Papers, PRO, PC 1.21 (A35a,b); PC 1.22 (A36b, A37). For a discussion of radicalism and millenarianism in the 1790s see J. K. Hopkins, 'Joanna Southcott: a Study of Popular Religion and Radical Politics, 1789–1814' (unpublished PhD thesis, University of Texas, Austin, 1972), chs 5 and 6.

39 E.g. when asked about the singing of the French revolutionary song 'Ça Ira', at a dinner on 2 May 1794, he said he approved of the music and had been told that the same tune was used by British troops in Europe. Sharp was reprimanded, and told not to evade the issue by pretending that 'Ça Ira' was a question of music and not of political sentiment.

40 Hopkins, 'Joanna Southcott', ch. 5; Thomas Holcroft, *Memoirs* (London, 1852), p. 184. Another radical who visited Brothers, and who found him 'insane on the one subject, sane on all others, and intelligent on many', was John Binns, a printer and leading member of the London Corresponding Society. See John Binns, *Recollections* (Philadelphia, 1854), pp. 48–50, and quoted in Garrett, *Respectable Folly*, p. 206.

41 Joshua Brooks (ed.), *A Dictionary of Writers on the Prophecies* (London, 1835), p. lxxi. A note in a contemporary hand on the title page of the copy of Towers' *Illustrations of Prophecy*, 2 vols (London, 1796), in the Divinity School Library, Harvard University, says that the work is very rare as most copies were suppressed by Pitt.

42 'The Great Prophet of Paddington Street: Nephew of God', *The Times*, 4 March 1795.

43 The full blast of this anti-masonic, anti-illuminati conspiracy theory was not felt, however, until after 1797, with the publication of John Robison's *Proofs of a Conspiracy against the Religions and Governments of Europe* (Edinburgh, 1797), and the Abbé Barruel's *Memoirs of Jacobinism*, 4 vols (London, 1797–8). These provided ammunition for the anti-Jacobin denunciations of Cobbett and Southey. See also Vernon Stauffer, *New England and the Bavarian Illuminati* (New York, 1918); and Richard Hofstadter, *The Paranoid Style in American Politics* (New York, 1965).

44 Halhed, *Testimonies*, in *World's Doom*, vol. II, pp. 107–8.

45 Christopher Frederick Triebner, *Cursory and Introductory Thoughts on Richard Brothers' Prophecies* [London, 1795]. Triebner was minister of the German Lutheran congregation of Great East Cheap, Cannon Street, London. On a similar theme see William Hamilton Reid, *The Rise and Dissolution of the Infidel Societies in this Metropolis* (London, 1800; repr. 1971 as *Literacy and Society*, ed. V. E. Neuburg.) Brothers was also associated in the press with Charles James Fox and the Whig

opposition. Cf. James Gillray's cartoon (published the day after Brothers' arrest) in which Brothers is shown as a *sans-culotte* carrying Fox and others on his back in a 'Bundle of the Elect'. Reproduced in Morton D. Paley and Michael Phillips (ed.), *William Blake: Essays in Honour of Sir Geoffrey Keynes* (Oxford, 1973), plate 65.

46 According to the Home Office check on him, Leigh was a member of the London Corresponding Society and lived at Newington, Surrey. He was 'paid' by a Mr Fields who lived near Blackfriars Bridge and was associated with the radical peer, Lord Stanhope. See Home Office Papers, PRO, HO 42/34 (letter from Edward Milward, Jr, to Duke of Portland, 1 May 1795).

47 Brothers, *A Revealed Knowledge*, bk II, in *World's Doom*, vol. I, p. 353.

48 HO 42 series, especially HO 42/34–5 (1795).

49 According to Halhed (*Testimonies* in *World's Doom*, vol. II, p. 102) Brothers was arrested 'on suspicion of treasonable practices'. *The Times*, 6 March 1795, stated more explicitly that the warrant was grounded on an Elizabethan statute, under which he was charged with 'unlawfully, maliciously, and wickedly writing, publishing, and printing various fantastical prophecies, with intent to cause dissension and other disturbances within the realm'. See also Paley and Philips, *Blake*, pp. 261–2.

50 E.g. the following (undated) handbill:
> *Thus Saith the Lord!* Thus saith the Lord, yet within five years shall this city, Babylon, be destroyed after the French have taken possession of England, and the inhabitants shall be carried away to the new heaven and the new earth to stand before the Son of Man in judgement; then the vile shall be separated from the precious, and I will grant eternal life to the precious saith the Lord God who ruleth in the armies of heaven and doeth that which seemeth good amongst the inhabitants of the earth.

A copy of this handbill is pasted inside the rear cover of a MS. vol. of the index of James Hayward, GLRO 1040/182.

51 Reid, *Infidel Societies*, pp. 14, 91.

52 R. Brothers, *A Letter from Mr. Brothers to Miss Cott, the Recorded Daughter of King David, and Future Queen of the Hebrews. With an address to the members of His Britannic Majesty's Council* ... (London, 1798), pp. 89–134. Frances Cott, the daughter of an Essex clergyman, was admitted to Fisher House asylum in the spring of 1797 and

Brothers fell in love with her. 'She is all that Solomon describes in the favourable part of his prophetic song', he declared (p. 143); and it was revealed to him that 'she is your sister, your married wife and acknowledged queen' (p. 159). But his love was unrequited, and Miss Cott left the asylum and was married.

53 R. Brothers, *A Description of Jerusalem: its Houses and Streets, Squares, Colleges, Markets, and Cathedrals, the Royal and Private Palaces, with the Garden of Eden in the Centre* ... (London, 1801). Also R. Brothers, *A Letter to the Subscribers for engraving the Plans of Jerusalem, the King's Palace, ...* (London, 1805).

54 *A Description of Jerusalem*, p. 49.

55 Henry Crabb Robinson, *Diary, Reminiscences and Correspondence*, ed. Thomas Sadler, 3 vols (London, 1869), vol. I, pp. 53–4.

56 See Ruthven Todd, *Tracks in the Snow* (London, 1946), pp. 54–5; Joanna Southcott, *Letters to the Clergy of Exeter from 1796 to 1800* (London, 1813), p. 7.

57 Brothers, *An Exposition of the Trinity*, pp. 26–9.

58 This was based largely on the prophecies in the thirteenth chapter of the apocryphal Book of Esdras II. Brothers had already identified himself as the 'man coming up from the midst of the sea' in verse 25. And Esdras' dream in verse 40 is interpreted by reference to the second coming:
> those are the ten tribes, which were carried away prisoners out of their own land in the time of Osea the king, whom Salmanasar the King of Assyria led away captive, and he carried them over the waters, and so came they into another land.

59 William Blake, *Poetry and Prose*, ed. Geoffrey Keynes (London, 1967), p. 463.

60 *Ibid.*, p. 375. Also Edward B. Hungerford, *Shores of Darkness* (New York, 1941), pp. 48–9.

61 Notably in the work of William Stukeley, Jacob Bryant, Edward Davies and Francis Wilford. Good secondary sources for the speculative mythologists are Todd, *Tracks in the Snow*, pp. 29–60; Hungerford, *Shores of Darkness*, pp. 62–91; Stuart Piggott, *The Druids* (London, 1968), ch. 4.

62 See Gwyn A. Williams, 'Welsh Indians: the Madoc legend and the First Welsh Radicalism', *History Workshop*, no. 1 (Spring, 1976).

63 Cf. also R. Brothers, *The Ruins of Balbec and Palmyra, from the plates of Robert Wood, Esq., Under Secretary of State, proved to be the*

Palaces of Solomon (London, 1815).

64 The full title suggests the argument of the book: *A correct Account of the Invasion and Conquest of the Roman Colony of Ailbane, or Britain, by the Saxons, never published before: and which is very Interesting to the present English, who are descended from those Great and Brave Men* (London, 1822). After the peak of his prophetic influence in 1795, Brothers modified some of his earlier views. In *Wisdom and Duty*, written in January 1801 but not published until 1805, he repudiated his republican sympathies and became almost chauvinist. He now defended monarchy as the best and divinely ordained form of government for both the Hebrews and Great Britain. Other nations might be more suited to republicanism (and this is agreeable to God). But 'the English have shown a similarity of wisdom to the Hebrews in the choice of their Sovereign; and he, like David, a due sense of his duty to support their freedom' (p. 6). And he concluded that the model Hebrew government which he would establish would be very similar to the English.

65 'A Descriptive Catalogue'. Blake, *Poetry and Prose*, pp. 609–10.

66 See *DNB* and T. Mordaf Pierce, *Dr W. Owen Pughe* (Caernarfon, 1914).

67 One of Pughe's co-editors in *The Myvyrian Archaiology of Wales* (n.p., 1801) was Edward Williams (the bard, Iolo Morganwg), who was a radical republican. Pughe visited William Winterbotham in Newgate during his imprisonment for sedition. W. D. Leathart, *The Origin and Progress of the Gwyneddigion Society of London* (London, 1831), pp. 67–9. See also note 22, p. 242.

68 Joanna Southcott, *The Trial of Joanna Southcott* (London, 1804), pp. 127–36.

69 This was the opinion of Southey, who wrote:

My old acquaintance William Owen,

now Owen Pugh ... found our Blake after the death of Joanna Southcott, one of whose four-and-twenty elders he was. Poor Owen found everything which he wished to find in the Bardic system, and there he found Blake's notions, and thus Blake and his wife were persuaded that his dreams were old patriarchal truths, long forgotten, and now revealed (*The Correspondence of Robert Southey with Caroline Bowles*, ed. E. Dowden (London and Dublin, 1881), pp. 193–4).

But in fact Pughe and Blake were almost certainly acquainted before the death of Joanna in 1814. Pughe's account of ancient Welsh mythology, including the Arthurian romances, is set out in *The Cambrian Biography: or, Historical Notices of Celebrated Men among the Ancient Britons* (London, 1803). The subject is explored further in Hungerford, *Shores of Darkness*, pp. 48–53, and Todd, *Tracks in the Snow*, pp. 50–4.

70 R. Brothers, *The New Covenant between God and his People; or the Hebrew Constitution and Charter ...* (London, 1830).

71 Taylor, *An Additional Testimony*, in *World's Doom*, vol. I, pp. 550–1.

72 Brothers, *A Revealed Knowledge*, pt II, in *World's Doom*, vol. I, p. 328.

73 See Morton D. Paley, 'William Blake, The Prince of the Hebrews, and the Woman clothed with the Sun', in Paley and Phillips (eds), *Blake*, to which I am indebted.

74 See his quatrain, 'On the Virginity of the Virgin Mary and Johanna Southcott', Blake, *Poetry and Prose*, p. 107.

75 Henry Crabb Robinson, *Diary*, entry for 30 January 1815.

76 *Ibid.*, letter to Dorothy Wordsworth, February 1826 (repr. in Henry Crabb Robinson, *Blake, Coleridge, Wordsworth, Lamb, etc., being Selections from the Remains of*, ed. Edith J. Morley (Manchester, 1922), p. 14).

77 Blake, *Poetry and Prose*, p. 466.

CHAPTER FIVE   THE WOMAN CLOTHED WITH THE SUN

(i) The Prophetess

1 William Sharp, *An Answer to the World* (London, 1806), p. 3.

2 Joanna Southcott, *The Strange Effects of Faith*, pt V (Exeter, 1801), p. 205. For the dating of this see Joanna Southcott, *The Controversy of the Spirit with the Worldly Wise* (London, 1811), p. 4.

3 *Joseph Southcott's Vindication of his Sister's Character* (London, 1804), p. 80.

4 Joanna Southcott, *The Strange Effects of Faith: being a Continuation of Joanna Southcott's Prophecies* (London, 1802), p. 84.

5 *Strange Effects of Faith*, pt I, p. 5.

6 The sixty-five books and pamphlets published by Joanna during her lifetime were numbered and indexed by Philip Pullen, a believer, in his *Index to the Divine and Spiritual Writings of Joanna Southcott*

(London, 1815). Believers usually referred to Joanna's works by the numbers given in Pullen. A fuller bibliography, but including the same numbers to the sixty-five works, was published by Daniel Jones, a believer, sometime after 1852, as *Catalogue of Books published by Joanna Southcott* (Bradford-on-Avon, [n.d.]). A useful descriptive bibliography is Charles Lane, 'Bibliography of Joanna Southcott', *Report and Transactions of the Devonshire Association for the Advancement of Science, Literature and Art*, vol. XLIV (Plymouth, 1912). This number of the *Report and Transactions* also contains a 'Life of Joanna Southcott' by the same author. The two articles were also published as a separate volume (Exeter, 1912). But the most complete bibliography is Eugene Patrick Wright, *A Catalogue of the Joanna Southcott Collection at the University of Texas* (Austin, Texas, 1968). Many of Joanna's pamphlets went through several editions before 1815. Daniel Jones of Bradford-on-Avon reprinted them, *c.* 1852; and Alice Seymour reissued the sixty-five works in 1912–24 (Plymouth and Ashford, Middx). Manuscript sources (communications, letters, etc.) are listed in chapter 5(i), note 21, and secondary material for Joanna's life in the bibliographical note at the end of this volume.

7 Joanna Southcott, *The Trial of Joanna Southcott* (London, 1804), p. 60.

8 Southcott, *Strange Effects of Faith*, pt I, p. 6.

9 Joanna Southcott, *The Second Book of Wonders* (London, 1813), p. 32.

10 For T. Brice, the Deist printer, see Joanna Southcott, *The Fifth Book of Wonders* (London, 1814), pp. 6–10; and *Divine and Spiritual Letters* (London, 1801), p. 9.

11 Richard Law, *Copy of an Epistle … to Henry Addington, Prime Minister* (London, 1803).

12 Joanna Southcott, *A Continuation of Prophecies* (Exeter, 1802), pp. 4–32.

13 Joanna's comments on Brothers are found throughout her works. But see in particular *Strange Effects of Faith*, p. 60; *Second Part of the Continuation of Joanna Southcott's Prophecies* (London, 1802), p. 68; *Divine and Spiritual Letters*, p. 11; *A Communication in Answer to Mr. Brothers' last Book* (London, 1802); and *Answer to Mr. Brothers' Book* (London, 1806).

14 The details are given in Southcott, *Trial of Joanna Southcott*.

15 The sealing is explained in Joanna Southcott, *Sound an Alarm in my Holy Mountain* (Leeds, 1804); and *A Caution and Instruction to the Sealed* (London, 1807). See

also *Divine and Spiritual Communications* (London, 1803), p. 20.

16 An amalgam of texts from 1 Peter 2:6 ('Behold, I lay in Zion a chief corner stone, elect, precious'); Ephesians 4:30 ('Grieve not the Holy Spirit of God, in whom ye were sealed unto the day of redemption'); Revelation 22:14 ('Blessed are they that wash their robes that they may have the right to come to the tree of life'); and Romans 8:17 ('If children, then heirs; heirs of God, and joint heirs with Christ').

17 BL Add. MSS. 26,039. f. 17; and 47,798. f. 13–14.

18 *Strange Effects of Faith*, pt 2, p. 49.

19 Joanna Southcott, *A Word to the Wise* (Stourbridge, 1803), p. 9.

20 Evelyn Underhill, *Mysticism* (London, 1911, repr. New York, 1961), p. 278.

21 According to Rachel J. Fox, *The Mystery of Joanna Southcott* (Plymouth, 1917), p. iii, there were fourteen sets of bound MS. communications, kept in the families of the believers who had originally copied them out. Some of these are now in the British Library, which holds the largest collection of Southcottian MSS. The main series are: Add. MSS. 26,038–26,039 (Hows); 27,919 (Warren); 32,633–32,637 (5 vols, Bird, Parker); 47,794–47,803 (10 vols, Underwood, Townley, Foley, Law, Parker, Wilson, Morison. This collection came from Joanna's home, Rock Cottage, Blockley, and probably belonged to Townley). The collection in the University of Texas Library came from the Bennett family, and contains at least part of the collection of Lavinia Elizabeth Chapman Jones. The Greater London Record Office has a smaller collection (Acc. 1040/1–319) which includes the papers and communications of James Hayward of Bridgwater and the Reverend Edmund Baker of Teddington, Middx, and Dowlish, Somerset. A fourth collection of MSS. and pamphlets is owned by the Blockley Antiquarian Society, Blockley, Gloucestershire. These were rescued after the fire which destroyed Rock Cottage in 1971. They were apparently collected originally by Alice Seymour, who bought Rock Cottage in 1917 and who lived there from 1919 with her secretary, Mary Robinson. The MS. volumes of communications relate to Foley, Judson, Pascoe, Parker, Molineaux, Hows, Turner, *et al.*; and there are odd letters to and from Foley, John Tolhurst, Jowett, Morison, W. B. Harrison, Liney, Turner and the Taylors

of Exeter. See A. W. Exell, *Joanna Southcott at Blockley and the Rock Cottage Relics* (Blockley, Gloucestershire, 1977). In addition there are the writings in the 'Great Box', which weighs 156 lbs. At Joanna's death this was in the custody of Sharp, but in 1816 it passed to Townley; thence in 1825 to Foley; and on his death in 1839 to his son, the Reverend Richard Foley. From 1861 it was in the hands of the Jowett family of Leeds, being passed on from father to son. Its present location is known only to a few believers, who from time to time appeal to the bishops to open it, in accordance with Joanna's instructions. See Mary S. Robertson, *Authentic History of the 'Great Box' of Sealed Writings left by Joanna Southcott* (Plymouth, 1929).

22 Joanna Southcott, *A Continuation of the Controversy with the Worldly Wise* (London, 1811), p. 36.

23 Joanna Southcott, *The Second Book of Wonders* (London, 1813), p. 3.

24 Joanna Southcott, *The Full Assurance that the Kingdom of Christ is at hand from the Signs of the Times* (London, 1806), p. 45.

25 G. Bennett, *The Cross and the Crown* ([n.p.], 1848): broadsheet in GLRO 1040/301. For Joanna's doctrine of the woman, see also BL Add. MSS. 47,799. f. 73.

26 Joanna Southcott, *The Third Book of Wonders* (London, 1814), p. 4.

27 The events of the final year of Joanna's life are covered in her pamphlets, *The Third, Fourth,* and *Fifth Book of Wonders* (London, 1814); and *Prophecies announcing the Birth of the Prince of Peace* (London, 1814). For the pregnancy and autopsy, Richard Reece, *A Correct Statement of ... the last Illness and Death of Mrs. Southcott* (London, 1815) is indispensable. This is reprinted in Alice Seymour, *The Express*, 2 vols (London, 1909), vol. II; as also are extracts from the reply by An Impartial Observer [Philip Pullen], *A Complete Refutation of the Statements and Remarks published by Dr. Reece* ... (London, 1815). There is a valuable account of Foley's visit to London in August 1814 in his Diary, reprinted in *The Express*, vol. II, pp. 344–53. Also of great use is the *Sunday Monitor* (London) for the period September 1814 to March 1815. Joanna's marriage is recorded in a letter from Underwood to Foley, 14 November 1814. BL Add. MSS. 47,800. f. 206. Details of Shiloh's cradle are from the *Penny Post* [c. 185?], a cutting in Foley Scrapbook, no. 1, p. 243, Palfrey Collection, Worcs. Record Office. Typical examples of the believers'

faith that the birth was spiritual are in the notebook of Edmund Baker (GLRO 1040/82) and in a letter from the Reverend Samuel Eyre to Charles Bowman, 14 March 1815 (GLRO 1040/92).

28 *Strange Effects of Faith*, pt V, p. 203. Also Theo Brown, 'The Black Dog in Devon', *Report and Transactions of the Devonshire Association*, vol. XCI (Torquay, 1959), pp. 38–44.

29 Joanna Southcott, *Copies and Parts of Copies of Letters and Communications* (London, 1804), pp. 1–2.

30 The following examples are from *ibid*. The story of Lord Burnet is in *What Manner of Communications are These?* (Stourbridge, 1804), pp. 89–96. Other versions of the ballad of 'Little Musgrave and Lady Barnard' are given in Francis James Child (ed.), *The English and Scottish Popular Ballads*, 5 vols (1882–98, repr. New York, 1965), vol. II, pp. 242–60. See also Arthur Quiller-Couch (ed.), *The Oxford Book of Ballads* (Oxford, 1932). More recently the ballad was popular as the (American) folk song, 'Matty Groves'.

31 *Copies ... of Letters and Communications*, p. 64.

32 Joanna Southcott, *The True Explanation of the Bible* (London, 1804), pp. 184–5.

33 Communication copied by William Parker, 8 May 1803. BL Add. MSS. 47,799. f. 77. The episode of the false teeth is in a letter from Townley to Foley, 3 July 1804. *What Manner of Communications are These?*, p. 109.

34 *Divine and Spiritual Letters*, p. 32.

35 Southcott, *Trial of Joanna Southcott*, pp. 59–60. Joanna's record as a prophetess is set out in *The First Book of Sealed Prophecies* (London, 1803), pp. 123–6; and *A Warning to the World* (London, 1804), pp. 26, 46.

36 Southcott, *The Strange Effects of Faith*, pt II, p. 77.

37 Joanna Southcott, *Astrology and Witchcraft* (Bradford-on-Avon, 1853), p. 4.

38 *Fairburn's Edition of the Prophetess, No. 2* (London, 1814) has a crude woodcut, 'Angels rejoicing at the birth of Joanna'. Another edition shows Joanna and the crib. *The Life and Death of Joanna Southcott* (London, [n.d.]) is an eight-page chapbook with a woodcut of the surgeons surrounding Joanna on the dissecting table. In the almanac style is *The Signs of the Times for 1810, being a full explanation of the prophecies of Joanna Southcott* (London, [n.d.]), roughly printed, on flimsy paper, and consisting of three prophecies and speculation about the coming of the millennium. Charles

Hindley, *The Life and Times of James Catnach* (London, 1878), p. 227 reprints a woodcut of Joanna in bed, with the crib labelled 'For the Shiloh', and the Duke of Wellington kneeling by the bedside.

39 The Horbury incident is described in *The Fifth Book of Wonders*, p. 16; and Baker's account is in a volume of copies of letters, GLRO 1040/209. There is also an account in Baker's notebook, GLRO 1040/81; and references in 1040/82 and 1040/18. For rough music, see E. P. Thompson, ' "Rough Music": Le Charivari anglais', *Annales*, vol. 27, pp. 285–312.

40 Joanna Southcott, *The Answer of the Lord to the Powers of Darkness* (London, 1802), p. 74.

41 *The Second Book of Wonders*, p. 89.

42 Details of Joanna's lovers are in *What Manner of Communications are These?*, pp. 33–5; and *Copies ... of Letters and Communications*, pp. 15–18, from which two pamphlets the quotations in this paragraph are taken. For psychological interpretations of Joanna, see Ronald Matthews, *English Messiahs* (London, 1936), chs 2 and 6; and

Hopkins, 'Joanna Southcott', ch. 1. Matthews, pp. 216–17, argues that Joanna's obsession with sealing has to be seen as a symbol of conception, and her repeated trials of her writings as symbolization of giving birth. 'When the seals are cut open and the doggerel pages examined and approved, is not the prophetess, under that cover, asking her followers to admire the child she will never be able to bear?' Her false pregnancy, he argues, was pseudo-cyesis, a by no means uncommon hysterical symptom, which has deceived doctors in other cases.

43 *What Manner of Communications are These?*, pp. 113–14. There are other sexual references in *A Communication ... in answer to Mr. Brothers' last Book*, p. 6 (circumcision); and in a communication dated 12 July 1802 about Bruce. See BL Add. MSS. 47, 801.B. f. 22.

44 See especially *The Second Book of Wonders*, pp. 90–101.

45 *The Strange Effects of Faith*, pt II, pp. 67, 70; pt V, p. 193.

(ii) True Believers

1 *A Warning to the World*, (London, 1804), pp. 70, 87.

2 Numbers of the sealed are given in Joanna Southcott, *Sound an Alarm in my Holy Mountain* (Leeds, 1804), p. 24; and in Philip Pullen, *Index to the Divine and Spiritual Writings of Joanna Southcott* (London, 1815), p. 170. Foley gives the figure of 14,000 by 1807 in a letter dated 12 October 1807 (BL Add. MSS. 27,919. f. 16), and also in a printed letter dated 2 September 1807 (Foley Scrapbook, no. 5. Palfrey Collection, Worcs. Record Office). See also communication dated 11 September 1808. Add. MSS. 47,800. f. 131. William Howard, *A Letter to Joanna Southcott, the pretended prophetess ...* (London, [n.d. 1810?]) says 20,000 were sealed. Elias Carpenter, *An Apology for Faith ...* (London, 1814), p. 164, says 40,000. The figure of 100,000 appears in many places. I have traced it in the *Phrenological Journal*, vol. VII (1831–2), pp. 360–1 (quoting the *London Encyclopedia*); John Wade, *British History Chronologically Arranged* (London, 1843), p. 716; and Robert Chambers, *The Book of Days*, 2 vols (London and Edinburgh, [n.d.]), vol. II, pp. 773–4.

3 In the University of Texas collection there are three scrolls (numbered 370, 371, 372, *Catalogue of the Joanna Southcott Collection*).

The largest is George Turner's list, which contains 4,062 names, arranged by place, but does not include addresses. The towns are wide-spread, but strongly Yorkshire and north of England. This scroll is undated, but appears to be *c.* 1815–16. A second scroll contains the names and addresses of 1,571 London believers from 1809 to 1908, but mainly in the period 1809–25. The third scroll has 1,291 names, and a few addresses, of believers in many parts of the country. It is undated, but the watermark reads 1816. The Greater London Record Office collection (GLRO 1040/1–2, 4) has two lists of members by the Reverend Edmund Baker. The first is of 125 members at Teddington, Middlesex. The second is for Dowlish, Somerset, and shows 304 names, *c.* 1813–14, and another 130 for the period 1816–88. There is another list of 227 sealed members in BL Add. MSS. 47,798. f. 164, but it is undated and gives no indication of place. Names of believers can also be gleaned from some printed sources. Pullen's *Index* lists about 70. The *Minutes of Conference, 19–25 November 1844* (GLRO 1040/297) gives the names and occupations of thirty-four Birmingham believers, 'who objected to the conference taking place, though professed Believers ... in Joanna Southcott.' The discussions in the 1840s about possible reconciliation between rival Southcottian groups produced printed documents which listed the names of the leading believers. In 1861, when the box of sealed writings was transferred to the custody of Samuel Jowett of Leeds, the election of the custodian resulted in the publication of the names of believers. See *List of the Names of the Friends who voted in appointing a Trustee of the Sealed Writings* (GLRO 1040/310) which lists 200 names from various towns but mainly in the north.

4 J. K. Hopkins, 'Joanna Southcott: a Study of Popular Religion and Radical Politics, 1789–1814' (unpublished PhD thesis, University of Texas, Austin, 1972), pp. 168–72, 418–26 gives a useful analysis of the membership on the three Texas scrolls, and the figures are taken from this breakdown. They need to be treated with caution, however, as they are obviously not complete: for instance Birmingham is shown as eight members, whereas there were many more believers than that. Similarly, there is no listing of Foley's group at Stourbridge. Dowlish, Somerset, which had over 300 members is omitted (unless it is included in the Crewkerne figure).

5 E.g. in the records of the Dowlish believers there are 104 signed testimonies of belief, and only three are signed with a mark (x). See GLRO 1040/5.

6 Hopkins, 'Joanna Southcott', p. 184. These figures should be regarded as highly tentative, as they were arrived at by classifying as 'family' those with the same surname or address and assigning the rest to the 'single' category.

7 GLRO 1040/1–2. Thirty-five members also paid 5s. 6d. each as 'subscription to Joanna's sickness'.

8 Letter, Foley to Robert Taylor, 6 July 1805. BL Add. MSS. 47,795, f. 20, 47, 49.

9 Joanna Southcott *The Trial of Joanna Southcott* (London, 1804), pp. 131–3.

10 *Census of Great Britain, 1851. Religious Worship. England and Wales. Report and Tables* (London, 1853), p. cxv. This possibly exaggerates the extent of the decline. In 1842 John Pye was able to contact twenty-two Southcottian meetings that were still active.

11 So called after Nicodemus, who was a secret believer in Jesus, and came to him by night: John 3: 1–15. This cautious policy, which must have restricted recruitment, is well illustrated by a letter from the Reverend Edmund Baker and his wife, Sarah, to Mrs Elizabeth Vile, 18 December 1842, in which they advise her not to discuss her beliefs with 'mockers', because this will only tend to shake her own faith in Joanna; but if people are seriously interested they should be lent one of Joanna's books. GLRO 1040/45.

12 Vol. 24 (1815), p. 470. Article by Francis Jeffrey (?), the editor.

13 The main collection of Foley's papers is at present untraceable, but in 1940 was apparently in the ownership of a descendant, a Miss Bache of Kidderminster (Foley's wife was née Bache). The Stourbridge historian and antiquarian, H. E. Palfrey, made notes from these papers after he discovered that they had been lent to Mr R. Todd of London, who intended to write a biography of Joanna. Todd lent his very copious extracts to Palfrey, who selected only some from 'a vast mass of correspondence, letters, etc., between T. P. Foley and Joanna Southcott, Townley, Underwood, and many others' (note by Palfrey, February 1940). This material is now in the Palfrey Collection, Worcs. Record Office (BA 3762. 899. 31). It includes extracts from Foley's diary and book accounts. There is also useful material in the Foley Scrapbooks, nos 1 and 5. An odd volume of Foley's diary for 1802–3 and a few letters from him are in the Blockley Antiquarian Society's collection. The only other source for Foley's diary is the extract for August 1814 in Alice Seymour, *The Express*, 2 vols (London, 1909) already quoted. A collection of Foley's letters (1802–30) is in BL Add. MSS. 47,795. The Palfrey extracts are used in H. J. Haden, 'Thomas Philip Foley', *Notes and Queries*, vol. 197 (1952), pp. 294–8. An earlier *Notes and Queries*, ser. 7, IV, 154 (20 August 1887) reprints the story of Foley's wild youth from Gunning's *Reminiscences of Cambridge* (2nd edn), vol. I, p. 63. Quotations in this and the next three paragraphs are from Palfrey's extracts, except where otherwise indicated. Foley's apologia is contained in Joanna Southcott's two pamphlets *What manner of Communications are these?* (Stourbridge, 1804); and *The Answer of the Rev. Thomas P. Foley to the World* (Stourbridge, 1805).

14 BL Add. MSS. 47,795. f. 86.

15 Quotations in this paragraph are from BL Add. MSS. 47,795. f. 10 and f. 22–3.

16 Joanna Southcott, *Divine and Spiritual Letters* (London, 1801), p. 4.

17 Thomas Webster, *Reasons for the Fall of Man* (London, 1804); *The Anagogue Analyzed by Joanna Southcott* (London, 1813), in which Joanna criticized his *Complete Anagogue*.

18 The main references to Mossop are in *The Answer of the Lord to the Powers of Darkness* (London, 1802), p. 83; *Divine and Spiritual Communications* (London, 1803), pp. 25–8; and Lavinia E. C. Jones (ed.), *Commentary upon the Prayers and Ordinances of ... the Church* (Bradford [n.d., 1863?]), pp. 66–8.

19 Letter of Joanna Southcott to Stanhope Bruce, 10 July 1802, copied by William Parker. BL Add. MSS. 47,799, f. 71. For Joanna and Swedenborgianism see also communications listed in University of Texas, *Catalogue*, items 121, 122.

20 Robert Hoadley Ashe, DD (1751–1826), Pembroke College, Oxford, held the living of Crewkerne from 1775 to 1826. See entry in *DNB*; and Balleine, p. 63. Information about Baker (?–1857) is from letters in the GLRO collection, 1040/7, 34, 47, 65.

21 Letters from Eyre are in BL Add. MSS. 47,798. f. 124; and GLRO 1040/90, 92. Foley visited Eyre at Bristol in 1808, and was impressed by the meeting of nearly a hundred believers, who included one rich family, 'that have near £3,000 a year and are very liberal upon all occasions.' BL Add. MSS. 47,795. f. 53. For details of Daniel and Lavinia Jones' publications, see GLRO 1040/304.

22 S. T. Coleridge, 'The Destiny of Nations', *Poetical Works* (London, 1974), p. 132. Coleridge was born in 1772 at Ottery St Mary, where his father was vicar and schoolmaster.

23 The phrase is used in a letter from Richard H. Norris of Birmingham to T. P. Hudson, 26 October 1843. Copy in a volume of Edmund Baker, GLRO 1040/79.

24 The fullest account of Turner is in Balleine, *Past Finding Out* (London, 1956), ch. 9. MS communications by, and letters to Turner (mostly 1821) are in the Blockley Antiquarian Society's collection. The BM *General Catalogue of Printed Books* lists fourteen titles by Turner, 1795–1821. Several of the later works, 1819–21, were published by S. Gompertz, a converted Jew who was an assistant preacher in one of the London Southcottian chapels, and who looked after Turner in his last years. Material in this and the following paragraph is from George Turner's *Wonderful Prophecies*, parts I–II (London, 1818–19); *The Rich Treasure of the Kingdom* (London, 1820); *The Armour of God* (London, 1821); *The Assurance of the Kingdom*, parts I–II (London, 1819–20); and *The Standard of Zion*, parts I–III (London, 1820). Details of the marriage ceremony are in *The Marriage of the Lamb* (London, 1820).

25 Samuel Jowett, *To the Believers of Joanna Southcott's Visitation* (Leeds, 1844), p. 7. Also quoted in Hopkins, 'Joanna Southcott', p. 385. Jowett (c. 1784–1876?) was a printer in Leeds; and was the author of *A Vindication of Joanna Southcott's Writings* (Leeds, 1805). He was elected trustee of the box of sealed writings in 1861. His son, John Marshall Jowett, of Bradford (also a believer) was a printer, and proprietor of *The Bradford Advertiser*. In a letter dated 15 April 1871, Samuel Jowett describes himself as 'a poor old man', and adds, 'I am pleased to learn that there is yet a few retaining the faith in those places where once was many.' BL Add. MSS. 47,798. f. 151. See also GLRO 1040/186.

26 *Copies ... of Letters and Communications*, pp. 52–3.

27 The chief Yorkshire references in Joanna's works are in *Joanna Southcott's Answer to Five Charges in the 'Leeds Mercury'* (London, 1805); and *The Kingdom of Christ is at Hand* (London, 1805). Pamphlets by John Crossley are *Letters and Observations to Ministers* (Leeds, 1806: 2nd edn. Bradford, 1814); and *The Master and Scholar Refuted* (Leeds, 1810). John Crossley (1777–1852) was born near Halifax and died at Derby. He married Hannah Jowett and had seven sons, one of whom was named Barnabas Southcott (two letters from his grandson, Fred. D. Crossley, 7, 15 October 1917; BL Add. MSS. 47,798. f. 196, 198). There is also a printed handbill, *The Old Religion; extracted from the Halifax Journal, August 4, 1810, with Additions*, by John Crossley (Taunton, 1810) in GLRO 1040/223d. In Bradford the believers were attacked by John Rushton, a glib versifier, in such effusions as *A Dessert of Nuts for the Southcottians* (Bradford, 1814); *The False Prophet Unmasked* [Bradford? n.d.]; and *A Scourge for Fanaticks* [n.p., n.d.]. A series of six broadsheets, with titles such as *A Fourth Letter of Prophecy, A Warning to the Bishops*, by Joanna Southcott, printed in York, 1813, is in the Houghton Library, Harvard University Library.

28 *Extraordinary Life and Character of Mary Bateman, the Yorkshire Witch* (Leeds, 1809). A twelfth edition was published in 1811. In the 1820s a shorter version appeared: *The Yorkshire Witch; or the extraordinary Life and Character of Mary Bateman* (Otley [n.d.]). See also Leman Thomas Rede, *York Castle in the Nineteenth Century; being an account of all the principal offences committed in Yorkshire, from*

the year 1800 to the present period (Leeds, 1831), pp. 30–59. There is a semi-fictitious account of Mary Bateman in Anthony Hunter, *The Last Days* (London, 1958), ch. VII.

29 Joanna Southcott, *The Answer to False Doctrine* [London, 1808], p. 17; *A True Picture of the World and a Looking-Glass for all Men* (London [1809]), pp. 7–11. The *Gentleman's Magazine*, vol. 79(2)(1809), p. 915, published a letter, signed 'M' and dated Leeds, 20 August 1809, in which the writer enclosed a seal found in Mary Bateman's cottage when she was arrested; it was in the name of John Bateman and dated 12 February 1806.

30 BL Add. MSS. 47,800. f. 45–6. Communication dated 26 January 1806.

31 Rede, *York Castle*, p. 59n.

32 Carpenter's chief writings, which contain some autobiographical references, are *Nocturnal Alarm: being an Essay on Prophecy and Vision* (London, 1803); *Modern Realities* (London, 1805); *Who are the Deluded?; or Mystery Unmasked* (London, 1805); *An Apology for Faith* (London, 1814), apparently published in parts, Part II entitled *Missionary Magazine*; *The Extraordinary Case of a Piccadilly Patient; or Doctor Reece physicked, by Six Female Physicians* (London, 1815). His wife, Catherine S. Carpenter, was also a believer, and wrote *Are These things so? Being Remarks on 'Demonocracy Detected'* (London, 1805). See also *Truth's Humble Appeal unto All Men* (Newington [n.d.]), signed 'Amraphel'; and *Religious Impostor Detected* (c. 1804, printed by Robins, Tooley Street.)

33 BL Add. MSS. 47,797. f. 59–60. Letter from Elias Jameson Field to Mrs Taylor at Exeter, 23 January 1804.

34 A collection of fourteen drawings by Prescott is in the Southcott Collection, at the University of Texas and seven of these are reproduced in the university's *Catalogue*. Joanna's interpretations are given in her *First Book of Sealed Prophecies* (London, 1803) and *A Word in Season to a Sinking Kingdom* (London, 1803). Other Southcottian collections also contain drawings of Joanna's visions. See BL Add. MSS. 26,038. f. 26–9; 32,636. f. 15; 47,794. f. 61–4, 70; and GLRO 1040/199–205, 223.

35 Detailed in Joanna Southcott, *The Controversy between Joanna Southcott and Elias Carpenter* (London, 1805). Also BL Add. MSS. 47,800. f. 21–3.

36 See p. 47.

37 Thomas Dowland, *Divine and Spiritual Communication ... to Elias Carpenter, for the British Nation* (London, 1848), p. 1.

38 *Crisis* (London, 14 June 1834), Vol. IV, p. 77.

39 *Memoirs of the Life and Mission of Joanna Southcott ... to which is added a Sketch of the Rev. W. Tozer, M.J.S.* (London, 1814). The sketch of Tozer is by 'Onesimus' and dated 28 August 1814.

40 Reece, *A Correct Statement*, repr. in Seymour, *Express*, vol. II, pp. 375–81.

41 Another Southcottian preacher was John Ingall, who had a chapel in London, and who wrote *Behold the Tent!* (London, 1804); and *A General Index to the Writings of Joanna Southcott, the Prophetess* (London [1805]). See also Theodore Turpin, *Extracts from Sermons preached at Different Chapels in the Years 1812, 1813, and 1814* (London, 1825).

42 BL Add. MSS. 47,794, f. 85–6. Letter, Joanna to Morison, 27 September 1806. Other letters to Morison are in Add. MSS. 47,794, f. 83, 128, 130. Morison's notebooks, which appear to be partly notes and references for preaching, are in Add. MSS. 47,803.

43 Jane Townley, *A Letter from Mrs. Jane Townley to the Editor of the Council of Ten* (London, 1823); and *Communications and Directions given to Mrs. Jane Townley* (London, 1824). Despite the title 'Mrs', Townley was unmarried, though not for lack of suitors. Richard Law, a believer, and author of *Copy of an Epistle to Henry Addington* (London, 1803), wanted to marry her; and BL Add. MSS. 47,796. f. 1–83 is a series of love letters which he wrote to her between 1816 and 1822. On 13 May 1816 he added a playful postscript:

> P. S. Townley, you and I are married by anagram, as for instance: Jane Townley – the letters of that name compose but one complete sentence which is as follows: Yet one in Law. How can you be divided from him?; there [is] something in all anagrams highly prophetic.

But when such entreaties were of no avail, he wrote angrily (11 June 1816):

> Come, come, don't puff yourself up about your virginity, it is through such proud, insolent, conceited Nuns as you that many a brave and proper man goes wifeless and childless to the grave, for there being an equal number of both sexes, the foolish celibacy of the one must deprive the other of his rightful partner to love and multiply by.

44 Joanna Southcott, *Copies and Parts of Copies of Letters and Communications*, p. 21.

45 Joanna Southcott, *Divine and Spiritual Communications*, p. 7 (introduction by Sharp).

46 Reece, *A Correct Statement*, repr. in Seymour, *Express*, vol. II, pp. 387, 389, 394.

47 It is possible that King had been a political radical and follower of Thomas Paine and had later apostasized. See Moncure Daniel Conway, *The Life of Thomas Paine* (London, 1909 edn), p. 155; and Hopkins, 'Joanna Southcott', p. 331. Joanna's treatment of the affair is given in her pamphlet, *An Account of the Trials on Bills of Exchange* (London, 1807); and there are letters referring to it in BL Add. MSS. 47,794. f. 100, 104.

48 William Sharp, *An Answer to the World* (London, 1806), p. 6. The quotations in this and the following paragraph are from the same source.

49 There is an entry for Pye in the *DNB*. Seymour, *Express*, vol. I, p. 204, has an illustration of a glass communion cup, engraved by Pye, and inscribed 'Presented by John and Ann Pye to William Tozer, November 16th, 1809'.

50 A flurry of pamphlets resulted from the exchange of views between believers in the London, Birmingham and Leeds congregations, and the main items are listed in Charles Lane, 'Bibliography of Joanna Southcott', *Report and Transactions of the Devonshire Association for the Advancement of Science, Literature and Art*, vol. XLIV (Plymouth, 1912), pp. 801–4.

51 The whole business can be followed in these pamphlets: *A Call to the Believers in the Divine Mission of the Lord to Joanna Southcott* (London, 1843); *An Address to the Protestants of England* (London, 1844); *The Indictment against that Tyrannical, Cruel, and Bloody*

Monarch, Satan (London, 1845); and *The Trial, Casting and Condemnation of the Prince of this World, the Old Serpent, Devil and Satan* (London, 1847).

52 Thomas Balston, *John Martin, 1789–1854: His Life and Works* (London, 1947); Ruthven Todd, *Tracks in the Snow* (London, 1946), 'The Imagination of John Martin', pp. 94–122.

53 Mrs Henry Wood, *East Lynne* (London, 1861), pt III, ch. 10, and quoted in Todd, *Tracks*, p. 96.

54 Todd, pp. 105, 120 quotes an advertisement in *A Divine and Prophetic Warning to the British Nation*, Christian Magia (London [c. 1845?]) for a British–Israelite book entitled *The Gathering Standard of the World, seen in the British Flag*, 'with designs by J. Martin'.

55 Peter Cunningham [John Martin's son-in-law], 'English Engravers. New Materials for their lives. William Sharp', *The Builder*, 29 August 1863, pp. 615–16.

56 W. B. Harrison, *A Letter Addressed to an Eminent Clergyman* (Leeds, 1842), p. 5. The next quotation is from p. 53.

57 Daniel Roberts, *Observations Relative to the Divine Mission of Joanna Southcott* (London, 1807), p. 23. Roberts (c. 1754–1811), was a Quaker merchant from Painswick, Gloucestershire, who became a believer and was disowned by the Society of Friends. In this pamphlet (p. 20) he complained that 'had [Joanna's] revelation taken place when the Friends first came forward as a religious people in the 17th century, there is every reason to believe it would not have been slighted and despised as by those of the present day.' Roberts had earlier written pamphlets defending the Friends against Unitarianism and Deism.

CHAPTER SIX FALSE PROPHETS

1 The best general account of these minor Southcottian prophets is in Balleine, *Past Finding Out* (London, 1956), ch. 8. Accounts of Sibley's riot are given in John Wade, *British History Chronologically Arranged* (London, 1843), p. 748; and in Charles Lane, 'Bibliography of Joanna Southcott', *Report and Transactions of the Devonshire Association for the Advancement of Science, Literature and Art*, vol. XLIV (Plymouth, 1912), p. 753. See also Crisis (London, 14 June 1834), p. 77. Sibley was the author of *A Copy of the Articles of Faith … of the Philadelphian Church, well-known by the name of the followers of the Divine Mission of Joanna*

Southcott (London, 1819), repr. as *The Indictment against Satan* (London [1843]), ed. D. Wells; and *Commentary upon the Old and New Testament* (Hoxton [1830]).

2 See the *Crisis* article above; and article by H. J. Haden in the *County Express* (Stourbridge), 18 March 1967. Zebulun was the author of *Joanna Southcott Vindicated by a Bruised Reed* [n.p., n.d.]; and *Songs of Royal Sion*; pts I–IV (London, 1831–2). In the University of Texas collection there are several copies of a broadside by Zebulun, 'The Seal of the Kingdom of Christ on Earth' (*Catalogue*, pp. 60–1).

3 BL Add. MSS. 47,795. f. 96. Letter from

Foley to Charles Taylor at Exeter, 5 April 1821. See also Add. MSS. 47,798. f. 104–5 (letter from Owen Pughe to Taylor, 8 April 1823); and the *Gentleman's Magazine*, vol. 95(1), May 1825, p. 460.

4 *Zion's Recorder and Truth's Advocate* [London, 1825], no. 1 [no further issues have been located].

5 The main source here is Wroe's *Life and Journal*, compiled from statements made by Wroe to his disciples, who took down the communications directly 'from John Wroe's mouth'. There are several editions of the work, the earliest being *The Life and Journal of John Wroe, with divine communications revealed to him*. (Ashton-under-Lyne, 1829). This was followed by *An Abridgement of John Wroe's Life and Travels* (Wakefield, 1837). Later came *The Life and Journal of John Wroe* (Gravesend, 1859–61), and also another edition of the *Abridgement* (Gravesend, 1851–5). The quotations in this and the following paragraphs, unless otherwise stated, are from the 1837 *Abridgement*. Also useful are John Wroe, *A Guide to the People surnamed Israelites* (Boston, Mass., 1848); Wroe, *Sermons selected from the Scriptures* (Ashton-under-Lyne, 1880); *The Faith of Israel* (Wakefield, 1843); *Extracts of Letters and other Writings of the Israelite Preachers, 1822–29* (Wakefield, [n.d.]); and *The Laws of God, as given to the Prophets* (Wakefield, 1843). There is an entry for Wroe in the *DNB*; and a review of his career in the *Leeds Times*, 6, 13, 20 June 1857.

6 E. Belfort Bax, *Reminiscences and Reflections* (New York, 1920), p. 50 recalls that Friedrich Engels was once mistaken for a Southcottian because he wore a beard.

7 W. B. Harrison, *A Letter Addressed to an Eminent Clergyman* (Leeds, 1842), p. 7.

8 *Letters of Israelite Preachers, 1822*, p. 7.

9 'Written from John Wroe's mouth by William Lees', Wroe, *Abridgement*, p. 133.

10 The prurient interest in the 'abominations' of Wroeism is largely based on this. T. Fielden, *An Exposition of the Fallacies and Absurdities of that Deluded Church generally known as Christian Israelites or Johannas* ... [n.p., Rawtenstall printed, n.d.] alleged that the woman administering corporal punishment grasped the man's genitals with one hand while laying on the strokes with her other. In Allan Stewart, *The Abominations of the Wroeites ... Exposed* [Melbourne, Australia, 186?] 'the woman held the man's private parts in her left hand and manipulated his posteriors with her

right during confession and cleansing from sin.' *The Laws and Commands of God for the Females* (Ashton, 1830) goes into intimate details of the ritual cleansing of women. Menstruation, the suckling of children, the covering and uncovering of the breasts are all subject to exact regulation.

11 James E. Smith, *The Coming Man*, 2 vols (London, 1873), vol. I, pp. 268–9. The quotations in the next three paragraphs are from this same volume.

12 W. Anderson Smith, *'Shepherd' Smith the Universalist* (London, 1892). Further details of Shepherd Smith's views and career are given in J. F. C. Harrison, *Robert Owen and the Owenites in Britain and America* (London, 1969). See also John Saville, 'J. E. Smith and the Owenite Movement, 1833–4', in Sidney Pollard and John Salt (eds), *Robert Owen: Prophet of the Poor* (London, 1971).

13 William Scruton, *Pen and Pencil Pictures of Old Bradford* (Bradford, 1889), pp. 244–7. The frontispiece of this volume is a drawing of the house in which Wroe was born.

14 The most useful source for the Ashton Wroeites is William Chadwick, *Reminiscences of a Chief Constable* (Manchester, [1900]). The following are mainly derivative, but each contains odd pieces of information not found elsewhere: Winifred M. Bowman, *England in Ashton-under-Lyne* (Ashton-under-Lyne, 1960); A. J. Howcroft, *Tales of a Pennine People* (Oldham, 1923); William Glover, *History of Ashton-under-Lyne*, ed. John Andrew (Ashton-under-Lyne, 1884); and Edwin Butterworth, *An Historical Account of the Towns of Ashton-under-Lyne, Stalybridge, and Dukinfield* (Ashton, 1842). In Ashton-under-Lyne Public Library there is a MS notebook of the Wroeite, Samuel Lees, for the period 1828–30: the entries relate to the making and wearing of jewellery by the women Israelites.

15 Account based on Smith, *The Coming Man*, vol. I, ch. 36.

16 There is an account of the allegations against Wroe and the riot in the Sanctuary in *The Voice of the People*, 5 March 1831. Christian Israelism was taken to Australia by Charles Robertson in the late 1830s, and Wroe first visited Australia in 1843–4. He met with considerable success and made subsequent visits. Sanctuaries were established in Sydney, Melbourne and Adelaide, and Wroeite congregations were wide-spread. Wroe's mansion at Wrenthorpe, near Wakefield, was built for him by his Australian followers in 1857, and

was called Melbourne House. See *Extracts of Letters from Charles Robertson and Charles Wilson, Israelite Preachers, Australia, 1841* [Wakefield, n.d.]; and Michael Roe, *Quest for Authority in Eastern Australia, 1835–1851* (Melbourne, 1965), p. 127; also Roe's entry for Wroe in the *Australian Dictionary of Biography* (Melbourne, 1966–), vol. 2, p. 625. After Wroe's death the leadership of the Christian Israelites was claimed by Daniel Milton, who established himself at Wakefield. He was an American and was born Daniel Trickey in 1821. He was a member of the Millerite congregation in Portsmouth, NH, but fell away after the failure of the second advent prophecy. In December 1844 he was converted to the Israelite church by two Wroeite preachers, John Bishop and his wife, Margaret. Early in 1845 he travelled to New York with the Bishops and married their daughter. From 1845 to 1854 he worked as a carpenter in New York and was an active Wroeite. He then changed his name to Milton. After some controversy with Bishop and other church members, Milton was arrested in 1858, and confined in a workhouse asylum until 1860. In that year he was released and went to England, where he continued his quarrel with Bishop at Wrenthorpe; and, after the death of Wroe in 1863, claimed the Shiloh succession. I am indebted to Professor Robert Fogarty for this information. There is a collection of posters, broadsheets and pamphlets by Milton in Wakefield Central Library.

17 *New York Daily Times*, quoted in Balleine, *Past Finding Out*, pp. 92–3.

18 W. Cooke Taylor, *Notes of a Tour in the Manufacturing Districts of Lancashire* (London, 1842), p. 234.

19 Attempts on Wroe's life are described in the *Abridgement*, pp. 386–7, 398. Mob violence at Bradford in 1824 is described by Elizabeth Elsworth in *Letters of Israelite Preachers, 1824*, pp. 8–9. For Mormonism see chapter 7.

20 *Abridgement*, pp. 68–9.

21 Wesley also warned against artificial curls. J. Wesley, *Advice With Regard to Dress* (1780); and John Walsh, 'Methodism at the end of the eighteenth century', in Rupert Davies and Gordon Rupp (eds), *A History of the Methodist Church in Great Britain* (London, 1965), vol. I, p. 311.

22 Figures from Edward Baines, *The Social, Educational, and Religious State of the Manufacturing Districts* (London, 1843). Also *Census of Religious Worship* (1853). The relative position of the Southcottians in Ashton is indicated by the numbers of nonconformists in the town in 1829: Southcottians, 548; Wesleyan Methodists, 1,000; New Connexion, 1,390; Primitive Methodists, 70; Independents, 800; Scotch Baptists, 50; Particular Baptists, 250; General Baptists, 260. Lancs. County Records Office, QDV. 9. Dissenters Returns, 1829, no. 249. I am indebted to Dr Peter Lineham for this information.

23 Following quotations from vol. I, pp. 274–6.

24 *Ibid.*, p. 294.

25 Communication dated 10 June 1832. *Abridgement*, p. 209.

26 See G. D. H. Cole, *Attempts at General Union* (London, 1953), pp. 46–52.

27 The following quotations are from the *Abridgement*, pp. 381–2, 384, and *Letters of Israelite Preachers, 1825*, pp. 8–9.

28 Published in his journal, *The Judgement Seat of Christ* (London), nos. 1–17 (June–October, 1831), pp. 65–75, from which quotations in this and the following paragraph are taken, unless otherwise stated. Biographical information about Ward is also contained in C. B. Holinsworth, *Memoir of John Ward* (Birmingham, 1881): and in two pieces by Shepherd Smith published in *The Crisis* (London, 24 August 1833), p. 275, and in J. E. Smith, *The Antichrist* (London, [1833]). There is an entry in the *DNB*. Ward's writings were edited and republished later by C. B. Holinsworth as *Zion's Works*, 12 vols (London, 1899–1901). This collection contains MSS. which Holinsworth says he had for over thirty years and which had not previously been published. Vol. I, pp. 304–11 lists thirty-seven titles by Ward. There is also a selection from Ward's papers in BL Add. MSS. 43,509. These are mainly letters to followers in Nottingham and Birmingham, 1829–31, and are largely reprinted in Holinsworth, *Zion's Works*, vol. XIV.

29 This was the Reverend J. L. Garrett who attacked Joanna in his *Demoncracy Detected* (London, 1805), provoking the reply, *Joanna Southcott's Answer to Garrett's Book ...* (London, 1805).

30 Ward's doctrines are set out in various works. This paragraph is taken in the first instance from *An Appeal to the British Nation* ([Birmingham?], 1832). But see also *The Vision of Judgement* (London, 1829); *Letters, Epistles and Revelations of Jesus Christ* ([Birmingham], 1831); and *The Doctrine of Zion*, pts I–III (Birmingham, 1874–5).

31 Carlile's transition to allegorical

Christianity can be followed in *The Isis* (London), May 1832, and in his later periodicals. A statement of his final position is given in Richard Carlile, *An Abstract ... of the Lectures delivered ... at Brighton and elsewhere in the year 1836, to prove that the Bible is not a Book of Historical Record, but an important Mythological Volume* (London, 1837). See also G. D. H. Cole, *Richard Carlile* (London, 1943); and Edward Royle, *Victorian Infidels* (Manchester, 1974), pp. 31–43; and *Radical Politics, 1790–1900: Religion and Unbelief* (London, 1971), pp. 32–4. Carlile's letter to Lees is in the *Republican*, 10 December 1824; and contacts with the Muggletonians, Southcottians and other sects are mentioned throughout the *Lion*, vols I–IV (1828–9).

32 Taylor's doctrines are set out in his *Syntagma of the Evidences of the Christian Religion* (London, 1828); *The Diegesis* (London, 1829); and *The Devil's Pulpit* (London, 1831; repr. 1879 and 1881). His visit to the Ashton Wroeites in 1829 is described in the *Lion*, 31 July 1829. Balleine, *Past Finding Out*, p. 95 states that Ward read Carlile in 1827 and was greatly impressed. For the possible influence of Taylor and his 'astronomico-theological discourses', see Ward, *The Judgement Seat of Christ*, pp. 106–68, where in an article on divine astronomy he argues that the signs of the zodiac are fulfilled in the Man of God, Zion.

33 Smith, *The Antichrist*, p. 125.

34 Shepherd Smith's *magnum opus* was *The Divine Drama of History and Civilization* (London, 1854), based on 'the science of historical analogy'. None of his earlier and more vigorous works contains a complete version of his 'dogma of universalism'; and the following outline of his principles is constructed from articles in *Shepherd* (London, 1834–5, 1837–8) and *Crisis* (London, 1832–4), supplemented with *The Antichrist*, and *The Little Book; or Momentous Crisis of 1840* (London, 1840).

35 *Shepherd*, 20 September 1834.

36 'Messiah's Kingdom', *ibid.*, 26 August 1837.

37 *Crisis*, 4 May 1833.

38 *Ibid.*, 31 August 1833.

39 John Ward, *Epistles and Revelations; Vision of Judgement; The Living Oracle; or the Star of Bethlehem ... in answer to a Letter of the Rev. T. P. Foley* (Nottingham, 1830); *A Letter addressed to the Believers in the Kingdom of God residing in London* [Birmingham, 1830].

40 Holinsworth, *Memoirs of John Ward*, p. 8.

41 *Crisis*, 31 August 1833.

42 See Elizabeth Fairlight [Farelight?] Vaughan [1772–1875], *A refutation to a Sermon preached by Robert Aitken, of Zion Chapel, Waterloo Road, upon the Second Coming of Christ* (London, 1839). Balleine, *Past Finding Out*, pp. 111–12 has biographical details. In 1855 her husband died and she married another believer named Peacock. She was for many years a colourful Southcottian prophetess in the Southwark area and died at the age of 103. See also *Western Antiquary*, vol. 7–8 (1887–9), pp. 243–4.

43 PRO, HO 64/11, 64/12.

44 For Ward's tone and arguments at this time see his pamphlets, *This Penny Book proves that the Bishops and Clergy are religious Imposters* (Birmingham, 1832); and *Dreadful Appearance of Choler[a] among the Wolves in Sheep's Clothing at Derby, on account of Two Strangers ...* [Birmingham, 1832]. A report of the trial appeared in Carlile's *Isis*, which Ward said was 'a fair account' (*Doctrine of Zion*, pt I, p. 53).

45 See Holinsworth, *Zion's Works*, vol. V, for a number of these epistles to Charles Bradley and others, written from Derby gaol. In a letter of 16 November 1833 he makes a passing reference to the great Derby Turn-Out of the silk workers: 'the Trades Unions go on well, we think; all the wheels are in motion' (vol. V, p. 55). At some point in his reading Ward became acquainted with the works of 'that sweet Prophetess, Jane Lead' (vol. II, p. 157; also vol. VI, p. 235). In his letters of 1829–31 he also mentions Behmen.

46 Details of Greaves can be found in Harrison, *Robert Owen and the Owenites*, pp. 127–31. See also Kathleen Raine and George Mills Harper (eds), *Thomas Taylor the Platonist: Selected Writings* (London, 1969), pp. 66–8. Ward's association with Greaves can be traced through the various letters to Greaves and to Miss Clissold (a follower of Greaves), 1834–5, in Holinsworth, *Zion's Works*, vols VI–IX, from which the quotations in this paragraph are taken. The continuity of the millenarian and mystical tradition is documented in the contact between Greaves and Christopher Walton, the theosophist and biographer of William Law (entry for Walton in *DNB*). See also letters to Walton from Dr Charles F. Zimpel of London, 1853–6. Zimpel, an admirer of Behmen and Law, was a Wroeite and believer in Joanna Southcott; and refers Walton to Mrs Peacock of Walworth for copies of Joanna's works, and to Mrs Dean of Gravesend for Wroe's writings. Walton MSS. 189.1

(100–104), Dr Williams's Library, London.
47 In Birmingham Charles Bradley and his
family, and later C. B. Holinsworth
remained faithful Shilohites. Ward's works
were published at intervals from the 1860s
to 1901 (see p. 254, note 28). At

Nottingham there is evidence of Shilohite
activity after Ward's death. See *Lord
Melbourne's Chain Unlinked* (Nottingham,
1840); and *The Way Searcher for Men*
(Nottingham, [n.d.]).

CHAPTER SEVEN   PECULIAR PEOPLES

1 Cf. the stimulating comparison with French
millenarian movements in Clarke Garrett,
*Respectable Folly: Millenarians and the French
Revolution in France and England* (London,
1975).
2 Two excellent modern studies of the
Shakers, to which I am heavily indebted, are
Edward Deming Andrews, *The People called
Shakers* (New York, 1953); and Henri
Desroche, *The American Shakers*, trans. and
ed. John K. Savacool (Amherst, Mass.,
1971). An indication of the large extent of
Shaker sources and literature is given in
these two volumes, especially in the notes to
Desroche; and there is a useful short
bibliography in Arthur Eugene Bestor, Jr,
Backwoods Utopias (Philadelphia, Pa., 1950),
pp. 255–8. A useful sociological study is
John MacKelvie Whitworth, *God's
Blueprints* (London, 1975). The two basic
Shaker texts are Benjamin Seth Youngs, *The
Testimony of Christ's Second Appearing*
(Lebanon, Ohio, 1808; 4th edn, Albany,
NY, 1856); and Calvin Green and Seth Y.
Wells, *A Summary View of the Millennial
Church, or United Society of Believers* (Albany,
1823; 2nd edn, 1848). These have to be
supplemented for the later period with F.
W. Evans, *Autobiography of a Shaker, and
Revelation of the Apocalypse* (Mt Lebanon,
NY, 1869); and his *Ann Lee ... a Biography*
(London and Mt Lebanon, 4th edn, 1858);
and Anna White and Leila S. Taylor,
Shakerism; its Meaning and Message
(Columbus, Ohio, [1905]). Of the many
accounts by outside observers the following
are particularly worth noting: William
Hepworth Dixon, *New America*, 2 vols
(London, 1867); John Humphrey Noyes,
History of American Socialisms (Philadelphia,
Pa., 1870; repr. New York, 1961); Charles
Nordhoff, *The Communistic Societies of the
United States* (New York, 1875; repr. 1961).
3 J. F. C. Harrison, *Robert Owen and the
Owenites in Britain and America* (London,
1969), pp. 53, 98–9, 108. See also F. Gerald
Ham, 'Shakerism in the Old West'
(unpublished PhD thesis, University of
Kentucky, 1962).
4 Andrews, *People called Shakers*, pp. 11–12.

5 Evans, *Autobiography*, pp. 58, 71–2, 89–148.
6 Green and Wells, *Summary View*, pp. 251–2.
7 Nordhoff, *Communistic Societies*, p. 133;
Green and Wells, *Summary View*, pp.
223–30.
8 Youngs, *Testimony*, pp. 2–3, quoted in
Desroche, *American Shakers*, p. 44.
9 Green and Wells, *Summary View*, p. 16.
10 In a Shaker hymn reprinted in Nordhoff,
Communistic Societies, pp. 120–2, Adam, in a
dialogue with his children, confesses the
nature of his trangression and the cause of
his fall.
11 Youngs, *Testimony*, p. 224.
12 Edward D. Andrews, *The Gift to be Simple*
(1940; repr. New York, 1962), p. 130.
13 'Millennial Laws', repr. in Andrews,
Shakers, pp. 243–89. For the relation of
Shaker architecture to Shaker beliefs see
Dolores Hayden, *Seven American Utopias: the
Architecture of Communitarian Socialism,
1799–1975* (Cambridge, Mass. and London,
1976), ch. 4.
14 Thomas Brown, *An Account of the People
called Shakers* (Troy, NY, 1812), quoted in
Symonds, *Thomas Brown and the Angels*
(London, 1961), pp. 116–17.
15 See Harrison, *Owen*, pp. 59–62.
16 Green and Wells, *Summary View*, ch. IV.
17 Symonds, *Thomas Brown and the Angels*, pp.
69, 83, 112–16, 138.
18 There are several well-documented cases of
this, e.g. the testimony of Mary Cummings
of New Hampshire, 1848, quoted in
Desroche, *American Shakers*, pp. 181–2.
19 Quoted in Andrews, *Shakers*, p. 28.
20 The Shaker usage of the term 'gifts' is from
St Paul (I Corinthians 12:4), 'there are
diversities of gifts, but the same Spirit.'
21 Details of Shaker dances are given in
Andrews, *Gift*, ch. III.
22 Quoted in Andrews, *Shakers*, p. 148.
23 Andrews, *Gift*, p. 7. On Shaker furniture
and craftsmanship, see Edward Deming
Andrews and Faith Andrews, *Shaker
Furniture* (New York, 1937).
24 Cf. also the experiences of W. M.
Wilkinson and his family in 1856 after the
death of his second son, when involuntary
drawings were directed by forces from the

spirit world. W. M. Wilkinson, *Spirit Drawings* (London, 2nd edn, 1864). Wilkinson was a brother of James John Garth Wilkinson, a homeopathic doctor and Swedenborgian.

25 Whitworth, *God's Blueprints*, p. 40.

26 E.g. Dixon, *New America*, vol. II, ch. 9. Also W. S. Warder, *A Brief Sketch of the Religious Society of People called Shakers* (1818), repr. in Robert Owen, *Life, by Himself*, 2 vols (London, 1857–8; repr. New York, 1967), vol. IA, Appendix K.; and 'Notes of Travel in the United States' by John Finch, the Owenite, in *New Moral World*, vol. 3, 10, February 1844.

27 Nordhoff, *Communistic Societies*, pp. 160–1.

28 Quotations in this paragraph are from Nordhoff, *ibid*, p. 163; and the 'Millennial Laws', in Andrews, *Shakers*, pp. 273, 277.

29 These examples are likewise taken from Andrews, *Shakers*, pp. 183, 267, 287.

30 Ham, 'Shakerism in the Old West', pp. 102–4.

31 Typical of this type of literature are J. B. Turner, *Mormonism in All Ages* (New York, 1842); and Henry Caswall, *The Prophet of the Nineteenth Century* (London, 1843). See also Davis Bitton, 'Anti-Intellectualism in Mormon History', *Dialogue*, vol. 1, no. 3 (Autumn, 1966).

32 Most useful for this account are Fawn M. Brodie, *No Man Knows my History: the Life of Joseph Smith, the Mormon Prophet* (New York, 1945; repr. London, 1963; 2nd edn, revised and enlarged, New York, 1971); and Thomas F. O'Dea, *The Mormons* (Chicago, 1957; repr. 1963). The official history of the church is Brigham H. Roberts, *Comprehensive History of the Church of Latter-day Saints, Century I*, 6 vols (Salt Lake City, 1930). Indispensable is the prophet's own account: Joseph Smith, *History of the Church of Jesus Christ of Latter-day Saints, Period I*, ed. Brigham H. Roberts, 7 vols (Salt Lake City, 1902–12, 1932; and later edns). His revelations are set out in *The Doctrine and Covenants* (Salt Lake City, 1968; and earlier edns). Also useful for the early days are the reminiscences of the prophet's mother: Lucy Smith, *Biographical Sketches of Joseph Smith, the Prophet, and his Progenitors for many Generations* (Liverpool and London, 1853; repr. New York, 1969).

33 Joseph Smith's autobiography (or sections of it) were reprinted in several places, including his *History of the Church* (1838). I have taken this quotation from the reprint in the *Cyclopaedia of Religious Denominations* (London and Glasgow, 1853), pp. 289–90.

34 *Cyclopaedia of Religious Denominations*, p. 291.

35 Smith, *Doctrine and Covenants*, 57:2.

36 [Charles Mackay], *The Mormons: or Latter-Day Saints. With Memoirs of … Joseph Smith, the 'American Mahomet'* (London [1851]), p. 113. See also Robert Southey, *Colloquies* (London, 1829), vol. II, p. 42, quoted in Caswall, *The Prophet*, p. ii.

37 Orson Pratt, *The New Jerusalem; or, the Fulfillment of Ancient Prophecy* (1849); and Tuveson, *Redeemer Nation* (Chicago, 1968), p. 184.

38 'Articles of Faith', printed in 1968 edn of *Doctrine and Covenants*.

39 E.g. Smith, *Doctrine and Covenants*, 43:17. Also Brodie, *No Man*, pp. 101–2; and Klaus J. Hansen, *Quest for Empire: the Political Kingdom of God and the Council of Fifty in Mormon History* (East Lansing, Mich., 1967), pp. 16–17.

40 *The Latter-day Saints Millennial Star* (Liverpool, 1840–) ran a regular feature headed 'Signs of the Times', in which were recorded disasters and unusual events in all parts of the world – to be interpreted as evidence of the last days before the second coming.

41 Walker, *Decline of Hell* (London, 1964), p. 250.

42 Parley P. Pratt, *Key to the Science of Theology* (Salt Lake City, 5th edn, 1891), pp. 138–9.

43 Tuveson, *Redeemer Nation*, p. 176; and 'A Note on the Millennial Beliefs of the Latter-day Saints', pp. 175–86. See also Hansen, p. 18; and Thomas G. Alexander, 'Wilford Woodruff and the Changing Nature of Mormon Religious Experience', *Church History*, vol. 45, no. 1 (March 1976).

44 *Cyclopaedia of Religious Denominations*, p. 290.

45 Hansen, *Quest for Empire*, pp. 28–31.

46 At a place he called Adam-ondi-Ahman in Daviess county, Missouri. Smith, *Doctrine and Covenants*, 116 and 117:8.

47 *Book of Mormon*, II Nephi.

48 See Brodie, *No Man*, pp. 45–6 for titles. The works of Josiah Priest are particularly relevant. In his *American Antiquities and Discoveries in the West* (Albany, NY, 1833) he claimed that there was evidence 'to show that America was peopled before the flood; that it was the country of Noah, and the place where the ark was erected.' His *A View of the Expected Christian Millennium* (Albany, NY, 1828) was an orthodox statement of post-millennialism. In *The Anti-Universalist* (Albany, NY, 1837) he dealt with the problems of the fallen angels,

Satan and the world of evil spirits. The book was produced in chapbook style, complete with woodcuts. Some of the ramifications of American–Israelism are seen in the career of Harriet Livermore (1788–1868), a school teacher and millenarian, who was the daughter of a US senator. She believed that the Indians were descendants of the Israelites, and so attempted to settle among the Indians at Fort Leavenworth, Kansas, but was prevented from doing so by the Commissioner on Indian Affairs, and then went to the Holy Land. See her *Millennial Tidings* (Philadelphia, 1839), a collection of pamphlets published 1831–9; and Robert Kieran Whalen, 'Millenarianism and Millennialism in America, 1790–1880' (unpublished PhD thesis, State University of New York at Stony Brook, 1971), pp. 48–9.

49 Brodie, *No Man*, p. 46; and ch. II *passim*.

50 O'Dea, *The Mormons*, p. 24.

51 See Whitney R. Cross, *The Burned-over District* (Ithaca, NY, 1950; repr. New York, 1965).

52 O'Dea, *The Mormons*, p. 27.

53 See the important article by Mario S. de Pillis, 'The Quest for Religious Authority and the Rise of Mormonism', *Dialogue*, vol. I, no. 1 (Spring, 1966), in which it is argued that early Mormonism successfully catered to the need for religious authority among rural Americans who were not satisfied by the claims of competing sects. Also useful is David Brion Davis, 'The New England Origins of Mormonism', *New England Quarterly*, vol. XXVI (1953).

54 Alexander Campbell, 'Delusions', *Millennial Harbinger*, vol. II (1831), p. 93; and see comment in De Pillis' article, 'Quest', pp. 79, 87.

55 Rigdon was in touch with the contemporary communitarian movement and had been present at Robert Owen's debate with Alexander Campbell at Cincinnati in April 1829. See Robert Owen and Alexander Campbell, *Debate on the Evidences of Christianity*, 2 vols (Bethany, Va., 1829). For Rigdon and the Campbellites see A. S. Hayden, *Early History of the Disciples in the Western Reserve, Ohio* (Cincinnati, 1875). Also Karl Keller (ed.), ' "I never knew a time when I did not know Joseph Smith": a son's record of the life and testimony of Sidney Rigdon', *Dialogue*, vol. 1, no. 4 (Winter, 1966).

56 E.g. Symonds Ryder, Oliver Snow and family (Campbellites), Ezra Booth (Methodist). Hayden, *Early History*, pp. 240, 245–53.

57 Campbell, *Millennial Harbinger*, vol. II (1831), p. 101.

58 Parley Parker Pratt, *Autobiography*, ed. Parley P. Pratt [his son] (Chicago, 1888), pp. 45–6.

59 Pratt, *Autobiography*, p. 35. Cf. the autobiography of the British preacher, William Huntington (the 'Sinner Saved') [1745–1813], *The Bank of Faith* (London, 1784; and later edns), in which he describes God's providences as cheques drawn upon the divine bank.

60 Pratt, *Key to Theology*, p. 49; and Davis, 'The New England Origins', p. 161.

61 Lucy Smith, *Biographical Sketches*. Quotations in this paragraph are from pp. 21, 37, 47, 90.

62 Caswall, *Prophet of the Nineteenth Century*, pp. 1–2, 9.

63 Turner, *Mormonism in All Ages*, pp. 280, 283.

64 Davis, 'The New England Origins', p. 156.

65 *Doctrine and Covenants*, 132. Verse 20 promises that a man and wife sealed for eternity 'shall be gods, because they have no end ... and the angels are subject unto them.' For a study of the wives sealed to Joseph Smith, see Brodie, *No Man*, ch. XXIV, and Appendix C.

66 The full story of the British Mormon emigration is admirably presented in P. A. M. Taylor, *Expectations Westward: The Mormons and the Emigration of their British Converts in the Nineteenth Century* (Edinburgh and London, 1965). See also James B. Allen and Malcolm R. Thorp, 'The Mission of the Twelve to England, 1840–41: Mormon Apostles and the Working Classes', *Brigham Young University Studies*, vol. 15, no. 4 (Summer, 1975); James B. Allen and Thomas G. Alexander (eds), *Manchester Mormons: the Journal of William Clayton, 1840 to 1842* (Salt Lake City and Santa Barbara, 1974); and Alexander, 'Wilford Woodruff'. Statistics of membership and emigration are from Taylor, *Expectations Westward*, pp. 19–21, 144–6; Mackay, *Mormons*, p. 249; and Frederick Hawkins Piercy, *Route from Liverpool to Great Salt Lake Valley*, ed. James Linforth (Liverpool and London, 1855); repr. and ed. Fawn M. Brodie (Cambridge, Mass., 1962).

67 Journal of Wilford Woodruff, 2 September 1840, quoted in Allen and Thorp, 'The Mission', p. 510.

68 Mackay, *Mormons*, p. 249 quotes figures of membership for the main Mormon conferences in 1850 as follow: London

2,529; Manchester 2,787; Liverpool 1,018; Glasgow 1,846; Sheffield 1,929; Edinburgh 1,331; Birmingham 1,909; Wales 4,342.

69 The Reverend Robert Aitken (1800-73) was ordained in the Church of England, became a Methodist preacher, then ministered to a sect of his own, and later returned to Anglicanism. See *DNB* and Taylor, *Expectations Westward*, p. 37.

70 Details in Allen and Thorp, 'The Mission', pp. 504-5.

71 E.g. members of the Lees family. The case of Elizabeth Lees is referred to in the *Millennial Star*, vol. X (1848), p. 256. The whole question of the relation between the Wroeites and Mormons is being examined by Professor Howard R. Murphy, using material in the archives at Salt Lake City. It would appear, tentatively, that some Wroeites and ex-Wroeites became Mormons, and that others were baptized posthumously through their descendants.

72 Allen and Thorp, 'The Mission', p. 516. This material is from the journals of the people concerned, in the LDS Church Historical Department.

73 Quoted in Brodie, *No Man*, pp. 264-5.

74 MacKay, *Mormons*, p. 250. The trades and professions of the Mormon emigrants are listed on p. 251 and include farmers, labourers, miners, engineers, joiners, powerloom weavers, shoemakers, tailors, watchmakers, stone-masons, butchers, potters, shipwrights, dyers, and other artisan trades. For an analysis of Mormon emigrants see Taylor, *Expectations Westward*, ch. 7.

75 *Millennial Star*, vols V (1844-5), pp. 180-2; IX (1847), pp. 231-3; XI (1849), pp. 202-7.

76 *Ibid.*, vol. X (1848), pp. 302-3, quoted from *Howitt's Journal*.

77 The standard Seventh-day Adventist history of Millerism is Francis D. Nichol, *The Midnight Cry* (Washington, DC, 1944: repr. pb. edn, n.d.); and there is also a very full account in LeRoy Edwin Froom, *The Prophetic Faith of Our Fathers*, 4 vols (Washington, DC, 1946-54), vol. IV. See also Clara Endicott Sears, *Days of Delusion* (Boston, 1924). A more recent interpretation is David T. Arthur, 'Millerism', in Edwin S. Gaustad (ed.), *The Rise of Adventism* (New York, 1974), which also has an extensive bibliography. Essential primary sources are William Miller, *Evidences from Scripture and History of the Second Coming of Christ* (Brandon, Vt, 1833; and later edns); Joshua V. Himes, *Views of the Prophecies and Prophetic Chronology*

(Boston, 1841); Sylvester Bliss, *Memoirs of William Miller* (Boston, 1853); Second Advent Library, nos I-XLVII (Boston, 1842-4) [a collection of tracts, individually paged, by leading Millerites]; and the two main Millerite periodicals, *Signs of the Times* [continued as *Advent Herald*] (Boston, 1840-4); and *Midnight Cry* [continued as *Morning Watch*] (New York, 1842-4).

78 Bliss, *Memoirs*, p. 77.

79 Miller, *Apology and Defence* (Boston, 1845), p. 12, quoted in Froom, *Prophetic Faith*, vol. IV, p. 474.

80 The Millerite calculations are described in detail in Froom, *Prophetic Faith*, vol. IV, ch. 37.

81 J. B. Cook, *A Solemn Appeal ... relative to the Speedy Coming of Christ*, Second Advent Library, no. XXXV (Boston, 1843), p. 37.

82 Froom, *Prophetic Faith*, vol. IV, p. 449.

83 Hiram Edson. Fragment of MS. on his life and experience, p. 8 [n.d.] quoted in Nichol, *The Midnight Cry*, pp. 263-4.

84 'A Scene of the Last Day', in Bliss, *Memoirs*, pp. 405-9.

85 Luther Boutelle, *Sketch of the Life and Religious Experience of Eld. Luther Boutelle. Written by Himself* (Boston, 1891), pp. 67, 69.

86 See Timothy L. Smith, *Revivalism and Social Reform* (New York and Nashville, 1957: pb. edn, New York, 1965), p. 228.

87 US Circuit Court, Massachusetts District, *Ezekiel Hale, Junior, versus Ezekiel J. M. Hale. May Term, 1845* (Boston, 1849). Copy in Haverhill Public Library, Haverhill, Mass. Quotations in this and the following paragraph are from pp. 78, 79, 90-1, 97, 115. See also Henry Hale Gilman, 'The Mill and the Millerite; or the Story of the Ezekiels' (undated typescript [c. 1920s?] by a grandnephew of the plaintiff, in Haverhill Public Library).

88 Bliss, *Memoirs*, pp. 70-2. Also in Himes, *Views of the Prophecies*, pp. 20-4; and in Apollos Hale, *The Second Advent Manual*, Second Advent Library, no. XXXVI (Boston, 1843), pp. 103-6.

89 Joseph Bates, *The Autobiography of Elder Joseph Bates* (Battle Creek, Michigan, 1868), p. 262; and quoted in Gaustad, *Rise of Adventism*, p. 176. Bates (1792-1872) was a sea captain from New Bedford, Mass., and became a Millerite in 1839. He was an active abolitionist and temperance reformer. After the great disappointment he became a Second Adventist, and moved to Battle Creek in 1858.

90 Details are given in Louis Billington, 'The

Millerite Adventists in Great Britain, 1840–1850', *Journal of American Studies*, vol. 1, no. 2 (October, 1967), pp. 191–212, to which I am indebted for most of the material in this paragraph. See also Froom, *Prophetic Faith*, vol. IV, pp. 713–18.

91 The most recent study is Herbert A. Wisbey, Jr, *Pioneer Prophetess: Jemima Wilkinson, The Publick Universal Friend* (Ithaca, NY, 1964). See also Robert P. St John, 'Jemima Wilkinson', New York State Historical Association, *Proceedings*, vol. XXVIII (1930). A contemporary, but hostile account is David Hudson, *History of Jemima Wilkinson, a Preacheress of the Eighteenth Century* (Geneva, NY, 1821). An article 'Jemima Wilkinson', in the *Millennial*

Harbinger, vol. II (1831), pp. 278–81, adds little to Hudson.

92 Recounted in fascinating detail by a local antiquarian in R. H. Taneyhill, *The Leatherwood God. An Account of the Appearance and Pretensions of Joseph C. Dylk: in Eastern Ohio in 1828* (Cincinnati, 1870, repr. with intro. by George Kummer, Gainesville, Florida, 1966). The story was also the basis of William Dean Howells' novel, *The Leatherwood God*, published in New York, 1916.

93 Taneyhill, *Leatherwood God*, p. 26.

94 Vol. II (1831), p. 357.

95 *Signs of the Times*, vol. 1 (1840), p. 56.

96 *Advent Herald*, vol. VIII (1844), p. 43.

CHAPTER EIGHT THROUGH A GLASS, DARKLY

1 Typically, a Dissenting lawyer in his reply to Burke, wrote:

> As I am a believer in Revelation, I, of course, live in the hope of better things; a millennium (not a fifth monarchy, Sir, of enthusiasts and fanatics), but a new heaven and a new earth in which dwelleth righteousness; or, to drop the eastern figure and use a more philosophical language, a state of equal liberty and equal justice for all men. (*A Letter to the Right Hon. Edmund Burke Esq., from a Dissenting County Attorney* (Birmingham, 1791), p. 147; and quoted in Peter H. Marshall, 'William Godwin: a Study of the Origins, Development and Influences of his Philosophy' (unpublished DPhil thesis, University of Sussex, 1976), p. 28).

2 Short accounts of Edward Irving (1792–1834) and Irvingism are given in LeRoy Edwin Froom, *Prophetic Faith of Our Fathers*, 4 vols (Washington, DC), vol. III, ch. 24; and in Sandeen, *The Roots of Fundamentalism: British and American Millenarianism, 1800–1930* (Chicago, 1970), ch. 1, which also has a useful bibliography. Irving's millenarian position appears in his publications, e.g. *Babylon and Infidelity Foredoomed of God: A Discourse on the Prophecies of Daniel and the Apocalypse*, 2 vols (Glasgow, 1826); Manuel Lacunza, *The Coming of the Messiah in Glory and Majesty*, trans. Edward Irving, 2 vols (London, 1827); and *The Last Days: A Discourse on the Evil Character of these our Times* (London, 1828). From the remnants of Irvingism came the Catholic Apostolic Church, for which see P. E. Shaw, *The Catholic Apostolic*

Church (New York, 1946).

3 Cf. Keith Thomas, *Religion and the Decline of Magic* (London, 1971), p. 469.

4 Ida Macalpine and Richard Hunter, 'The Pathography of the Past', *The Times Literary Supplement*, 15 March 1974.

5 Two basic works on the treatment of the insane in Britain at this time are Kathleen Jones, *Lunacy, Law and Conscience, 1744–1845* (London, 1955); and William Ll. Parry-Jones, *The Trade in Lunacy* (London, 1972). For changing concepts of madness, see George Rosen, *Madness in Society* (New York, 1969); Max Byrd, *Visits to Bedlam* (Columbia, South Carolina, 1974); and Michael V. Deporte, *Nightmares and Hobbyhorses* (San Marino, California, 1974).

6 *Great News from Bedlam!; or the Wonderful Prophecies of Margaret Nicholson; which were found written in a letter under the walls of Bedlam. Being her account of a vision which appeared ... and related to her the most wonderful things which will happen in Europe* [n.p., n.d.]. See also *Prophecy on Prophecies: being a true and exact account of the dream of Margaret Nicholson ...* [n.p., 1787?]; and *A True and Particular Account of Margaret Nicholson's Attempt to stab His Most Gracious Majesty, George III, ... at St. James's on the 2d. of August, 1786* (London, 1786).

7 *The Complete Trial of James Hadfield ... charged with High Treason for ... firing at the King in Drury Lane Theatre, on the 15th of May last ... to which is added some account of James Hadfield* (London, [1800?]). See also *Sketches in Bedlam* (London, 1823), pp. 14–18

8 *Bell's Weekly Messenger*, 18 May 1800 (account of the interrogation of Truelock

before the Privy Council). The remaining quotations in this paragraph are from *Sketches in Bedlam*, pp. 19–26.

9 *The Life of Jonathan Martin, of Darlington, Tanner. Written by Himself* (Darlington, 1825). Information about other editions of this chapbook, and details of Martin's life, are given in Thomas Balston, *The Life of Jonathan Martin, Incendiary of York Minster* (London, 1945).

10 Vol. LXXXV, pt I (1815), pp. 599–602. The *Quarterly Review*, vol. XXIV (1821), pp. 184–9, also discussed the 'very delicate and interesting topic' of whether religion was a cause or an effect of insanity, in a review of George Man Burrows' book, *An Inquiry into Certain Errors relative to Insanity* (London, 1820).

11 W. A. F. Browne, 'Observations on Religious Fanaticism; illustrated by a comparison of the belief and conduct of noted religious enthusiasts with those of patients in the Montrose Lunatic Asylum', *Phrenological Journal and Miscellany*, vol. IX (1834–6) and vol. X (1836–7).

12 George Man Burrows, *Commentaries on Insanity* (London, 1828), quoted in Vieda Skultans, *Madness and Morals: Ideas on Insanity in the Nineteenth Century* (London, 1975), p. 41. But this view was contested by Samuel Tuke in his *Description of the Retreat* (York, 1813; repr., with intro. by Richard Hunter and Ida Macalpine, London, 1964), pp. 208–10, who said that very few cases admitted to the Retreat in York were connected with 'religious impressions' (unlike Bethlem, where the apothecary claimed that Methodism was the cause of many of the derangements of his patients). Similar charges and rebuttals were made in America, especially in connection with the Millerites. See Francis D. Nichol, *The Midnight Cry* (Washington, DC, 1944) ch. 24 and Appendices E, F. A fascinating modern study is Milton Rokeach, *The Three Christs of Ypsilanti: a Psychological Study* (New York, 1964).

13 Beatrice Webb, *My Apprenticeship* (London, 1926), p. 13; Georgina Meinertzhagen, *From Ploughshare to Parliament* (London, 1908), pp. 191, 200, 223.

14 John Perceval, *A Narrative of the Treatment experienced by a Gentleman during a State of Mental Derangement*, 2 vols (London, 1838–40; repr. as *Perceval's Narrative: A Patient's Account of his Psychosis, 1830–1832*, ed. Gregory Bateson, Stanford, California, 1961; and London, 1962), pp. 11, 30. The subsequent quotations in this paragraph are from pp. 19, 271.

15 There is an entry for Tom in the *DNB*. But the fullest account is P. G. Rogers, *Battle in Bossenden Wood: the Strange Story of Sir William Courtenay* (London, 1961), which also has a short bibliography. A number of contemporary sources were published, of which the most useful are Canterburiensis, *The Life and Extraordinary Adventures of Sir William Courtenay* (Canterbury, 1839); and *An Account of the Desperate Affray ... in Blean Wood near Boughton, ... 31st May 1838* (Faversham, 1838). Complete runs of Courtenay's periodical, *The Lion*, 1833, are scarce, but the eight numbers are reprinted in *The Eccentric and Singular Productions of Sir W. Courtenay* (Canterbury, [1833]). A volume of pamphlets and press cuttings from local papers is in the British Library, reference 809 f. 32 (1–9).

16 F. Liardet, 'State of the Peasantry in the County of Kent', *Central Society of Education. Papers. Third Publication* (London, 1839; repr. London, 1968), pp. 89–90. Liardet, a barrister-at-law, was commissioned by the CSE to make a detailed report on the neighbourhood in July 1838, following the Bossenden affair. He interviewed as many people in the area as he could, and the result is an invaluable case-study of millenarians.

17 Liardet, 'State of Peasantry', pp. 90–1. Quotations in the next paragraph are from pp. 91, 92–3.

18 Kenneth Leech, 'Christianity and the divine madness', *The Times*, 27 April 1974.

19 There is a discussion of Blake and madness in Byrd, *Visits to Bedlam*, ch. 6, to which I am indebted.

20 Blake, *Poetry and Prose*, ed. Geoffrey Keynes (London, 1967), 'Notes on Spurzheim's "Observations on the Deranged Manifestations of the Mind, or Insanity",' p. 817.

21 *Ibid.*, p. 652, 'A Vision of the Last Judgment'.

22 Alexander Gilchrist, *Life of William Blake*, 2 vols (London, 1880), vol. 1, p. 370.

23 Thomas Carlyle, 'Natural Supernaturalism', *Sartor Resartus* (London, 1834), bk III, ch. VIII.

24 Nathaniel Brassey Halhed, *The Whole of the Testimonies to the Authenticity of the Prophecies and Mission of Richard Brothers* (London, 1795), pp. 6–7.

25 James Jenkins, 'Records and Recollections, 1761–1821', 4 vols [see chapter 4, note 22 for source location], pp. 273, 345–7.

26 The most complete development of this

theory is Michael Barkun, *Disaster and the Millennium* (New Haven and London, 1974).

27 Bryan R. Wilson, *Magic and the Millennium: a Sociological Study of Religious Movements of Protest among Tribal and Third-World Peoples* (London, 1973).

28 Liardet, 'State of Peasantry', p. 96.

29 Wilson, *Magic and Millennium*, p. 7.

30 I am indebted to Dr J. Ann Hone for this information. See also her unpublished DPhil thesis, 'The Ways and Means of London Radicalism, 1796–1821' (Oxford, 1975).

31 Courtenay is said to have contacted the Spenceans during a visit to London in 1821. See Canterburiensis, *Life of ... Courtenay*, pp. 62–70; and Rogers, *Battle in Bossenden Wood*, pp. 4–5, 211.

32 Liardet, 'State of Peasantry', p. 133.

33 E.g. Marie Louis Reybaud, *Études sur les Reformateurs contemporains, ou Socialistes modernes*, 2 vols (Bruxelles, 1843), vol. II, pp. 51–3.

34 Thomas Dudgeon, *Moral and Theological Axioms* (Auburn, New York, 1839), p. 7. His other writings were *Lectures on a literal Transcript of Ancient Prophecies* (Edinburgh, 1841; another edn, New York, 1844); *A Nine Years Residence ... in New York and Pennsylvania* (Edinburgh, 1841); *Prophetic Chronology of Daniel and Revelation* (Detroit, 1846); and *Lecture on Radical and Practical Chartism* (London, 1848).

35 The four letters (dated 1841–7 and written by William Loveless from Pymore, Bridport, to his brother, George, who lived first near Chipping Ongar, Essex, and later near London, in western Ontario) are in the possession of Miss M. E. Loveless (a grand-daughter of George Loveless) of Regina, Canada. Copies have been deposited in the Regina Office of the Archives of Saskatchewan. I am grateful to Professor C. B. Koester of the University of Saskatchewan, Regina, Canada for supplying me with copies of the letters and for information about the Loveless family. Quotations in this paragraph are from the letters dated 10 December 1841 and 25 December 1847.

36 As E. P. Thompson, *Making of the English Working Class* (London, 1963), pp. 388–91, speculates in the case of religious revivalism; though with the important caution that to substantiate this oscillation hypothesis we should need to know about 'not the years of revivalism, but the months; not the

counties. but the towns and villages'.

37 Isaac Watts' *Hymns and Spiritual Songs* was first published in 1707. See the edition by Selma L. Bishop (London, 1962), p. 230.

38 Hymn no. 846, *Methodist Hymn Book* (London, 1904). It is dated 1802–19.

39 Chapter 4, note 7; chapter 6, note 29. Also George Horne, *Sound Argument dictated by Common Sense; in answer to ... Richard Brothers* (Oxford [1795?]); William Wales Horne, *Jesus Christ, the only true and divine Shiloh ... in refutation of ... Joanna Southcott* (London, 1814); R. Hann, *The Prophecies of Joanna Southcott* (London, 1810); *A Letter to ... the Bishop of London concerning ... Joanna the Prophetess* (London, 1810); *Charges against Joanna Southcott* (London, [n.d.]).

40 A fascinating modern study of how the failure mechanism works is Leon Festinger, Henry W. Riecken, and Stanley Schachter, *When Prophecy Fails* (New York, 1966).

41 J. B. Phillips, *The Book of Revelation: a new Translation of the Apocalypse* (London, 1957), pp. xii–xiii. See also Tuveson, *Redeemer Nation* (Chicago, 1968), pp. 6–11.

42 Philip Pullen, *Hymns on the Millennium composed from the Prophetic Writings of Joanna Southcott* (London, 1808), p. 94, no. XCIV.

43 William Wordsworth, preface to 'Lyrical Ballads', in *Poetical Works*, ed. E. de Selincourt and Helen Darbishire, 5 vols (Oxford, 1944–9), vol. 2, p. 397.

44 I am indebted to my colleague, Dr Michael Wadsworth, for pointing out the similarity between Ward and Rudolph Bultmann. See Bultmann, 'New Testament and Mythology', in Hans Werner Bartsch (ed.), *Kerygma and Myth* (London, 1960).

45 All the collections of Southcottian manuscripts include such material. Typical is James Hayward's (MS.) two-volume index to his collection of Joanna's communications (also in manuscript), GLRO, 1040/182–198. As early as 1805 a *General Index to the Writings of Joanna Southcott, the Prophetess* by John Ingall was published in London, and Philip Pullen's *Index to the Divine and Spiritual Writings of Joanna Southcott* (London, 1815) went through several editions.

46 John Ward, *Doctrine of Zion* (Birmingham, 1874–5), pt I, p. 18.

47 Joanna Southcott, *Divine and Spiritual Letters* (London, 1801), p. 11.

48 Blake, *Poetry and Prose*, p. 825. Annotations to Dr Thornton's 'New Translation of the Lord's Prayer', London, 1827.

BIBLIOGRAPHICAL NOTE

There is a very large literature on the millennium and millenarianism, but much of it is not relevant to the purposes of this book. To guide the inquiring reader, and to set this particular aspect of millenarianism in perspective, a few remarks on the material used may therefore be appropriate. All the main sources are quoted in the Notes and References, and details need not be repeated. This note is a critical evaluation of that material, not an additional bibliography. It is a rough map to help those travellers for whom millenarianism is a rather strange and still largely unexplored territory.

Some idea of the variety and amount of recent millenarian scholarship can be gained from Hillel Schwartz, 'The End of the Beginning: Millenarian Studies, 1969–1975', *Religious Studies Review*, vol. 2, no. 3 (July, 1976). When this is supplemented with David E. Smith, 'Millenarian Scholarship in America', *American Quarterly* (Fall, 1965), a substantial bibliographic introduction is available. Ernest R. Sandeen, *The Roots of Fundamentalism: British and American Millenarianism, 1800–1930* (Chicago, 1970) has a valuable bibliographic essay; and for earlier writers (as for much else in the field) the indispensable work is LeRoy Edwin Froom, *The Prophetic Faith of Our Fathers*, 4 vols (Washington, DC, 1946–54).

A small corpus of work, produced during the last twenty years, is now familiar to social historians and is quoted when the subject of millenarianism is raised. Probably the best-known work is Norman Cohn, *The Pursuit of the Millennium* (London, 1957; and later edns). This influential book is a good starting place for the historical study of millenarianism; but the book is based on material from the Middle Ages and the Reformation period, and it would be dangerous to extrapolate Cohn's conclusions and hypotheses for the popular millenarians of the nineteenth century. Nearer to our own concerns are E. J. Hobsbawm, *Primitive Rebels* (Manchester, 1959); and parts of E. P. Thompson's widely read *Making of the English Working Class* (London, 1963). Sylvia L. Thrupp (ed.), *Millennial Dreams in Action* (The Hague, Netherlands, 1962) is a collection of comparative studies by historians, anthropologists and sociologists which gives a sense of context and perspective. Also to be included in the list of basic reading are Ernest Lee Tuveson's two books, *Millennium and Utopia* (Berkeley and Los Angeles, Cal., 1949; New York, 1964); and *Redeemer Nation* (Chicago, 1968).

Much of the present day interest in millenarianism comes from anthropologists and sociologists, and some of their work is of direct concern to the historian, even though it deals with contemporary sects or with the Third World. Max Weber's classic study, *The Sociology of Religion*, trans. Ephraim Fischoff, intro. Talcott Parsons (Boston, Mass., 1963), provides seminal ideas which have been followed by scores of lesser writers. Peter Worsley, *The Trumpet Shall Sound* (London, 1957), and Vittorio Lanternari, *The Religions of the Oppressed*, trans. Lisa Sergio (New York, 1963) are frequently quoted, but have not contributed much to this present study. More useful have been Bryan R. Wilson, *Magic and the Millennium* (London, 1973); Kenelm Burridge, *New Heaven New Earth* (Oxford, 1969); Michael Barkun, *Disaster and the Millennium* (New Haven and London, 1974); and Hildred Geertz and Keith Thomas, 'An Anthropology of Religion. Two Views', *Journal of Interdisciplinary History*, vol. VI (i) (Summer, 1975).

The historian who has profited most from anthropology and sociology is Keith Thomas, whose magnificent *Religion and the Decline of Magic* (London, 1971) has much to say on themes which are echoed by millenarians in the nineteenth century. Other works on seventeenth-century history are also useful in suggesting a continuous millenarian tradition, particularly those listed in chapter 2, notes 4 and 7.

A bane of millenarian literature, which the inquiring reader is sure to meet sooner or later, is the semi-popular synopsis which provides a rag-bag of freaks, curiosities, imposters and 'unbelievable' characters. Such productions have a long history; witness M. Aikin, *Memoirs of Religious Imposters* (London, 1823); [Richard Alford Davenport], *Sketches of Imposture, Deception and Credulity* (London, 1837); John Timbs, *English Eccentrics and Eccentricities* (London, 1898). Modern versions are little better. Apart from their inaccuracy (being based on secondary accounts and unsubstantiated assertions), they have the effect of trivializing and reducing their subjects. Millenarians are presented as specimens of abnormality and deviancy – good for a smile or a warning, but not to be taken seriously in these enlightened days. Alternatively they are explained away by a few references to Freudian psychology, or expansively patted on the head as evidence of the great British love of eccentricity. Examples of this genre include John Montgomery, *Abodes of Love* (London, 1962); Anthony Hunter, *The Last Days* (London, 1958); Jack Gratus, *False Messiahs* (London, 1976); and E. R. Chamberlin, *Antichrist and the Millennium* (New York, 1975). Ronald Matthews, *English Messiahs* (London, 1936) is a rather more serious work which uses a psychological interpretation.

Biographies and studies of individual millenarians are not plentiful. The only full-length biography of Richard Brothers is Cecil Roth, *The Nephew of the Almighty* (London, 1933), which is seriously deficient. Roth presumably came upon Brothers through an interest in Anglo-Jewish history, and the significance of the prophet in the context of his times is not brought out. The most useful study of Brothers (and of the whole millenarian tradition in the late eighteenth century) is Clarke Garrett's *Respectable Folly: Millenarians and the French Revolution in France and England* (Baltimore and London, 1975). Joanna Southcott still awaits a modern published biography, but until it appears J. K. Hopkins, 'Joanna Southcott: a Study of Popular Religion and Radical Politics, 1789–1814' (unpublished PhD thesis, University of Texas at Austin, 1972) is the most authoritative work available. The entries for Brothers, Joanna and other millenarians in the *Dictionary of National Biography* should not be overlooked. They are usually concise, accurate and sometimes based on sources not now traceable (e.g. Riebau's manuscript memoir of Brothers). However, for an introduction to Brothers, Joanna and the later Southcottians, G. R. Balleine, *Past Finding Out* (London, 1956) can be recommended. Despite its tantalizing omission of all sources and references, the book is based on primary material, and is in general balanced and reliable. An older study by Charles Lane, *Life of Joanna Southcott* (Exeter, 1912) has some useful additional details. Modern Southcottians have not produced any official life of Joanna; the nearest to this being Alice Seymour, *The Express*, 2 vols (London, 1909), which relies mainly on autobiographical passages from the prophetess's writings. A recent short account of Brothers, Joanna and other early nineteenth-century messiahs and millenarians is chapter 7, 'Sectarian Movements'; in Alan Smith, *The Established Church and Popular Religion, 1750–1850* (London, 1971).

At some stage the serious inquirer will want to read the original works by millenarians, and these are not too easy to find. Collections of Brothers' pamphlets may be found in major libraries, e.g. the British Library, Harvard University Library (Houghton Library) and Leeds University Library (Cecil Roth collection). Similarly with Joanna's writings; but these may be more accessible, as there were many editions and printings. Moreover, the whole canon of sixty-five titles was republished in paperback form by Alice Seymour (Plymouth and Ashford, Middx, 1912–24). Philip Pullen's *Index to ... Joanna Southcott* (London, 1815; repr. 1925) is very useful when working on her writings, as it gives a complete analysis and index of persons, themes, and places. Copies of John Wroe's works are scarce, even though the Wroeites continued into the second half of the nineteenth century. John Ward's writings were republished as *Zion's Works*, ed. C. B. Holinsworth, 12 vols (London, 1899–1901) and are available in the British Library. Details of the main collections of Southcottian manuscripts in the British Library, University of Texas Library, Greater London Record Office, and the Blockley Antiquarian Society are given in chapter 5 (i), note 21.

Scholarly work on the three American millenarian movements is more plentiful than for their British counterparts. For preliminary reading on the Shakers the various works of Edward Deming Andrews, especially *The People Called Shakers* (New York, 1953), cannot be bettered. And for the Mormons,

BIBLIOGRAPHICAL NOTE

Fawn M. Brodie, *No Man Knows my History* (New York, revised edn, 1971) is a fascinating and highly readable account of Joseph Smith and the early (millenarian) days of the Saints. Most accounts of the Millerites are by sympathetic Seventh-day Adventists, and the best is still Francis D. Nichol, *The Midnight Cry* (Washington, DC, 1944: repr. paperback edn, n.d.).

Beyond these specifically millenarian movements and prophets, this book has branched out in many directions. Contacts have been made with folklore, mysticism, astrology and madness. But the traveller who wishes to explore such regions must look elsewhere for authoritative guidance. This author has been able to provide only a few sign-posts on the way.

INDEX

The notes and references have not been indexed, except for millenarians not mentioned in the text.

Berlin, 70
Bermondsey, 67, 92, 116, 124–6
Berwick, 148
Best, Samuel, 30–1
Bethlehem, 40
Bethlem, 210–11
Bible, 14, 44, 46, 50, 59, 61, 73, 84, 187, 192,
200–1, 230; illustrations of, 131–2
Bigbury, 110, 139
Binns, John, *Recollections*, 243
Birch, James, 24
Birmingham, 14, 110, 130, 158, 160
Bishop, John, 254
Bishop, Noah, 106
Black Torrington, 107
Blackley, 42
Blake, William, 17, 18, 19, 20, 41, 72, 74,
80–5, 130, 182, 216–17, 229, 230; *Four Zoas*,
84; *Jerusalem*, 80; *Milton*, 81
Bliss, Sylvester, 259
Blockley (Gloucestershire), 96, 246
Blore (Derbyshire), 24
Blyth, 158
Boehme, Jakob, 19–23, 24, 40, 72, 84, 103,
118, 159; *Aurora*, 19
Bolton, 21–2, 28
Boon, Mary, 137–8, 154
Borough, 116; Chapel, 158–9
Bossenden Wood, 213–14, 221
Boston (Mass.), 193
Boudinot, Elias, *Star in the West*, 183
Boutelle, Luther, 197
Bradford, 110, 138, 140, 146–52
Bradford Turn-Out, 151–2
Bradford-on-Avon, 118
Bradley, Thomas, 37
Bramley (Leeds), 41
Brice, T., 246
Bristol, 22, 27, 29, 43, 53, 59, 71, 77, 110, 111,
117, 153, 159
British Convention, 75
British Israel, 61, 79, 80–3, 121, 132, 183; *see
also* Judaism; Wroe
Brixham, 110
Brooke, Henry, 233, 235
Brooks, Joshua, *Dictionary of Prophecies*, 243
Brothers, Richard, 23, 29, 31, 38, ch. 4 *passim*,
86, 91, 120, 124, 185, 188, 210; arrested and
declared insane, 60, 77–8; and Blake, 84–5;
early career, 58–9; effect of confinement on
followers, 79, 86; engraving by Sharp, 74
and plate 1; intercedes with God to save
London, 62; lodgings in Paddington Street,
60, 63; Nephew of the Almighty, 60;
political content of writings, 77; Prince of
the Hebrews, 60–1, 63, 64, 67, 68, 74;
prophetic mission, 59–60; and radicalism,
223–4; and Satan, 62, 130; and Joseph

Smith, 183; social programme, 83–4; visible
and invisible Hebrews, 61, 80; *Correct
Account*, 82; *Description of Jerusalem*, 79, 82;
Revealed Knowledge, 60–3, 64, 66, 67, 68, 71,
77, 79, 84
Brown, James, 37
Brown, John, 30
Brown, Thomas, 168, 170, 171, 173
Bruce, Colonel Basil, 66, 67, 91, 116
Bruce, Mrs Basil, 91
Bruce, Reverend Stanhope, 67, 86, 90, 103,
113, 116–17
Bryan, William, 69–72, 88, 91
Bryant, Jacob, 82
Buchan, Elspeth (Mrs Luckie), 32–8, 207, 209
Buchan, Robert, 32
Buchanites, 33–8, 164
Bulkeley, Sir Richard, 27
Bunhill Fields, 26
Bunyan, John, 44, 101, 119; *Pilgrim's Progress*,
44, 119
Burned-over District (N.Y.), 183
Burns, Robert, 236
Burrows, George Man, 212, 213
Burton, Robert, *Anatomy of Melancholy*, 46
Busby, Mr, 60
Butts, Thomas, 18

Campbell, Alexander, 184, 185
Campbellites (Disciples of Christ), 179, 184–5,
186, 203, 205; *Millennial Harbinger*, 205
Cambridge, 27
Cambridge University, 6, 43, 112
Camden Town, 93
Camisards, 25–9
Canterbury, 213
Carlile, Richard, 155–6, 158–9, 211, 224
Carlyle, Thomas, 208, 217
Carmarthen, 153
Carpenter, Catherine S., 251
Carpenter, Elias, 92, 94, 124–7, 135, 158;
Nocturnal Alarm, 124
Carrickfergus (Ireland), 21
Caswall, Henry, 187–8
Cataclysm, 4, 9, 167, 199
Catholic Apostolic Church, 208
Census of Religious Worship, 203
Cévennes, 25, 28
Chapbooks, 39, 45, 52–4, 98, 105, 118
Charisma, 11–12, 38, 150, 199
Charlottesville (Va.), 37
Charms, magic, 46
Chartism, 133, 151, 224; Christian, 190; Land
Plan, 225
Chatham, 139
Chester, 22
Chesterfield, 110, 158
Child, Thomas, 113

INDEX

Lavington, George, 16
Law, Richard, 91
Law, William, 19, 21, 22, 24, 159
Lawson, Joseph, xiii
Leach, Reverend Mr, 89
Lead, Jane, 23, 27, 38, 59; *A Fountain of Gardens*, 23, 59
Leadbetter, J., 22
Lee, Mother Ann, 28–9, 37, 164–76, 209; and ascetic feminism, 167–70; compared to Joanna Southcott and Mrs Buchan, 166, 169, 207; as second Eve, 169
Lee, Sarah, 22
Leeds, 41, 67, 69, 91, 110, 111, 122–3, 159, 203
Lees, Edward, 140
Lees, Elizabeth, 259
Lees (brothers), Henry, Samuel, William, 146, 155
Leicester, 110
Leigh, 22
Letsham, Elizabeth, 22
Liardet, F., 221, 261
Lightbourne, James, 113
Lilly, William, 47
Limping Billy, 42
Lincolnshire, 41
Lindsay, Alexander, 137, 139
Lisbon earthquake, 5
Litch, Josiah, 193, 202
Little flock of sheep, story of, 99–100
Livermore, Harriet, 258
Liverpool, 66, 67, 126, 138, 190, 203
Livingston, John H., 5
Llanfihangel, 32
Locke, John, 16–17, 216
London, 16, 23, 24, 25, 29, 47, 52, 58, 59, 62, 69, 91, 110, 127, 136–7, 189, 203
London Corresponding Society, 75, 223
Long Acre (London), 59
Lord Burnet, ballad of, 101–2
Louis XVI, 63, 67
Loutherbourg, Philip de, 74
Love, Christopher, 54, 71, 124
Loveless, George, 224–5
Loveless, William, 224–5
Lovett, William, 41
Luke, John, 69
Lukins, G., 53
Lunacy, *see* Madness
Lymington, 64

Macclesfield, 110
Madness, 11, 54, 57, 83, 108–9, 120, 132, 209–18; Brothers's, 78; divine, 215–16
Madoc, 82
Magic, 9, 21, 39–40, 46, 50, 93, 123
Manchester, 22, 28, 54, 73, 75, 110, 133, 166, 170, 189

Mann, Samuel, 22
Mansfield, 110
Margarot, Maurice, 75
Mari (y fantell wen), *see* Evans, Mary
Mark, Gospel according to St, 130
Market Deeping, 116
Marriage, 36, 38, 52, 121, 168; plural, 188
Martin, John, 131–2, 196, 211
Martin, Jonathan, 132, 211; *Life*, 211
Mason, John, 69
Mather, Ralph, 21–3, 69
Matthew, Gospel according to St, 49, 135, 154
Maxfield, Thomas, 30
McNemar, Richard, 164
Meacham, Joseph, 164–5, 166, 167
Mede, Joseph, 5
Medicine, popular, 21, 49, 115
Melancholia, 209, 210
Melbourne (Australia), 147
Merioneth, 32, 82
Merlin, 51, 53
Mesmerism, 70, 74
Messiah, 5, 61, 66, 157, 177, 204, 213–15
Methodism, xiv, 15–17, 22, 28, 29, 32, 37, 42, 54, 67, 87, 89, 111, 117, 119, 148–9, 153, 160, 185, 189, 190, 211, 230
Mexborough, 110
Microcosm, 20
Middle Ages, 7, 144, 216
Middleton (Lancs.), 42
Midnight Cry, 5, 34, 173, 194
Millenarianism, 41; Anglo-American, 205–6; and astrology, 49–50; comparative study of, 163, 205–6; culture of, 131, 196, 215; definition of, 3–4, 7–8; difficulties in understanding, 3; and disaster, 220; and evangelical Protestantism, 226; and family, 169; fusion of past and present, 191; imagery of, 195–6, 227–8; institutions of, 85; intellectual appeal of, 226–9; and Owenites, xv; political, 74; popular, 5, 69, 208, 226; psychic benefits from, 220, 228; psychological explanation of, 209–18; and radicalism, 74–9, 83, 158–9, 223–6; and relative deprivation, 221–2; respectable, 5, 207–8; as salvationism, 8; secular, 10; sensibility to, 83; in seventeenth century, 14, 124; and social change, xvi, 148–9, 202, 219, 222; social context of, 218–21; tradition of, 84; typology of, 8–9; and 'vital' Christianity, 65; and witchcraft, 46–7
Millenarians, and almanacs, 52; as God's chosen people, 183; mentality of, 115, 186, 215; recruitment of, 38; social composition of, 29, 37, 110–11, 189–90, 221
Millennialism, 5; distinguished from millenarianism, 5–6; postmillennialism, 4, 6–7, 181, 197; premillennialism, 4, 181